# INTERGENERATIONAL SOLIDARITY IN CHILDREN'S LITERATURE AND FILM

Children's Literature Association Series

# INTERGENERATIONAL SOLIDARITY IN CHILDREN'S LITERATURE AND FILM

EDITED BY
JUSTYNA DESZCZ-TRYHUBCZAK
AND ZOE JAQUES

University Press of Mississippi / Jackson

The University Press of Mississippi is the scholarly publishing agency of
the Mississippi Institutions of Higher Learning: Alcorn State University,
Delta State University, Jackson State University, Mississippi State University,
Mississippi University for Women, Mississippi Valley State University,
University of Mississippi, and University of Southern Mississippi.

www.upress.state.ms.us

The University Press of Mississippi is a member
of the Association of University Presses.

Copyright © 2021 by University Press of Mississippi
All rights reserved

First printing 2021
∞

Library of Congress Cataloging-in-Publication Data available

ISBN 9781496831910 (hardback)
ISBN 9781496831927 (trade paperback)
ISBN 9781496831934 (epub single)
ISBN 9781496831941 (epub institutional)
ISBN 9781496831958 (pdf single)
ISBN 9781496831965 (pdf institutional)

British Library Cataloging-in-Publication Data available

# CONTENTS

Acknowledgments . . . . . . . . . . . . . . . . . . . . . . . . . . . . . . . . . . . . . . . . . . ix

Towards Intergenerational Solidarity
in Children's Literature and Film . . . . . . . . . . . . . . . . . . . . . . . . . . . . xi
Justyna Deszcz-Tryhubczak with Zoe Jaques

## PART ONE: TRADITION OF INTERAGE KINSHIPS IN CHILDREN'S BOOKS

1    From Solitary to Solidary: Intergenerational Relationships
in the Representation of Full Lives . . . . . . . . . . . . . . . . . . . . . . . . . . . . .3
Clémentine Beauvais

2    *Pollyanna*'s Intergenerational Gladness: Examining Porter's Novels
in the Digital Humanities. . . . . . . . . . . . . . . . . . . . . . . . . . . . . . . . . . . .18
Ashley N. Reese

3    "You and Me, Alfred": Intergenerational Solidarity in the Emil Series .31
Björn Sundmark

## PART TWO: CHILD-ADULT ALLIANCES IN CONTEMPORARY NARRATIVES

4    Crossing the Divide: How Death and Dementia
Develop Understanding between Young and Old
in Contemporary Children's Literature . . . . . . . . . . . . . . . . . . . . . . . 47
Jean Webb

5  From Juxtaposition to Interweave: Intergenerational Collaboration
   in the Works of Brian Selznick .................................. 58
   Terri Doughty

6  Envisioning Solidarity: Disrupting Linear Temporality
   in Studio Ghibli's *Howl's Moving Castle*
   and *When Marnie Was There* ...................................... 70
   Aneesh Barai and Nozomi Uematsu

7  "Remember Me": Intergenerational Dialogue
   in Disney-Pixar Animation ........................................ 85
   Zoe Jaques

## PART THREE: CHILDREN'S LITERATURE AS INTERGENERATIONAL MEMORY

8  Trains to Life—Trains to Death: Judith Kerr's Writing
   and Drawing from and about Childhood Exile in
   the Nazi Era as Intergenerational Solidaristic Practice ............ 101
   Lucy Stone

9  Nadja Halilbegovich's *My Childhood Under Fire: A Sarajevo Diary*:
   The Intergenerational Self and the Kinship Model ................. 116
   Anastasia Ulanowicz

10 Imagined Genocides, Multidirectional Memory,
   and Intergenerational Solidarity in
   Ransom Riggs's *Miss Peregrine* Trilogy .......................... 130
   Marek Oziewicz

## PART FOUR: CHILDREN'S LITERATURE AND INTERGENERATIONAL PROJECTS

11 "Something There Is That Doesn't Love a Wall":
   The Mediating Child and the Ethics of Cohabitation ............... 147
   Blanka Grzegorczyk

12 A Grand Cause: Representations of Children's Contributions
   to Regenerative Agriculture in Picturebooks ...................... 162
   Michelle Superle

13  Gardening and Intergenerational Solidarity in
    Contemporary American Children's Literature ................... .176
    Aneta Dybska

### PART FIVE: REWRITING AETONORMATIVITY WITH YOUNG READERS

14  The "Lynx-Eyed Sagacity" of the "Schoolboy":
    William Godwin and the Juvenile Library (1805–1825) ............. 191
    Malini Roy

15  Building Bridges: Intergenerational Solidarity
    in the Works of Aidan Chambers ............................. 205
    Vanessa Joosen

16  The Mingling of Teenage and Adult Breaths:
    The Dutch *Slash* Series as Intergenerational Communication ....... .218
    Helma van Lierop-Debrauwer and Sabine Steels

Afterword: The Case of the Evil (Step)mother, or the Impossibility of
Intergenerational Solidarity ..................................... .231
Maria Nikolajeva

About the Contributors ........................................ 247

Index ....................................................... .251

# ACKNOWLEDGMENTS

This project is an output of ChildAct: Shaping a Preferable Future: Children Reading, Thinking, and Talking about Alternative Communities and Times, which received funding from the European Union's Horizon 2020 research and innovation program under Marie Skłodowska-Curie grant agreement no. 745888.

We are immensely grateful to the initiative for providing the funding to support this research and to Anglia Ruskin University for hosting the project grant. Special note should be given to Eugene Giddens for his advice and guidance on the work and to the Centre for Research in Children's Literature at Cambridge University for organizing the conference from which this collection has developed.

Finally, we would also like to thank our contributors for their trust, patience, and timeliness while this volume was taking shape.

# TOWARDS INTERGENERATIONAL SOLIDARITY IN CHILDREN'S LITERATURE AND FILM

Justyna Deszcz-Tryhubczak with Zoe Jaques

Our initial work on this book coincided with US student-led protests against gun violence after the mass shooting at Marjory Stoneman Douglas High School on February 14, 2018. The "March for Our Lives" campaign, inspired and organized by students in response to silent acceptance of school shootings as a feature of the post-Columbine reality, has been actively supported by adults, including lawmakers and politicians. We hope that young people's critical engagement with the adult-dominated political and sociocultural reality in the US will bring about change to intergenerational agreement on gun laws in the the country, so that their voices have a major impact on policy making. But such change may occur only as a result of a systematic cross-age effort. An important example of a successful child-adult alliance has been the climate strike movement, initiated by teen activist Greta Thunberg, later joined by thousands of younger and older people all over the world.[1] While the climate crisis will most probably never be over, the UK government's commitment to reduce greenhouse emissions to zero by 2050 is certainly a significant step forward. Most recently, intergenerational connectivity has become a crucial element of societies' response to the COVID-19 pandemic, which is affecting people of all ages in material and psychological ways. Social distancing seems a misnomer: we are all obliged to follow rules of physical distancing, but this does not mean we cannot intensify mental and emotional bonds, especially those uniting generations.

Responding to the growing awareness of the necessity and transformative potential of cross-age interdependencies, *Intergenerational Solidarity and*

*Children's Literature and Film* explores diverse ways in which children's culture contributes to the development of a solidaristic consciousness so essential for the emergence of a more sustainable and just world. It argues that (1) texts for young audiences stimulate intellectual and emotional appreciation of multifaceted connections between generations through representations of intergenerational solidarity; and that (2) children's and adults' joint engagements with such texts may turn into collaborative cultural practices around reading that strengthen intergenerational bonds. Hence this project is not only likely to advance an innovative approach to children's literature studies, but it also expresses the contributors' commitment to enhance the relevance of this field to current political, societal, and cultural needs and to strengthen its impact outside academia.

## INTERGENERATIONAL SOLIDARITY IN THEORY

Generation is usually seen as an intersection of the phenomena of age groups, birth cohorts, and family time. Its significance can also result from the maturation of one's individual consciousness of how these diverse influences shape one's behavior. In *Generational Intelligence: A Critical Approach to Age Relations* (2011), Simon Biggs and Ariela Lowenstein argue that although all these categories are the fundamental organizing principles of our lives, our generational identity is rarely experienced as fragmented: it is rather the "meeting point of birth cohort, familial lineage and personal maturation [that] creates a three-dimensional space in which the immediate experience of generational identity [. . .] exists and is given holistic expression" in our thoughts, feelings, attitudes, and actions to ourselves and to others (6). As they further argue, such an approach relies less on formal distinctions and categories and more on "personal and collective experience and self-conscious identity" (8). A sense of solidarity with one's "age other"—that is, someone perceived as belonging to a different group because of particular age (xii)—is thus an expression of one's awareness of and ability to act on one's generational status.

The notion of intergenerational solidarity, developed by Vern Bengtson in the late 1960s and '70s as a term referring to cohesiveness among grandparents, parents, and children within the family, has come to be defined as "[t]he social compact [. . .] based on reciprocity and the belief that society progresses because of the investments past generations have made in carrying knowledge and culture forward. It recognizes that people of all generations [. . .] are bound together in order to survive and thrive" (Butts, 83). In *Intergenerational Solidarity: Strengthening Economic and Social Ties* (2010), Maria Amparo Cruz-Saco argues that intergenerational solidarity is present in all societies as "a core element of IG [intergenerational] relationships" and that it "bonds generations that share common interests, feelings of affection and affinity, reciprocity, mutual care, and protection" (10). Intergenerational solidarity is also regarded as a basis for personal and social security as such bonding results in the emergence of "social networks of care," generating opportunities for the personal and professional development and integrity for everybody (2). Cruz-Saco and Zelenev conclude that intergenerational solidarity "could justifiably be considered the root of a healthy society" both today and in the future (212); the corollary is that when such solidarity is sundered, as we have found in recent political events, then society itself faces crisis.

The concept of intergenerational solidarity has been theorized in a number of ways, all of which reveal both the complexity of this phenomenon and its significance for the well-being of individuals and societies. Cruz-Saco offers a thorough overview of these approaches, beginning with Bengtson's proposition that intergenerational solidarity and affective ties between people naturally coexist with conflicts (Bengtson 2001), reflecting "the complex balancing of bonding" (Cruz-Saco, 19).[2] Bengtson and Schrader (1982) distinguish the following conceptual dimensions of intergenerational solidarity applicable to relationships within families and in larger communities:[3]

1. *affectual or affectional solidarity* (sense of closeness among family members and the reciprocity of these sentiments);
2. *associational solidarity* (the structure of contacts and interactions in diverse activities);
3. *consensual solidarity* (sharing the same worldview and value system among family members);
4. *functional solidarity* (financial and nonfinancial exchanges among family members);
5. *normative solidarity* (sense of responsibility and obligation to care or the recognition and adherence to the norms of family solidarity);
6. *structural solidarity* (cross-generational contacts enabled by geographic proximity) (Cruz-Saco, 19–21).

Some of these types of intergenerational solidarity can be found in all contributions to this volume: for instance, Astrid Lindgren's Emil series (1963–71), discussed by Björn Sundmark, abounds with examples of associational and normative solidarity, while Nadja Halilbegovich's *My Childhood Under Fire: A Sarajevo Diary*, the focus of Anastasia Ulanowicz's chapter, contains exemplars of affectional and associational solidarity. In Ransom Riggs's *Miss Peregrine* trilogy, analyzed by Marek Oziewicz, these two types of solidarity are closely interlinked with consensual solidarity. Functional solidarity is the core of William Godwin's creative collaboration with children, discussed by Malini Roy, while structural solidarity can be found in Blanka Grzegorczyk's reading of Sita Brahmachari's *Tender Earth* (2017) and Rachel Anderson's *Asylum* (2011) as narratives concerned with communication across young Britons and migrants. These understandings of intergenerational solidarity reveal the many ways in which it shapes and fosters relationships formed in individual families and the larger networks of communities and nations.

Greater solidarity obviously generates more connectivity and vice versa, which, in turn, may result in the alleviation of conflicts and tensions. The intensification of effective intergenerational affiliations is increasingly urgent in the face of global aging, changes in family structure, transnational family separation, precariatism, as well as political trends pitting younger and older generations against each other, as has been the case with Brexit or the last US election. According to the United Nation's 2017 *World Population Aging. Highlights* report, by 2030, older persons will outnumber children aged 0–10 years (1.41 billion vs. 1.35 billion); by 2050, there will be more people aged 60 or over than adolescents and youth aged 10–24 years (2.1 billion vs. 2.0 billion) (1). Population aging will lead to an increasing number of older adults who may support younger relatives, performing housekeeping chores, helping with raising children, and passing on traditions and values to younger generations (Cruz-Saco, 10). On the other hand, children will be required to take care of their aging relatives and friends. Simultaneously, as Cruz-Saco and Zelenev point out, the transition from adolescence to adulthood has become uncertain because of precarious employment and economic insecurity, which has made Western young people less willing to become parents: "Young people may sometimes prefer nonmarital cohabitation, postponing or forgoing children, remaining single, or adopting nontraditional lifestyles in order to meet educational challenges or find the types of jobs that can bring income security" (217). Young people are also more exposed to labor flexibility and periods of unemployment. In some countries, preteens and teenage children have to undertake jobs to cope with poverty, which, in turn, limits the educational opportunities they need to improve their economic situation (217).

## YOUNG GENERATIONS AND INTERGENERATIONAL SOLIDARITY

While intergenerational solidarity can be promoted and practiced through partnerships involving all social groups, children and youth, who constitute more than one-quarter of the global population, play a crucial role in establishing and maintaining cross-age connectivity. Cruz-Saco and Zelenev argue that the social contract of intergenerational solidarity is repeated with every new generation: "from childhood until old age [...], each person's participation in the 'give' and 'take' of the IG [intergenerational] continuum evolves and plays the roles that pertain to childhood, youth, adulthood, and old age" (226). Therefore, it is essential to implement pedagogies, programs, and policies aimed at encouraging young members of a given community or society to learn about and experience intergenerational solidarity as in this way they will gain knowledge and expertise as to how to carry it into the future.

Promoting two-way intergenerational relationships and developing new ways of communicating between generations is especially imperative in view of the structural age apartheid affecting both interpersonal relationships and political, social, and cultural life, which prevents the development of age diversity at all levels of our societies. Age segregation is currently one of the most aggravating factors fueling intra-social divides harming communities. As an example of state-sanctioned age segregation, in 2016 the Polish parliament ratified a regulation forbidding local authorities to locate child care homes and elderly people care homes in the same building or so close to one another that they share a courtyard. The regulation was justified with the scientifically unconfirmed claim that the presence of older people affects children negatively and will intensify the former's alienation because "children raised around old age, sickness and death face the drama of the loneliness experienced by people who are often deprived of the support of their closest kin" (Justyna's translation). Therefore, as the explanation continues, "functioning in such an environment is very difficult for adults and it is hard to see why it is adequate for children's emotional development and the proper shaping of their attitudes." Yet research shows that separating older people from children, who spend most of their time surrounded by their peers, limits young people's exposure to diverse adult role models.[4] This lack of opportunities to share interests and concerns, as well as to build reciprocal trust, hinders the development of generational intelligence—that is, the capability for "recognising and valuing generational differences, finding common ground, plus negotiating social and practical outcomes from the situation" (Haapala et al., 457). Generational intelligence not only facilitates the establishment of sustainable relations among generations, but also implies the awareness of "the way that our ideas about generations and age groups are shaped by society, rather than just assuming that these attitudes are normal or self-evident. Sometimes they are shaped deliberately and sometimes in ways that we are unaware of" (459).[5] Generational intelligence renders the above-mentioned regulation absurd in light of the state-initiated patriotic remembrance in Polish culture, which depends on the intergenerational transmission of knowledge, values, and emotions. Such contradictory approaches to old age as a problem and as a resource to be mined for ideological purposes are examples of age-imperialism, "[t]he colonization of the goals, aims, priorities and agendas of one age group by another" (Biggs, 103). Generational intelligence is crucial in understanding complex social and political contexts motivating the emergence of ageist attitudes.

Age apartheid also manifests itself in adultism. Thirty years since the proclamation of the United Nations Convention on the Rights of the Child, which is itself controversial because of its focus on Western childhoods, children's rights continue to be violated in a number of ways. While the respect for children's rights undoubtedly depends on cultural and political contexts, there exist more fundamental factors hindering the successful implementation of the CRC. As Nick Lee argues in *Childhood and Human Value*, some adults reject the idea of children's rights as they fear losing whatever power they have over children. Others resist children's rights because they see them as "corrod[ing] relationships between adults and children" (4) and "bring[ing] all familiar ways of valuing children, all traditional means by which ideas of human value are passed on, to an end" (69). Yet Lee argues that the issue is more complex: some adults mistake children's separability—that is, their autonomy alternating with attachment and mutual dependence, all of which are necessary in human life—for separateness and independence. Lee sees the latter as a "strategic" delusion guaranteeing the superiority of adulthood over childhood, although in reality "everyone depends on someone for something" (Lee 2005, 22) and we are never completely separated (156). Lee further argues that children's rights are not about separating children from adults but about establishing "partial and temporary separability between children and adults" (70). It is especially the case with children's rights to participation, perhaps the most challenging of all the CRC provisions but at the same time most crucial for intergenerational solidarity; for Lee, they do not imply the absence of adults from children's lives but "suggest a situation in which children are with adults rather than surrounded by them, accompanied rather than possessed" (18). Priscilla Alderson refers to the idea of separateness between adults and children as a founding narrative that needs to be retold with a focus on continuities among different age groups and through a life-course approach: "If societies are to draw together in greater justice, informed by empathy and mutual understanding, adults would question the distancing and diminishing of children, and of their own earlier childhood years" (153). Hence one of the most crucial elements of this retelling is to show "how children and adults have so much in common in relation to [. . .] global matters and to good societies" (164) and, one should add, how much both groups can contribute to creating a better future through compromise and cooperation.

Children's and young people's contributions to the project of intergenerational solidarity in diverse settings, among them home, school, and community, are indeed crucial for the creation of good societies. *Participation, Citizenship and Intergenerational Relations in Children and Young People's Lives: Children and Adult in Conversation* (2014)—a collection coauthored by adults, young people, and children to document the 2012 conference of the International Childhood and Youth Research Network—is a rare example of intergenerational collaboration in academia and in specific social contexts. The goal of the network is "to promote, internationally, the inter-disciplinary study of children and young people in order to further awareness and understanding of issues that affect their well-being" (n.p.). The collection includes chapters co-written by young researchers, who contributed their feedback on how to conduct effective research with young scholars. The adult editors see the collection as an example of "true collaborative conversations between the research community and children and young people" (156). The book also recounts a number of child-led initiatives aimed at improving children's and adults' lives; one of the chapters discusses Neighborhood Children's Parliaments set up in villages in South India, whose members (between six and eighteen years old) conduct research to determine the most urgent problems faced by children and adults in particular villages (e.g., the removal of an illegal liquor store) (Crowley, 32). However particularistic in scope, this and other examples of cross-age collaborations and partnerships mentioned in the collection testify to the socially, culturally, and politically transformative potential of leveling age hierarchies as a gateway to a greater social cohesion.[6] In *Strains of Commitment: The Political Sources of Solidarity in Diverse Societies* (2017), Keith Banting and Will Kymlicka point out that "as societies become more diverse, historic forms of solidarity need to be stretched to incorporate newcomers" (24), which means that we need "the new champion of inclusive solidarity" (24). While the feminist, LGBT, multiculturalist, or environmental movements have served "as the new bearers of solidarity" (24), childism—understood in positive terms as the recognition of children as a social group with its own viewpoints and experiences (Wall, 71)—can become a "champion" of intergenerational solidarity as constituting inclusive solidarity.

## TOWARDS INTERGENERATIONAL SOLIDARITY IN CHILDREN'S LITERATURE STUDIES

Children's literature scholarship is well placed to contribute to the emergence of solidarity between generations despite the adult-dominated nature of the cultural production for children and the many ways in which it emphasizes childhood and adolescence as categorically distinct from adulthood. As Lydia Kokkola argues in *Fictions of Adolescent Carnality: Sexy Sinners and Delinquent Deviants* (2013), adolescence has been seen as a period of rebellion to reinforce the Romantic view of the child and "to prevent it from crumbling under the onslaught of counter-evidence" (36). For Kokkola, the young generation, and especially adolescents, are expected to be rebellious and punished for their misbehavior to maintain adult normativity (23). These constructions of childhood and adolescence have obviously been circulated in the culture of childhood, forming its most recurrent motif (Nikolajeva, 8).[7]

Yet the attempts to expand the focus of the field beyond aetonormativity—understood not only as the usual subject matter of texts for young audiences, but also as the fundamental organizing principle of child-adult relations in real life, reflected, for example, in the production, distribution, and use of children's literature—have been gradually intensifying, as evidenced in such groundbreaking studies as Karen Sánchez-Eppler's *Dependent States: The Child's Part in Nineteenth-Century American Culture* (2005), Marah Gubar's *Artful Dodgers: Reconceiving the Golden Age of Children's Literature* (2009), and Robin Bernstein's *Racial Innocence: Performing American Childhood from Slavery to Civil Rights* (2011).[8] Gubar and Bernstein, in particular, postulate that although children are born into an adult-controlled world, they are nevertheless capable of engaging in practices actively shaping their childhoods. Gubar exemplifies this thesis by providing evidence for child-adult creative collaborations in Victorian England. Bernstein shows that children's play, including their engagement with literature, is both "scripted" to reflect adults' worldviews and never fully under adult control.

Of foundational importance for this new interest in diverse aspects of non-aetonormativity have also been the two forums on recent changes in approaches to real, imaginary, and conceptual child-adult relations in research into children's and youth culture, which appeared in the 7.2 (2015) and 8.1 (2016) issues of *Jeunesse: Young People, Texts, Cultures*. The 2015 forum, entitled "Keywords in the Cultures of Young People," includes a contribution by Lisa Weems, who emphasizes the impossibility of upholding binaristic conceptions of child-adult relations. In "Theorizing Resistance and Intimacy in Youth Studies," Weems proposes to look at the concept of resistance as referring not only to "fighting an outside oppressive force" but also as signifying "the affective dimensions of difference, conflict, and the struggle of everyday life" (144). To this end, she complicates it with the notion of intimacy as an analytical tool enabling researchers to acknowledge "an affective dimension to particular relationships" and their being structured both by "domination and coercion as well as through carefully crafted systems of trust and interdependence" (138). As

Weems sees it, we should pay attention to "the spatial connections between and among youth and adults (both real and imagined) produced through various events, documents, images, and narratives in specific times and places" (144). Such an approach thus requires the examination of children's and adults' power and agency "beyond the binaries of oppression/ resistance or fear/confidence that structure nostalgia and protectionism" (144). Significantly, the revision of these binaries has nothing to do with the temporary carnivalesque empowerment of children, which, as Julie Cross points out, "is a socially sanctioned method relieving tension, and normally involves a return to social norms" (41). The contributions to our volume exemplify the critical practice proposed by Weems in that they all focus on images of relationships between young and old that complicate the aforementioned binaries.

The 2016 forum, entitled "Divergent Perspectives on Children's Agency," includes contributions by Richard Flynn and Marah Gubar, both of whom advocate the acknowledgment of children's agency as relational and emerging out of interactions with others, just as is the case with adults' agency. Flynn recognizes asymmetrical power relations between children and adults and "the immense power that social, historical, and ideological constructions have in shaping children's—or, for that matter, adults'—subjectivities" (259). Yet he disagrees that "the relationship between adults and children (or between adult writers and child readers) is inherently oppositional" (256) and instead proposes a model of children's agency in which children are perceived as capable, which corresponds to the approach proposed by Biggeri et al. in *Children and the Capability Approach* (2011). Biggeri et al. contend that "children should be seen as agents in the process of developing their capabilities and well-being" (4), including, one might add, their interactions with culture. Flynn suggests that such a model also implies the life course perspective and the recognition that both children and adults have varied competences and capabilities that are subject to change throughout their lives (262–63).

The approach proposed by Flynn shapes Victoria Ford Smith's *Between Generations: Collaborative Authorship in the Golden Age of Children's Literature* (2018), which recuperates and examines the rich tradition of fictive and real adult-child collaborations in nineteenth- and early twentieth-century British children's literature and culture. As Ford Smith argues, many of these alliances reflect the emergence of new concepts of childhood, acknowledging children's agency. As she explains, "the partnerships I examine, taken separately and read together, elucidate the contours of real children's participation in their own literature and culture and challenge popular narratives of children's literature that read actual young people solely as idealized listeners or passive muses" (7). Yet, while Ford Smith emphasizes partnerships between child and adult creators, she does not explore them as potential channels of intergenerational solidarity. Several contributions to our volume—by Vanessa Joosen, Malini Roy, and van Lierop-Debrauwer and Steels—expand Flynn's and Ford Smith's claims as they not only center on particular cases of such creative collaborations between writers, critics, and readers, but also show their broader sociocultural significance as a form of intergenerational connectivity. Moreover, Ford Smith does not position the field itself as a site of cross-generational connectivity. This discipline-shifting claim drives *Intergenerational Solidarity in Children's Literature and Film.*

Marah Gubar's thought-provoking and influential contribution, "The Hermeneutics of Recuperation: What a Kinship-Model Approach to Children's Agency Could Do for Children's Literature and Childhood Studies,"[9] expands the idea of possible similarities between childhood and adulthood. Gubar discusses the "kinship model" of child-adult relations in which "children and adults are fundamentally akin to one another, even if certain differences or deficiencies routinely attend certain parts of the aging process" (299). Of particular significance for children's literature studies is Gubar's plea to consider working outside the foundational paradigm of the field proposed by Jacqueline Rose (1984); as Gubar argues, it would be more constructive, and in fact more commonsensical, to "start from the kinship model premise that younger people, like older ones, are involved in various and complex ways with children's literature" (306). Such a shift in how we think about young and adult readers is a gateway out of our habit-driven thinking about children's literature as a tool used by adults to colonize young generations (Nodelman, 33). It results in novel methodologies that enable an exploration of the multifaceted importance of children's literature and culture in past and present societies, including intergenerational bonds, explored in detail throughout this collection.

A pioneering line of research into connections between generations in children's books was initiated by Vanessa Joosen in "Second Childhoods and Intergenerational Dialogues: How Children's Literature Studies and Age Studies Can Supplement Each Other" (2015). In her study, she proposes to combine insights from age studies with children's literature research to interrogate images of old age, and in particular "four ageist tropes: the decline narrative, the infantilized senior, the disregard of the old body, and the wise old mentor" (128), in selected twenty-first-century children's texts. Significantly, Joosen also points out that relatively little attention has been given to "the generation in between" (128), that is, the working generation, thereby reinforcing some generational conflicts while alleviating others (138). Cultural representations of interdependencies between childhood and senescence in popular media, and their influence on our perception of age and aging, are also the subject of

*Connecting Childhood and Old Age in Popular Media* (2018), a collection edited by Joosen. The collection explores "the various ways in which characters of different ages can be linked and opposed to each other" to "offer ways to think about intergenerational relationships beyond clichés, prejudices, and cheap sentimentalism, recognizing instead the multifaceted nature of each stage of life, and the complexity of relationships across age groups" (5). Nevertheless, even though the collection argues for the importance of cultural age literacy or being "agewise" (22) in times of global wrinkling, only one contribution, "Representations of Intergenerational Relationships in Children's Television in Turkey" by Gökçe Elif Baykal and Ilgım Veryeri Alaca, emphasizes the significance of children's media in the promotion of intergenerational alliances. Moreover, in contrast to *Intergenerational Solidarity in Children's Literature and Film*, the collection lacks the metacritical interest in new theoretical paradigms emerging in children's literature studies and in the crucial role of our field in fostering intergenerational connectivity. Joosen develops her interest in intergenerationality in *Adulthood in Children's Literature* (2018), which aims to decenter the prevalent interest in constructions of childhood in texts for young readers to representations of adulthood. Joosen shows how adulthood is performed by adult characters, examining metareflections about this phase of life conveyed in children's texts. She proves that children's literature is an important source of messages advocating certain age norms and potentially affecting how we act our own age and how we see others' enactments of their age (12). However, intergenerational solidarity as such is of marginal interest to this study.[10]

## CHILDREN'S CULTURE AND INTERGENERATIONAL SOLIDARITY

These diverse propositions dismantle the long-standing dogma of children's literature studies—the binary between child and adult—for the sake of emphasizing interdependencies between children and adults. Of greater importance is the fact that they reflect the growing awareness of both the complex nature of the concept of generation and generational identity and of the importance of intergenerational bonds for the sustainability and welfare of contemporary societies. As such, they make children's literature studies constructively relevant to the urgent challenges posed by the rapid aging of the global population. *Intergenerational Solidarity in Children's Literature and Film* addresses these challenges by exploring the role of children's and YA literature and film in propagating and facilitating a culture of generational interconnections. We propose that this role may be understood in the following interrelated ways:

1. cultural products addressed to young audiences contain representations of subjective experiences related to the attainment and practice of intergenerational solidarity, which, in turn, may hone readers' generational intelligence;
2. narratives addressed to children not only depict instances of solidaristic endeavors but also constitute vital elements of broader intergenerational ventures;
3. the creative process itself may constitute an intergenerational solidaristic practice of reciprocal exchange and empathy between adult authors and young audiences;
4. as academic interest in children and childhood affects "the constitution of children's lives" (Lee 2001, 47), applying the concept of intergenerational solidarity may enable children's literature researchers to respond to and engage in the process of creating an intergenerational-friendly world.

The first two sections of our volume show the sustained presence of the motif of intergenerational bonds in children's literature and film. Section one, "Tradition of Interage Kinships in Children's Books," opens with Clémentine Beauvais's exploration of intergenerational connectivity as it emerges in the depictions of full lives in children's books. Analyzing both biographies for children and stories belonging to other genres, for example Anne-Laure Bondoux's *L'aube sera grandiose* (2017) and Will Buckingham's *Lucy and the Rocket Dog* (2017), Beauvais argues that such texts enable the representation of age-related topics, including the significance of intergenerational others. Ashley N. Reese reflects on Eleanor Porter's *Pollyanna* (1913) and *Pollyanna Grows Up* (1915) to show that, in orphan girls' literature, the young heroines engage in intergenerational communication and actively co-construct the society around them, strengthening its integrity. In the final chapter in this section, Björn Sundmark rereads the Emil trilogy to reveal its reliance on relational solidarity between the child and adult characters as a communal value, reflecting and anticipating changes in perceptions of childhood in twentieth-century Sweden.

Section two, "Child-Adult Alliances in Contemporary Narratives," offers insights into contemporary representations of generational interdependences in children's texts as sources of well-being and self-fulfilment. Jean Webb focuses on depictions of dementia and the age divide in contemporary Western books for young readers. Discussing *The Granny Project* (1983) by Anne Fine, *Billy Elliot* (2001) by Melvin Burgess and Lee Hall, *Unbecoming* (2008) by Jenny Downham, *Grandpa's Great Escape* (2015) by David Walliams, and *The Dementia Diaries* (2016) by Matthew Snyman and the Social Innovation Lab Kent, Webb argues for the potential of literature to facilitate the transfer of knowledge and experiences across generations. In the subsequent chapter, Terri Doughty continues Webb's argument by examining Brian Selznick's preoccupation with the benefits of intergenerational relations in *The Invention of Hugo Cabret* (2007), *Wonderstruck* (2011), and *The Marvels* (2015). As Doughty's readings show, the novels present child-adult collaboration and empathy as enabling the protagonists to live more meaningful lives. Less straightforward but equally productive processes of intergenerational solidarity are discussed by Aneesh Barai and Nozomi Uematsu in their joint essay on children's film. They propose to explore nonlinear age-bending transformations and the intergenerational alliances they catalyze in *Howl's Moving Castle* (2004) and *When Marnie Was There* (2014), fantasy animated films based on British children's books, by Diana Wynne Jones and Joan G. Robinson, respectively. Uematsu and Barai contend that both films move away from a narrative of child-adult progression to emphasize the potential childness of adults or adultness of youths. Finally, Zoe Jaques's contribution to this section continues the interest in animated film, turning attention to the case of Disney-Pixar animation. The Disney tradition tends to focus on generational rifts, but Jaques argues that two recent Disney-Pixar animated efforts—*Up* (2010) and *Coco* (2017)—have offered dialogic models for intergenerational solidarity. While the former focuses on the possibilities of communal exchange between neighbors and the latter finds purpose in the ties that bind families, both films are invested in highlighting connections forged not only between living subjects, but with those remembered from previous generations.

Chapters in section three, "Children's Literature as Intergenerational Memory," provide insights into the role of children's literature as a bridge connecting generations across time through the joint memory work related to national and individual trauma. Lucy Stone's chapter documents the trajectory from Erich Kästner's *Emil und die Detektive* (1929) to Judith Kerr's *When Hitler Stole Pink Rabbit* (1971), influenced by Kerr's preoccupation with Kästner's novel, to reflect on the construction, transmission, and reception of intergenerational trauma. Anastasia Ulanowicz traces the realization of the kinship model in Nadja Halilbegovich's *My Childhood Under Fire* (2008), a young person's firsthand account of her war experience supplemented with later annotations by the now-adult author. Ulanowicz argues that this palimpsestic combination of content and form emphasizes both the relatedness between children and adults and the intrasubjective connection between one's past and present selves. Finally, Marek Oziewicz reads Ransom Riggs's *Miss Peregrine* trilogy (2011–15) within the framework of multidirectional memory to argue that the protagonist's slipping back in time can be seen as an attempt at forging intergenerational solidarity, which turns out to be the only way to subvert a genocidal regime.

Section four, "Children's Literature and Intergenerational Projects," delves further in the uses of children's texts to propagate intergenerational solidarity in specific social contexts. Grounded in postcolonial and human rights studies, Blanka Grzegorczyk's chapter examines Sita Brahmachari's *Tender Earth* (2017) and Rachel Anderson's *Asylum* (2011) as narratives that counter the mainstream media's anti-immigrant rhetoric by showcasing cosmopolitan solidarity effected through intercultural and intergenerational cooperation. Grzegorczyk's contribution is followed by two chapters on texts that propagate children's active participation in communal projects and focus on children's interactions with nature. Michelle Superle's child-centered reading of children's texts focuses on picturebooks depicting children as collaborating with adults to ensure food safety. Superle argues that these narratives may inspire young readers to participate in communal efforts to make the world better for everyone now rather than in the future, when they become adult citizens. Aneta Dybska focuses on children's books related to the community garden phenomenon in the United States, whose crucial element is a model of place-based sociality based on intergenerational cooperation, reciprocity, and solidarity. Looking, for example, at DyAnne DiSalvo-Ryan's *City Green* (1994) and Rebecca Elliott's *The Last Tiger* (2013), Dybska identifies the centrality of the theme of neighborhood regeneration through gardening, including resolving conflicts between strangers of different ages, ethnicities, and social backgrounds. For Dybska, such motifs are examples of the fictional renditions of the concept of the city as an intergenerational polity.

The fifth section, "Rewriting Aetonormativity with Young Readers," examines intergenerational connections emerging from children's and adults' joint engagement with texts, addressing specifically the status of children's literature as a means of maintaining age hierarchies. Malini Roy sheds new light on William Godwin as an author who tried to develop intergenerational dialogue with child readers, both those from his family circle and the general young audience. Roy traces Godwin's abundant comments addressed directly to children and reflecting his respect for their intellectual capabilities. Vanessa Joosen relies on a genetic perspective to explore Aidan Chambers's construction of adolescence as shaped particularly by his correspondence with adolescent readers to inform his knowledge about this phase of life. Finally, Helma van Lierop-Debrauwer and Sabine Steels present the kinship model in action: their chapter discusses Edward van de Vendel's *Slash* series (2008–2017), which resulted from the collaboration between young adults and well-known children's authors, and the empirical research aimed at revealing the *Slash* coauthors' perceptions of the collaborative life writing projects as spaces fostering child-adult partnerships and alliances. The collection concludes with Maria Nikolajeva's reflection on the tensions between intergenerational solidarity and intergenerational conflict in children's and young adult fiction from two theoretical perspectives: bio-psychological and aesthetic. Nikolajeva argues that since children's literature is predominantly premised on the idea of children's revolts against their parents, full intergenerational solidarity in children's texts is impossible. We hope that the deliberately provocative nature of this polemic will encourage a further critical interrogation of the spectrum of child-adult relationships in children's literature.

Differences and conflicts between younger and older generations do exist and they have proven to be a very popular trope in world literature and culture, including texts for young audiences. They have also been abundantly acknowledged in children's literature criticism. *Intergenerational Solidarity in Children's Literature and Film* breaks new ground by exploring approaches to texts, authors, readers, and scholarship itself that acknowledge and examine the diversity of intergenerational connections represented in children's literature. The collection also testifies to the cultural, social, and political significance of children's culture in the development of generational intelligence and empathy towards age-others. Finally, it innovatively positions the field of children's literature studies as a site of intergenerational solidarity, opening possibilities for a new socially consequential inquiry into the culture of childhood.

## NOTES

1. Following the practice of age studies, we use "older" instead of "elderly" whenever relevant to the context. See Dale Avers, et al., "Use of the Term 'Elderly,'" *Journal of Geriatric Physical Therapy* 34, no. 4: 153–54.

2. See Vern L. Bengtson, "The Burgess Award Lecture: Beyond the Nuclear Family: The Increasing Importance of Multigenerational Bonds," *Journal of Marriage and the Family* 63, no.1 (2001): 1–16.

3. See Vern L. Bengtson and S. S. Schrader, "Parent-Child Relations." *Research Instruments in Social Gerontology*, eds. D. J. Mangen and W. A. Peterson, vol. 2 (University of Minnesota Press, 1982), 115–28.

4. See Barbra Teater and Jill M. Chonody, "Stereotypes and Attitudes toward Older People among Children Transitioning from Middle Childhood into Adolescence: Time Matters," *Gerontology & Geriatrics Education* 38, no. 2 (2016): 204–218. See also Margaret C. Skropeta, Alf Colvin, and Shannon Sladen, "An Evaluative Study of the Benefits of Participating in Intergenerational Playgroups in Aged Care for Older People," *BMC Geriatrics* 14 (2014): 109.

5. For more on generational intelligence, see Simon Biggs and Ariela Lowenstein. *Generational Intelligence: A Critical Approach to Age Relations* (Routledge, 2011).

6. For an example of such a collaboration in the field of children's literature studies, see Ewa Chawar, Justyna Deszcz-Tryhubczak, Katarzyna Kowalska, Olga Maniakowska, Mateusz Marecki, Milena Palczyńska, Eryk Pszczołowski, and Dorota Sikora, "Children's Voices in the

Polish Canon Wars: Participatory Research in Action," *International Research in Children's Literature* 11, no. 2 (2018): 111–31.

7. Maria Nikolajeva's concept of aetonormativity relates to "adult normativity that governs the way children's literature has been patterned. [...] Nowhere else are power structures as visible as in children's literature, the refined instrument used for centuries to educate, socialize and oppress a particular social group. [...] Yet, paradoxically enough, children are allowed, in fiction written *by adults* and for the enlightenment and enjoyment of children, to become strong, brave, rich, powerful, and independent—on certain conditions and for a limited time" (Power 8, 10).

8. For a discussion of Sánchez-Eppler's book, see Marah Gubar, "The Hermeneutics of Recuperation: What a Kinship-Model Approach to Children's Agency Could Do for Children's Literature and Childhood Studies," *Jeunesse: Young People, Texts, Cultures* 8, no. 1 (2016): 291–310.

9. See also her "On Not Defining Children's Literature," *PMLA* 126, no. 1 (2011): 209–216 and "Risky Business: Talking about Children in Children's Literature Criticism," *Children's Literature Association Quarterly* 38, no. 4 (2013): 450–57.

10. For more on intergenerationality in children's literature, see also the special issue of *Literatura Ludowa* 3 (2018), available at http://apcz.umk.pl/czasopisma/index.php/LL/issue/view/1472/showToc.

## WORKS CITED

Alderson, Priscilla. *The Politics of Childhood Real and Imagined, Volume 2: Practical Application of Critical Realism and Childhood Studies*. Routledge, 2016.

Bernstein, Robin. *Racial Innocence: Performing American Childhood from Slavery to Civil Rights*. New York University Press, 2011.

Biggeri, Mario, Jerome Ballet, and Flavio Comim, eds. *Children and the Capability Approach*. Palgrave Macmillan, 2011.

Biggs, Simon. "Narratives, Masquerades, Feminism, and Gerontology." *Journal of Aging Studies* 18, no. 1 (2004): 45–58.

Butts, Donna M. "Key Issues Uniting Generations." In *Intergenerational Solidarity: Strengthening Economic and Social Ties*, eds. María Amparo Cruz-Saco and Sergei Zelenev, 83–97. Palgrave Macmillan, 2010.

Cross, Julie. *Humor in Contemporary Junior Literature*. Routledge, 2011.

Crowley, Anne. "Evaluating the Impact of Children's Participation in Public Decision-Making." In *Participation, Citizenship, and Intergenerational Relations in Children and Young People's Lives, Children and Adults in Conversation*, eds. Joanne Westwood, Cath Larkins, Dan Moxon, Yasmin Perry, and Nigel Thomas, 29–42. Palgrave Macmillan, 2014.

Cruz-Saco, María Amparo. "Intergenerational Solidarity." In *Intergenerational Solidarity: Strengthening Economic and Social Ties*, eds. María Amparo Cruz-Saco and Sergei Zelenev, 9–34. Palgrave Macmillan, 2010.

Cruz-Saco, María Amparo, and Sergei Zelenev, eds. "Conclusions: Putting It All Together." In *Intergenerational Solidarity: Strengthening Economic and Social Ties*, 199–210. Palgrave Macmillan, 2010.

Flynn, Richard. "What Are We Talking about When We Talk about Agency?" *Jeunesse: Young People, Texts, Cultures* 8, no. 1 (2016): 254–65.

Ford Smith, Victoria. *Between Generations: Collaborative Authorship in the Golden Age of Children Literature*. University Press of Mississippi, 2018.

Gubar, Marah. *Artful Dodgers: Reconceiving the Golden Age of Children's Literature.* Oxford University Press, 2009.

Gubar, Marah. "The Hermeneutics of Recuperation: What a Kinship-Model Approach to Children's Agency Could Do for Children's Literature and Childhood Studies." In *Jeunesse: Young People, Texts, Cultures* 8, no. 1 (2016): 291–310.

Haapala, Irja, Laura Tervo, and Simon Biggs. "Using Generational Intelligence to Examine Community Care Work between Younger and Older Adults." *Journal of Social Work Practice* 29, no. 4 (2015): 457–73.

The International Childhood and Youth Research Network ICYRNet. http://www.icyrnet.net/. Accessed January 20, 2018.

Joosen, Vanessa. *Adulthood in Children's Literature.* Bloomsbury, 2018.

Joosen, Vanessa. "Introduction." In *Connecting Childhood and Old Age in Popular Media*, 3–20. University Press of Mississippi, 2018.

Joosen, Vanessa. "Second Childhoods and Intergenerational Dialogues: How Children's Literature Studies and Age Studies Can Supplement Each Other." *Children's Literature Association Quarterly* 40, no. 2 (2015): 126–40.

Kokkola, Lydia. *Fictions of Adolescent Carnality: Sexy Sinners and Delinquent Deviants.* John Benjamins, 2013.

Lee, Nick. *Childhood and Human Value: Development, Separation and Separability.* Open University Press, 2005.

Lee, Nick. *Childhood and Society: Growing Up in an Age of Uncertainty.* Open University Press, 2001.

Nikolajeva, Maria. *Reading for Learning: Cognitive Approaches to Children's Literature.* John Benjamins, 2014.

Nodelman, Perry. "The Other: Orientalism, Colonialism, and Children's Literature." *Children's Literature Association Quarterly* 17, no. 1 (1992): 29–35.

Rose, Jacqueline. *The Case of Peter Pan, or the Impossibility of Children's Fiction.* University of Pennsylvania Press, 1984.

Sánchez-Eppler, Karen. *Dependent States: The Child's Part in Nineteenth-Century American Culture.* University of Chicago Press, 2005.

"Sejm: dom dziecka nie może być w jednym budynku z domem pomocy społecznej." *Rzeczpospolita*, July 22, 2016. http://www.rp.pl/Zadania/307229950-Sejm-dom-dziecka-nie-moze-byc-w-jednym-budynku-z-domem-pomocy-spolecznej.html. Accessed November 20, 2017.

United Nations, Department of Economic and Social Affairs, Population Division (2015). "World Population Ageing 2017—Highlights (ST/ESA/SER.A/397)." http://www.un.org/en/development/desa/population/publications/pdf/ageing/WPA2017_Highlights.pdf. Accessed February 18, 2019.

Wall, John. "Childism: The Challenge of Childhood to Ethics and the Humanities." In *The Children's Table: Childhood Studies and the Humanities*, ed. Anne Mae Duane, 68–84. University of Georgia Press, 2013.

Weems, Lisa. "Theorizing Resistance and Intimacy in Youth Studies." *Jeunesse: Young People, Texts, Cultures* 7, no. 2 (2015): 134–47.

Westwood, Joanne, Cath Larkins, Dan Moxon, Yasmin Perry, and Nigel Thomas, eds. "Conclusion: Moving Forward Participation, Citizenship and Intergenerational Relations—Ongoing Conversations and Actions." In *Participation, Citizenship, and Intergenerational Relations in Children and Young People's Lives, Children and Adults in Conversation*, 155–62. Palgrave Macmillan, 2014.

# PART ONE

## TRADITION OF INTERAGE KINSHIPS IN CHILDREN'S BOOKS

# 1

# FROM SOLITARY TO SOLIDARY

## INTERGENERATIONAL RELATIONSHIPS IN THE REPRESENTATION OF FULL LIVES

Clémentine Beauvais

> A classic adult novel frequently follows the character from birth to death—a biographical plot. For obvious reasons, such a plot would not work in children's fiction.
> (Nikolajeva 2005, 101)

In this chapter, I am interested in what happens to questions of intergenerational solidarity when a children's book does undertake to represent the full lives of its main character(s). By *full*, I do not mean interrupted by premature death, but rather from childhood to middle or indeed even old age. Such books are quite rare primarily because, as Nikolajeva says, the concept violates some of the most fundamental narrative and ideological expectations of children's literature. Yet such texts do exist, and the very fact that they run counter to the most evident expectations we may hold about a children's book makes them theoretically interesting. The only genre within children's literature to have developed specific narrative and aesthetic strategies for the representation of full lives is the biography, a varied category of texts which has known a remarkable comeback in very recent years. Additionally, a hodgepodge of isolated examples, from picturebooks to children's and adolescent novels, follow fictional characters throughout full lives.

Reflections around intergenerational solidarity arise with particular intensity throughout children's books depicting full lives, because in them, intergenerational relationships are not—and, indeed, cannot be—represented statically. Vanessa Joosen (86) has analyzed the "seesaw effect" of intergenerational relationships in children's literature, showing that compassion and complicity among the very young and the very old can occur to the detriment of intermediary generations ("adults"). This age-related seesaw effect, intriguingly, seems to imply an evolution, throughout the life course, of one's attitude towards other generations. If a child character and an older character are portrayed helping each other while adults look on unmoved, it suggests that the child is expected to be, in the future, that selfish adult, and that the older character is assumed to have been, in their past, that selfish adult, too. Such lifelong dynamics in and out of intergenerational solidarity are made available by children's books representing full lives, because they must show us, so to speak, the seesaw in movement.

In this chapter, therefore, I look at what children's literature makes of the evolution of intergenerational solidarity as its protagonists themselves revise their vision of, and modify their attitude to, younger and older characters throughout life. What changes, and what remains, in the character's perspective on intergenerationality, and of their own place in the generational landscape of their world, as they grow old?

The first part of this chapter is devoted to theoretical reflection on what the lack of full lives in children's literature means for the representation of intergenerational relationships, finishing with how we may define intergenerational solidarity as evolving throughout the life course. In the second part, I look at full lives in biographies for children. The purpose of exemplarity of the genre means that intergenerational solidarity is frequently presented as the handing down of values, which the child character gratefully receives from helpful adults, and that the aging character, in turn, has the duty to pass on. In such books, intergenerational solidarity is perceived as asynchronous: one will be generous towards the future generation as the past generations were once generous to one, but the individual cannot reciprocate to the older figure at the moment of giving. In the third part, I look at a more haphazard selection of stories that represent full lives, highlighting their more ambivalent portrayals of intergenerational solidarity. There, the synchronous nature of intergenerational solidarity is more evident, but also more fraught. I will not attempt to propose an all-encompassing theoretical framework of such works, which is impossible given the fragmentary nature of the corpus. Rather, I will suggest that representing full lives in children's literature allows for an exploration of age-related topics that the wider canon tends to ignore. Among those are the fear of obsolescence, the impossibility of redemption, and ambivalence towards intergenerational others in the creation of one's existence.

## INTERGENERATIONAL RELATIONSHIPS IN (MOST) CHILDREN'S LITERATURE: A STATIC CONCEPT

As a category of text bound to the *Bildungsroman*—and, in Roberta Seelinger Trites's famous analysis, the *Entwicklungsroman* for adolescent literature (*passim*)—the children's book, in theory, traditionally focuses on processes of growth. This does not rule out the portrayal of full lives, but in practice it is difficult to find examples of children's books that take their protagonist from an early age to midlife and/or senescence. There exists a number of such books that, although originally published for adults, have been beloved by younger readers over the centuries. Herman Hesse's *Siddhartha* (1922) is perhaps the most radical example; Charlotte Brontë's *Jane Eyre* (1847), though a more limited timespan, would arguably qualify. But those *de facto* crossover celebrities are red herrings; by far the most widespread type of texts that represent "full lives" to child or young adult readers are texts in which the life ends abruptly. From Werther to Augustus Waters, many protagonists do live full lives in children's, young adult and crossover texts, but that is because they live fast and die young.

Rarely do we even see representations of "full young lives"—namely, from childhood to late adolescence. J. K. Rowling's *Harry Potter* series (1997–2007) is a striking counterexample, but generally it is unfashionable to have characters cross the gap, especially within one book, between childhood and adolescence. Editorial categories may be to blame in part for that state of affairs, but there is also something more profound at stake; as Lydia Kokkola explores, adolescence has been historically and culturally set up as a "buffer zone" (33) between childhood and adulthood, its fabled Sturm und Drang preserving the purity of childhood by contrast. The thresholds between childhood and adolescence, and between adolescence and adulthood, are everywhere hinted at yet often offstage—their crossing is made *obscene*.

This segmentation of protagonists' existences in children's and young adult literature into short narrative timeframes means that we only get snapshots of intergenerational relationships. Those relationships are solidified; even when they are presented in nuanced ways, their descriptions cannot involve evolution and re-evaluation throughout the life course of the main protagonist, because the main protagonist simply does not have time to re-evaluate those relationships. There is little opportunity for self-reflectiveness about intergenerational relationships, since so little temporal distance is available to the protagonists. Most prominently, they lack the experience of being part of another generation. Whenever such retrospective evaluation occurs, it is generally given rather awkwardly, in the form of an epilogue, postface, or paratext. The infamously clunky epilogue to the *Harry Potter* series, in which the once-young characters are put in the position of (still relatively young) parents, is one such example, but we can also mention the very end of José Mauro de Vasconcelos's *My Sweet Orange Tree* (1968), in which Vasconcelos—suddenly endorsing an authorial, rather than narratorial, position—reflects upon his changed perception of the older protagonist, in the light, so to speak, of new evidence—his own evolved vision of intergenerational relationships. It is not clear whether this self-reflective ending should be seen as text or paratext, and this is part of the point: in children's literature, reflections on how the protagonist's later life modified their perceptions of other generations hover in an uneasy narrative space.

The tendency for children's literature to present only "snapshots" of intergenerational relationships is one of its elementary characteristics. It is narratively, structurally, and aesthetically "correct," from the viewpoint of children's literature theory, that intergenerational relationships should be thus reified. There is even clear ideological purpose to that reification; the teenage crisis, for instance, and what it implies of conflictual relationships with adults, has been quite rightly posited by Trites (passim) as a founding component of young adult literature, with both narrative and didactic purpose. The lack of retrospective evaluation of intergenerational relationships is one of those essential features that allow children's and young adult literature to achieve poetic, ideological, and formal stability.

We know, of course, that it is not existentially accurate to think of intergenerational relationships, and especially of intergenerational solidarity, as static. One gains and loses a sense of connectedness with older and younger generations, and indeed with one's own generational contemporaries, as one grows and as one endorses the generationally specific roles that were once only witnessed from a distance. Furthermore, child perspectives on intergenerational solidarity—for instance, knowing that flying a kite with a grandfather may be an equally enjoyable activity for the grandfather—may be eminently different to that of older people, whose enjoyment of said activity may be layered with their own memories of that shared activity with their own grandparent, with the joy of giving pleasure to the child, and yet also with a conflicting desire to sit down with a nice glass of Chianti and a good book.

Therefore, for a literature so eminently concerned with age—aetonormative, as Nikolajeva (2010) has argued, and maintaining adulthood as an aspirational norm (see also Nodelman)—children's literature is also limited in its perceptions of the lifelong changes in interactions with generational others. This makes the very concept of intergenerational solidarity difficult to accommodate in such a literature. I am here defining the concept as mutual well-wishing and trust, evidenced by, for instance, reciprocal acts of help, kindness, or generosity between members of two different generations. It is difficult to accommodate intergenerational solidarity within narratives occurring over a brief timespan, because that exchange of favors is most often solely understood in specific contexts intensified by narrative necessity, rather than envisaged as existential, continuing, and evolving through time, subject to constant reconsideration, and tinged with memories of previous encounters.

## THE BIOGRAPHY FOR CHILDREN: INTERGENERATIONAL SOLIDARITY AS AN ABSTRACT CONCEPT

Biographies for children, as I have discussed elsewhere, form an undertheorized, though currently thriving, genre that encompasses a wide variety of works. The genre is comprised of biographies and autobiographies of real people, although *fictional* (auto)biographies of characters set up as historically significant may also be included, as well as works inscribed within the nineteenth-century tradition of fictional biographies of things or animals, such as Anna Sewell's *Black Beauty* (1877), which I have no space to tackle within this chapter (see Pickering). Biographies are among the oldest kinds of children's literature, with historical, narrative, and aesthetic ties to other literary genres, including hagiography and memoir. I am working, within this analysis, on the assumption that the biography for children *de facto* has an exemplary purpose, in that the presentation of eminent individuals is at least partly intended to elicit admiration in the young reader. The inspirational nature of the genre is still a clear overall purpose of that corpus, as evidenced by the proliferation in recent years of biographies of influential women (see, for example, the hugely popular series "Little People, Big Dreams"). This definition suffers nuances, not least that the aspirational nature might be counterbalanced by the presentation of their contribution to knowledge or the history of ideas; however, straightforward counterexamples, such as biographies of evil people, are exceedingly rare in children's literature.

Biographies for children, particularly preoccupied with the question of what makes an exemplary existence, generally put emphasis on those aspects of a person's early life that may predispose them to lead said existence. This is where, often, formative experiences are described in relation to older, parent or mentor, figures whose patient understanding and help accompanies the child. There is clear didactic content in such relationships in the simplest sense of the word—that is, an adult leading a child towards knowledge—but also a markedly child-focused view of the adult as intensely concentrated on the child's success. Narratively as well as ideologically, the intergenerational relationships in such books tend to focus on the handing down, by adults, of intellectual, moral, and physical tools to enable the child's self-realization.

I will take here as an example the Chinese-box treatment of such child-adult relationships in the building of a great existence, in Nikki Grimes and Bryan Collier's *Barack Obama, Son of Promise, Child of Hope* (2008). This picturebook biography of the former US president, which devotes time to little Barack's education, is framed by a fictive relationship between a mother narrator and a child narratee; the (black) mother tells the child about Barack Obama's life, himself presented in a close relationship to his mother.[1] The double layer of child-adult intimacy, clustered around the great man's achievements, is reinforced still by another intergenerational relationship it implies—that of its own possible reading event by a parent-child couple together. The implications are clear: as the great man was helped by the benevolent, caring mother, so the child can be great, if protected, assisted, and loved by an adult.

Other biographies present the same theme in reverse, underlining, instead, the existential weight of an absent parent. Amy Novesky and Isabelle Arsenault's *Cloth Lullaby* (2016), a highly stylized biography of Louise Bourgeois, emphasizes the death of Louise's mother, triggering the protagonist's grief, which leads to her own success as an artist. Louise, left alone, undertakes to piece her life together, using the legacy of her mother's craf, symbolized alternatively by spiders, rivers, constellations, and tapestries. While *Cloth Lullaby* is decidedly darker than *Barack Obama, Son of Promise, Child of Hope*, and stamped throughout by loss—of the mother, of a sense of self, of the meaning of existence—it relies on a similar kind of premise: that the adult's role in the child's life is that of a giver, hander-down, protector, and helper. As far as those biographies are concerned, the child at the time of blossoming is in a position primarily of receiver. This is not intergenerational solidarity, but a one-directional duty of care from the adult to the child. Nurturing, it is understood, flows overwhelmingly in one direction.

Clearly, this treatment echoes what critics have identified as the role of the helper, the parent or the person *in loco parentis* in children's literature more generally. It also recalls a Rousseauist view of education, in which the carer is placed in the position of a gardener (Rousseau's Jean-Jacques in *Emile* is a "tuteur," which can mean both a tutor and a gardening-stake around which a plant coils). As such, there should be nothing especially noteworthy about this perception of transgenerational help. Yet this is not the full story, because, of course, in the biography the child character ultimately grows into an adult, then (potentially) an older person. And it is then their turn to repay the favor.

Here intergenerational solidarity arises in biography for children, where it acquires a presence, importance, and conceptual vigor so strong as to become quasi-philosophical. For, eminently, the grown man or woman of the biography for children is most often, in turn, placed in the role of the inspirator, helper, protector, carer, and giver. Having received the attention of adults as children—or having suffered from that lack of attention—they are placed in the position of someone who has, so to speak, contracted a kind of existential debt. It is striking, in biographies for children, that many of them end with the middle-aged or elderly character in a mentoring position for much younger characters, or that the whole story is framed by a didactic situation in which there is in effect a didactic narratee. Those narratees or child characters are frequently fictional, sometimes plucked out of the great historical figure's created universe (as is the case, for instance, with Peter Sís's 2014 *The Pilot and the Little Prince*), sometimes real (for instance, the children who died with Janusz Korczak in Philippe Meirieu and Pef's 2012 biography of that figure), and at other times wholly invented, present verbally, and/ or visually among the pages (for instance, in Doreen Rappaport and Bryan Collier's 2001 *Martin's Big Words*).

Of course, to those intradiegetic relationships and addresses, we must add the extradiegetic parameters of the reading situation itself: the very act of proposing a biography—namely, the narrative of a full life—to a young reader can be considered in itself as a handing down of values and knowledge from an experienced elder to an individual still in development. While the didactic situation is certainly not necessarily authoritarian (as I have argued at length elsewhere, there are many gaps in such texts, allowing the reader to see themselves on different tracks to that exemplary model), most acts of intergenerational generosity in such texts are non-reciprocal.

If, that is, by *reciprocal* generosity we mean generosity towards *the same person* that is being generous to us. But while there is rarely any reciprocity between two given characters of different generations in the biography for children, intergenerational solidarity is ineluctably present and indeed even arguably an essential aspect of the genre. It is, however, to be averaged out over a whole life course. In other words, in the biography for children, intergenerational solidarity works as an abstract concept, a kind of guiding philosophical principle, whose effects are understood to be distributed across an individual's existence. As the child has benefited from the adult, the adult will later benefit new children. Intergenerational solidarity works over a length of time rather than within a given moment.

As befits the genre, this vision of intergenerational solidarity as asynchronous is quite traditional, if not conservative—rarely does a younger person help an older person—yet it also makes the statement that human existence is defined by a transgenerational debt of solidarity. While not, properly speaking, progressive, that statement is certainly future-oriented. There is true exchange, ultimately, between young and old, but that exchange is asynchronous, occurring at an incommensurably greater distance of time and space than that traditionally allowed by the briefer timespans of other stories for children. More significantly, perhaps, there is nothing regulating that exchange but an unspoken trust that it will indeed occur, that the selfish receiving, in earlier life, will turn into selfless giving, in later life. This is what I mean when I say that intergenerational solidarity is forever present abstractly in the biography for children. It exists as a self-evident, but delayed, moral imperative, rather than as a concrete necessity pressed onto the characters by narrative contingency.

In keeping with the "seesaw effect," it is not unusual to see the intermediary stages of characters' lives—adolescence or young adulthood, the time of blossoming into the great historical figure—as a time of solitude. Ensconsed in self-reflectiveness, characters may go traveling, choose to stay alone, or plough through episodes of doubt and lack of motivation. It is only once they have experienced, to keep Kokkola's term, that "buffer zone" (33) of trouble or solitude that the solitary protagonist can become *solidary* towards younger generations.

The biography for children presents an intriguing example of intergenerational solidarity in children's literature because the uncommonly long timespan of is narratives exacerbates the didactic imperative, present in other children's literature in much more condensed forms, that children once grown older should help children just as they were once helped by older individuals. Intergenerational solidarity over the life course becomes, in the biography for children, a kind of genre expectation, both intra- and extra-diegetically. The genre thus allows us to observe, with, of course, many nuances and variations, how children's literature addresses young readers as current benefiters of adult help and care, and always-already, by necessity, also as future benefactors.

## INTERGENERATIONAL RELATIONSHIPS IN UNCATEGORIZABLE TEXTS: AMBIGUOUS SOLIDARITIES

I now turn to a much more mismatched corpus, composed of some of those rare texts in which we also see full lives represented in children's literature, but not within the genre of the biography or autobiography. Such texts are, obviously, hugely varied. There are some recognizable traditions, not least of which some fairy and folk tales turned into children's stories or picturebooks—there exists an Aarne-Thompson-Uther classification for stories about the stages of human life (173), the most famous of which is the Brothers Grimm's "The Duration of Life"—though that short tale of genesis is, not inexplicably, very rarely adapted specifically for children. Retellings of Greek or other myths for children may also present whole lives, or at least from infancy to middle age; again, though, it is not surprising that it was Telemachus, rather than Oedipus or Odysseus, who was cast as one of the first characters of children's literature.

Now and then, a rara avis flies in the face of generic, narrative, and ideological conventions of children's literature and young readers are given, for instance, Will Buckingham's atypical children's novel, *Lucy and the Rocket Dog* (2017). The book is a philosophical tale of sorts, as well as a light-touch science-fiction story, dreamlike and full of existential reflections. The story follows a young girl, Lucy, who builds a rocket in her back garden. Promptly, said rocket accidentally launches, with one sole passenger on board: Lucy's dog, Laika. For the duration of the novel, Laika is in outer space; Lucy, however, grows older, becoming a scientist who wins the Nobel Prize. In the last part of the story, Lucy, now retired, spends time in her own garden talking to the neighbors' young daughter, Astrid, while communicating to her the wonders of science. Laika returns from her space travels, having not aged as fast as a normal dog on Earth (for which relativity is to be thanked), and Lucy and Laika are reunited in the twilight of both their lives.

In many ways *Lucy and the Rocket Dog* abides by the categorical imperative of "lifelong intergenerational solidarity," averaged out over a whole existence, which I have detailed earlier. Although the story starts with a clear indication that Lucy and her parents lead independent lives despite their mutual affection, young Lucy is cared for and helped by them, and she gains other mentor figures. In return, Lucy, once old, is automatically placed in the position of having to care for, help, and guide a child, Astrid. In a minimal way, the relation between the elderly Lucy and the young Astrid is reciprocal: "Lucy was pleased to have Astrid's company; and Astrid was full of questions" (136). The trading of pleasant company (for the older person) and knowledge (for the younger one) is conventional enough. But it is clear that the two characters are looking not at each other but towards the sky, and thus the future; this future is mostly Astrid's, and no longer Lucy's.

Particularly interesting within this framework, however, is the space devoted to the transition between the "receiving" state of earlier life and that later state of giving. Lucy's realization that she can no longer be helped by members of the older generation is given considerable thought. We begin to see hints of that realization when her teacher, Mr. Kingham, is no longer able—nor, indeed, very willing—to help Lucy, still a child, with her calculations and understanding of science. But a more poignant moment occurs later, when a young adult Lucy tells her parents that she is planning to build another spaceship. Her bewildered but still caring parents attempt to help; her mother offers her soldering iron. "Will any of this help?" she asks. "Just let me know what you need, and I'll do my best to give you a hand" (89). But her father more shrewdly realizes that their assistance is now obsolete. "A *very* interesting project. I'm afraid that, unlike your mom, I can't give you any practical help" (89.). He then offers her to "come perambulating" with him, in order to think it through. Lucy's simple reply, which closes the chapter, is: "Thanks . . . I'll let you know" (89).

Following that (most British) polite rebuke, it is clear that the story enters a second stage, one in which Lucy gathers momentum to become, in turn, a "giving" adult, who will help the younger generations. From then on, Lucy, having received the Nobel Prize, tells the world her story, and the story of science, lavishing upon society the treasures that the older generations once so tenderly helped her find. Lucy's parents, once central to the picture, have become obsolete, but not absent; they are pictures on the wall, part of her story, smiling faces at the Nobel ceremony. They finally fade away into the distance; at the beginning of one chapter, they are "no longer around" (129), and that is precisely the chapter in which Lucy meets Astrid. We have been given a gentle and detailed portrayal of the protagonist's relationship to other generations developing over her life course; now the loop of lifelong intergenerational solidarity is about to close.

Laika's return adds another symbolic layer to the intergenerational dynamics in the story. By being reunited with the dog, Lucy is metaphorically reunited with her childhood dream, the one she had launched into space all those years ago. That dream, it is understood, is only allowed to return once Lucy has transmitted it, as an elderly woman, to another child. Laika, aside from being a big basset hound, is the recompense in old age of a life led in accordance to one's youthful dreams. There is intergenerational solidarity there, radically, across the life course of a same individual: having allowed her future self to become a renowned scientist, Lucy is rewarded in old age with the rediscovery of a central joy of her child self—her beloved pet and friend.

While Lucy's story remains ideologically conventional in regards to the logic of intergenerational solidarity in children's books that represent full lives, there are more ambivalent representations in other texts for children. One famous classic in which we find a representation, albeit fragmentary, of a full life is Philippa Pearce's *Tom's Midnight Garden* (1958). Not unlike *Lucy and the Rocket Dog*, Pearce's novel plays with time travel, but within her text the relationship between the young Tom and the old-but-young-but-old Hatty exacerbates the ambiguity of intergenerational relationships—and the fraught possibility of reciprocity, making true solidarity difficult—over the life course. In the fantasy setting of the novel, the intergenerational exchange between the two protagonists is always at once synchronous and asynchronous. The twist of the novel, of course, is that Tom has always *been there* for Mrs. Bartholomew, including at a time when he was not born yet, and Hatty has helped him, reciprocally, in her own past and his present. The temporal slipperiness, however, only allows for a frustratingly fluid understanding of when those episodes of mutual recognition take place and of their consequences. Sometimes their relationship deploys when they are the same age; sometimes they are at different ages. Yet even when they are of the same age—and therefore their relationship could be characterized as *intra*generational—Hatty and Tom paradoxically always belong to historically different generations. Despite their points of contact, there remains an unbridgeable temporal gap, and their fusional relationship is throughout tinged with ambiguity, frustration of abandonment, on the part of young Tom, and an implied resentment of Tom's presence, on the part of the elderly Mrs. Bartholomew, whose *present* self, in a highly symbolic manner, is almost always relegated to a narrative offstage.

Thus, while Tom and Hatty's relationship is intensely solidary within the timeslips and lingers in their minds, the two protagonists never fully coincide. While their final meetup is an occasion for discussing what happened, it is clear by then that their relationship is one of benevolent didacticism and that their generation gap is always in sight:

> "And since you've come to live here, you've often gone back in time, haven't you?"
> "Gone back in time?"
> "Gone back into the Past."
> "When you're my age, Tom, you live in the Past a great deal. You remember it; you dream of it." (222)

The poignancy of the celebrated final scene comes in only partly resolving this tension; the episode of physical contact, as if between two children, is offset by the humorously stilted dialogue, as if between a child and an elderly woman: "'Good-bye, Mrs Bartholomew,' said Tom, shaking hands with stiff politeness; 'and thank you very much for having me.' 'I shall look forward to our meeting again,' said Mrs Bartholomew, equally primly" (226). The memories they share—the assistance, help, and affection they brought each other in the enchanted garden—are not enough for neat ideological and narrative wrap-up. The novel implies that there is something unbridgeable in generational gaps that forever precludes simple reciprocity, and thus, probably, true solidarity. Moreover, the "equation" of lifelong intergenerational solidarity described previously is turned on its head in this novel. While both children have benefited from the presence and affection of each other, Hatty, in order to grow old, had to forego Tom, and it is understood that Tom, in order to grow old, must now forego Hatty. Thus, the sense of loss that inhabits *Tom's Midnight Garden* strongly derives from the fact that the relationship deploys over Hatty's life course, in which the move towards a solitary, rather than solidary, existence, is made palpable in the long term.

A similar reflection on the difficulty, or indeed impossibility, of fully satisfactory, lifelong, and rewarding intergenerational solidarity dominates the last novel I will tackle in this chapter: French writer Anne-Laure Bondoux's celebrated recent YA novel *L'aube sera grandiose* [*Dawn will be magnificent*] (2017). This complex novel sees a middle-aged mother, Titania Karelman, telling her teenage daughter, Nine, the story of her own life, as well as that of her own mother, Rose-Aimée, whom Nine has never known. That story is articulated around a family secret that provides a narrative pretext for the telling, but the most significant aspect of the novel is its exploration of the last few decades of the twentieth century, attempting to bridge, through storytelling, the generational gaps between grandmother, mother, and daughter. While the story takes place over a single night, with precise indications of time (mother and daughter are locked in a log cabin in the woods), the story-within-the-story develops over more than thirty years.

That well-rehearsed strategy allows the novel to insert the description of a full life—deep time—within a very brief narrative timeframe; it also presents, in "real time" on the first diegetic level, the evolution of the teenager's feelings towards that recounted full life. At first, Nine is resentful at being, as she sees it, whisked away by her mother, without explanation, to the woods. Gradually, however, as her mother's and grandmother's life stories develop, Nine's interest increases, and she engages more firmly in reciprocal exchanges with her mother. The whole reason for the night, as Nine (and therefore the young reader) comes to understand, is for a woman of one generation to unburden herself of a tale she could not previously tell to a woman of a younger generation who will, in the process, learn something about herself that she could not previously have known. Both protagonists benefit: they will be reappropriated through that exchange, a far-reaching past cementing their identities. In the mother's case, that can only occur through the telling, and in the daughter's case, through hearing; once the tale is told and heard, as Titania says many times, they will see how "everything is connected" (255).

Yet the two protagonists are never placed in stable positions as active teller and passive listener. Nine interrupts her mother, rebels against her conclusions, finds connections to her own life, resents being locked up, asks for more, and re-evaluates her own relations to her parents. Titania, by the same token, focuses greatly on the evolution of her relationship to other generations, weaving into her tale her own hesitancies towards her own mother—who has abandoned her—and, later, her ambivalent feelings about her own daughter, who arrived without warning.

Whenever it looks like the protagonists may be working through those ambivalences to find in each other comfort, help, and mutual assistance, doubt is instilled in light touches. "I had never been so happy," asserts Titania, referring to the birth of Nine; Nine retorts, "so you say" (286), forcing her mother to launch into a labored and clichéd explanation that such things are difficult to comprehend for young people. The intergenerational understanding that existed only a few instants before, in a suspended moment of mutual recognition, is broken, as if it were impossible to maintain a coherent, mutually intelligible, mutually beneficial tale in the face of generational difference. Titania's full life can no more contain her daughter's than the short night can contain Titania's life; any storytelling, for the purpose of getting a younger generation to understand one's life, is always a failed affair. When dawn is supposed to bring closure, in the concrete form of the grandmother's return, it brings, unexpectedly, yet another escape: Nine decides she cannot "face in the flesh the characters that have peopled her night" (288). She escapes the log cabin, goes for a swim in the lake, checks her phone—in other words, checking in with her own contemporaries, with the flat surface of her daily life. Eventually, her mother finds her again, and leads her back. But the novel ends: we are not privy to her final reunion with the "character" of her grandmother; that final intergenerational relationship will remain forever off-stage. A closing redemptive meeting of the three generations—the only possibility, perhaps, for true intergenerational solidarity in the novel—cannot take place within its pages.

This tour of children's literature from the particular angle of intergenerational solidarity in representations of full lives has been by necessity fragmentary, in some ways too specific, in some ways too general, and, for want of space, lacking in close-reading; such is the nature of broad topics not much previously explored. But if some general conclusions may be drawn of a theoretical order, they would be as follows. Firstly, the question of intergenerational relationships in children's literature must be understood as *de facto* complicated by the fact that the narratives are often temporally condensed; thus, books that do not abide by that norm are worthy of investigation for the evolutive portrayal they imply of such relationships. Secondly, stories that present full lives and, therefore, show an evolution of intergenerational relationships, often represent intergenerational solidarity as distributed across a life course, and therefore are fundamentally asynchronous, as part of a general moral imperative and existential ideal, rather than a contingent necessity. This is eminently the case, as I have discussed, for the genre of the biography.

Thirdly, and most crucially, much can be gained from studying "odd ones out," that is, those stories that depict intergenerational relationships as evolving across a lifetime, because they can nuance optimistic portrayals of intergenerational solidarity. In such works—probably in part due to their very atypicality in a children's market dominated by short narrative timeframes—there can be resistance to tales of straightforward intergenerational solidarity. The examples presented here speak of imperfect storytelling across generations, of the impossibility to help each other fully when two people—adult, child—are separated by a temporal gap, and yet of the intense efforts on either side to forge that connection. We see in such stories a number of age-related fears—impending death, obsolescence, redemptive relationships to one's children—that present one's attitude to other generations as forever modified, re-evaluated, and renegotiated throughout the life course. Young readers may choose to think of such a realization as soothing, or perhaps not; but they might be braced for their own slow sliding through time, until the strange moment where they find themselves, suddenly, part of "an older" generation, and no longer sure how they feel about their younger and older peers.

## NOTE

1. For a closer analysis of this book, see Philip Nel, "Obamafiction for Children: Imagining the Forty-Fourth US President," *Children's Literature Association Quarterly* 35, no. 4 (2010): 334–56.

## WORKS CITED

Beauvais, Clémentine. "Bright Pasts, Brighter Futures: Inspirational Biographies for Young Children in the Early 21st Century." In *The Twenty-First Century and the Child*, ed. Nathalie Op de Beck. Palgrave, 2020 (in press).

Brontë, Charlotte. *Jane Eyre*. 1847. Wordsworth, 1999.

Bondoux, Anne-Laure. *L'aube sera grandiose*. Gallimard, 2017.

Buckingham, Will. *Lucy and the Rocket Dog*. Alfred Knopf, 2017.

Grimes, Nikki, and Bryan Collier. *Barack Obama: Son of Promise, Child of Hope*. Simon & Schuster, 2008.

Hesse, Hermann. *Siddhartha: An Indian Tale*. 1922. Trans. Hilda Rosner. Penguin, 2008.

Joosen, Vanessa. "Age Studies and Children's Literature." In *The Edinburgh Companion to Children's Literature*, eds. Clémentine Beauvais and Maria Nikolajeva, 79–89. Edinburgh University Press, 2017.

Kokkola, Lydia. *Fictions of Adolescent Carnality: Sexy Sinners and Delinquent Deviants*. John Benjamins, 2013.

Mauro de Vasconcelos, José. *My Sweet Orange Tree*. 1968. Trans. Alison Entrekin. Pushkin, 2018.

Meirieu, Philippe, and Pef. *Korczak, pour que vivent les enfants*. Rue du Monde, 2012.

Nikolajeva, Maria. *Aesthetic Approaches to Children's Literature: An Introduction*. Scarecrow Press, 2005.

Nikolajeva, Maria. *Power, Voice and Subjectivity in Literature for Young Readers*. Routledge, 2010.

Nodelman, Perry. *The Hidden Adult: Defining Children's Literature*. John Hopkins University Press, 2008.

Novesky, Amy, and Isabelle Arsenault. *Cloth Lullaby: The Woven Life of Louise Bourgeois*. Abrams, 2016.

Pearce, Philippa. *Tom's Midnight Garden*. 1958. Oxford University Press, 2008.

Pickering, Samuel F. "The Evolution of a Genre: Fictional Biographies for Children in the Eighteenth Century." *Journal of Narrative Technique* 7, no. 1 (1977): 1–23.

Rappaport, Doreen, and Bryan Collier. *Martin's Big Words: The Life of Martin Luther King, Jr.* Hyperion, 2001.

Rowling, J. K. *Harry Potter and the Philosopher's Stone*. Bloomsbury, 1997.

Sewell, Anna. *Black Beauty*. 1877. Wordsworth, 1993.

Sís, Peter. *The Pilot and the Little Prince*. Pushkin, 2014.

Trites, Roberta Seelinger. *Disturbing the Universe: Power and Repression in Adolescent Fiction*. University of Iowa Press, 1998.

# 2

# *POLLYANNA'S* INTERGENERATIONAL GLADNESS
## EXAMINING PORTER'S NOVELS IN THE DIGITAL HUMANITIES

Ashley N. Reese

Eleanor H. Porter's eponymous protagonist of *Pollyanna* (1913) and its sequel, *Pollyanna Grows Up* (1915), is often not recognized for her agency. This quality, as Justyna Deszcz-Tryhubczak and Zoe Jaques have noted in the introduction, is often key to intergenerational solidarity (see introduction). Yet critics have acknowledged Pollyanna's influence on the town of Beldingsville, where she moves to live with her aunt at the beginning of the first novel (Avery 181; Griswold 18; O'Keefe 105). To wield this influence, Pollyanna utilizes the glad game, a game invented by her father to help her find the positive in a negative situation. For this reason, as Alice Mills observes, "the Glad Game is emphatically Pollyanna's paternal inheritance" (89). Already this link between Pollyanna and her father begins to establish the intergenerational connection in Porter's novels. However, it also highlights Pollyanna's debt to her father, situating the girl as dependent on him for what little agency she may possess. Pollyanna in essence masters a patriarchal tool, the glad game, to change the adults around her.

Furthermore, Pollyanna has agency by virtue of being a so-called Romantic child and possessing attributes of innocence and spiritual wisdom. These presumed qualities reverse the traditional power structure between adults and children. As Jackie C. Horne observes, "[r]ather than in need of teaching by adults, [. . .] the Romantic child could serve as exemplar to them" (94). The

Romantic child harnesses a supposedly angelic nature to inspire change in authority figures, underscoring the idea of more reciprocal generations. This influential child type is particularly prevalent in North American orphan girls' novels, wherein protagonists change their mother figures. L. M. Montgomery's 1908 eponymous heroine in *Anne of Green Gables* (1908) might eventually begin to blend into societal expectations by talking less and making somewhat fewer mistakes, but, as Joe Sutliff Sanders has argued, Marilla's change from a bitter, lonely woman to a laughing, motherly one is at the heart of the novel (93). Similarly, Elnora in Gene Stratton-Porter's *A Girl of the Limberlost* (1909) must contend with her unkind mother to get an education of her own accord. Towards the end of the novel, it is Elnora's mother, not Elnora, who has made a significant change, becoming more of an ideal mother. Porter's *Pollyanna* follows a similar model: Pollyanna, the perpetuator of the glad game, wherein she finds something for which to be glad, no matter the circumstances, comes to live with her harsh, unkind Aunt Polly. Through the course of the novel, Pollyanna manages to transform Aunt Polly into an idealized nineteenth-century woman, becoming both mother to Pollyanna and wife to Dr. Chilton. Unlike Elnora and Anne, Pollyanna's influence extends beyond her home, and she manages to transform the majority of the town of Beldingsville with her unbridled optimism, what Jerry Griswold refers to as "a contagious and redemptive effect in her community" (19). Alternatively, as I have written elsewhere, Pollyanna serves as a domestic missionary, sharing the so-called gospel of gladness (Reese, 167).

The cult of domesticity and the idealized femininity promoted in United States at this time was central to society's expectations for women: the way for a "nineteenth-century American women to gain power [was] through the exploitation of their feminine identity as their society defined it" (Douglas, 8). This "power" is more akin to influence, which is confined to the home and female-appropriate spaces, such as the Church and its charitable societies. Nineteenth- and early twentieth-century heroines are expected to "grow down," as posited by Annis Pratt, to become smaller in personality and influence (14). An adult Pollyanna can no longer admonish adults to be glad. Instead, the adults are expected to contribute to the heroine's "downward" growth, which Vern Bengtson and Sandi Schrader call "normative solidarity" (117), wherein the townspeople recognize their responsibility to teach Pollyanna the societal norms of behavior. Similarly, though, as a child Pollyanna teaches the adults and co-constructs a society that better embraces the ideals Pollyanna purports. Pollyanna creates "consensual solidarity" (117), in which the adults now share Pollyanna's positive worldview. The interchange between the orphan girl and her community creates an intergenerational solidarity.

It is Pollyanna's influence—namely, the glad game—that reforms the community's "consensus among beliefs and values" (118), enabling consensual solidarity. Significantly, though, because Pollyanna is only temporarily empowered as a Romantic child, her awareness of her influence is limited, even nonexistent. In this way, the consensual solidarity is able to thrive, as Pollyanna is not threatening or challenging the normative solidarity expressed through typical power dynamics—namely, that between adults and children. Even though she has influence over adults, with whom she should have no power, she still outwardly adheres to the role of child, one who must obey the adults around her, seeming to uphold normative solidarity. Thus, unaware of her supposed power, Pollyanna expects to be treated as a child and readily accepts her limited societal role, outlined in normative solidarity, when she enters adulthood.

In this chapter, I argue that Eleanor H. Porter's *Pollyanna* and its sequel, *Pollyanna Grows Up*, feature a heroine who changes the society around her, while operating within a patriarchal society's standards. Porter's novels contain representations of intergenerational communities: they depict an important reciprocity through which Pollyanna makes lasting changes in the townspeople. Nevertheless, these changes also usher her into the cult of domesticity. In order to look more closely at this tension in the text, I use the digital tool Voyant, a free open-access digital software. It provides a digital reading of the two novels, using results such as word frequency graphs, word clouds, and word correlations. In order to arrive at a more accurate interpretation of the material, I have scrubbed the texts to eliminate copyright wording, chapter headings, and illustration captions. Additionally, the "stop word" list provided by Voyant was also used, so that so-called common words, such as "and," "the," and "to," did not interfere with the tool's textual analysis. As Michaela Mahlberg observes, the "application of corpus techniques to the study of literary texts has to combine quantitative and qualitative analyses to provide useful insights" (298). In particular, computational methods "help [with] identifying and assessing literary patterns" (Wilkens, 11). While we might know from close-reading Porter's novels that the word "glad" pervades much of the narrative, using Voyant will help us know how this pattern emerges in both novels and provide better insight into at what point and by whom the word is used. Matthew Wilkens argues that "[l]iterary scholars often underestimate [. . .] the extent to which their claims are implicitly quantitative, pattern-based, and dependent on reductive models of the texts they treat" (11). Just as close-reading can overlook the larger patterns in a book, so distant reading may provide a "superficial," or even inaccurate interpretation. For this reason, I incorporate what Frederick Gibbs and Dan Cohen call a "combinatorial" approach (70, 76).

## WHOSE GAME?

Pollyanna's influence over the town of Beldingsville, resulting in consensual solidarity, is rooted in the glad game. Her now-deceased father taught her this game before she came to live with Aunt Polly. Her father was a missionary to those living the American West, and it is while they depended on donations from those "back east" that the glad game was invented. As Pollyanna tells anyone who will listen, she asked for a doll to be donated, but when crutches arrived instead, her father told her to "be glad" that she did not need the crutches. This story, and Pollyanna's consequent emphasis on gladness, underpin the entire first novel. Pollyanna tells this transformational narrative to each new person she encounters, and it is ultimately a metamorphic medium for the entirety of the town.

But whose story is it? In order to better measure Pollyanna's influence over her town, we must first assert whose power she is wielding. While Pollyanna is undoubtedly the mouthpiece of the story, it is her father's game. She continually contributes the game to his invention, emphasizing the solidarity between the two generations. In fact, her father's involvement is the reason Pollyanna waits to tell Aunt Polly about the game, because Aunt Polly has forbidden Pollyanna to speak of her father (*Pollyanna*, 248). In some ways, then, the glad game can be seen as a reinforcement of the patriarchy, or, as Laura Robinson phrases it, as "a strange invention of the patriarchal authority; Pollyanna's insistent repetition of the game with each new person she meets reasserts, queerly and fearfully, the power of the father" (48). One might imagine that a grown man, even if he is a minister, would receive a different, more resistant response when telling people to "be glad." It is because Pollyanna is young and naïve (and, in many ways, is unconscious of preaching) that people willingly accept and even begin playing the game. A young female is an unusual wielder of what Robinson calls the tool of patriarchal authority, highlighting the tensions present for the Romantic child. In order for there to be true solidarity, Pollyanna must take the game for her own, not just parrot her father's beliefs.

The fact that the game becomes Pollyanna's, as she takes her father's ownership away to an extent, is corroborated by a textual analysis. Upon searching for the words "father*" and "game" in Voyant (see graph 2.1), we see a clear transition as *Pollyanna*'s plot progresses.[1] At first, "father" and its derivatives ("father's" specifically) take precedence over "game"; in the first segment, "father*" comes up thirteen times, while "game" only appears three times. These results confirm an initial close-reading of the novel, as when Pollyanna first arrives, she discusses her father with both Aunt Polly and the servant, Nancy. Her focus

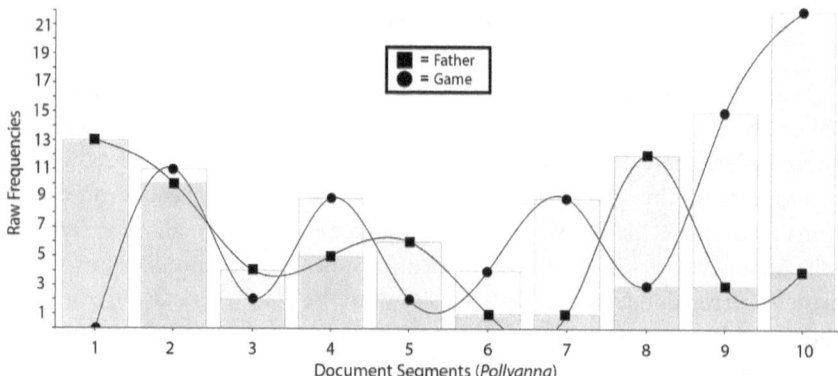

**Graph 2.1** The Raw Frequencies of "Father*" and "Game" in *Pollyanna*.

on the glad game specifically does not come until the text has established that Pollyanna is an orphan.

After the novel introduces the importance Pollyanna places on her father, she begins meeting new people and telling them about her father and the game. These two things are often spoken of in the same dialogue, as she rarely preaches the value of the glad game but instead shares the example of how her father taught her the importance of being glad. The relative closeness of these two terms is established as the middle segments of the novel show the terms at relatively the same word frequency. The term "father*" appears fifty-nine times in the text; of these, fifty-three references apply to Pollyanna's father specifically.[2] These fifty-three references are often in the context of Pollyanna explaining the origins of the game.

About halfway through the novel, the term "game" begins to take precedence in the text. This shift happens after Pollyanna has told the majority of the named characters, with the exception of Aunt Polly, about the game. Here the game is being played and referenced, but Pollyanna is no longer making the active connection to her father; arguably, the game is now Pollyanna's, not his. It is not until Pollyanna refuses to play the glad game (after she learns that she will never walk again) that Nancy intervenes by telling Aunt Polly about the game. At this point, "father*" is used more than "game" ("father*" is used twelve times and "game," four in Segment 8). This increase in the use of "father*" is not because the game is associated with Pollyanna's father, as much as Nancy must address the complicated relationship between Pollyanna's father and Aunt Polly. After Aunt Polly learns about the game, "game" resumes having a higher frequency than "father*" (thirty-eight times in the last two segments, in comparison to seven times for "father*"). The consistent frequency of "game" without "father*" shows Pollyanna's ownership of the game her father once taught her. In honoring her father by keeping the game alive, while still making the game her own tool to transform the adults around her, she enters into a form of the asynchronous reciprocity that Clémentine Beauvais identifies in her chapter (see chapter 1). Yet, in contrast to Beauvais's observances about other texts, Pollyanna remains a child when she influences the new adults in her life. Although Pollyanna lacks some childhood qualities by no longer being under the authority of her now-deceased father, she still possesses an unusual amount of influence for a child character.

## POLLYANNA'S INFLUENCE

Pollyanna uses her father's game to change the lives of the adults around her—from the cranky Mrs. Snow, who, despite her inability to walk, learns to be grateful she can use her arms to knit for those in need, to the ill-reputed Mrs. Payson, whom Pollyanna convinces not to divorce her husband. Influence over adult females is not uncommon in girls' literature. Influence over male characters is rare, as in a patriarchal society it infers a greater societal shift. As Deborah O'Keefe observes, "[t]he more exciting transformations were those in which a girl conquered a man. [. . .] The reformation of a man character had wider social implications than the merely domestic softening of a woman—more of the sense that a breach in the community was being healed. The power of female virtue was at its most triumphant in these relationships" (105–106). Over the course of the first novel, Pollyanna influences three such pillars in the community: the head of the religious community, Rev. Ford; the wealthiest man in town, Mr. Pendleton; and the town doctor, Dr. Chilton. Each character represents a branch of authority: the church, wealth, and medicine. Robinson refers to Pollyanna's influence here as the "disrupt[ion of] the authority of [. . .] patriarchal figures" (48). When Pollyanna meets these men, they do not necessarily invite her intervention in their lives, but in typical Pollyanna fashion, she shares the glad game's origins whether or not they are interested. While a Romantic orphan child's power is almost to be expected in this context, the fact that these men have power, which in some ways they surrender to Pollyanna by playing her game, tells the extent of Pollyanna's influence and her ability to foster intergenerational solidarity.

Arguably the most prominent example of Pollyanna's influence is Mr. Pendleton's transformation. He begins the novel a frowning, taciturn figure, whom Pollyanna encounters on walks. Yet his manner does not prevent the girl from befriending him, and before long she has told him of the glad game. While he perhaps is the most reluctant, second only to Aunt Polly, to begin playing the game, his change is also the most dramatic. He stops leading a lonely life, allowing Pollyanna to befriend him, and eventually adopts the orphan Jimmy Bean. At the end of *Pollyanna Grows Up*, Mr. Pendleton proposes marriage to Mrs. Carew, the widow whom Pollyanna transforms in the first half of Porter's sequel. In this way, Pollyanna continues to confirm the patriarchal norms like she does for Aunt Polly at the end of *Pollyanna*. Because of Pollyanna's influence (and arguably only because of her influence), Mr. Pendleton and Mrs. Carew will form a nuclear family, two parents and two children (as each adopted an orphan boy at Pollyanna's insistence).

Interestingly, Mr. Pendleton is aware of his evolution and accredits it to Pollyanna. Towards the end of *Pollyanna Grows Up*, Mr. Pendleton tells Pollyanna that because of her and her glad game, "all these years I've been gradually growing into a different man" (*Grows Up*, 287). This changed man still reinforces patriarchal norms but fulfills the role generally given to mother figures, such as Marilla and Elnora's mother, in turn-of-the-century children's novels. As we see in Mr. Pendleton's conversation with Pollyanna, the text gives space for the male characters' reactions to Pollyanna and her glad game. This recorded male reaction complies with Peter Stoneley's argument that "when a girl's or a woman's power is at issue, men's power must be accommodated and dealt with" (131). On the contrary, Aunt Polly as a mother figure rarely acknowledges the changes that Pollyanna has enacted and becomes uncomfortable when Dr. Chilton implies that Pollyanna's efforts act as "medicine" (*Grows Up*, 15).

Although Mr. Pendleton's change is evident as we are reading the novels, a textual analysis of the two novels combined reveals that "Pendleton*" and "glad*" have a correlation rate of 0.050007, indicating a lack of meaningful correlation. This result means that, while the word "Pendleton*" occurs frequently throughout the two novels (a total of 291 times), "glad*" is seldom associated with it.[3] While this correlation might lead us to believe that Mr. Pendleton's reformation is not as definitive as initially thought, I would argue that the change exists, but that it remains less effusive or emotional than the change Pollyanna brings about in other, less masculine characters. Mr. Pendleton changes, as evidenced by his friendship with Pollyanna among other actions, but he remains true to the patriarchal expectations for an emotionless masculinity (Nelson, 4). As Sanders observes, "Pendleton's reformation is a microcosm of the changes Pollyanna makes throughout the community en route to the climatic transformation of Aunt Polly" (108). Mr. Pendleton represents the transformation of Beldingsville, both as a central character in the novel and as the representative of patriarchal power.

Pollyanna walks a fine line between being a powerful force in the community and convincing those around her that she is the ideal girl. An ideal girl would almost never be synonymous with a powerful force, especially in a patriarchal community. One way that *Pollyanna* subverts this expectation is by reaffirming patriarchal values, one of which is the importance of the home. As John Seelye observes, "the orphan trope in *Pollyanna* is used by way of emphasizing the importance of the domestic core—expanded to include the surrounding community—the essential familial note in sentimental fiction" (330). While Seelye's statement is based only on *Pollyanna*, his observed emphasis on the domestic is important for *Pollyanna Grows Up*, as Pollyanna must operate within the domestic realm as she enters adulthood, succumbing to a "normative integration" (Bengtson and Schrader, 118) into the community. No longer can she go from house to house proselytizing about the game. She must focus on her own home, on herself, and on Aunt Polly.

## POLLYANNA IS GROWN UP

Porter's sequel begins with fourteen-year-old Pollyanna living briefly in Boston with Mrs. Carew, who resembles Aunt Polly. There, Pollyanna replicates her earlier influence, changing the lives of Mrs. Carew, the orphan Jamie, and the working-class Sadie Dean. Almost exactly halfway through the novel, the timeline shifts, and readers learn that Pollyanna has spent six years abroad with her aunt and Dr. Chilton. Dr. Chilton has since died, and Aunt Polly and Pollyanna have reduced wealth as a result. Now that Pollyanna is twenty years old, the text's treatment of her shifts. She is no longer permitted to be the naïve, optimistic orphan spreading her glad gospel around town. Instead, she must act in a manner acceptable for an adult woman.

Such a narrative shift is most notable during a conversation between the once-orphaned Jimmy and his adoptive father, Mr. Pendleton. Mr. Pendleton, who has seen Pollyanna recently, assures Jimmy that Pollyanna is still glad, which Jimmy notes "sounds like the old Pollyanna"; Mr. Pendleton replies, "Oh, you'll still find her—Pollyanna" (*Grows Up*, 167). There is this sense that for Pollyanna to be herself she must be synonymous with the glad game. Having grown up, she is no longer the proselytizing girl but has softened and adapted to society's expectations of womanhood. Mr. Pendleton instead notes, "I imagine she plays [the game], but she doesn't say much about it now, I fancy" (*Grows Up*, 168). This silencing is reminiscent of Anne Shirley's assurance that "[i]t's nicer to think dear, pretty thoughts and keep them in one's heart, like treasures"

(Montgomery, 307). In that manner, Pollyanna adopts the quiet that accompanies genteel womanhood.

This silencing does not eliminate the use of "glad," as a textual analysis of Porter's sequel shows (see graph 2.2). *Pollyanna Grows Up* includes the word "glad" 212 times, of which eighty-five times occur in the second half, roughly after Pollyanna has grown up. As an adult, the term is spoken by Pollyanna directly only forty times. These numbers can be compared to the eighty-seven times that Pollyanna directly uses the word "glad" in the first half of the novel. Child Pollyanna uses "glad" almost twice the amount that adult Pollyanna does, epitomizing Pratt's aforementioned "growing down" or silencing. Instead, the townspeople have taken up the mantle of gladness, using the word "glad" almost as many times (thirty-three times total) as Pollyanna in the novel's second half.[4] This interchange of Pollyanna embracing "proper" womanhood as decided by society (falling into line with Bengtson and Schrader's normative solidarity), and the people of Beldingsville sharing in Pollyanna's worldview (or consensual solidarity), shows the intergenerational solidarity at work by the end of the two-book series.

While Pollyanna still uses the word "glad," she no longer refers to the game by name. The narrator still references the game in relation to Pollyanna; when relaying Pollyanna's reduced circumstances, the text observes that "Pollyanna would need some kind of a game if ever anybody did" (*Grows Up*, 170). Nowhere does the narration suggest Pollyanna should go so far as to talk about the game. The majority of the time the glad game itself is referenced, it is by another character, such as when Aunt Polly becomes frustrated by Pollyanna's constant use of the word "glad," despite their unfortunate circumstances. Aunt Polly assumes that, in using the word "glad," Pollyanna is playing the game, observing that "it's a very good game, too; but I think you carry it altogether too far" (*Grows Up*, 265). Interestingly, in this exchange and the one that follows Pollyanna's consequent attempt not to use the word "glad," Pollyanna herself never references the game.[5] Instead, it serves as the framework other characters use to understand how they *should* approach life based on Pollyanna's childhood teachings, demonstrating the community's consensual solidarity about the glad game.

The second half of *Pollyanna Grows Up* serves as a coda to Porter's original novel, as Pollyanna returns to the community where people speak of gladness and the game in a way that Pollyanna no longer does. Her childhood effect on the townspeople is lasting, still prevalent in day-to-day lives, despite the eight years that have passed since the end of the first novel. This association serves as proof that Pollyanna's influence on the town extends beyond just that of a town indulging an orphan girl's fancies. Before Pollyanna leaves for Boston at the beginning of *Pollyanna Grows Up*, the narrator observes that "[e]verybody

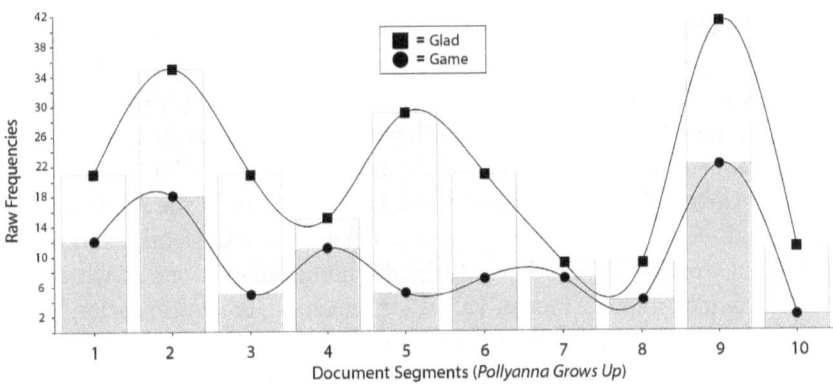

Graph 2.2 The Raw Frequencies of "Glad" and "Game" in *Pollyanna Grows Up*.

in the little Vermont village knew Pollyanna now, and almost everybody was playing the game with her. The few who were not, were not [sic] refraining because of ignorance of what the glad game was" (23). Pollyanna's game has transformed an entire town. This idea is expanded upon later in the novel when Pollyanna goes to visit Mrs. Snow and her daughter, both of whom are miserable when Pollyanna first meets them in *Pollyanna*. Now, the text notes, "[in] no home in Beldingsville was the glad game more ardently played than in the Snows'" (249). Not only is Pollyanna's lasting impression clear, but there is a further emphasis on the far-reaching change Pollyanna has caused. Mrs. Snow lists aloud all of the places that people play the glad game, rippling out into different communities because of Pollyanna's influence, including Massachusetts, where Mrs. Payson (the woman Pollyanna saved from divorce) now lives. In Mrs. Snow's opinion, this movement has momentum. As she observes, "now not only do [Mrs. Payson's neighbors] play it themselves, but they've got quite a lot of others playing it down there, and THEY'RE getting still others. So you see, dear, there's no telling where that glad game of yours is going to stop" (*Grows Up*, 252, emphasis in original). Pollyanna has not only changed the town of Beldingsville and a pocket of Boston, but the text seems to imply that she has the potential to change the world. As Björn Sundmark notes in his chapter, for solidarity to occur, a power divide must be crossed (see chapter 3). For a young girl's game of gladness to have reached and transformed whole communities requires a certain amount of power, one which would not be typically assigned to a child, much less a female orphan.

Now that Pollyanna has influenced the community, in a shift appropriate for a turn-of-the-century woman, her focus becomes the household. In becoming an adult, Pollyanna has taken the responsibility in the household but does so in a genteel manner. For example, Pollyanna never shows her own grief in an attempt to spare her aunt, and since they cannot afford help, she declares, "I'm going to do the work" (*Grows Up*, 179). As a result, she conveniently converts their home into a boarding house where her Boston friends can pay to stay with her. She makes money without having to leave home or interact with strangers. From a modern viewpoint, Pollyanna's shift in influence becomes smaller. Glenna Matthews observes the centralization of the home for the nineteenth-century community: "in so doing, they and the female exponents of the cult created yet another role for the home, an epic one in which the home provided a touchstone of values for reforming the entire society" (35). In many ways, by conforming to the cult of domesticity and centering her focus on the domestic realm, Pollyanna continues to be a force of change in the community, just a culturally "appropriate" force, similar to the manner in which she operated as a Romantic child.

While Pollyanna does continue to bring gladness to her friends and Aunt Polly, by the end of the novel, the person who needs the glad game is Pollyanna herself. This shift from Pollyanna needing the invention of the glad game when she receives crutches instead of a doll to being a grown woman in need of the game because of heartbreak creates a cyclical pattern that re-situates Pollyanna into a diminutive position, this time limited in her power because she is an adult woman. As she prepares for marriage and stepping into the ultimate role in the cult of domesticity, she needs the glad game more than ever. Pollyanna incorrectly believes that Jimmy Bean Pendleton is in love with Mrs. Carew, and as a result, she "tried, with a tearful smile, to put [this belief] to the test of the glad game" (*Grows Up*, 259). The difference is that instead of her father, Pollyanna becomes her own ambassador for the game. While Pollyanna never has a definitive moment in the text where she realizes her love for Jimmy, her inability to successfully play the glad game catalyzes Pollyanna's romantic epiphany:

> She was reminded then of something Nancy had said to her years before: "If there IS a set o' folks in the world that wouldn't have no use for that 'ere glad game o' your'n, it'd be a pair o' quarrellin' lovers!" "Not that we're 'quarrelling,' or even 'lovers,'" thought Pollyanna blushingly; "but just the same I can be glad HE'S glad, and glad SHE'S glad, too, only—" Even to herself Pollyanna could not finish this sentence. (*Grows Up*, 259, emphasis in original)

Somewhat fittingly, when she and Jimmy are officially engaged, her response returns her to her game: "Why, Jimmy, I'm glad, GLAD, *GLAD* for—everything, now!" (*Grows Up*, 307, emphasis in original). Pollyanna has successfully stepped into the role the patriarchal society has set out for her and that she has helped those around her adhere to as well. The glad game has served its purpose for the community, but also for its prophet, confirming the consensual solidarity of a shared worldview.

Patriarchal authority, partnered with the power of the appeal of the Romantic child, enables Pollyanna to have greater influence over her town when she is young. Pollyanna invokes her father's authority when she tells people about the game, but rarely tells them directly to play the game. When she herself becomes an adult, she loses her connection to that authority and has to turn her advice towards herself. Because she already influenced her community, the glad game is part of the lives of those around her. Her childhood legacy lives on, implying that intergenerational communication is only possible when the child is not perceived as a threat to the society. Her influence is not taken seriously, and it is for this reason that she is able to change the town of Beldingsville. Significantly, her powers remain within the boundaries of the patriarchal norm. Even when Pollyanna is able to exert influence, it is in such a way to restore a degree of patriarchal order, such as in Aunt Polly's marriage, Mr. Pendleton's adoption of Jimmy, and the restored marriage of Mrs. Payson. Thus, Pollyanna continues to operate within the "appropriate" boundaries of early twentieth-century society, and by doing so, is able to enact change and create solidarity in a way that the town considers acceptable, even though it comes from a child, and a female child at that.

## NOTES

1. Because Pollyanna frequently uses the term "glad" and often refers to the "game" generally without the adjective "glad," I chose to use just the term "game" for this analysis.

2. Two references at the beginning of the novel refer to Polly's father (*Pollyanna*, 6), two refer to the story which the minister uses to illustrate a point (194–95), one refers to Mr. Pendleton's father as the source of his wealth (77), and the other is a reference to Aunt Polly's hired man's father (59).

3. Significantly, in the second novel, Jimmy Bean becomes Jimmy Bean Pendleton, so some of the occurrences of "Pendleton" refer to him, not Mr. Pendleton.

4. The narration comprises the remaining twelve times "glad" is used.

5. The text makes it clear that Pollyanna is still playing the game. The narrator notes that "Pollyanna was not finding it very easy these days to play the game, but she was playing it faithfully, valiantly" (*Grows Up*, 261).

## WORKS CITED

Avery, Gillian. *Behold the Child: American Children and their Books, 1621–1922*. Bodley Head, 1994.

Bengtson, Vern, and Sandi S. Schrader. "Parent-Child Relations." In *Research Instruments in Social Gerontology, Volume 2: Social Roles and Social Participation*, eds. David J. Mangen and Warren A. Peterson, 115–28. University of Minnesota Press, 1982.

Douglas, Ann. *The Feminization of American Culture*. Alfred A. Knopf, 1977.
Gibbs, Frederick W., and Dan J. Cohen. "A Conversation with Data: Prospecting Victorian Words and Ideas." *Victorian Studies* 54, no.1 (2011): 69–77.
Griswold, Jerry. *Audacious Kids: Coming of Age in America's Classic Children's Books*. Oxford University Press, 1992.
Horne, Jackie C. *History and the Construction of the Child in Early British Children's Literature*. Ashgate, 2011.
Mahlberg, Michaela. "Corpus Linguistics and the Study of Nineteenth-Century Fiction." *Journal of Victorian Culture* 15, no. 2 (2010): 292–98, doi: 10.1080/13555502.2010.491667.
Matthews, Glenna. *"Just a Housewife": The Rise and Fall of Domesticity in America*. Oxford University Press, 1987.
Mills, Alice. "Pollyanna and the Not So Glad Game." *Children's Literature* 1, no. 27 (1999): 87–104, doi: 10.1353/chl.0.0228.
Montgomery, L. M. *Anne of Green Gables*. 1908. Puffin Classics, 1995.
Nelson, Claudia. *Boys will be Girls: The Feminine Ethic and British Children's Fiction, 1857–1917*. Rutgers University Press, 1991.
O'Keefe, Deborah. *Good Girl Messages: How Young Women were Misled by Their Favorite Books*. Continuum International Publishing, 2000.
Porter, Eleanor H. *Pollyanna*. 1913. Puffin Classics, 1994.
Porter, Eleanor J. *Pollyanna Grows Up*. Page Company, 1915.
Pratt, Annis. *Archetypal Patterns in Women's Fiction*. Indiana University Press, 1981.
Reese, Ashley N. "'The "Veritable Bugle-Call': An Examination of *Pollyanna* through the Lens of Twentieth-Century Protestantism." In *Eleanor H. Porter's* Pollyanna: *A Children's Classic at 100*, eds. Roxanne Harde and Lydia Kokkola, 121–36. University Press of Mississippi, 2014.
Robinson, Laura M. "'Aggressive Femininity': The Ambiguous Heteronormativity of *Pollyanna*." In *Eleanor H. Porter's* Pollyanna: *A Children's Classic at 100*, eds. Roxanne Harde and Lydia Kokkola, 44–57. University Press of Mississippi, 2014.
Sanders, Joe Sutliff. *Disciplining Girls: Understanding the Origins of the Classic Orphan Girl Story*. The Johns Hopkins University Press, 2011.
Seelye, John. *Jane Eyre's American Daughters: From* The Wide, Wide World *to* Anne of Green Gables: *A Study of Marginalized Maidens and What They Mean*. University of Delaware Press, 2005.
Sinclair, Stéfan, Geoffrey Rockwell, and the Voyant Tools Team. *Voyant Tools* (web application), 2012.
Stoneley, Peter. *Consumerism and American Girls' Literature, 1860–1940*. Cambridge University Press, 2003.
Stratton-Porter, Gene. *A Girl of the Limberlost*. 1909. Indiana University Press, 1984.
Wilkens, Matthew. "Digital Humanities and Its Application in the Study of Literature and Culture." *Comparative Literature* 67, no. 1 (2015): 11–20, doi: 10.1215/00104124-28619.

# 3

# "YOU AND ME, ALFRED"

## INTERGENERATIONAL SOLIDARITY IN THE EMIL SERIES

Björn Sundmark

Children's literature is built on a paradox: it is expected to help and empower the child reader, but, at the same time, it maintains and inscribes the adult-child dichotomy on which the generational social order is constructed. Both of these (seemingly contradictory) aspects are foundational to children's literature. Juvenile reading in itself is potentially empowering—it makes it possible for children to learn by themselves. Moreover, the very content of children's literature—from Robinson Crusoe to Harry Potter—regularly encourages children's agency and independence, but the opposite is also true. Reading can be seen as a regulatory regime, teaching lessons and discipline. In consequence, childhood itself is often represented as either a nostalgic Neverland or a dystopian prison. The way in which children's literature resolves (or fails to resolve) this paradox is the subject of substantial critical work, both because of the ideological and pedagogical-political implications and because of the challenging complexity of the issue. Perry Nodelman's "hidden adult" metaphor and Maria Nikolajeva's concept of aetonormativity (the norm of adulthood), for instance, both show how adult desires and ideas about childhood shape children's literature. My own position, exemplified in the introduction to *Child Autonomy and Child Governance in Children's Literature* (2016), focuses more on the liberating and empowering potential of children's literature, which, of course, also can be the aim of the "hidden, aetonormative adult" lurking in the text, but if so, it is an adult who encourages liberation. The aim of this chapter, however, is to bypass the entrenched positions by underplaying both the signs of adult agenda (aetonormativity) and examples of children's subversiveness and autonomy. Instead, I will look at what happens at a relational level between adult and child in children's literature. My focus will be on representations of intergenerational solidarity between children and adults, with the main examples taken from the Emil trilogy by Astrid Lindgren (1963, 1966, 1971).

"Solidarity" as a key critical term does not ignore the reality of two unevenly matched parties (in terms of power—the adult and the child) but crosses the power divide between the two. The adult aids the child; the child helps the adult. Meaning is established in what happens in-between, and not in recognizing who is the stronger party. To my mind, such an approach aligns with that suggested by Marah Gubar's "child is kin" metaphor. She writes that the "concept of kinship encapsulates this delicate balancing act and, in so doing, helps us to perform it. Unlike models linked to analogies like 'the child is an alien other' or 'the child is a universal novice'" (300). In this chapter, the concepts of generation and child(hood) will be used relationally rather than as fixed categories. This means that instead of attributing specific traits and powers to one generation, each member of an age group is dynamically defined in relation to other age groups. Such a relational approach also leads to a focus on how individual relationships play out rather than on the characteristics of cohorts and classes of people.

It should be noted that the "child" is different from other social categories such as ethnicity, gender, or sexual orientation since children's relative marginalization and disempowerment can be motivated on developmental grounds (Alanen 2001). As Gubar puts it, the child is "another kind of other": children "enter the world in a state of dependency that makes it not merely justifiable but ethically incumbent upon their caregivers to treat them in ways that would seem offensively authoritarian if applied to other historically marginalized groups" (296). As I see it, however, there is more to children's specific "otherness" than their state of dependency. Unlike other social categories, "the child" is an inherently dynamic state of being. Literature can of course nostalgically freeze the idea of childhood in time—and often does so—but, biologically and culturally, childhood is a transitory state. You are a child, then you grow up, and then you are no longer a child. This dynamism makes children's relative lack of agency more acceptable—since this too will pass—and it explains why children's literature is so concerned with gaining agency and growing up.

The second point that can be made about the child as "another kind of other" is that unlike other social binaries (such as man-woman, black-white, homosexual-heterosexual), the child is constructed and defined in opposition not only to the category of the "adult," but also to the category of "parent" (mother, father). In other words, we find two dichotomies at work at the same time: child-adult and child-parent. Through life, we remain the children of our parents even as we have long since grown into adulthood ourselves. In other words, where the child-adult pairing is based on age and ability (and expressed through power), the child-parent binary is relational and based on kinship and solidarity, and therefore capable of bypassing aetonormativity. Obviously, these two systems of categorization overlap; nevertheless, I believe the distinction is both important and useful. A systematic combination of the two binaries is close to the idea of intergenerational solidarity. For instance, a grownup (whether a parent or an adult) exercising age-based authority over a child runs the risk of draining the relationship of solidarity; conversely, an adult who develops a kinship-based relation with a child builds intergenerational solidarity. It is possible to turn it the other way round, too, for a child can (at least to some extent) choose to relate to adults as "kin" or regard them as anonymous representatives of adult authority. In my reading of the Emil trilogy, intergenerational solidarity, kinship, confrontation, and redistribution of power/ agency are central. We see examples of intergenerational solidarity, as well as instances when kinship-based agency is (temporarily) obstructed in Emil's relations to his family (father, mother, sister), to the farmhand Alfred, and to the farming community of Lönneberga, where the stories are set. In a wider context, Astrid Lindgren's questioning of the adult-child norm can be seen as being in harmony with changing perceptions of childhood in the Nordic countries from 1950s and onwards. The changing view of children and childhood can be traced in legislation, in child psychology, and in children's literature (see Kåreland 1999). To what extent children's literature was responsible for the "scripting" of a more liberated child is of course hard to gauge. In line with Gubar's reasoning about "looping" (294–95), one could hypothesize that these fictional accounts of superhuman Pippis and mischievous Emils have, at least partly, shaped contemporary Scandinavian ideas of what it is to be a child, an adult, a family, and a society.

## THE EMIL BOOKS

Astrid Lindgren's three books about Emil have not been as widely discussed as her books about Pippi Longstocking. Still, there is a body of critical work in Swedish on the books that has focused on the narration (Boethius 1990), the biographical elements (Edström 1992; Strömstedt 1977), folk genres (Nettervik

1996), and verses and songs (Sundmark 2011). There is also an interesting Marxist-psychoanalytic reading of the Emil books by Eva Adolfsson, Ulf Eriksson, and Birgitta Holm (1971), to which I will return later.

Emil is a good-natured and enterprising boy endowed with enormous energy and inventiveness. He is five in the first book and seven in the third. Although he never intends any harm, his actions and (mis)deeds frequently land him in trouble, especially with his father, Anton. When this happens, Emil is locked in the woodshed. While his father bars it from the outside to prevent Emil from getting out, Emil locks it from the inside to prevent his father from coming in. Emil's mother, Alma, worries about her son but insists that he is "a good boy." She keeps a diary where Emil's "hyss" (pranks/deeds) are scrupulously recorded. The narrator of the Emil stories seemingly relates what can be gleaned from Alma's notes and sometimes comments on the mother's concerns about her son, as we see in book two:

> But there were new days to come, and more mischief to get up to. Emil's mother wrote in the blue notebook until her arm ached and until the book was full of her scribbling, both backwards and forwards and up and down. "May God give me strength with that lad," she wrote. 'He'll go far if he lives long enuf to be grown wich his father does not believe will happen." (41)

The diary-style of the narrative is also reinforced by the chapter headings, which relate what Emil did on a particular day. One such day and chapter from book two will be examined in some detail: "Monday the twenty-sixth of December: When Emil had the Great Obliteration Party at Katthult and Trapped the Sergeant-Major in the Wolf Pit" (91–147).

## THE GREAT OBLITERATION PARTY

In this chapter, Emil is inspired by old Krösa-Maja's stories of wolves and werewolves and decides to make a wolf trap. Alfred, the farmhand, helps him with the digging. A few days later, snow covers the trap and everything else at Katthult. The Christmas preparations are in full swing. The household prepares great quantities of food for the season. Emil's father even provides a couple of sheaves of corn for the sparrows although he thinks of it as "madness right enough [. . .] but I suppose the sparrows have got to survive, them too at Christmas time" (103). They also think about and help the people who have to "survive Christmas time: all the destitute old people in the poorhouse" (103). With the description of the poorhouse, the narrator turns directly to the reader:

> I don't expect you to know what destitute means, or what a poorhouse is, come to that, and be glad you don't. The poorhouse was something they had in the old days and if I were to tell you what it was really like, well, that would be far worse than all Krösa-Maja's stories about murderers and ghosts and wild animals. Can you imagine a small, run-down cottage with a couple of rooms full of poor, worn-out old people who have nowhere else to go and who live there all together in one big muddle of dirt and lice and hunger and misery, well, then you know what it is to be destitute and live in the poorhouse. (103–4)

The Lönneberga poorhouse is run in a tyrannical fashion by the so-called "Sergeant-Major." She is described in the following way:

> The Sergeant Major was one of the poor people, too, but she was the biggest and the strongest and the most bad-tempered and that's why she had been put in charge of the poorhouse, which would never happened if Emil had by this time been a grown-up and leader of the local council. But for now he was still a little boy and could do nothing about the Sergeant Major. (104)

One of the inmates of the poorhouse is Alfred's grandfather, Batty Jack. A few days before Christmas, Alma prepares a large basket full of delicious food: "sausages of every kind, there was ham and bacon, there were loaves of bread and black pudding dumplings, saffron buns and ginger biscuits, there were candles and a little pouch of tobacco for Batty Jack" (105). Emil and Ida take the basket to the poorhouse, where the Sergeant Major takes it and says that it shall be saved until Christmas Eve. On Boxing Day, Emil's parents have been invited to a party in Skorphult, some miles away (there are no children invited, because of Emil's reputation). Alfred stays to look after Emil and Ida. Soon after the family has left, Batty Jack comes wandering to Katthult. He is crying and confused, telling them that the Sergeant Major has taken everything: "We ain't had none of them black pudding dumplings. No sausages neither. And I ain't had me to-to-tobacco" (111). This throws Emil into a mighty rage, but then he forms a plan: there is going to be "an enormous party like never before and every single person in Lönneberga poorhouse was going to come to Katthult, right at that very moment" (114). Ida asks whether this is not one of his pranks, something that worries Alfred, too, but Emil tells them that it is "a good deed which would make God's angels clap their hands just as much as they had cried over the miserable Christmas in the poorhouse" (114). They then lure away the Sergeant Major by telling her about the party in Skorphult, and she immediately sets off with her begging bowl. Emil leads the motley crew from the poorhouse to Katthult. Emil announces, "Let the party begin!"

Soon, however, Ida begins to worry again that this is a prank after all. She remembers that the next day their relations from Ingatorp are supposed to come to Katthult:

> And here was all the food disappearing in all directions. She listened to the crunching and munching and the slurping and the smacking of lips around the table. It was as if a herd of ravenous wild animals had thrown themselves over the bowls and dishes and plates. Little Ida understood that only desperately hungry people eat like that, but it was still a terrible thing to hear. (126)

When she reminds Emil about the upcoming Ingatorp party, he says, "They're fat enough as it is [. . .] surely it's better the food goes where it's needed most" (126). When a plate has been completely emptied, the one who takes the last morsel calls out that it has been "obliterated." Soon everything has been "obliterated," and "that is why to this very day the party has been known as 'The Great Obliteration Party at Katthult' and it was talked about for ages in Lönneberga and the villages around, I can tell you that" (127).

After the party, Alfred drives the inmates back to the poorhouse on a log sledge. While this has been going on, the Sergeant Major has returned from Skorphult, found the poorhouse empty, and gone looking for the rest at Katthult. At that moment, the spying Sergeant Major sees a sausage on a stick. She tries to take the sausage-bait and falls into Emil's wolf pit. Returning from Katthult, Emil, Ida, and Alfred hear "a howling enough to make your blood run cold" (134). Overjoyed Emil thinks a wolf has landed in his trap, but then they hear that it cries for help. At that Emil's eyes light up: "a werewolf!" But then he sees that it is the old Sergeant Major. First, he is disappointed, but then he decides to teach her a lesson and shouts to Alfred and Ida:

> "Oh-ho! Come over here! Come and have a look at this ugly old beast!" And they stood there all three, staring down at the Sergeant Major who, in her grey shawl, did look something like a wolf.
> "Are you sure that's a werewolf?" said little Ida, her voice shaking.
> "It certainly is," said Emil. "A bad-tempered old lady werewolf is what it is, and they are the most dangerous of all."
> "Yep, for them's so greedy," said Alfred. (136)

They discuss what to do ("hand me my gun, Alfred!"), comparing wolves and werewolves favorably to the greedy Sergeant Major just to teach her a lesson. When she admits to everything and shows remorse, they "recognize" her and help her out of the pit; she immediately hurries back to the poorhouse. The next day, there is only freshly salted pork and potatoes to offer the relations from Ingatorp. The narrator writes:

> Emil's mother was very sad when she wrote in her blue notebook that evening, I have to admit, and to this day the page has stains just as if someone's tears had dropped onto it. "Writing on the day after Boxing Day, in the evening, with grate sadness," was the heading she wrote. And below: "Today he has sat in the woodshed the hole day, the poor child. Of corse he is reely good that lad only sumtimes I think how he has lost his senses." (142)

## EMIL'S ACT OF INTERGENERATIONAL SOLIDARITY

One way to analyze the Great Obliteration Party is to focus on Emil's agency and subversiveness. He is the driving force behind everything that happens in this story. He undermines the authority of the Sergeant Major, as well as that of his parents, whose property he spends. Savior-like, he takes it on himself to feed the hungry and chastise the tyrant of the poorhouse. It is an excellent example of child autonomy and child governance. However, even this can be turned around. One can stress that in the end Emil is punished and contained (literally) for his transgressions. Moreover, the values imparted in this episode are in line with the values that parents usually wish to teach their children, such as generosity, resourcefulness, and bravery. The hidden adult can be heard applauding in the background.

An alternative approach is to focus on the relational aspects of the story. In this episode, Emil acts out of solidarity with the old inmates of the poorhouse, and he does everything in his power to help them. In an interesting aside, the narrator reveals that the Sergeant Major would never have been put in charge of the poorhouse "if Emil had by this time been a grown up and leader of the local council" (104). As the narrator goes on, "[b]ut for now he was a little boy and could do nothing about the Sergeant Major" (104). This remark of course points out the limitations imposed even on exceptional children like Emil. The quotation also highlights the dynamic nature of the category of childhood—the lack of agency is only temporary for the individual, and not a fixture. What matters is each person's individual qualities and characteristics, regardless of age. Finally, contrary to what the narrator says, even as a child, Emil is nevertheless able to do something about the Sergeant Major.

Marah Gubar writes that "the child is kin" (299), which may mean that the relationship between adults and children is fundamentally characterized by solidarity, affinity, and caretaking. In other words, the relationship between adults and children should be modeled on a (functioning) family model. Hence, the existing generational power imbalance between adults and children (as social categories) can be counterbalanced by positive outcomes of kinship and solidarity. In the Emil books, a great deal of the narrative force (and humor) stems from the clash between recognizing Emil as kin (and "kind") and seeing him as a wayward, "lost" child. Alma's diary notes after the Great Obliteration Party reflect this split perception: "Of corse he is reely good that lad only sumtimes I think how he has lost his senses" (142). But, even in this hour of need, Alma shows solidarity with Emil and refuses to think of him as bad. An even more striking example can be found in the first chapter of book two, when Emil has scared the people of Lönneberga so much that they collect money to send him off to America. When the parishioners present their business to Alma, she is furious and throws the money back at them "and it flew all over Lönneberga." Alma goes on to say: "Emil is a lovely little boy. [...] We love him just as he is" (4). This incident provides a nice twist to the saying that it takes a village to raise a child, since, in this case, they do not want to do just that. Instead, the villagers have given up on Emil and want him out of their way. In other words, they no longer see him as kin.

Thus, the model presented in the Emil books shows some adults giving Emil unconditional support. Besides Emil's mother, it is Alfred, the farmhand, who is the boy's staunchest adult supporter. As we see in the Great Obliteration Party, Alfred helps Emil at every turn of events. However, one could argue that Emil shows little solidarity with his parents and relatives when he empties the larders to feed the inmates of the poorhouse. One could further argue that commitment, solidarity, and taking care of one's kin (despite their flaws and weaknesses) should be grounded in reciprocity, and that Emil's overriding concern should be the welfare of his immediate family. If Emil had reasoned in that way, he would surely not have organized the Great Obliteration Party. My view, however, is that Emil extends the notion of kinship to include also those who live as outcasts in the community and takes on the responsibility of a neighbor who is relatively well off and has something to spare, which would normally be an adult duty. In the context of kinship, it is interesting, too, that the inmates are not represented as an anonymous horde but are singled out and named: Batty-Jack, Karl the Spade, Johan One Kronor, Crazy Niklas, Mia-Fia, Little Iris Tubs, Big Hat Bettan, Holy Amalia, and the Sergeant Major. Each of them is a poor neighbor with a personality and a history. Batty Jack is also Alfred's grandfather. By contrast, the acquaintances in Skorphult and the relations in Ingatorp remain unnamed and anonymous. When Emil defends the "obliteration" to Ida, he says about the people of Ingatorp that they are "fat enough as it is" (126). I do not take this as disparagement of his parents or as disloyalty on a deeper level. After all, Alma is widely known in Lönneberga as someone "who is kind to the poor" (111), and she is the one that prepares the big basket of food to be delivered to the poorhouse. In a sense, Emil follows her example but takes it a step further. It is also worth noting that the only adult who would have direct family-kinship reasons to set things straight with the Sergeant Major and to provide food for the inmates is Alfred. But if he had been the one to arrange the Obliteration Party, the consequences would of course have been direr. Emil's child (kin) status gives him some protection (and agency) where the farmhand has none.

Lindgren's stories often hinge on the confrontation between adulthood and childhood. It is certainly easy to regard the antagonism between father (Anton) and son (Emil) as epitomizing such a confrontation or to see Emil's showdown with the Sergeant Major as another instance of a generational conflict. Yet alternative ways of looking at the child-adult relations in the series may be equally productive. In the light of solidarity and kinship, Anton's vain attempts at imposing discipline and a hierarchical (patriarchal?) order seem childish and petulant, whereas some of Emil's acts appear magnanimous, selfless, and mature. It is also hard to see the conflict with the Sergeant Major as a generational conflict; rather, it is a conflict between the inmates of the poorhouse and the Sergeant Major, while Emil intervenes out of solidarity. By enabling the poor to escape temporarily from the poorhouse, providing them with food, and humbling the Sergeant Major, Emil partially rights the power imbalance in the poorhouse. He does not gain any power or agency for himself by doing it; instead, he has to sit the whole day in the woodshed and do penance. What matters is that something good has happened: the hungry have been fed, and the downtrodden have been given some dignity.

### THE NOBLE DEED

My second example is from the final story in book three. The chapter heading is "Saturday, the eighteenth of December, when Emil did such a noble deed that the whole of Lönneberga was proud of him and all his past tricks were forgiven and forgotten." In this chapter, Alfred cuts his thumb while making wooden teeth for a rake and gets a fever from blood poisoning. Unfortunately, that night a snowstorm rages over the county of Småland, and Emil's parents are unable to take him to the doctor in Mariannelund. The storm continues during the day, and in Katthult the whole farmyard is "covered in one big soft white snowdrift" (157). When Emil has shoveled his way to Alfred's hut, the stove is not lit, and Alfred does not want to eat. Emil wants to take Alfred to the doctor immediately, but the snowstorm is still raging. His father tells him: "We can't do anything, Emil. You know we can't" (161). Emil then decides to stay in Alfred's hut to keep him company, but he cannot get to sleep and realizes that Alfred is getting worse. At four o'clock in the morning, he decides to take Alfred to Mariannelund himself, "even if he and Alfred died in the attempt" (163). He harnesses his horse Lukas and manages to get Alfred into the sleigh before anyone else is awake at Katthult. What follows is an epic account of how Emil and Lukas battle through the snow until, a mere mile from Mariannelund, neither he nor Lukas have any strength left. Eventually, Emil falls asleep and dreams of summer but is woken up by the sound of sleigh bells; a snow plough is clearing the way from Mariannelund, which makes it possible for them to continue. Thirty minutes later, they arrive at the doctor's, where Alfred can be saved. When they all return the day before Christmas Eve, "the whole of Lönneberga learned about his noble deed, and everyone felt very proud of him" (174). Emil even has it in writing, for the doctor has written a letter to Emil's mother and father in which he states, "You have a boy you can be proud of" (174).

In this episode, Emil shows solidarity when he puts his own life at risk to save his friend, Alfred. It does not matter to Emil that Alfred is a grownup or that he is not a member of his own family; Emil sees him as the closest of kin. That is why he stays beside him for a day and a night and why he makes the foolhardy attempt to save his life. First, he tries to persuade his mother and father to take Alfred to the doctor, but there is no real confrontation when Anton says that it is impossible. Emil does realize that it cannot be done as long as the storm is raging. And when he eventually leaves with Alfred, he does so before anyone else has woken up, thus avoiding another confrontation. Everyone in Lönneberga, including his father, now see that Emil is not driven by self-interest and mischievous ill will. Coming as the last of Emil's adventures in book three and in the trilogy as a whole, the chapter provides a reading instruction to the whole series. It strikes a happily-ever-after chord. Emil's mother says that she has a feeling that Emil will "be very important one day," adding that maybe someday he will be president of the local council (181). His father concedes that Emil "might turn out to be a good citizen" (181). All of these predictions are true to some extent. Having just saved Alfred's life, Emil has already established himself as an important and good citizen.

### EMIL: MONSTER OR MODEL?

It is possible to pursue a contrary (or counter) reading of the Emil books as well. By focusing on Emil's progress from a fearsome bad boy to hero (in the eyes of the community), by looking at the power struggle between him and his father, and by noting Emil's entrepreneurial skills (acquisition of farming animals and money), one can construct a counter-narrative in which Emil acts out of self-interest and successfully dethrones his father. In such a reading the Great Obliteration Party merely provides an alibi for the existing capitalist order and the Noble Deed is the final nail in the coffin for Anton as head of the Svensson household. In such a reading, the Noble Deed shows Emil once and for all as more of a man than his father. Accordingly, Emil's actions are not expressions of free play but are either acts of learning (to be a landowner) or more or less conscious Oedipal efforts at undermining the father's authority (in order to take his place). This is not just a hypothesis; an interpretation along these lines was proposed in a controversial but interesting essay from 1971 (Adolfsson, Eriksson, and Holmberg). However, such a reading is only meaningful if solidarity across age and social boundaries is taken out of the equation. In such a reading, solidarity becomes charity. If Emil's father had decided to treat the inmates of the poorhouse to a feast, it would certainly have been a charitable act, but it would not necessarily have been an act of solidarity. Emil is socially superior, too, of course, but as a child he is also subordinate and formally powerless. By the same token, he cannot escape the consequences of his act; in fact, he is punished for it. The inmates are not in a position to help Emil in any concrete way, but they become "kin," not least through Alfred's grandfather, Batty-Jack. Alfred, in turn, is the one adult who is always on Emil's side, who shows him solidarity and helps him out. This is why the final Noble Deed is also an act of solidarity rather than a one-sided mad act of heroism. The formulation of their intergenerational friendship is expressed in the following phrases exchanged between Emil and Alfred: Emil's "you and me, Alfred" and Alfred's "you and me, Emil."

Emil is at one point asked how he comes up with his tricks and pranks, and he answers that he does not know beforehand how they will turn out. Similarly, the overall narrative and the narrator's asides show us that his acts eventually will make him a respected and successful member of society. If this had been Emil's intention all along, this would certainly have made him into a true monster, one that premeditates his father's downfall and his own success. But again, this is not what drives him. He does not always know why he does the things he does or how they will turn out. His acts can just as well kill him, which his father considers to be likely. Thus, while Adolfsson et al. see his play and mischief as didactic exercises full of purpose, I regard them as examples of free play. Neither do I agree that Emil's predicted future success reinforces the social status quo. Instead, I recognize a utopian drive in Lindgren's stories. My reading, just as that of Adolfsson et al., is shaped by the circumstances; that is, the time and place of reading and writing. However, I find it ironic that the

Marxist analysis does not recognize the Emil books as being about solidarity whereas mine does (although it represents a twenty-first-century liberal and individualistic standpoint).

I have endeavored to show that intergenerational solidarity is central to the Emil books by Astrid Lindgren, and that the reciprocity of kinship relations is a meaningful addition to approaches that focus on the distribution of power (or its subversion). Moreover, I contend that it is useful to broaden the definition of childhood by acknowledging that it is a dynamic social category. It is temporary for the individual, and it is defined through two dichotomies, not one: child-adult and child-parent. Finally, I think that Astrid Lindgren's Emil books can be thought of in terms of looping, that is, that they reflect and anticipate changing views of children and childhood in Sweden during the twentieth century.

## WORKS CITED

Adolfsson, Eva, Ulf Eriksson, and Birgitta Holm. "Anpassning, flykt, uppror: barnboken och verkligheten." *Ord och Bild* 79, no. 5 (1971): 299–314.

Alanen, Leena. "Explorations in Generational Analysis." In *Conceptualizing Child-Adult Relations*, eds. Leena Alanen and Berry Mayall, 11–22. Routledge, 2001.

Boethius, Ulf. "Konsten att göra sig rolig: Skazen i Astrid Lindgrens Emil i Lönneberga." *Tidskrift för litteraturvetenskap* 3 (1990): 51–65.

Edström, Vivi. "Emil och skrattet." *Kvällsdoppet i Katthult: Essäer om Astrid Lindgren diktaren*, 129–65. Rabén & Sjögren, 1992.

Gubar, Marah. "The Hermeneutics of Recuperation: What a Kinship-Model Approach to Children's Agency Could Do for Children's Literature and Childhood Studies." *Jeunesse: Young People, Texts, Cultures* 8, no. 1 (2016): 291–310.

Kåreland, Lena. *Modernismen i barnkammaren: Barnlitteraturens 40-tal*. Stockholm: Rabén & Sjögren, 1999.

Lindgren, Astrid. *Emil and the Piggy Beast*. 1971. Illus. Björn Berg, trans. Michael Heron. Follett, 1973.

Lindgren, Astrid. *Emil in the Soup Tureen*. 1963. Illus. Björn Berg, trans. Lilian Seaton. Brockhampton, 1970.

Lindgren, Astrid. *Emil's Pranks*. 1966. Illus. Björn Berg, trans. Susan Beard. Follett, 1971.

Lindgren, Astrid. *Samuel August och Hanna i Hult*. Svanbäck & Nyman, 1973.

Nettervik, Ingrid. "Illbattingen Emil: Om folkligheten i Emilböckerna." In *Astrid Lindgren och folkdikten*, ed. Per Gustavsson, 89–110. Carlssons, 1996.

Nikolajeva, Maria. *Power, Voice, and Subjectivity in Literature for Young Readers*. Routledge, 2010.

Nodelman, Perry. *The Hidden Adult. The Hidden Adult: Defining Children's Literature*. Johns Hopkins University Press, 2008.

Strömstedt, Margareta. *Astrid Lindgren: En levnadsteckning*. Rabén & Sjögren, 1977.

Sundmark, Björn. "Introduction." In *Child Autonomy and Child Governance in Children's Literature: Where Children Rule*, eds. Christopher Kelen and Björn Sundmark, 1–15. Routledge, 2017.

Sundmark, Björn. "The Sound and Music of Astrid Lindgren." In *Beyond Pippi Longstocking: Intermedial and Interntational Aspects of Astrid Lindgren's Works*, eds. Bettina Kümmerling-Meibauer and Astrid Surmatz, 201–218. Routledge, 2011.

# PART TWO

## CHILD-ADULT ALLIANCES IN CONTEMPORARY NARRATIVES

# 4

## CROSSING THE DIVIDE
### HOW DEATH AND DEMENTIA DEVELOP UNDERSTANDING BETWEEN YOUNG AND OLD IN CONTEMPORARY CHILDREN'S LITERATURE

Jean Webb

An increasingly aging population across Europe raises the issue of understanding between the young and older generations, a topic that is especially important in the light of the continuing rise in dementia in older people. Alzheimer's Research UK predicts an escalation in cognitive problems in the aged, stating that "[t]here are 850,000 people with dementia in the UK. This will increase to over one million by 2025 and over two million by 2050" (Alzheimer's Research UK 2019). Consequently, the question arises as to how such relationships are represented in fiction for children, for fiction vicariously enables the reader to engage with the gaps between generations. The following discussion considers how contemporary writers for children have approached crossing the divide between the young and the old. Understanding and trust, key factors which alleviate the problems caused by Alzheimer's disease and dementia, are now more widely represented in contemporary fiction for children as they are part of present day reality.

*The Granny Project*, originally published in 1983 by Anne Fine, *Billy Elliot* (2001) by Melvin Burgess and Lee Hall, *Unbecoming* (2008) by Jenny Downham, *Grandpa's Great Escape* (2015) by David Walliams, and *The Dementia Diaries* (2016) by Matthew Snyman and the Social Innovation Lab Kent, each take differing approaches to the problems of dementia. However, they have a common intention of demonstrating how intergenerational understanding and solidarity can be developed in living with those suffering from dementia and Alzheimer's disease.

My discussion of approaches towards dementia and Alzheimer's disease in English children's literature begins with Fine's *The Granny Project* as it was one of the first, if not the first, to deal with this subject. Short-listed for the prestigious *Guardian* Children's Fiction Award in 1984, and subsequently published as a play as well the as a text for older children, it is used in schools in the UK to educate children about living with and caring for someone with these conditions. It is a groundbreaking work interrogating the effect on a family who are caring for a grandmother with degenerative disease which is both physical and mental. There are four children in this middle-class family; their father, Henry, is a teacher, and their mother, Natasha, is Russian. This is a family which is somewhat out of control. The opening scene is of the doctor's visit to discuss the grandmother's condition while the teenage children (Ivan, Sophie, Tanya, and Nicholas) are eating their meal. Their table manners are appalling. Neither parents are dining with the children, as they are conversing with the doctor about the grandmother. The doctor's diagnoses are all associated with aging. He uses formal, dehumanizing language to identify her problems, such as "characteristic volar subluxation and ulnar deviation of the phalanges instead of saying 'bent fingers" (Fine, 5). In the same manner he describes her deafness and deteriorating cognitive functions. The information Natasha and Henry supply in response to the doctor's questioning reveals the grandmother's behavior as bizarre. She will eat anything, including ornamental garden plants and feathers, and she shuffles because she has taken her son's slippers which are far too large for her. The doctor's conclusion is that she is not actually technically ill at present. His action is to put in process the paperwork to have her removed to a care home. Fine's representation of the doctor's approach is indirectly critical, for he makes no sympathetic comment on the pressures on the family resulting from the old woman's behavior. His approach is coldly clinical, drawing satisfaction from the fact that he can complete his forms rather than humanitarian concern for his patient. The grandmother's odd behavior generates tension, for Tanya describes her grandmother as greedy while Natasha declares, "She is not *my* mother!" (7). Natasha's comment epitomizes both a lack of empathy for the old woman's condition and the pressures of looking after an in-law. However, the emotional climate is not as clear-cut as it might at first seem as the children are shocked when they realize that the decision may very well be to put their grandmother into care. The parents are also uncomfortable about their pending decision, with Henry telling his children that there is nothing to worry about, while Natasha's response is a folk proverb which she delivers in Russian, the translation being, "You can't hide sharp steel spikes in soft cloth bags" (8). Throughout the text, Fine uses various Russian proverbs, which, Natasha says, originate in her village. They serve as pithy comments on the various situations which arise, acting, as it were, as a summary of the emotional and practical situation at the time.

Following their parents' decision to place their grandmother in a home, the children hold a secluded meeting. The first question they ask of themselves is whether they actually care. Their response is unanimously positive. They then have to decide on a course of action to persuade their parents not to go ahead with the placement. They consider antisocial behavior directed at their parents, such as a code of silence, not helping with chores, or putting emotional pressure on their parents by their disturbing their sleep with the younger children faking nightmares supposedly brought about by the threat of losing their grandmother. Their deliberations then move in a more calculated and organized direction. The two teenage children, Ivan and Sophie, have been assigned a project for Social Science which they decide to use to put pressure on their parents. They combine information about the general circumstances of older people in the UK with a case study of their own family dynamics. Thus their "Granny Project" is born. The brilliance of Fine's creation is that within the fiction she embeds factual information about the actual circumstances of older people in the UK, enabling her readership in the twelve plus age group to engage with these problems. Furthermore, the family story built around these characters reveals the realities of the pressures on carers such as the hard and often unpleasant work and the draining fulltime physical and emotional commitment. Fine also demonstrates how understanding and empathy can be developed and grow—how the generations can come to know each other. This does, however, take time, work, and patience, which is reflected in Fine's narrative being organized around a series of climaxes. The first is the doctor's visit, the second the children's decision to engage in their "Granny Project," and the third is the moment when a place becomes vacant in a local care home. The grandmother is left with Sophie, while the rest of the family visit the care home. Being confronted with the reality of taking his mother to the care home for good, Henry breaks down in tears. The family return home; a decision is put on hold. Sophie then hands over the "Granny Project" notebook entirely to Ivan. Although Ivan is intellectually very able, he lacks empathy. His focus is on facts and information. Ivan carries on with the project in order to blackmail his parents into abandoning the care home proposition by using the study to confront them with the actualities of their treatment of the grandmother and to make them feel guilty.

The fourth climax comes when the "Granny Project" is complete. Ivan leaves the notebook on the kitchen table for his father to find. Henry is shocked, furious, and deeply upset at what he reads, for Ivan has not softened the account in any way. He has recorded all of the unsympathetic thoughts generated by the pressures and fatigue of caring for someone with cognitive impairment that would otherwise remain unspoken. For instance, he records Henry's comments on the costs of electricity required to keep his eighty-seven-year-old mother warm:

> *A calculation of the exact number of hours that her fire was actually on in one typical winter week gives the lie to the frequently expressed claim by Mr H. that "If it weren't for her and her multi-kilowatt gobbling fire, I reckon all our heating bills would be a quarter of what they are."* (97, italics in original)

Ivan's account is unflinching and unsympathetic, revealing personal and painful information and conversations concerning the impact his parents' looking after their elderly relative has on them. Henry is understandably enraged and hurt. The situation is exacerbated by the fact that Ivan attends the school where Henry teaches. If Ivan does submit his project, then many of the details would very likely become part of staffroom gossip. Henry's reputation would be ruined, leading him to be exposed as shameful and uncaring. Both Ivan and Henry know that the presentation of the "Granny Project" is a means of blackmail to enable the grandmother to be kept at their home.

Henry and Natasha share their reaction to Ivan's actions and the contents of the "Granny Project" and are so upset and angry that they contemplate beating him up or throwing him out of the house. Fortunately, Natasha comes up with a new plan; since the prospect of putting their grandmother in a care home is so repulsive to the children, they should take over looking after her. Ivan is to become the sole carer for his grandmother, while the other children will take the responsibility for the other household requirements, such as cooking, shopping, and cleaning. This leaves the parents free time to enjoy their own pursuits, which they have put aside for years. The children have no option but to accept. The irony here is that when Sophie looked after her grandmother for one evening when the rest went to see the care home, she found it challenging and exhausting and at one time felt very frustrated and angry. On the other hand, Ivan has to date had little individual contact with his grandmother as he prefers not to engage in normal emotive relationships. The children happily agree to the proposition, having "won." Yet their triumph is short-lived after they realize what they will have to do, and it is even more so when they actually start running the household and Ivan cares for his grandmother.

This turn of events enables Fine to show both how challenging it is to look after a person with the problems of cognitive and physical deterioration which come with old age. The grandmother can be difficult and demanding; she can either be engaged in the present or living in a world of her memories. She will need her food prepared in a particular way so that she can easily eat, and she will want her routines in terms of television programs. She will need her environment to be completely attuned to her desires and needs, which she expects Ivan and the others to know irrespective of whether they have been told of her requirements. Her behavior may also be eccentric and strange at times. For Ivan, the learning process is taxing and draining. He is not used to or willing to have to fully accommodate someone else's needs and demands over his own but he has no option. The other children also learn that running a household takes a lot of work, organization, and a considerable amount of their personal time, a series of facts to which they have previously been oblivious. In contrast, Natasha and Henry have regained their freedom and now have personal time to spend together, which they take advantage of by going dancing, an activity they have not been able to do for years.

Fine uses the interaction between Ivan and his grandmother to demonstrate how intergenerational understanding can be developed. In being forced to spend so much time looking after his grandmother, Ivan gradually comes to know her and earns her trust . In her more lucid moments, she uses her childhood memories to tell him about her life. Ivan writes them down in his new version of the "Granny Project," which has become a personal account rather than a cold exercise in facts and figures. He now understands why his parents may have expressed their frustrations in negative ways and also why his grandmother's behavior was seemingly eccentric, for she is living out her memories in the unfamiliar context of the present day. For Ivan, the learning experience is not only one of how to be a carer, but also of how to engage with his emotions, to understand himself. The story concludes with the grandmother's death. As a family, they now have an understanding of this woman who was initially seen only as a burden and a stranger lost in her own world. Thanks to Ivan's record of her life and his time with her, they now have memories to cherish. The change brought about in Ivan is that he is determined in his forthcoming adult life to help others, knowing now that small changes can bring about positive revolutions through caring. The intergenerational understanding and sense of solidarity brought about by initially adverse circumstances will continue to make a difference in the future.

Whereas the focus in Fine's *Granny Project* is on the depth and breadth of the effect of dementia, in Burgess and Hall's *Billy Elliot*, the occurrence of the grandmother's Alzheimer's disease is part of a much wider plot examining the difficult times of the miners' strike in England in the 1970s and the experiences of Billy, whose talent and passion for dancing make him an outsider in this very male-orientated community. Prime Minister Margaret Thatcher's decisions to close coal mines for economic reasons caused hardship, anger, distress, and rioting against the police in the mining area of the north of England. Against all cultural mores of this community, which is very conscious of protecting its identity in these stressful times, Billy has a desire to be a ballet dancer, secretly joining a ballet class. Matters are compounded by the fact that Billy's mother is dead. His father is raising his two boys and looking after the grandmother, who suffers from Alzheimer's disease. The taxing nature of their lives is exacerbated by divisions in the once close mining community caused by those men who are on strike and those who break the picket lines of strikers and continue to work. Solidarity was an important concept to the miners who were pitted against the government and the police. Paradoxically, it is the miners' sense of self and masculine identity that threatens to break the solidarity of Billy's family. When Billy's secret is out, he faces a tense discussion with his father. Billy tries to defend himself and courageously expresses his point of view: "'So what's wrong with ballet?' I said." Confounded and increasingly angry Billy's father responds:

> "What's wrong with ballet? Look at me, Billy. Are you trying to wind me up?"
> "It's perfectly normal," I said, turning to face him.
> "Normal?" I was scared. He'd gone all white round the lips. (48)

The grandmother unusually enters into the conversation, breaking out of her enclosed world when she says, "I used to go to ballet" (48), which would have been exceptional for a working-class woman whose young years would have been in the early decades of the twentieth century. The episode with Billy and his father wakens her memory of her love of ballet, for a few days later she plays a recording of *Swan Lake* which had lain silent and neglected for years. Nan begins to dance. Billy had seen her dance before, but now he recognizes her movements as balletic for she used to take classes as a girl. She tells Billy that she could have been a professional dancer. The demonstration of how much dancing means to her and what it could potentially mean for Billy eventually results in his becoming a professional dancer, in a way fulfilling her own crushed ambitions. In the grand finale of the novel, Billy is a principal dancer in a production of *Swan Lake* at Covent Garden. The importance of the link across the generations is paramount, for this is an example of intergenerational solidarity at the heart of a family which is potentially being rendered asunder by cognitive disease, stress, poverty, and cultural norms. Links have been made between Billy and his Nan through the creative experience of dance and the love of music and movement. Nan can express herself through the memory of movement in ways that are lost to her through more usual means of communication and simultaneously she can make an important difference to her grandson's life.

Downham's *Unbecoming* also features a grandmother suffering from Alzheimer's disease and dementia. Mary is the grandmother of the family from which she has been estranged for years. Initially reluctant, they help Mary to make sense of her history and unlock the silences of the past. The novel begins when Caroline, a single parent, is called unexpectedly to the hospital to collect her mother. Much to her surprise and discomfort, Caroline has been identified as the next-of-kin being named on a medical bracelet. Katie, the teenage daughter, has accompanied her mother to the hospital. Mother and daughter are faced with Mary, who is confused, noncommunicative, and detached from reality. Mary will have to go home with them as there is no provision available from Social Services. This is a complex situation, for Mary had left her illegitimate baby, Caroline, in the care of her sister, Pat. Caroline is angry and resistant to having an unwanted stranger, albeit her blood mother, foisted upon her. Katie is more sympathetic as she does not have the complex emotional relationship her mother has with this stranger, who is her grandmother.

For Mary, memories come and go, and reality appears and fades; people are known to her, but then she is unable to recognize or remember them. Mary's inner experiences, which are hidden from outsiders, are captured in italics. Here the reader has insight into the confusion, desperation, and heartbreak of someone suffering from Alzheimer's disease and is made aware of the difficulties of communication and language. Fortunately for Mary, Katie breaks through by her persistence, curiosity, and compassion. The strategies which Downham writes into the approaches taken by Katie are those used in accord with the recommendations of bodies involved in research into dementia and care, among them the National Health Service. These strategies emphasize the need for the recognition of personhood for those who are cognitively challenged (NHS, "Simple Ways...," 5). Like Ivan in *The Granny Project*, Katie persists with conversation and keeps a diary of their exchanges, using notes to remind Mary of everyday matters such as her name and those of family members. A relationship is gradually built up between them. For Mary, it also means regaining a knowledge of herself. Storytelling is at the center of this approach; the diary is a series of stories, building the fragments which Mary recalls from the fog of her past. What they discover is that Mary had been a lively and outgoing person, one who was in love with life and unafraid to embrace the richness and the sorrows that it brought. Unlike her grandmother, Katie is shy and reserved but is spurred on by Mary to confront the girls who are bullying her. Encouraged by Mary, she accepts her own sexuality and finally tells her mother that she is gay. Mary's condition will only worsen, but, with the strength given by her grandmother, Katie will confidently emerge into her chosen lifestyle. *Unbecoming* is a complex novel which begins with a family fractured over generations. Through compassion, striving to understand, and the courage to confront difficult and disturbing memories, they piece together and consolidate the past so that finally they can move together with the strengthening attitude of solidarity across the generations into a healed and more positive future. Although at times emotionally searing, *Unbecoming* is a novel of encouragement and hope.

Walliams's *Grandpa's Great Escape* is a high-speed comic adventure. Emotionally light as it is for younger children, it nonetheless centers on coping with dementia and Alzheimer's disease. Twelve-year-old Jack's Grandpa was in the Royal Air Force in World War II. He was as a Spitfire pilot and was thus involved in the vital Battle of Britain, one of the turning points in the war that helped Britain towards victory. However, the glory of those days is far from the lived reality of Grandpa in his old age. Walliams begins with a prologue charting Grandpa's deterioration from being somewhat forgetful: making tea and forgetting that he had done so, or leaving the bath taps running flooding the downstairs flat (23).

> *Over time, Grandpa started to forget bigger things. What year it was. Whether his long-deceased wife Peggy was alive or not. One day he even stopped recognizing his own son.*
>
> *Most startling of all was that Grandpa completely forgot he was an old age pensioner.* (25, italics in original)

Grandpa now lives in his past. The stories he told Jack of his wartime adventures have become his reality. Jack is the only member of the family to understand this situation. Jack is a shy and retiring boy who is happiest playing out the air battles of World War II with his model airplanes. In his games and his dreams, he can be a hero like his grandfather, but those games and dreams are far from the reality they both live. Jack's favorite time is when he is with his grandfather. At one time, they had regularly visited the Imperial War Museum in London. Afterwards, Grandpa would regale Jack with his stories of wartime. Now, sadly, Grandpa's condition has deteriorated to the extent that he is not safe to be out by himself. Throughout, Walliams inserts comic scenes of the disjunction between Grandpa re-living his war exploits and reality as when he decides that a supermarket trolley is a Lancaster bomber plane which he "pilots," "hurtling down the aisles on a top -secret mission, hurling huge bags of flour," thinking they were bombs (42). He is consequently banned from the supermarket. Comedy is also juxtaposed with the sadness of his condition as when "the old man would call for his Darling Peggy as if she was in the next room" (43). Matters come to a climax when Grandpa can no longer be trusted to live independently, for he develops a tendency to wander and go missing. As with *The Granny Project*, the question of the elderly person being moved into a care home becomes the crux of the story; here it is both for Grandpa's safety and to relieve pressures on Jack's parents. As a compromise, Grandpa moves in to live with Jack and his parents, where he shares a room with Jack. Now their time together is more than Jack listening to the stories, for Grandpa incorporates the boy into the memories he is re-living. On his first night with Jack, Grandpa stands listening acutely for any sound of Luftwaffe planes. Jack joins in as he is bidden: "[he] cleared his mind of thoughts and concentrated hard on listening. It was absurd, if you thought about it. Here they were in 1983, listening out for planes that hadn't flown over the British Isles for nearly half a century. But it was so real in grandpa's mind, Jack couldn't help believe it too" (126). As their adventures develop, Jack plays up more and more to being a wartime character, with Grandpa acting as his respected commanding officer. Jack is therefore able to gently guide his Grandpa as required, thus averting difficult situations. For example, when Grandpa goes missing from home, Jack guesses that he will have returned to a place which reminds him of his wartime adventures. The boy does find him at the Imperial War Museum, fast asleep in the cockpit of the Spitfire suspended high above the ground. Grandpa is then sent to a local care home, which is actually a cover for a fraudulent scam. The inmates are poorly treated, locked in their rooms and drugged with sleeping pills, the "nurses" are local criminals, and the matron is the vicar in disguise.

This all sets the scene for a quasi-wartime escape headed by Grandpa and helped by Jack, who breaks into the care home. The model Grandpa initially uses is what is known as the Great Escape, when British soldiers dug a tunnel to escape from the prisoner of war camp Stalag Luft III. However, Grandpa is persuaded by Jack, who fully plays the part of Grandpa's Squadron Leader, that this will take far too long. The final great escape for the elderly inmates is done via a daring descent from the top floors using ladies' silk knickers knotted together. To get to this point, Grandpa has shown the other inmates how to circumvent their being drugged with the sleeping pills, leading them through the window and across the roof to safety. The dastardly "matron" and her "nurses" are arrested by the police, with their true identities revealed. Grandpa is now the hero of the hour in real time as well as in his memories. Thus, the way in which Walliams portrays Grandpa is both sensitive and demonstrates respect: despite his loss of contact with reality, he is still able to solve problems as long as the realities are embedded in a wartime context that he is capable of understanding. Grandpa is hailed as a hero, while Jack also knows that he has played an important part in helping the old man triumph. Jack no longer needs to hide behind his shyness, for his Grandpa has given him confidence.

While *Grandpa's Great Escape* is a rollicking fantasy comic adventure built around the serious realities of the problems of dementia, *The Dementia Diaries* (2016) by Matthew Snyman and the Social Innovation Lab Kent is firmly based in reality. The diary entries, which have been shaped by a professional writer, draw on the experiences of teenagers who have grandparents suffering from dementia. In her foreword, Angela Rippon, a celebrity and advocate for older people and co-chair of the Prime Minister's Dementia-Friendly Communities Champion Group, makes the following comment: "I think it's brilliant to see Brie [. . .] representing a dementia aware generation who will mature into a society in which dementia is understood, dementia patients are respected and the word "stigma" will no longer be part of the Dementia Dictionary. These aren't just diaries; they are beacons of hope for the future" (7). Brie writes that she wants to "share the sort of stories that are hard to talk about" (13). The diaries recount important and painful times in the relationships across the generations, for instance when the grandparent first tells of their condition, or the teenager fully realizes that something is wrong and that it will not get better. In addition to these personal accounts, the third chapter focuses on ways of coping with dementia, such as keeping to a regular timetable for family meals, and at times of heightened stress just to "relax and accept them as they are" (45). Activities are suggested at the end of each chapter as the text makes a progression through various stages of the illness and its potential effects for the grandparent, the teenager, and their family. The text also points out the things that teenagers should look out for in their grandparents, such as loss of memory, mood changes, and difficulties in communication. *The Dementia Diaries* is informative, poignant, and also funny, stressing human communication across the generations where the young and old are working together with a sense of solidarity so as not to allow this disease to destroy their quality of life.

In conclusion, the above readings of selected texts for young readers demonstrate how children's literature authors engage the younger generation in concrete approaches aimed at reducing the generational divide and bringing about greater solidarity. It is notable that over the past decade the number and range of books addressing dementia has increased considerably, with lists now available from associations such as the Book Trust or Young Dementia UK. Picturebooks designed to appeal to younger readers, which displace the subject into a fantasy world of animals, are also becoming increasingly common. The drive toward intergenerational understanding is becoming stronger as writers for children use their creative and powerful imaginations to address dementia, using their work to help and support the increasing number of children who are having to cope with this problem.

## WORKS CITED

Alzheimer's Research UK. https://www.dementiastatistics.org/statistics-about-dementia/prevalence/. Accessed February 15, 2019.
Burgess, Melvin, and Lee Hall. *Billy Elliot*. Chicken House Books, 2001.
Downham, Jenny. *Unbecoming*. David Fickling, 2016.
Fine, Anne. *The Granny Project*. Corgi Yearling, 2006.
"The Granny Projec't [sic!]." http://www.annefine.co.uk/books/granny.php. N.d. Accessed October 1, 2019.
NHS. "Simple Ways to Help Someone Living with Dementia." https://www.whittington.nhs.uk/document.ashx?id=2103. Accessed February 15, 2019.
Snyman, Matthew *The Dementia Diaries*. Jessica Kingsley, 2016.
Walliams, David. *Grandpa's Great Escape*. HarperCollins Children's Books, 2017.

# 5
# FROM JUXTAPOSITION TO INTERWEAVE
## INTERGENERATIONAL COLLABORATION IN THE WORKS OF BRIAN SELZNICK
Terri Doughty

In his trilogy *The Invention of Hugo Cabret* (2007), *Wonderstruck* (2011), and *The Marvels* (2015), Brian Selznick explores the possibilities inherent in child-adult relationships, particularly how children and adults can stimulate one another creatively and establish mutually beneficial communities. The books may not seem to be a trilogy because they share neither characters nor plot elements. However, Selznick has stated that he is "comfortable thinking of them as [such]" (quoted in Henderson), since not only are they united in their experimentation with form, but they are also united in theme: the nature of family. They share, as well, a celebration of creativity: film in *Hugo*, dioramas in *Wonderstruck*, and stage design in *The Marvels*. As Roni Natov observes, the arts are important tools to stimulate imagination (165), but I am more interested in creative activities as loci for cross-generational collaboration. This chapter considers Selznick's use of the orphan plot in all three books and then focuses on *Wonderstruck* and *The Marvels*, which structurally take a more sophisticated approach to intergenerational relationships, juxtaposing and interweaving stories focalized through different generational perspectives to demonstrate intergenerational solidarity. In *Wonderstruck*, there is a vivid connection between a grandmother and grandson as we read about the parallel adventures of Rose and Ben. In the final section of the book, parallelism is replaced by intersection when the now aged Rose meets Ben. The very structure of the narrative emphasizes cross-generational cooperation. Similarly, in

*The Marvels* a family history presented entirely in pictures is succeeded by a word-only narrative of Joseph trying to untangle the mysteries of his Uncle Albert's life. The narratives are connected by clever incorporation of visual and verbal clues, and Albert comes to find in Joseph a creative collaborator. In the end, Joseph makes a story of his own adult life that both pays homage to and is enabled by his uncle's story. In both works, the narratives of children and adults become symbiotic, highlighting the degree to which the generations thrive when they collaborate in telling their stories and helping one another find purpose and place in the world.

## ORPHANS AND CROSS-GENERATIONAL RELATIONSHIPS

Initially, Selznick's child protagonists are either literally or figuratively orphaned: Hugo's and Ben's parents are dead; Rose's mother rejects her and her father is distant; and Joseph's parents send their son to a boarding school to prevent him from disrupting their lives. Despite their seeming powerlessness, though, these children seek agency in running away from circumstances in which their development is stunted. Maria Nikolajeva has addressed the carnivalesque freedom provided by the runaway plot (20). Yet, she argues, such plots always end in restoring the usual power structure that privileges adulthood. To be sure, there are many social and legal structures in place that prevent children from having autonomy. However, while I take Nikolajeva's point that much children's literature is aetonormative, preserving and normalizing a power imbalance between children and adults, I also find in some contemporary texts, such as Selznick's, a more nuanced treatment of the relationship between child and adult, wherein child characters exercise agency by, as Michelle Superle argues, "collaborat[ing] with adults to realize goals and intentions, [. . .] seek[ing] to realize their rights and/or responsibilities, and [. . .] demonstrat[ing] critical thinking and/or problem solving capacities" (152). Moreover, Richard Flynn suggests that, rather than re-inscribing a hard boundary between adult and child, setting the two in a binary relationship that privileges the adult, we think instead of "the life course as a continuum [. . .] and [recognize] the intersection of the natural with the cultural and of modes of being and becoming that persist throughout our lives" (262–63). Selznick's books show that viewing adults as well as children as beings who differ in abilities and agency allows us to identify spaces where adults and children can interact and cooperate for mutual pleasure and benefit.

For Selznick, one of those spaces is the creative and identity-forming process of telling stories. *The Invention of Hugo Cabret* has been rightly celebrated for its innovative formal hybridity. Nevertheless, it is relatively conservative in its use of the orphan plot to celebrate cross-generational relationships. Critics have described the sentimental arc of the orphan story in which (usually) a girl, embodying childhood innocence and optimism, finds a home and reforms the fallen adults around her into a caring, supportive community (see Mills, 230; Nelson, 66; Sanders, 42; and Reese's chapter in this volume). Hugo is, of course, not a girl, nor is he the embodiment of the Romantic child. He is an orphan in Paris who has run away from an unsympathetic uncle to live in hiding in a train station. Here he steals to stay alive, but also to pursue his dream of fixing his dead father's automaton. Hugo believes this object, salvaged from a museum fire, contains a final message from his father. When the shopkeeper from whom Hugo steals turns out to be the film pioneer Georges Méliès, and Hugo is befriended by Méliès's goddaughter, Isabelle, Hugo repays the family for taking him in by reviving Méliès's creative passion. Hence, an intergenerational exchange occurs by which Hugo has achieved a home wherein his imagination is valued and nurtured, and, through shared interests in magic, automata, and film, he has also transformed the life of a depressed adult who has lost his way. In this regard, Hugo does work similar to that performed by orphan girls such as L. M. Montgomery's Anne Shirley, who is nourished by her life at Green Gables and brings a renewed sense of family and community to the adults there. Like the story of Anne, Hugo's story, although told inventively through words and images, is always Hugo's. There is no intersection of adult and child perspectives.

In contrast, both *Wonderstruck* and *The Marvels* present different generational points of view intersecting and collaborating to describe the formation of families by individuals who have been prevented from growing and developing in their families of origin. In his May Hill Arbuthnot Honor Lecture on queerness and families in children's books, Selznick uses Andrew Solomon's term "horizontal" to describe the identities of children who find themselves in this situation ("'Love is a Dangerous Angel,'" 6). *Wonderstruck* opens with the story of two children living in separate time frames: New Jersey in the 1920s and Minnesota in the 1970s. Rose's parents, in the earlier period, seem uninterested in their daughter as an individual; they see only her disability. Ben's mother, in the 1970s, loves him, but for her own reasons she has cut him off from any knowledge of his father; when she dies, Ben is left with his well-meaning aunt and uncle, neither of whom share his interests. In *The Marvels*, in the contemporary setting in England, Joseph's absent father is obsessed with his career, and his mother has abandoned her youthful creativity in exchange for economic security. His parents find Joseph, at best, inconvenient and, at worst, an embarrassment. These children are cut off from their roots; they do not seem to belong within their families. This generates one of the most popular tropes of the relationship between older, non-parental adults and children: the adult as caring elder or mentor who passes on knowledge that helps the child understand themselves and their place in the world (Scheffel, 178; Joosen, 128). Joosen identifies this motif as ageist, potentially ignoring the needs of the older adult (137). However, Selznick resists this in two ways. First, while the adult Rose provides Ben's family history, the structure of *Wonderstruck* parallels Rose's story with Ben's, and the adult Rose needs Ben's story to fill in her knowledge of her descendants. Second, in *The Marvels*, Uncle Albert participates in cross-generational creative activity while establishing his living museum-house and the story of its fictional family, eventually welcoming Joseph as a collaborator, which meets his own needs while supporting those of his nephew. For Selznick, sharing and creating stories allows different generations to create spaces to find themselves and find meaningful cross-generational connections.

## INTERSECTING CROSS-GENERATIONAL NARRATIVES IN *WONDERSTRUCK*

Perry Nodelman argues that it is difficult, perhaps even impossible, for readers to identify with two protagonists in a single book (7). As he is talking about two narratives addressing the same events, this conclusion may not seem applicable to *Wonderstruck*. Yet readers of Selznick's book encounter a serious challenge in the opening: a series of illustrations of wolves running in the snow give way to pages set in 1977 in Gunflint Lake, Minnesota, introducing Ben, who has been dreaming of the wolves; then the book cuts to a new title spread identifying the setting as 1927 in Hoboken, New Jersey, and introduces a new main character named Rose, who is obsessed with a silent film star and surrounded by paper skyscrapers for a cityscape in her bedroom. Just as readers see Rose issuing a cry for help after she observes a man arriving at her house, the story cuts back to Ben, who is struggling to cope after his mother's death. The only thing linking the parallel stories is that both children are clearly unhappy. Even the forms of the narratives are separate, with Ben's story told all in words and Rose's all in pictures. It might seem easier for readers to identify with Rose's graphic narrative, given the power of images such as the double-page spread close-up of Rose that highlights her unhappiness and perhaps fear. However, readers encounter Ben first, and they get exposition of his circumstances and feelings in the words. Nodelman notes that twice-told tales move "attention away from what the characters experience onto *how* they experience it (7). In *Wonderstruck*, with characters experiencing events fifty years apart, the *how* becomes focused on figuring out what the relationship is between the two stories. How is Ben's story connected to Rose's story?

The key word here, of course, is "relationship." Eventually, Rose is revealed as Ben's grandmother, but even though they do not know each other for most of the book, they have much in common. Rose is deaf; Ben is born deaf in one ear and loses the hearing in his functional ear after being struck by lightning. Both Rose and Ben are desperately unhappy, and both run away to New York: Rose to find her mother and Ben to find his father. Both find themselves, literally and metaphorically, at the Museum of Natural History, which becomes central to their family story, and both encounter people who help them: Rose's brother, Walter, and a boy who befriends Ben, Jamie.

The stories are not only parallel for the first two parts of the book, but the form cleverly interweaves them. As Virginia Zimmerman notes, "certain pictures co-exist in both storylines and thus function like artifacts that mean different things to people of different times" (48). Similarly, Katherine Eastland describes these convergences of word and image as a form of translation (40). I am not sure either of these fully captures the connection, though. In an online interview, Selznick states that he arrived at the intersection of words and pictures because he wanted to draw the lightning that strikes Ben; since Ben's narrative is in words, Selznick had to introduce lightning in Rose's story (Jules). Selznick uses the lightning link twice. First, Rose leaves home to attend a silent film, *Daughter of the Storm*, featuring her actress mother carrying a baby and fleeing amid a storm, an ironic commentary on Rose's situation, as her mother does not wish to care for her own child. Yet when the screen (a double-page spread) fills with lightning, the book switches to Ben's narrative, when Ben is in his former home during a storm (126). Having discovered information about a man he believes to be his father, Ben calls the man's phone number. Selznick ends here with a cliffhanger of the phone ringing (137). In the ensuing visual narrative, Rose leaves the cinema and is herself caught in a storm. Immediately after a second double-page spread of lightning, we return to Ben, now deaf in both ears after lightning has traveled through the phone line (156). This is a dramatic interweaving of picture and word, but the narrative technique begins much earlier in the book. Ben's first narrative section ends with his mother's favorite line from Oscar Wilde's *Lady Windermere's Fan*: "We are all in the gutter, but some of us are looking at the stars" (27). When we turn to Rose's narrative, she *is* looking at a star, the film star who is her mother. Then we return to Ben, looking at a shooting star from his aunt's house (56–57). Likewise, just as he sneaks out to go to his old home, we turn the page to see Rose sneaking out of her house to go to the cinema. The interweaving continues throughout the book: when Ben discovers the Museum of Natural History (311), a turn of the page brings us to a double-page image of the museum, with another turn of the page showing this to be a postcard from her brother in Rose's hands. Again, when Rose is safe with her brother, Walter is reading the book *Wonderstruck* in bed, and he is on the same page that Ben looks at in his copy of the book (482). There is more going on here than simply translating experiences, and rather than objects meaning different things to different people across time, the objects actually serve to highlight shared interests and pleasures between generations.

In part three of the book, Ben finds Rose, now an adult. He learns that she is his grandmother; his father is dead. From this point onward, words and pictures come together not to tell parallel, interwoven stories, but to tell a single story that Ben and his grandmother share as they piece together their family story; the narrative is mostly focalized through Ben, but large chunks of inserted written narrative are by Rose. The book *Wonderstruck* is the touchstone for the family connection: a catalogue for an exhibit on Cabinets of Wonders that Walter, a museum exhibits worker, gave his sister, who gave it to her son Danny, Ben's father, who gave it to Ben's mother. The book, as both an artifact and a metatextual device, "holds these people (and the reader) together" (Zimmerman, 48). Everything in the book is about connection, as readers must solve the puzzle of the interwoven narratives to figure out how characters are connected to place and to each other. When Ben first sees the aged Rose in the museum, she is just another old lady to him. When he later looks at her, knowing she is his grandmother, "Rose's face somehow change[s] before his eyes. Her skin, her white hair, and her slender fingers no longer [belong] to a stranger" (520). Ben finds a missing part of himself in Rose: "It was odd to touch his grandmother's face, almost as though her skin were somehow a part of his own face, and his father's (579). Ben has felt like Major Tom from his mother's favorite David Bowie song, "Space Oddity," imagining that he, like his father before him, has been floating, disconnected from the earth. Now Rose tells Ben that not only did his father have connections, but so does he. Ben's love of collecting things is something he shares with his father: Daniel was a diorama designer, sharing this activity with his mother, Rose. When Ben first sees Rose at the Museum of Natural History, she is looking at a wolf diorama based on Daniel's research in Gunflint Lake, which ties the three of them together.

Rose also takes Ben to the Queens Museum of Art, where she shows him a scale model of New York that she helped make for the 1964 World's Fair. This brings her story full circle, as it links to her paper models from her childhood bedroom. She shows Ben how she has curated a history of Daniel's life in the model. In the hospital where Daniel was born, she has placed a baby photo of him; in his former school, one of his pencils; and so on. Inside the model of the

Museum of Natural History is a child's drawing of the wolf diorama, made by Ben. In this moment, Ben realizes that even though he does not remember his father, he has always been connected to him: "in some strange way it all made sense. His need to collect things, his interest in museums, the wolf dreams . . . it all came into focus sort of like one of those polaroid pictures. [. . .] Ben's dreams hadn't come from nowhere. He'd been dreaming of his *father's* wolves, which he'd *seen*" (577). Ben marvels at the connections that have led him to this moment, concluding that "[t]he world is full of wonders" (609). In the end, as he sits during a blackout in New York, not in the gutter but on a rooftop, looking up at the stars with his grandmother and his new friend, Jamie, Ben realizes that no matter what happens to him in the future, he has found his place and the family where he belongs.

When the narratives come together, Rose's story seems to be taken over by Ben's: despite her contribution of a lengthy handwritten narrative, she has become an adjunct character in his narrative. This could reflect a similar situation in Philippa Pearce's *Tom's Midnight Garden*, in which a boy staying with family connects through a fantastical manifestation of a young girl, discovered eventually to be an aged neighbor dreaming of her childhood. Once this is revealed, the book is over and the boy returns home, perhaps never to see the old lady again. Joosen talks about such books as providing a model of backtracking in which "elderly characters re-embody their former childlike selves in order to bond with the young" (129). However, Ben has not been interacting with the child Rose; it is the reader who has been making that connection, and having learned to identify with Rose's emotions, the reader can also see that Rose is profoundly affected by finding Ben. While Ben has been cut off from part of his family's past, Rose has been cut off from her family's future. Scholars exploring the geographies of age have discussed how the aged and children in Western societies are seen as existing on the margins. This is challenged by Peter Hopkins and Rachel Pain, who suggest it might be more productive to think about age geographies as relational: "identities of children and others are produced *through* interactions with other age/generational groups and are in a constant state of flux" (288–89). Applying this to Rose and Ben alerts us to how not only is Ben's identity transformed by what he discovers from Rose about his family history, but Rose's identity is also transformed by learning that she has a grandson who carries on her family history. As Rose sits with her grandson and his friend during the blackout, the narrative shifts to pictures, which readers have come to associate with Rose's perspective. Over three pages, the boys look at each other, then a double-page spread shows just Rose, looking at her grandson. The love in Rose's smile shows that she benefits from this discovery of a grandson and a new life stage for herself as grandmother.

Katharina Mahne and Oliver Huxhold summarize research that indicates the importance of the grandparent role in the well-being of older adults (225). They apply to grandparent-grandchild relationships the intergenerational solidarity model developed by Vern Bengtson (see the introduction to this volume). Most dimensions of the model are apparent in the relationship between Rose and Ben. Associational solidarity addresses "frequency of contact and shared activities" (Mahne and Huxhold, 227); although Rose and Ben have been denied contact for much of Ben's life, they discover that they have practiced similar activities in collecting and curating: there is an inference that they will share these activities as often as they can be together. Affectual solidarity addresses "the emotional bonds between family members" (227). The reader perceives emotions and experiences shared by Rose and Ben, and once the two characters meet, the emotional bond is reciprocal. Consensual solidarity refers to values and beliefs shared across generations (227). This is subtle in the book, but Rose and Ben clearly share values related to family connections and the importance of creative activities. Finally, functional solidarity addresses mutual helpfulness across the generations (227), and this is manifested in the ways Rose and Ben help each other discover their shared history and their resultant new identities. It seems clear at the end of the book that Rose will support Ben as he moves forward, and Ben anticipates being able to spend time with Rose, perhaps helping with her diorama work. *Wonderstruck* interweaves cross-generational narratives to show how adults and children can become collaborators in storytelling and identity formation.

## CROSS-GENERATIONAL CREATIVE COLLABORATION IN *THE MARVELS*

*The Marvels* also intertwines cross-generational narratives. As in *Wonderstruck*, the reader is presented with a puzzle: the first 387 pages, all in images, tell the history of five generations of a London theatre family, from Billy Marvel and his brother Marcus in 1766, through orphan baby Marcus raised by Billy; disruptive Alexander, son of Marcus; greatest actor of his generation Oberon, son of Alexander; and finally hapless Leontes (Leo), son of Oberon but uninterested in theatre. The narrative then jumps decades to 1990, when Joseph's story is told entirely in words. Just as Joseph becomes fascinated by the clues about the Marvels in his uncle's house, the reader is also looking for connections to understand the relationship between the Marvel family and Joseph. Selznick states in a television interview that his interest in this book is exploring "memory and storytelling and family and the way people pass down stories from generation to generation" ("Making of Brian Selznick's *The*

*Marvels*"). The Marvel family history, however, is a fiction, created through an intergenerational collaboration between Joseph's Uncle Albert, his lover, Billy Marvel, and their neighbor's son, Marcus Bloom, to establish a unique home for their queer family. The ensuing narrative of Joseph's evolving relationships with his new friend Frankie and Albert, which weaves motifs from the fiction to reveal the answers to the mystery, is then followed by another fictional—or not—narrative presented in images depicting Joseph growing up to live happily in his uncle's house with his friend Blink and a baby. Billy's motto—"You either see it or you don't" (451)—not only refers to clues to his, Albert's, and Marcus's relationship hidden within the Marvel stories and the house, but also, as Joseph learns, to how one might see that there is truth in stories (544).

*The Marvels*, then, is about how generations create and share stories that allow individuals to define themselves. Most discussions of cross-generational creative work focus on the adult as the guide directing the child to develop more advanced skills (see, for example, Kouvou, 275–76). Hausknecht et al. suggest that, via collaborative storytelling while playing alternate reality games, adults and children can "form new understandings through the coming together of differing perspectives" (48). Similarly, sharing the stories of Albert's house and the Marvels, Albert and Joseph develop new understandings of their relationship to one another and others, as well as of their own identities. Joseph learns to revision his family history and his own identity: "perhaps his ancestors really *had* been actors and artists! What if [his] cold, rich parents were the *exceptions* on his family tree, not him? Maybe every other generation, the ones he'd never known, had been full of brilliant adventurers and romantic dreamers, like himself" (480). Likewise, Albert has woven the stories of the Marvels with the collaboration of Billy and Marcus, creating a family that is "restorative, founded [in] similar views and interests" (Natov, 173). For all that, after the deaths of Billy from AIDS and Marcus in a car accident, Albert has become reclusive and initially resists the new opportunity for cross-generational solidarity presented by Joseph. He tells his nephew that he cannot continue the Marvel stories without Billy and that the blank page at the end of the drawings signifies time has stopped (550–51). However, in telling the history of the stories to Joseph, Albert finds that time begins again. As he says to Joseph, "'I'm glad you came and found me. [. . .] I'd hate to think what I'd be doing right now without you" (558). Perceptively, reviewer Sarah Hunter notes that both Joseph *and* Albert find home (66). With Joseph now his family, Albert finds his house a home again, and he welcomes Joseph as co-caretaker of the house and its stories.

When time progresses, though, there must be change. Albert dies of AIDS, and Joseph again is left to the mercies of his parents. This book may seem to be aetonormative, insofar as the child Joseph is limited in his options. He is able to question his mother, insisting that she consider that her and his father's vision of what is best for him might be wrong for who he really is (597), but he must still carry on at school, and his mother only promises to listen and talk to him about the house, his uncle, and their family at a later date. Nevertheless, on what might be his last night in the home he shared with his uncle, Joseph looks through Billy's drawings of the Marvels and comes to realize that the "story within the story" is "the real gift Albert Nightingale had given him. [...] It [is] *his* story now, and he kn[ows] his own story [is] as unfinished as Leo's" (602). Joseph has identified with Leo Marvel, as he too has felt that he did not belong in his family. Now, though, Joseph knows that there is a blank page after the flames that trap Leo and his grandfather in the theatre, so "Joseph turn[s] the page" (603). The remainder of the book is a visual narrative, presumably by Joseph, that encompasses both entrapping flames and a cozy fireplace reminiscent not only of Joseph's happy memories of his grandfather but also of his uncle. Then a series of double-page spreads show us this is the home of Albert and Joseph, eventually arriving at a framed photo on a bedside table of Albert protectively holding Joseph in front of the house, with a smaller double photo frame holding Leo's drawing of the angel Marcus and a picture of a young man, perhaps Leo. Leo has survived, as will Joseph. As the image of Albert and Joseph is reproduced in successive close-ups, we finally focus on Joseph, and just as Billy's drawings showed Billy Marvel growing up, the final close-ups show Joseph transforming into an adult. Then we see that he is reading a postcard from Frankie, off pursuing her dreams of travel, addressed to "Joe and George." A turn of the page shows Joe and another adult man, presumably George, reading before a fireplace, with a baby in a cradle between them. The proper name of Joseph's school friend Blink is George Patel, so the inference is that Joseph and George have found one another again, and they are now a family. Baby Albert is their child, named after Joseph's uncle. The final spread is a close-up of the infant's alert gaze, with blank pages left for the next part of the story. The postscript, from director Wim Wenders's *The Act of Seeing*, presents a question and an answer: "'Is this a true story?' [...] 'It is now.'" Continuing his uncle's story allows Joseph to invent the future he wants. *The Marvels*, like *Wonderstruck*, demonstrates that cross-generational creative activities benefit adults and children by helping them develop new relational identities and opportunities to become their authentic selves. The truth lies within the creative act.

Selznick uses creative activities as spaces where members of different generations join to share interests and stories, as well as find opportunities for transformation. In *Wonderstruck*, Rose and Ben fill in gaps in each other's family narrative with their interweaving narratives, and both are empowered by new identities shaped within their cross-generational relationship. Their curating becomes a form of self-invention for each. In *The Marvels*, Albert and Joseph come to share the narratives of their house, both in the fictive and dynastic sense. After all, as the book teaches, stories can be both nonfactual and true. Just as the original stories are the products of intergenerational collaboration between Albert, Billy, and Marcus, so the final story becomes an act of collaboration as Joseph carries the stories forward, only to leave space for the next generation. These books reinvent the concept of family, allowing those who shape their own non-normative families to also reshape themselves within these family identities. In Selznick's trilogy, there is no fixed boundary between adult and child, and not all adult norms are upheld. Cross-generational relationships are shown to have capacity for creative invention of the self (whether that self is young or old) within dynamic collaborations. You either see it or you don't.

## WORKS CITED

Eastland, Katherine. "Deaf Meets *Wonderstruck*." *Humanities* 33, no. 1 (January-February 2012): 38–42. EBSCOhost, ezproxy.viu.ca/login?url=http://search.ebscohost.com/login.asp x?direct=true&AuthType=ip,cookie&db=a9h&AN=71408441&site=ehost-live.

Flynn, Richard. "What are We Talking about When We Talk about Agency?" *Jeunesse: Young People, Texts, Cultures* 8, no. 1 (2016): 254–65. Project MUSE, doi:10 .1353/jeu.2016.0012.

Hausknecht, Simone, Carmen Neustaedter, and David Kaufman. "Blurring the Lines of Age: Intergenerational Collaboration in Alternate Reality Games." In *Game-based Learning across the Lifespan: Cross-Generational and Age-Oriented Topics*, eds. Margarida Romero, Kimberly Sawchuk, Josep Blat, Sergio Sayago, and Hubert Ouellett, 47–64. Springer, 2016. ProQuest Ebook Central, ebookcentral.proquest.com/lib/viu/detail.Action?docID=4723011.

Henderson, Jane. "Inventions of Brian Selnick: Latest Book Makes Unusual Trilogy." *St. Louis Post-Dispatch*, September 20, 2015, http://www.stltoday.com/entertainment/books-and-litera ture/book-blog/inventions-of-brian-selznick-latest-book-makes-unusual-trilogy/article _6651a90e -726b-50e3-b999–20b579c00bfd.html. Accessed February 21, 2018.

Hopkins, Peter, and Rachel Pain. "Geographies of Age: Thinking Relationally." *Area* 39, no. 3 (2007): 287–94. JSTOR, www.jstor.org/stable/40346044.

Hunter, Sarah. "Safe Harbor." *Booklist* 111, no. 21 (July 1, 2015): 66. EBSCOhost, ezproxy.viu.ca/login?url=http://search.ebscohost.com/login.aspx?direct=true&AuthType=ip,cookie&db=aph&AN=108581903&site=ehost-live.

Joosen, Vanessa. "Second Childhoods and Intergenerational Dialogues: How Children's Literature Studies and Age Studies Can Supplement Each Other." *Children's Literature Association Quarterly* 40, no. 2 (2015): 126–40. Project MUSE, doi:10.1353/chq .2015.0016.

Jules [Julia Davidson]. "My Conversation with Brian Selznick: On *Wonderstruck, Hugo*, and the Terror and Joy of Creating Children's Books." *Seven Impossible Things Before Breakfast*, October 27, 2011, blaine.org/sevenimpossiblethings/?p=2228. Accessed March 6, 2017.

Kouvou, Ourania. "Drawing with Children: An Experiment in Assisted Creativity." *International Journal of Art and Design Education* 35, no. 2 (2016): 275–90. *Wiley Online Library*, doi:10.1111/jade.12056.

Mahne, Katharina, and Oliver Huxhold. "Social Contact between Grandparents and Older Grandchildren: A Three-Generation Perspective." In *Contemporary Grandparenting: Changing Family Relationships in Global Contexts*, eds. Sara Arber and Virpi Timonen, 225–46. Policy Press, 2012. *ProQuest Ebook Central*, ebookcentral.proquest.com/ lib/viu/ detail.action?docID=922865.

"The Making of Brian Selznick's *The Marvels*." Canada AM-CTV Television, Toronto, October 15, 2015. *ProQuest*, ezproxy.viu.ca/login?url=https://search-proquest-com.ez proxy.viu.ca/ docview/1722258722?accountid=12246.

Mills, Claudia. "Children in Search of Family: Orphan Novels through the Century." *Children's Literature in Education* 18, no. 4 (1987): 227–39. *Springer*, doi: 10.1007 /BF0 1141754.

Natov, Roni. *The Courage to Imagine: The Child Hero in Children's Literature*. Bloomsbury Academic, 2018.

Nelson, Claudia. *Little Strangers: Portrayals of Adoption and Foster Care in America, 1850–1929*. Indiana University Press, 2003.

Nikolajeva, Maria. "Theory, Post-Theory, and Aetonormative Theory." *Neohelicon* 36, no. 1 (2009): 13–24. *Springer*, doi: 10.1007/s11059-009-1002-4.

Nodelman, Perry. *Alternating Narratives in Fiction for Young Readers: Twice Upon a Time*. Palgrave Macmillan, 2017. *ProQuest Ebook Central*, ebookcentral.proquest.com/lib /viu/ detail.action?docID=3661.

Sanders, Joe Sutliff. "Spinning Sympathy: Orphan Girl Novels and Sentimental Tradition." *Children's Literature Association Quarterly* 33, no. 1 (2008): 41–61. *Project MUSE*, doi:10.1353/chq.2008.0005.

Scheffel, Tara-Lynn. "The Heart of the Matter: Exploring Intergenerational Themes in Children's Literature." *Journal of Intergenerational Relationships* 13, no. 2 (2015): 167–81. *Taylor and Francis*, doi:10.1080/15350770.2015.1028259.

Selznick, Brian. *The Invention of Hugo Cabret*. Scholastic, 2007.

Selznick, Brian. "'Love is a Dangerous Angel': Thoughts on Queerness and Children's Literature." *Children and Libraries* 13, no. 4 (2015): 3–12. *EBSCOhost*, ezproxy.viu.ca/ login?url =http: //search.ebscohost.com/login.aspx?direct=true&AuthType=ip,cookie&db =aph &AN=111472063&site=ehost-live.

Selznick, Brian. *The Marvels*. Scholastic, 2015.

Selznick, Brian. *Wonderstruck*. Scholastic, 2011.

Superle, Michelle. "The United Nations Convention on the Rights of the Child: At the Core of a Child-Centred Critical Approach to Children's Literature." *The Lion and the Unicorn* 40, no. 2 (2016): 144–62. *Project MUSE*, doi:10.1353/uni.2016.0017.

Zimmerman, Virgina. "The Curating Child: Runaways and Museums in Children's Fiction." *The Lion and the Unicorn* 39, no. 1 (2015): 42–62. *Project MUSE*, doi: 10.1353/uni .2015.0008.

# 6

# ENVISIONING SOLIDARITY

## DISRUPTING LINEAR TEMPORALITY IN STUDIO GHIBLI'S *HOWL'S MOVING CASTLE* AND *WHEN MARNIE WAS THERE*

Aneesh Barai and and Nozomi Uematsu

This chapter discusses adult-child relations in two Japanese animated fantasy films that are based on English children's literature and that involve characters who are not the age they appear. *Howl's Moving Castle* (2004; hereafter *Howl*), directed by Hayao Miyazaki and *When Marnie Was There* (2014; hereafter *Marnie*), directed by Hiromasa Yonebayashi were both produced by renowned Japanese animation company Studio Ghibli. Both films are based on British children's books, by Diana Wynne Jones and Joan G. Robinson respectively, but transpose their texts both literally (from Norfolk to Hokkaido, for *Marnie*) and figuratively (into Japan's political and military context, for *Howl*). Both films draw strongly on the age-bending elements of their source texts, with Sophie in *Howl* transforming from an eighteen-year-old into an older woman, and in reverse, Marnie transforming from the heroine Anna's grandmother into her young friend (around age twelve). As we will argue, both films utilize the mode of fantasy to present conversations across generations that appear to be between equals, thus removing preconceptions that age can give rise to, and providing mutual benefit to both younger and older people. *Marnie* presents Anna and Marnie as both traumatized by their childhood experiences and their feelings of being different from others, undermining ideas of childhood "innocence." They are able to overcome their traumas through the encounter Anna has with a young-looking Marnie, and the revelation of their secrets to each other. *Howl* takes a less psychological and personal approach to the issue of solidarity across the generations, and more of a sociopolitical stance, using Sophie, who defies categorization by age, as a spokeswoman for pacifism, and emphasizing the need for people of all ages to speak out against war.

## AGE, FANTASY, AND POWER RELATIONS

We contend that these two films, through their age-bending elements, push against the adult authority that typifies children's literature and media. As Jacqueline Rose famously proposed, the fact that children's literature (and media) is made by adults for children means that adult power over children is the fundamental basis of children's literature. Maria Nikolajeva has expanded this broad sense of adult authority over children through coining the term "aetonormativity"; that is, the adult is taken as the norm, and the child as the deviation from that norm, by society ("Theory," 16). It is undeniable that such power relations exist, are codified in law in what children are not allowed to do that adults can, and are expressed everywhere in culture in the assumed limitation of children's interests, desires, and needs (for example, in terms of sexual, economic, intellectual, and social engagement). Nevertheless, many authors and artists have sought ways to diminish or trouble their own authority, in an effort to empower their young readers. Fantasy as a mode has great potential towards subverting adult authority, as Nikolajeva asserts (17). Indeed, Rosemary Jackson attests to the power of fantasy to challenge norms and hierarchies of all kinds: "fantastic literature points to or suggests the basis upon which cultural order rests, for it opens up, for a brief moment, on to disorder, on to illegality, on to that which lies outside the law, that which is outside dominant value systems" (4). Through the magical affordances of fantasy—ghostly visitations, shape-shifting, and the literalization of metaphors—the very category of "age" can be undermined, as happens in these two films, imagining worlds where "adult" and "authority" are not necessarily aligned.[1]

It can be useful to consider what impact age-swapping has in other fantasy movies, to see where Studio Ghibli's films mark themselves as distinct. At the end of the classic age-swapping story *Big* (1988), the hero Josh (played by Tom Hanks) chooses to break off a potential romance and return to his childhood self. Fowkes comments on this ending: "Ironically, the fantasy device of allowing child and man to become conflated ultimately serves not so much to erase the distinction between childhood and adulthood as to reinforce that very rift" (113). Fowkes further teases out the gendered implications in *Big* of valuing boyishness, in itself, and as a kind of freedom for adult men, but often simultaneously undermining girlishness in order to do so (Fowkes, 112–13). In the films we will be discussing here, the ultimate effect of their age-switching elements is not to reaffirm the binary of young and old, nor is it to value the "innocence" of the child as an attitude that adults or adult men should aim to reclaim as a kind of charming boyishness. These films focus more significantly on girlhood and crone-hood, to connect younger and older people, and disrupt ideas of chronological "progression" from youth to old age. In changing the appearance of characters, allowing for others to perceive them as being a particular age (younger in *Marnie*, older in *Howl*), conversation can be seen as being among equals, empowering engagement between young and older people.

Interestingly, Perry Nodelman has recently challenged some figurations of the adult-child power relationship by noting that we are all subjects to social power, and in fact that this is something that adults and children have in common (265, 278). Given this commonality, perhaps there can be a mutual liberation if adults and children form alliances against wider social powers, whether this be as individuals who are "outsiders" to the norm (as we will discuss below in *Marnie*) or in response to political shifts, such as declarations of war (as we will discuss in relation to *Howl*). These fantasy films imagine such possibilities, through their disruptions of linear narratives of aging.

## WHEN MARNIE WAS THERE

In this section, we will read the animated film *When Marnie Was There* as depicting Anna constantly "outside" of the norm and connecting as an outsider with her grandmother, for them to both overcome the traumas they have experienced. Through the film's representation of queer girlhood, questioning assumptions about childhood "innocence," *Marnie* presents girls' development neither through linear temporality nor usual bildungsroman narratives, but through tracking back and reconnecting with the temporality of the protagonists' pasts. The mode of fantasy enables disruption and subversion of the normative temporality of child development, especially for the queer child.[2] As Anna encounters and interacts with Marnie, who it turns out is/was her own grandmother in the past, she is able to disentangle the past and forgive those who have passed. Forging intergenerational solidarity through temporal disruption allows Anna to break free from the suffering and pain in her past and live the moment of "now" by communication and ultimately through art.

In the film, the location has changed from England to Japan, more specifically from Norfolk to Hokkaido, which is in the north part of Japan. Anna, an adopted girl who lives in Sapporo, a city in the Hokkaido prefecture, suffers from asthma, and her doctor suggests that she should temporarily relocate herself to the countryside for her recovery. In the countryside in Hokkaido, her foster mother's relatives, Kiyomasa and Setsu, whose daughter has grown up and left their house, look after her. Near their place is a large European-style manor, known as the "Marsh House," which Anna immediately finds herself attracted to; she starts to sketch the house from the other side of the shore and goes to explore it.

Anna, similar to in the source text, is indeed a "difficult" girl: cynical, grumpy, and depressed. The film starts off with a monologue from Anna, referring to an "invisible magical circle":

> Anna: [voiceover] In this world, there's an invisible magic circle.
> There's inside and outside.
> These people [her schoolmates chattering with friends and a teacher] are inside.
> And I'm outside. But I don't really care.
> [Her teacher comes up to her]
> Teacher: How's it coming?
> Anna: I . . . kind of messed up . . .
> Teacher: Let me have a look.
> Anna: [hesitates; the teacher is distracted; voiceover] I . . . I hate myself.

In this scene, children ranging in age from kindergarten pupil to secondary school student all mingle in a lively way. Anna and her classmates are engaging in an outdoor art activity. As she monologues on the "magic circle" above, there is a long shot of a sandpit in the shape of a circle, where the preschool pupils are making a sandcastle. Outside of the round sandpit, she sits alone in the shadow of a tree. Such shyness and introversion prevent Anna from interacting with others, and she shields herself from the world with her sketchbook and her grumpy and indifferent face. In contrast, a group of girls chat and tease each other, and when a male teacher talks to them, they easily communicate with him. When he comes to ask how Anna's drawing is going, reaching his hands out to her, his face is cut off at the top of the screen, implying a child's-eye-view, from Anna, unable to take in his whole, larger body. This view, and the scene generally, suggest that she cannot connect with any adults or children who are "inside" the magical circle.

We could perhaps read the "inside" of this magic circle as a place where the norm is secured, and the place defines how people should behave, in particular, how children should behave based on adult expectations towards childhood. Anna's sense of exclusion and isolation from this circle implies that she is not a normal or ordinary child in her perspective. Indeed, in the village where she stays for the summer, they celebrate the *tanabata* festival on the 7th of July, and she makes a wish on a bamboo tree—"I wish for a normal life every day"—which is questioned and interrogated by her acquaintance, Nobuko. Nobuko, who is always leading the group of students and dominating the conversation and space, is unable to comprehend the meaning of "normal" here. If one is inside the norm, like Nobuko, it is hard to take distance from it and understand what it is. Anna is painfully aware of the norm, and of her own separation from it, unable to get in to the circle of friends.

The audience is told, later in the film, that Anna's self-loathing comes from having found out that her foster parents receive monthly financial support from the council, from which she feels betrayed and sees herself as merely a commodity. When she faints during school time and is released from hospital, she apologizes to her foster mother that her sickness will cost them. In *Don't Tell the Grown-Ups*, Alison Lurie talks about the taboos of children's literature: "Of the three principal preoccupations of adult fiction—sex, money, and death—the first is absent from classic children's literature and the other two either absent or much muted" (xiv). Classic children's literature's frequent disengagement from death, money, and sex indicates that they disturb the concept of childhood innocence. However, *Marnie* involves all these three and, in so doing, it undermines the presumptions that adults have on childhood innocence. Anna suffers from the death of her biological family, feels betrayed when she discovers that her foster family receives money to raise her, and she is attracted to a mysterious girl, Marnie. Against the expectations of childhood innocence, she is on the verge of entering into adolescence, losing such "innocence," or feeling disturbed by the pressure to retain it: thus, she is outside of the circle, the norm of childhood innocence. Ultimately, Anna knows far too much of the world.

In *Inside/Out*, Diana Fuss contests conventional binaries, such as heterosexuality and homosexuality, in the rise of queer theory to explore the meaning and mechanism of inside and outside: "Inside/outside functions as the very future for signification and the mechanisms of meaning production. It has everything to do with the structure of alienation, splitting, and identification which together produce a self and an other, a subject and an object, an unconscious and a conscious, an interiority and an exteriority" (1–2). Just as Fuss shows, the figure of being inside or outside of the "invisible magic circle" has numerous analogies and layers of significance in Ghibli's *Marnie*. It represents not only exclusion from the group of Anna's schoolmates or expectations from adults, but it also implies the tidal shift between reality and fantasy that Anna encounters with Marnie. When she sees and communicates with Marnie, it almost always happens in relation to her dreams and the movement of the tides. On the cover image for the DVD, Marnie and Anna are standing ankle-deep in the water of the marsh, emphasizing this movement and the liminality of their meetings (between land and water).

Before meeting her, Anna initially dreams about Marnie, looking up at the window of the Marsh House where Marnie sits, with her maid combing her hair fiercely, and she later rows there when the tide is high. Her close relationship and intimacy with Marnie work to uncoil this rigid but invisible circle and become part of a process of exploring her memory and unconscious, inside out, connecting to the world. In this sense, Anna's psychological development does not follow and adhere to the linear model of the bildungsroman but brings the past into the present time and again.

In Robinson's *Marnie*, Anna and Marnie recreate the magic circle for themselves:

> "Sometimes I feel I'm the luckiest girl in the world!"
> "I think you are, too," said Anna. "But now I've got you I'm even luckier!" Marnie flung her arms round Anna's waist. "You don't know how much I wanted someone like you to play with! Will you be my friend for ever and ever?" And she would not be satisfied until they had drawn a circle round them in the sand, and holding hands, vowed eternal friendship. Anna had never been so happy in her life. (128)

In Robinson's text, Anna and Marnie become, so-to-speak, bosom friends, like Anne and Diana in *Anne of Green Gables*, and Anna is now able to be "inside" the circle. This chapter comes soon after they share the secret of Anna's foster parents receiving payments from the council, and Marnie's secret (that her nanny and maids abuse her by scaring her and brushing her hair painfully). While they confess that they know and have experienced more than children "should," they take a vow to keep it secret, something that they feel should be hidden. Creating their own invisible magic circle and sharing a secret, they break down the hierarchical assumption that adults know more than children.

Interestingly, this recreation of the magic circle is not literally reproduced in the film, but instead, holding hands and building a sand castle visually represent their strong bonding. Sand acts as a significant material in the film, for its flexibility and variability of forming and holding shapes, indeed only holding a shape temporarily. This changeability of sand creates a space and sense of a brief encounter and temporality that Marnie and Anna share, just as fantasy creates a space and moment that is hard to define, existing as it does on the fine line between reality and the impossible. When Marnie and Anna share their secrets—in particular, Marnie confessing that she has been abused by her nannies and neglected by her parents—Marnie is making a sandcastle. This is

DVD cover art for *Omoide no Marnie* [*When Marnie Was There*].

the moment that both girls, who have dark clouds in their minds and who are outside the norm and circle of childhood innocence, bond and empathetically support each other. Making the sand castle, a temporary structure, symbolizes the moment that they can emotionally connect and briefly form an emotional solidarity across generations.

In this key scene, when Marnie and Anna confess their love to each other and jealousy of each other, they help each other to overcome their traumas. Through the repetition of each other's lines ("I wish I was you") and the mutual support they provide each other, this becomes an empowering dialogue among equals. Even though Marnie is Anna's deceased grandmother, and part of Marnie's sorrow (it is revealed later) is her regret at leaving Anna behind in her death, there is no sense here of either Anna as a more innocent child, nor Marnie as a more knowing adult. Together they face their traumas and, through their love for each other, they both find strength and comfort. While both are outsiders, Marnie is best able to engage Anna in conversation and help Anna to open up by appearing to her as a child of her age. The DVD case image centralizes this sense of equality between them, as they stand back-to-back at the same height, as well as pointing to their physical intimacy, since they hold hands. The fantastical affordances that show her visually as an equal to Anna mean that Anna and the viewers of the film can shed preconceptions about the stark age difference between them and recognize that they have much to offer each other through their solidarity.

### *HOWL'S MOVING CASTLE*

Similarly, *Howl's Moving Castle* challenges the adult-child binary through multiple characters who conceal or change their age, also engaging with what is expected of the child, in centralizing Sophie's response to war. Sophie, the teenage main character, is a hatter. One day, she is cursed by the Witch of the Waste to become an older woman of around ninety years; she leaves the hat shop and puts herself in the service of the wizard Howl as a cleaning lady, while secretly making a deal with the fire demon, Calcifer, in his castle in order to break the age curse upon her. The key difference between the film and the book is the element of war that Miyazaki adds to the plot: while pending war is briefly alluded to in the novel, it is at the forefront of the film, leading the story in a new direction. Part of that includes the expansion of Suliman, the royal wizard, who is a man and is missing for most of the book, but is turned into a woman, and in charge of the war effort, in the film. We will discuss Sophie's encounter with Madame Suliman and the consequences of the war narrative in more detail below.

A fascinating aspect of Jones's novel that a number of critics have focused upon (Mendlesohn 2005; Nikolajeva 2002) is that Howl's castle door opens onto multiple locations—not only onto other parts of Sophie's world, Ingary, but also onto our real-world Wales, which is where Howl is originally from. This makes the novel into a kind of "portal fantasy" (Mendlesohn, 41), but reverses the typical shape of a portal fantasy by having our world as the exotic and strange "other" to what for Sophie is the ordinary and known world. In the film, the fourth door does lead to Howl's childhood home, but it is simply another place within Ingary. Matt Kimmich is disappointed that this element of the book has not been transferred, as it means that the film does not present the same "ontological" challenge as the book (131). However, Kimmich does not mention or reflect upon the final door of the film, which appears after the castle has collapsed. Initially, it also seems to lead to Howl's childhood home, but once Sophie passes through it, she sees Howl as a child catching a shooting star, and while she cannot hear the words that pass between them, the scene appears to be a vision to Sophie of the contract between Calcifer and Howl. The space Sophie has entered begins to collapse, and as she flees it, she calls out to Calcifer and Howl to find her. At this moment, we realize that what had appeared to be a vision, of which Sophie was a distant observer, is, in fact, a time-slip, and Sophie has integrated herself into the initial contract between Howl and Calcifer, making herself a third party to it. In telling them to find her, she effectively sets into motion all the events we have just seen, including Calcifer letting Sophie into the castle in the first place. She becomes the author of her own adventure. In these ways, although the film does not allow for crossings between worlds, it makes time itself something potentially flexible and controllable, thus building further on the blurring of ages that we encounter in the book.

The film shows many characters shifting in age, rendering those shifts more extreme than in the book, including Howl, his apprentice, Markl, and the Witch of the Waste. Markl (named Michael in the book), for example, is fifteen years old in the book and romantically entangled with Sophie's younger sister Martha. In the film, by contrast, he is considerably younger, around ten years old. When answering requests as Howl's apprentice, he transforms himself into an older man with an enormous beard, changing his voice and speech patterns from those of a child to those of an older person—changes that are very clear in Japanese, in speech markers such as his choice of personal pronoun (*washi* as an older man, and *boku* as a boy). His character brings an extra sense of age fluidity to the story: Markl is treated with great respect by customers who see him as an older man, and he is able to perform this older age perfectly as a separate identity from his child self.

Howl himself becomes an impossible hybrid of young and old at the end of the film, when he is reunited with his heart. Sophie takes Howl's heart from Calcifer and, holding it, says, "It's all warm and fluttery like a little bird." Calcifer explains that this is because the heart is still the heart of Howl as a child. With a child's heart in an adult's body, Howl literally holds the "other" within him, upsetting any efforts at distinction between adult and child since he is simultaneously both.

Sophie, too, finds her body ultimately transformed in ways that defy singular categorization by age. In the film, we see Sophie regularly switching between various ages; she reverts to her youthful, real age when she is asleep as well as when she gains in confidence, as in her discussion with Madame Suliman (discussed further below). When she is first transformed, and when she is most self-conscious of being an older lady, she is withered, hunched-over, and speaks with a cracked voice.

At other times, she is an older lady, but with better posture and a firmer voice. In representations of all ages, after her initial transformation, her hair is gray, and even after the curse is broken at the end of the film, and she is once again in her younger form, her hair remains gray. The gray hair with the younger body visually suggests a blurring of categories, of Sophie as not just young or old but both at once, thus challenging the binary between the two.

The implication of this, never made explicit, is that it is her own will that is maintaining the spell cast upon her, and that it is strengthened or weakened by her own self-confidence or self-belief. In the key scene of the film, when Sophie speaks out against Madame Suliman, and against war, she transforms for the first time fully back into her youthful self, with brown hair. At this point, Sophie's transformations have to do with more than her own agency and independent choices, and reach out into ideas of the child's engagement with wider society and politics, tying the film to its context in 2004 and to the *oeuvre* of Miyazaki as its director.

Kimmich notes that "the closest the film comes to a traditional, sustained antagonist is Madame Suliman, but one could see war as the real enemy" (133). Jones herself, in an interview about the film adaptation, notes Miyazaki's strong interest in war as an issue and comments: "Miyazaki and I were both children in World War II and we seem to have gone opposite ways in our reactions to it. I tend to leave the actual war out (we all know how horrible wars are), whereas Miyazaki (who feels just the same) has his cake and eats it, representing both the nastiness of a war and the exciting scenic effects of a big bombing raid" (Jones, 316). Indeed, the film puts forward a direct and unambiguous rejection of war, as in the following exchange between Sophie and Howl:

DVD cover art for *Howl's Moving Castle*.

Sophie: Is it the enemy's or one of ours?
Howl: What difference does it make? Murderers.

In condemning both sides, the film implicitly rejects the idea of a "just war." Daisuke Akimoto convincingly argues that the film provides a set of parallels with Japan's postwar circumstances and various kinds of pacifism. After the Second World War, Japan agreed upon the USA's conditions to have no army whatsoever, codified in law as Article 9 of the Japanese constitution. However, Japan does have military power in the form of the Self-Defense Forces, controlled by the Ministry of Defense. Akimoto likens Calcifer to the Self-Defense Forces, allowing Howl to operate a kind of passive pacifism: he does not seek out warfare but Calcifer gives him the strength to fight in order to defend himself and his home. Sophie rejects this willingness to self-defense, thinking to herself it would be better for Howl to remain a "coward" and not fight to defend them; in this "absolute pacifism," Akimoto argues, Sophie represents Article 9 (n.p.).[3]

We contend that Sophie's absolute pacifism is most strongly and effectively conveyed in the film by her encounter with Madame Suliman. It is during this meeting that Sophie finds the strength and desire to speak out and to challenge authority. The mission that Howl is being summoned for in the film is not merely to find a missing person (as in the book) but to spearhead a military effort, and it is at this moment that all ages come together to challenge military pursuits and reject war. In the first place, it is because of Sophie's older body that this meeting can take place: her apparent age lends her the authority to speak to a powerful woman who appears to be about the same age. During Sophie's heartfelt speech against Madame Suliman, we watch her body transform step by step from older to younger and revert back to older age again moments later. This not only suggests the personal agency that Sophie is expressing, which brings her closer to her youthful self, but can also be interpreted as Sophie speaking for all ages of people in Japan, of her being a spokeswoman for older and younger people alike in her rejection of war.

Moreover, as Miyazaki has commented in interviews, there was a particular reason for him to return to discussing war at this moment, with the outbreak of the Iraq War (Akimoto, n.p.), to which Japan contributed its Air and Ground Self-Defense Forces in 2003. Wilson and Wilson have noted that the disturbing creatures that first chase Sophie and Howl, and recur through the film, are distinctly oil-like, which can be linked to Miyazaki's deeply critical message about the Iraq War: "they represent the covert interests of big companies that are happy to exploit people's inane justifications for self-perpetuating war, while being complicit in profitable attempts to find further sources of oil" (193). As

Jones noted the impact of war on her own childhood, as well as Miyazaki's, the implication of this film responding to the Iraq War is that its own young viewers are also growing up in a world at war. The film implicitly engages with two wars, and Sophie responds to war as both an older woman and a youth, linking together the past and present war, the current generation and the older generation. This conflation of past and present wars forms an intergenerational push for peace, which, like Sophie and Howl, transcends any singular age category or classification. Through this film's age-bending elements and intergenerational alliances, Miyazaki calls for his viewers to recall the horror of past wars and connect them to the dangers of the war being entered into by the current generation.

Both films empower their young female protagonists to connect with others, regardless of age, and to undermine the very category of "age" itself, through their magical elements. Moreover, these two films suggest something about the very nature of animation as a medium that facilitates these connections with others. For *Howl*, the element of fire plays a key role, with Calcifer forming the heart of the household, which he can reshape and relocate at will. Eisenstein takes up the instability of fire as a form (not solid, liquid, or gas, but plasma) as an analogy for the transmutability of objects that animation allows (24–33). This "plasmaticness" (5) is seen everywhere in the film, as no character is what they seem, and transformation—of appearance, of material, of time, and of reality itself—becomes the new norm. In *Marnie*, a parallel is silently drawn in the film between Anna sketching and the elderly artist Hisako painting, as they line up on the shore, facing the Marsh House. While they are parallel but distant early on in the film, the resolution of the film, and the final realization of who Marnie is, comes from talking with Hisako. Anna and Hisako bond over their artwork and, just as Hisako's story links together past and present generations, it is thus suggested that art too has the capacity to connect across generations. The still shots we see of their art, framed neatly within the screen for us to view head-on, are reminiscent of the kinds of sketches and paintings that the animation house would have had to produce in preparation for the film we are watching. In these ways, the two films meta-visually emphasize the power and value that artwork and animation can have in bringing together children and adults alike.

Studio Ghibli's films target both adult and child audiences, without distinguishing between what is deemed "acceptable" or "unacceptable" content, and without seeking to diminish either audience (see Prunes 2003). Complex, troubling, and timely issues, such as trauma, adoption, abuse, economics, and war, are engaged with in uncompromising terms, in order to bring together the mixed-age audience, to make them into a community, and to show their commonalities. Through the affordances of animation as a medium, and fantasy as a mode, these two films challenge the separation of adult and child into distinct realms and envision the mutual support that can come from bringing adults and children together into conversation, as equals.

## NOTES

1. For reasons of space, we will not engage here in the long debate over the definitions and boundaries of fantasy as a genre. Rather, in line with the fantasy film critics Furby and Hines, we believe that fantasy can fruitfully be seen as a "mode" that operates across genres and in different historical and social contexts (28).

2. See Kathryn Bond Stockton, *The Queer Child: or, Growing Sideways in the Twentieth Century* (Duke University Press, 2009).

3. Article 9 has recently returned as a key issue in Japanese politics, as the former prime minister, Shinzō Abe (2012–2020), wanted to overturn the law and aim for a more militaristic future for Japan.

## WORKS CITED

Akimoto, Daisuke. "*Howl's Moving Castle* in the War on Terror: A Transformative Analysis of the Iraq War and Japan's Response." *Electronic Journal of Contemporary Japanese Studies* 14, no. 2 (2014), www.japanesestudies.org.uk/ejcjs/vol14/iss2/akimoto.html. Accessed June 12, 2017.
Eisenstein, Sergei. *Eisenstein on Disney*, ed. Jay Leyda. Seagull, 1986.
Fowkes, Katherine A. *The Fantasy Film*. Blackwell, 2010.
Furby, Jacqueline, and Claire Hines. *Routledge Film Guidebooks: Fantasy*. Routledge, 2012.
Fuss, Diana. "Decking Out: Performing Identities." In *Inside/Out: Lesbian Theories, Gay Theories*, ed. Fuss, Routledge, 1–13. Routledge, 1991.
Jones, Diana Wynne. *Howl's Moving Castle*. 1986. HarperCollins, 2010.
Kimmich, Matt. "Animating the Fantastic: Hayao Miyazaki's Adaptation of Diana Wynne Jones's *Howl's Moving Castle*." In *Fantasy Fiction into Film*, eds. Leslie Stratyner and James R. Keller, 124–39. McFarland, 2007.
Lurie, Alison. *Don't Tell the Grown-Ups: Subversive Children's Literature*. Bloomsbury, 1990.
Mendlesohn, Farah. *Diana Wynne Jones: The Fantastic Tradition and Children's Literature*. Routledge, 2005.
Miyazaki, Hayao, dir. *Hauru no ugoku shiro* [*Howl's Moving Castle*]. Studio Ghibli, 2004.
Nikolajeva, Maria. "Heterotopia as a Reflection of Postmodern Consciousness in the Works of Diana Wynne Jones." In *Diana Wynne Jones: An Exciting and Exacting Wisdom*, eds. Teya Rosenberg et al., 25–39. Peter Lang, 2002.
Nikolajeva, Maria. "Theory, Post-theory, and Aetonormative Theory." *Neohelicon* 36, no. 1 (2009): 13–24.
Nodelman, Perry. "The Hidden Child in *The Hidden Adult*." *Jeunesse* 8, no. 1 (2016) : 266–78.
Prunes, Mariano. "Having It Both Ways: Making Children Films an Adult Matter in Miyazaki's *My Neighbor Totoro*." *Asian Cinema* 14, no. 1 (2003): 45–55.
Robinson, Joan G. *When Marnie Was There*. 1967. HarperCollins, 2014.
Rose, Jacqueline. *The Case of Peter Pan, or The Impossibility of Children's Fiction*. Macmillan, 1984.

Stockton, Kathryn Bond. *The Queer Child: or, Growing Sideways in the Twentieth Century*. Duke University Press, 2009.

Wilson, Carl, and Garrath T. Wilson. "Taoism, Shintoism, and the Ethics of Technology: An Ecocritical Review of *Howl's Moving Castle*." *Resilience: A Journal of the Environmental Humanities* 2, no. 3 (2015): 189–94.

Yonebayashi, Hiromasa. *Omoide no Mānī [When Marnie Was There]*. Studio Ghibli, 2014.

# 7

# "REMEMBER ME"

## INTERGENERATIONAL DIALOGUE IN DISNEY-PIXAR ANIMATION

Zoe Jaques

Generations are meant to relate to each other through connections, not conflict. After all, it is about building a world that values and engages all generations in a community not a competition.
(Butts, 96)

The tradition of Disney animated film is one predicated on generational rifts. The movies themselves are, of course, "family viewing"; they invite intra-age cinematic experiences, encourage dialogues about stories, and offer what Nadia Crandall calls a "vehicle for the transmission of cultural heritage from generation to generation and from community to community" (181). Yet their subject matter, substantially derived from folk and fairy-tale traditions and invariably detailing the challenges of coming of age, tends to heighten the tensions between aged subjects, particularly female ones, and most often in the context of extended or otherwise non-nuclear families. From *Snow White and the Seven Dwarfs* (1937) to *Tangled* (2002), Disney stories have shown a long commitment to variously highlighting, and then conservatively healing, fissures between generations. Younger characters are invariably rebellious or naïve; older ones ineffectual, overbearing, or villainous (with the exception of the occasional, venerated sage). If, as Donna M. Butts argues, intergenerational solidarity is forged through practices that prompt connection over conflict, the Disney animated feature is a highly constricted space for promoting such endeavors.

Disney-Pixar collaborations, however, offer a broader spectrum of possibilities in imagining how senescence and youth might intersect. Two recent films, invested particularly in exploring the relationship between male youth and old age, provide somewhat more nuanced—but notably distinct—takes on intergenerational dialogue. *Up* (2010) looks beyond the confines of the family to imagine positive intra-age relationships formed through greater communal ties in an increasingly urbanized America; *Coco* (2017), conversely, locates intergenerational solidary in the context of an idealized, but rather detached, rendering of the familial traditions of Mexican culture. Both are curiously similar in their attentive, if somewhat conflicting, stances on the challenges and rewards of intergenerational solidarity, inflecting that understanding through their negotiations of the lives and deaths of older characters. This chapter will interrogate these differing takes, calling attention to the distinctive modes by which the stories explicate how the lives of the living intersect with those of the dead and dying, pointing to an intergenerational solidarity that operates both within, but also extends beyond, a single lived experience.

### "NOBODY CAN BE UNCHEERED WITH A BALLOON": ON AGING *UP*

Disney-Pixar's narrative of the unlikely relationship between Carl Friedricksen, an irascible balloon salesman, and Russell, a young boy-scout some seventy years his junior, takes a multilayered approach to reflecting on the relationship between age and youth. Few children's fictions are comfortable focalizing stories through the lens of older characters, and while *Up* is unusual in negotiating the majority of the plot through the eyes of senior citizen Carl, it offsets that peculiarity by opening the film with a wistful montage of Carl's life from youth to adulthood. This backstory centers on Carl's childhood relationship with Ellie, a spirited young girl who eventually becomes his wife and lifelong partner into old age. It purposefully inflects a sense of the past—and thus childhood—with color, imagination, and "the spirit of adventure," which then dwindles and recedes with the passing years as the aging couple come to terms with the realities of a contrasting adulthood. They face minor disasters, distressing disappointments, and a degree of drudgery, albeit offset by their love for each other. The story is affectingly insular, as the filmmakers include a scene in which the couple learn they cannot have children and then heighten their isolation through depicting limited interaction or dialogue with the wider world throughout their all-too-quickly replayed lives (a literalizing of the adage that life is too short). The poignancy of their seclusion is underscored—in a mode not uncommon to Disney's aesthetic drive to "make a play for our feelings" and to "court and cultivate sentiment" (Whitley, 2)—when the montage concludes with Ellie's death marked by a funeral that only Carl, seemingly, attends. Much as in *Bambi* (1942), in which the mother's death is signaled rather than seen, the emotive impact of the moment is registered and foregrounded largely through "[i]ssues of abandonment and separation, rather than actual death" (Spitz, 123), as Carl's isolation is centralized. While Maria Nikolajeva asserts that the pervasive presence of "separation, death and grief" in children's fiction tends to be "introduced in diluted forms" (83), there is little doubt that the loss here is meant to pack a heady emotional punch for both child and adult viewers.

The opening tableau of *Up* is demonstrably nostalgic, resonating with Jacqueline Rose's oft-cited case that children's literature is predicated upon an adult sense of "lost childhood, nostalgia or innocence" (137), which is necessarily backwards glancing. Yet it also functions to remind viewers from the outset of the generational connections within the self, inviting them—perhaps—to think more in terms of Madeleine L'Engle's stance: "For, after all, I am not an isolated fifty-seven years old; I am every other age I have been, one, two, three, four, five, six, seven, all the way up to and occasionally beyond my present chronology" (16). In offering a quick-cut biographical montage, Disney-Pixar highlights the connections between one age and another, forming the basis for the main story of Carl's adjustment to life without Ellie and, in turn, his relationship to the wider community. In doing so, the film's take on intergenerational solidarity is established: not on an easy or uncontested cohesion between old age and youth (either within the self or without), but on dialogue between the ages that sees each as mournfully, tensely, reluctantly, but necessarily connected to the other. It is a narrative that—ultimately—values an ethics of community, but not unquestioningly, insisting upon respect for and recognition of the individuation (including the sometimes curmudgeonly detachment) of those involved.

The transition into Carl's aged circumstances is highly self-aware and critically attentive to stereotypical expectations as to what being old—or young—means in Western culture. Our reintroduction to Carl shows him navigating his early morning routine: he struggles to rise from bed, utilizes a mechanical stairlift, and traverses rooms stocked with medications. When he exits his home to sit on the porch, viewers watch as he wrestles with an excessive number of door locks—a wry nod to stereotypes of the senior citizens' overzealous security measures and a first clue as to his radical spatial autonomy. Seen from outside, it becomes clear that Carl's community has drastically changed from the rural idyll of his youth, with his and Ellie's house now the one remaining discernable residential plot in an urbanized space marked by high-rise constructions and the commercial franchises of Sushi Pronto and Lazer Tan. This setting is demonstrably incongruent with ideals about aged lifestyle; as Michael K. Gusmano writes: "[h]igh levels of congestion, pollution and crime rates, as well as the high cost of housing and social polarization in world cities may undermine the quality of life for older people" (398). The persistence of the out-of-place and out-of-time homestead, with its cantankerous lone resident, is an inconvenience to cityscapers, and Carl finds himself encouraged to move to the more pastorally imagined Shady Oaks Retirement Community. There is a nuanced playfulness around the notion of what makes for effective communal living in old age here; the sense of forced interaction with others—noticeably absent from Carl's life with Ellie—is subtly disparaged in the saccharine inauthenticity of adverts for Shady Oaks, and viewers are encouraged to empathize with Carl's repeated resistance to such an "idyllic" fate as more than merely peevish.

Urban community programs that artificially link the old with the young are also subject to critique in the early stages of the film, as they fail to attend to the individuality of the participants. Elizabeth Larkin makes the case that "[i]n today's world, it often takes targeted policies and specialized programming to connect and support people across ages, so that they can recognize mutual benefits in caring for each other and continue to live interdependently" (99). The introduction of young Russell is situated in this "targeted" context: as a member of the Wilderness Explorers scouting group, he must successfully "assist" an "elderly" member of the community in order to fulfill the requirements to become a Senior Explorer. Vanessa Joosen has pointed out that "nature has been a constant factor in connecting childhood and old age since romanticism" (*Connecting*, 15), and there is more than a little ironic mockery in the film's awkward alignment of youth and "seniority," "urbanity," and "wilderness" in parodying social structures like Shady Oaks and the Wilderness Explorers. More important, however, is Russell's early inability to engage in any meaningful dialogue with Carl as a person, as he reads by rote from his manual:

> Russell: Good afternoon. My name is Russell. And I am a Wilderness Explorer in Tribe 54, Sweatlodge 12. Are you in need of any assistance today, sir?
> Carl: No.
> Russell: I could help you cross the street.
> Carl: No.
> Russell: I could help you cross your yard.
> Carl: No.
> Russell: I could help you cross your . . . porch?
> Carl: No.
> Russell: Well, I gotta help you cross something.

The moment recalls Maria G. Cattell and Steven M. Albert's sense that "the elderly" are often "lumped [...] into one undifferentiated category using chronological age as the defining characteristic" (115). Russell's—and, by association, his scouting group's—failure to delineate between generic assistance (for personal gain) and genuine care is here lampooned, with Carl playfully and self-deprecatingly labeling himself "elderly and infirm" and then, in turn, mocking Russell's own childish naivete about the wild by sending him to "assist" by catching the "snipe bird" who "every night [...] sneaks in my yard and gobbles my poor azaleas." Such an exchange draws attention to the homogenization and stereotyping of old and young alike in the context of "specialized programming."

That Carl and Russell's relationship begins in a tokenistic manner—whereby the child sees the adult only through the lens of the coveted "assisting the elderly badge"—is one of several instances where Disney-Pixar use talismanic objects to make playful connections between one age and another, keeping the viewer lightly attuned to a relationship that is complex and crucially nonlinear through multiple symbolic cues. Balloons, of course, provide an overarching symbol for childhood and freedom in the film; they both connect Carl with his past and become the link to his future as the means by which he, his house, and, by unwitting circumstance, Russell, travel to Paradise Falls and ultimately engage in an adventure that sees them connect on a more meaningful level. Birds are similarly pervasive—emerging and remerging in fantastical, pictorial, and souvenir forms as a secondary connection to flight and escaping the mundane—while Carl's hybrid walking cane yokes together the youthful (in the form of tennis balls) with its aged function. Yet most crucial to the narrative and its eventual resolution is Ellie's Adventure Book: a photograph-album-cum-scrapbook she creates as a child and which is comprised mostly of blank pages saved "for all the adventures I'm gonna have." We see Ellie with this book on several occasions during the opening montage, including on her deathbed; it is the pervasive guilt over Ellie's missed adventures represented in those blank pages that prompts Carl to make his final, unorthodox voyage. It is only late into his journey, when he settles their disheveled house atop of Paradise Falls, that he discovers that Ellie has, in fact, filled the pages with photographs of their life together.

The surprise discovery of these images and their networked alignment of age with youth is significant. Victoria Ford Smith's work on the "lively practice of adult-child collaborations" has located real instances of coauthorship as providing "creative thresholds where both adults and children can meet" (261). In this iteration, though fictional, we are invited to reflect upon a child-into-adult collaboration, in which an intergenerational pictorial adventure is formed within a single lifetime, speaking back to the narrative's investment in making connections between the age we are and the age we were or will be. The images that comprise the story are in keeping with such dialogue; the album begins with "ritual photographs" that mark "different stages of the life course" (Gomila, 67)—the couple's wedding, birthdays—but soon morph into the stuff less frequently memorialized: car journeys, feeding birds, or simply sitting by a window. There is an explicit sense of absence here as the photographer—what Roland Barthes terms the "*Operator*"—is unaccounted for. Yet the compilation, and its purpose, makes greater sense when considered in terms of its "*Spectator*":

> The *Spectator* is ourselves, all of us who glance through collections of photographs—in magazines and newspapers, in books, albums, archives. [. . .] And the person or thing photographed is the target, the referent, a kind of little simulacrum, any eidolon emitted by the object, which I should like to call the Spectrum of the Photograph, because this word retains, through its root, a relation to "spectacle" and adds to it that rather terrible thing which is in every photograph: the return of the dead. (9)

This return of the dead, however, is fleeting and purposeful here; below the final photograph, Ellie thanks Carl—in a handwritten message—"for the Adventure" and invites him to "go have a new one!" That the images included in the album tend towards the commonplace acts as a salient reminder to all spectators, both within the context of the film and its viewing audience, that "adventure" can take many forms.

Much of *Up* does not concern a close intergenerational adventure between an old and young person. It is a story of loss, change, aging, forced connections, happenstance, stereotypes, awkwardness, and difference—in short, the challenges of intergenerational solidarity. Yet it is also a narrative invested in negotiating a space wherein old and young might have a productive relationship that, in Elizabeth Larkin's terms, has "mutual benefits in caring for each other." Crucial to *Up* is the notion that such bonds can—and indeed sometimes must—operate outside of traditional kinship ties. In addition to foregrounding Carl and Ellie's involuntary childlessness, the narrative also slowly reveals Russell's non-nuclear family dynamics, as we learn of his father's remarriage and the subsequent decline of their relationship (the film makes many references to alternative family structures, including a "mother" bird named Kevin). Carl's eventual extra-familial role in Russell's life reflects strategies for what care might look like in modern, urban America, where displacement, divorce, and a rethinking of what counts as "kin" are common. Thus, when Carl attends Russell's Explorer ceremony, "elderly assistance" is revaluated:

> Carl: Russell, for assisting the elderly, and for performing above and beyond the call of duty, I would like to award you the highest honor I can bestow: the Ellie Badge.

Carl's gift of the final simulacrum of his and Ellie's youth, in the form of the grape-soda badge she gave to him as a child, transforms the impersonal and tokenistic "badge" of the program into a meaningful connection. In doing so, *Up* stresses that intergenerational relationships are most valuable when they are nuanced, dialogic, and particular.

## "BUT, OF COURSE, IT ISN'T REALLY GOOD-BYE": *COCO*'S INTERGENERATIONAL REMEMBERING

While *Up* is invested in outlining the barriers to intergenerational solidarity in urbanized America, and then navigating a pathway through them, *Coco* works to reverse that structure. Beginning with the premise that such solidarity is fundamental to the context of a Mexican family, the majority of the film attends to the many challenges of maintaining and nurturing relationships between, and across, generations. As in *Up*, the film commences with a reflective introduction, immediately attuned to its interests in family bonds and quarrels. This opening montage, told in papel picado and narrated by young Miguel, reveals the conflict that will structure the narrative: the love for music expressed by his great-great-grandfather, Héctor, led him to leave his family to pursue his dream "to play for the world." In turn, his great-great-grandmother, Imelda, banished all music from their family and began a profession in shoe-making—a literally down-to-earth occupation to offset the more ethereal symbolism of her deserting husband's trade. The resulting generations of the family are thus all shoemakers, bonded "as the only family in Mexico who hates music." The main storyline of *Coco* naturally concerns Miguel's growing resistance to this benevolent but insular structure, so that he might realize his own ambition to become a musician and connect to the rest of the world, in a broader understanding of "familia."

The initial barrier to Miguel's aspirations is represented in the figure of his abuelita (grandmother), Elena, who showers him with a domineering affection and whose rule of "no music" is absolute. Their relationship is one of loving struggle, as Miguel fails to truly acknowledge or comprehend the important traditions of their family while his abuelita routinely interferes and manipulates his life in an attempt to protect him from the perceived dangers of music. A spatial disjuncture can be seen to underpin their conflicting interests from the outset, with Elena committed to keeping her grandson firmly rooted in the home and all that it signifies –a space occupied by an extended, but entirely consanguineal and affinal family—while Miguel is drawn to the music and conversations of the town's central plaza, a space which functions as "the open-air heart of every Mexican neighbourhood, town and city—it's communal living room" (Wagner et al., n.p.). Yet while Miguel's grandmother might be his initial foil, their discord is not the film's primary interest: *Coco* is invested in exploring the strata of connections across multiple generations as opposed to problematizing or focusing on a singular relationship between one generation and another. Vanessa Joosen has highlighted a "seesaw effect" that occurs in narratives which focus upon "the special relationship" between age and youth: "the parental generation in between is, at best, absent from the intimate moments, and more often depicted as shallow, preoccupied, unhappy, and unimaginative" ("Second Childhoods," 132). Both *Up* and *Coco* tend to this pattern; *Up* almost entirely excludes any parental presence (Russell's mother is onscreen, silent, for fewer than five seconds), and, while Miguel's parents are firmly rooted in his life and household, they are secondary in focus to the living elders or dead ancestors of the family. Indeed, *Coco* is keen to keep looking back, to move in reverse through the generations of this single family in the context of its heritage and specifically through celebrating those connections and opening up dialogues with them on Día de Muertos. Thus, the majority of the film takes place in the Land of the Dead, with the opening section's focus on the Land of the Living—or the present—directly entangled with that afterlife. As Octavio Paz puts it: "Our cult of death is also a cult of life. [. . .] [L]ife and death mingle together" (24).

The positioning of the film's eponymous character is perhaps the most intriguing example of such mingling. The narrative offsets Miguel's taut relationship with his abuelita with that of her own mother; we are invited to see the connection between Miguel and Mamá Coco as tender and dialogic by comparison, for, as he explains, "I tell her pretty much everything." But it is an unequal partnership; Mamá Coco is infirm and restricted to a wheelchair, limited in her ability to communicate directly with Miguel or the rest of her family and losing her memory and self-awareness. Mamá Coco is simultaneously the center of the household and at its margins. The family interacts with her lovingly but in a manner that resonates with Jenny Hockey and Allison James's (1993) case that older and disabled people experience infantilizing practices as part of everyday social discourse. Thus, the affectionate intergenerational connections represented here align with the more problematic and overt modes by which childhood and old age are obviously aligned as stages of life marked by vulnerability, physical fragility, and limited social status. Such a depiction lacks the self-reflexive lampooning of *Up*, but gestures to a tension in the family's treatment of Coco and contextualized celebration of Día de Muertos. As Clive Seale writes: "[i]n spite of symbolic attempts to transform death into hopes of immortality, to create a sheltering canopy of culture against nature, for people facing death these human constructions appear fragile. Disruption of the social bond occurs as the body fails, self-identity becomes harder to hold together and the normal expectations of human relations cannot be fulfilled" (149). It is telling that, although Coco is among the living, she is already crossing into the afterlife both physically, as her body begins to fail, and symbolically, through photography. Her daughter, Elena, explains to Miguel, that the ofrenda and its photographs provide a crucial function in connecting the family across generations:

> Elena: Día de los Muertos is the one night of the year our ancestors can come visit us. We've put their photos on the ofrenda so their spirits can cross over. That is very important! If we don't put them up, they can't come! We made all this food, set out the things they loved in life, mijo. All this work to bring the family together.

Yet Mamá Coco's place and image sit awkwardly in this context. She is positioned in her wheelchair in front of the ofrenda but simultaneously appears on it: the portrait of her enterprising mother Imelda and "walkaway musician" father, Héctor (whose face has been torn away in an attempt to forget him), also includes the image of her childhood self. Although she still lives, this photograph represents her as at once dead and alive, comingling one existence with another and playing with Roland's Barthes sense that the "rather terrible thing that is in every photograph" is the "return of the dead." The very purpose of the photograph on the ofrenda is to permit the return that Barthes finds so uncomfortable, and its discomfort is not one of return but of preemption and fusion. In the image of Mamá Coco, we are forced to encounter both *Spectrum* and *Spectator*. The result is both uncannily unsettling and compellingly connective.

The almost silent Mamá Coco thus ironically provides the family's point of dialogue between its living members and dead ancestors. Miguel's revised quest once he enters the Land of the Dead is to unpack a story of murder and betrayal that casts Mamá Coco's father's disappearance in a more positive light and, in turn, serves to heal the familial rift that has extended beyond the grave. The majority of the narrative therefore develops the relationship between young Miguel and his great-great-grandfather, Héctor, transforming their initial encounter as two strangers attempting to exploit the other into a buddy bond of shared ancestry. Such a focalizing relationship between a child character and one three generations his senior is, of course, unusual; it is made possible through a fantastical transition into the afterlife and its associated dismantling of the limits of the human body in both being and time. As with most narratives that place senescence and youth in dialogue, Mamá Coco's aged stasis is contrasted to Miguel's youthful vitality in a mode that is both comically caricatured (such as in Miguel's attempts to include her in his wrestling play) and somewhat dismal (in that Mamá Coco has no autonomy in the game). In the afterlife, however, great-great-grandfather Héctor's "dead" skeletal body is spry and agile, recalling an age many years his junior and simultaneously partaking of the creative possibilities of disarticulation that themselves recall the near-century-old playfulness of Disney's 1929 animated short *The Skeleton Dance*. The connection that is forged between the two male characters across the generations thus creates a form of agelessness in the childlike-yet-ancestral, skeletal-yet-living Héctor that inverts the aged-yet-infantilized, alive-but-dead Mamá Coco. It is one of many spirited ontological paradoxes in which the film revels, hinting at the dividing lines that separate one generation from another, or life from death.

Yet, while the film might be said to tease viewers with what age or youth might mean in the context of a shared ancestral history and a body beyond the grave, other tensions are less easily resolved. The connection to the Land of the Dead (symbolized through an exquisitely conceived marigold bridge and satirized border-control agency) provides a point of return to the living world for those who have passed on. But it relies upon the currency of memory and representation; as one border officer puts it, "No photo on the ofrenda, no crossing the bridge." Being is here subject to proof of identity in photographic form—to live, it seems, is to have been imaged—relying upon the maintenance of generational connections that the dead themselves cannot affect. Moving through a degraded shanty town, devoid of color and peopled by "all the ones with no photos or ofrendas, no family to go home to," Héctor introduces a multistaged death. As Alexandra Mendoza Covarrubias writes:

> The Day of the Dead comes of the Indigenous belief in three deaths: the first is the physical death of the body; the second death, the death of the spirit, comes with the spirit's return to mother earth and ascent to the sun; and the third death is the death than Indigenous peoples truly feared—the death of the soul that occurs after there is no one left alive to remember or welcome the soul home. El Dia de los Muertos represents a means through which to spare ancestors from this third death. (403)

In keeping with such belief, the narrative quest invests in protecting Héctor from what he calls "the Final Death" by reinstating his photo on the ofrenda and reigniting Mamá Coco's ailing memory of him through his music. She now might tell his story before she too crosses over. Yet, while *Coco* here takes pains to particularize the moment in the context of Riveria family line and to resolve it discreetly, there are fuzzy elements to the resolution that somewhat haunt the close. We are reminded by Héctor, albeit glibly and fleetingly, that this final death "happens to everyone eventually." Although passed over quickly, such an allusion to the inevitability and universality of a final death of forgetting, to the fact that all intergenerational connections will be lost to time, is both at odds with the narrative's focus and strangely central to it. After all, the ofrenda which dominates the film's plot has a starting point and thus also an absent *beyond*, even for the family at its center. In emphasizing the connections between a physical image and the feelings brought forth when memorializing story, *Coco*'s stance on intergenerational dialogue conversely proves a disconnect between one and the other, recalling Barthes's stance that "[n]ot only is the Photograph never, in essence, a memory [. . .] but it actually blocks memory, quickly becomes counter-memory" (91). The photograph alone, without a surrounding narrative, recalls nothing from death; what Coco considers the final death of when no one remembers, is for Barthes the "*flat Death*" (92) of the photograph itself.

*Coco*'s narrative concludes with a buoyant song that declares to its audience: "Let it be known / Our love for each other / Will live on forever." It is the film's most affirmative statement of intergenerational solidarity, and perhaps the most emotive scene in Disney-Pixar animated history, as generations of Riverias, living and dead, gather in the courtyard of their family home, brought together by song. Yet the tension that opens the film—the family's insular seclusion from both music and the wider world—remains only partially resolved, despite the celebratory aesthetic and compelling refrain that "the world es mi familia." The Riveria home is as impenetrable to the outside world as before, now transformed into a tourist attraction and thus arguably even more removed from local communal connections as a detached, objectified commodity. Such concluding sequestration, however beautifully rendered, reflects a mild suspicion of extra-familial relationships that can be traced throughout the film, from the neglected "nearly forgotten" denizens of the shanty town, who "call each other cousin, or tío, or whatever," to the comical stigmatizing of second marriage and its implications for negotiating living-nether world crossovers: "[w]e are *not* visiting your ex-wife's family for Día de Muertos!" Thus, while *Up* lauds intergenerational relationships which broaden what counts as family, *Coco* insists than only the bonds of traditional family structures can promote lasting connection and offer true kinship. The two films are Janus-like in their dual cases for a dialogue between the ages, with Carl Friedricksen looking forwards and recasting memories of the past to foreground future relationships beyond the family, and Miguel Rivera journeying backwards through the generations to remember and reaffirm ancestral ties with the present. Crucial to both narratives, however, is the sense that intergenerational solidarity must negotiate death as much as it interrogates life, even if their stances on death stare firmly in two different directions.

■ ■ ■

I opened this chapter by referencing the traditions of intergenerational conflict in Disney animation, particularly in stories of female relationships across age divides. It is telling that the stories most committed to offering a more nuanced reflection on the relationship between age and youth do so principally through the lens of male characters. Dennis Tyler is somewhat critical of Disney-Pixar's deferment of Ellie's dream in *Up* as "beyond her ability to pursue it" and substitution of her dreams "for a lifelong pattern of repetitive domestic service" (274). Certainly such a criticism aligns with Disney's overt position on gendered identity; the marginalization of Ellie and her spirit of adventure—which must be lived out by her husband and which sees her reduced to hazy memories and tokenistic simulacra—is in keeping with a longstanding tendency to reduce female experience to a limited number of roles. The same might be said of *Coco*, which gives its female cast more voice and agency, but in conventional modes that tend towards the fractious, reducing its centralized female character to silenced agedness and placing her in a corner for most of the story. It is easy to forget that the film is entitled *Coco* and not *Miguel* or *Héctor*. While the narratives might be said to uphold many of the stereotypical generational rifts that pepper Disney's animated history, however, they also take a revisionist look at that model, making a case towards a solidarity between the ages that—although distinctive in each case—recognizes the complexities involved and resists easy resolution. Both are tales of the realization—in life and in death, in age and youth—that we do not always know others as well as we might. In arguing for greater knowing within, between, and across generations, *Coco* and *Up* find value in a dialogue of youth and senescence, forging connections through as well as beyond conflicts and clashes, and making meaningful and multifaceted conversations in ways that are as complex and contradictory as they are compelling.

## WORKS CITED

Barthes, Roland. *Camera Lucida: Reflections on Photography*. Trans. Richard Howard. Hill & Wang, 1980.
Butts, Donna M. "Key Issues Uniting Generations." In *Intergenerational Solidarity: Strengthening Economic and Social Ties*, eds. María Amparo Cruz-Saco and Sergei Zelenev, 83–97. Palgrave Macmillan, 2010.

Cattell, Maria G., and Steven M. Albert. "Elders, Ancients, Ancestors and the Modern Life Course." In *The Cultural Context of Aging: Worldwide Perspectives*, ed. Jay Sokolovsky, 115–44. 3rd ed. Praeger, 2009.
*Coco*. Dir. Lee Unkrich. Walt Disney Pictures and Pixar Animation Studies, 2017.
Covarrubias, Alexandra Mendoza. "Dia de los Muertos." In *Celebrating Latino Folklore: An Encyclopedia of Cultural Traditions*, vol. 1, ed. Maria Herrera-Sobek, 403–414. ABC-CLIO, 2012.
Crandall, Nadia. "The Fairy Tale in the 21st Century: Shrek as Anticipatory Illumination or Coercive Ideology." In *Turning the Page: Children's Literature in Performance and the Media*, eds. Fiona M. Collins and Jeremy Ridgman, 165–84. Peter Lang, 2004.
Ford Smith, Victoria. *Between Generations: Collaborative Authorship in the Golden Age of Children's Literature*. University Press of Mississippi, 2017.
Gomila, Antònia. "Family Photographs: Putting Families on Display." In *Families and Kinship in Contemporary Europe: Rules and Practices of Relatedness*, eds. Riitta Jallinoja and Eric D. Widmer, 63–91. Palgrave Macmillan, 2011.
Gusmano, Michael K. "Growing Older in World Cities: Benefits and Burdens." In *The Cultural Context of Aging: Worldwide Perspectives*, ed. Jay Sokolovsky, 395–417. 3rd ed. Praeger, 2009.
Hockey, Jenny, and Allison James. *Growing Up and Growing Old: Ageing and Dependency in the Life Course*. Sage, 1993.
Joosen, Vanessa. "Introduction." In *Connecting Childhood and Old Age in Popular Media*, ed. Vanessa Joosen, 3–25. University Press of Mississippi, 2018.
Joosen, Vanessa. "Second Childhoods and Intergenerational Dialogues: How Children's Literature Studies and Old Age Studies Can Supplement Each Other." *Children's Literature Association Quarterly* 40, no. 2 (2015): 126–40.
Larkin, Elizabeth. "Who is Needy and Who should Give Care? Promoting Intergenerational Solidarity." In *Intergenerational Solidarity: Strengthening Economic and Social Ties*, eds. María Amparo Cruz-Saco and Sergei Zelenev, 99–125. Palgrave Macmillan, 2010.
L'Engle, Madeleine. *The Irrational Season*. Seabury Press, 1976.
Nikolajeva, Maria. *Reading for Learning: Cognitive Approaches to Children's Literature*. John Benjamins, 2014.
Paz, Octavio. *The Labyrinth of Solitude*. 1950. Trans. Lysander Kemp. Grove Press, 1977.
Rose, Jacqueline. *The Case of Peter Pan or The Impossibility of Children's Fiction*. 1984. University of Pennsylvania Press, 1992.
Seale, Clive. *Constructing Death: The Sociology of Dying and Bereavement*. Cambridge University Press, 1998.
*Snow White and the Seven Dwarfs*. Dir. David Hand. Walt Disney Productions, 1937.
Spitz, Ellen Handler. *The Brightening Glance: Imagination and Childhood*. Random House, 2006
*Tangled*. Dir. Nathan Greno and Byron Howard. Walt Disney Studios Motion Pictures, 2010.
Tyler, Dennis. "Home Is Where the Heart Is: Pixar's Up." In *Diversity in Disney Films: Critical Essays on Race, Ethnicity, Gender and Sexuality*, ed. Johnson Cheu, 268–83. McFarland, 2013.
*Up*. Dir. Pete Docter. Walt Disney Pictures and Pixar Animation Studies, 2009.
Wagner, Logan, et al. *Ancient Origins of the Mexican Plaza: From Primordial Sea to Public Space*. University of Texas Press, 2013.
Whitley, David. *The Idea of Nature in Disney Animation*. Ashgate, 2008.

# PART THREE
## CHILDREN'S LITERATURE AS INTERGENERATIONAL MEMORY

# 8

# TRAINS TO LIFE—TRAINS TO DEATH

## JUDITH KERR'S WRITING AND DRAWING FROM AND ABOUT CHILDHOOD EXILE IN THE NAZI ERA AS INTERGENERATIONAL SOLIDARISTIC PRACTICE

Lucy Stone

In March 1933, when children's author-illustrator Judith Kerr was nine years old, her family was forced to flee Berlin. Her father, writer Alfred Kerr, had been placed on the *Erste Schwarze Liste* (first blacklist) in the *Völkischer Beobachter* because of his mocking broadcasts about Hitler.[1] Tipped off by an anonymous policeman of the Nazis' intention to capture him, Alfred Kerr was on a train out of Germany within two hours. Kerr and his wife, Julia, feared the Nazis would try to take the family as hostages to force his return, so as soon as the house was packed up, the rest of the family—Julia, Judith, and her brother, Michael Kerr—also boarded a train to meet him in Zurich (*Eine eingeweckte Kindheit* [*A Pickled Childhood*], 35–36). Twenty-four hours after the family was reunited, the Nazis went to their Berlin home to confiscate their passports. The tension accompanying the Kerrs' journey features powerfully in Judith Kerr's fictionalized three-part autobiography, Out of the Hitler Time (1971–78).[2] The specific fear of discovery at the German-Swiss frontier is a climactic moment in the first volume, *When Hitler Stole Pink Rabbit* (1971). Even more terrifying is the moment when the family mistakenly starts to board a train bound back to Germany rather than on to France.[3]

Although they were technically safe, the Kerr family continued to feel the effects of the Nazis' rise to power. During the spring of 1933, Alfred Kerr's books were among those in the Nazi book burnings and his German citizenship was revoked, which made it impossible for the family to return to Germany under the Nazi regime. The exile that the children had been told would be temporary became permanent. By the end of 1935, the family's financial circumstances were so reduced that they could not afford to stay together. The children were sent alone by train to the south of France to stay with their maternal grandparents. During this stay, writing and drawing took on heightened significance for the young Judith Kerr. What had been pastimes and modes of play in Berlin[4] became means of maintaining a "spatial connection" (Weems 144)[5] with her parents. Her letters to them show that parents and daughter were in conversation about the development of their daughter's creative productions at this time.[6]

Judith Kerr deposited examples of these productions to Seven Stories: The National Centre of Children's Books in the United Kingdom in 2008. While Kerr's literature *about* childhood exile has received critical attention,[7] her literature *from* childhood has all but been ignored. This chapter is the first academic publication to bring a selection of the juvenilia to light.[8] In so doing, we can explore how the young Kerr drew on her craft to create a "spatial connection" with her parents on the page. Through close-readings of two of the illustrated stories, *Pierre and Michelle* (*Pierre et Michelle*, JK/01/01/01) and "The Journey" ("Die Reise," JK/01/01/02), both of which fictionalize her and her brother's unaccompanied train travel from Paris, I argue that Kerr began to creatively reconstruct her exilic train travel as a child.[9] Through close-readings of these texts, this chapter establishes the "spatial connection" Kerr was able to forge with her parents on paper. Although she had her personal experience of real-life railway journeys to call on in her juvenilia, as a tyro author-illustrator she would also have been aware of the way other writers and illustrators had created narratives about trains, including writer Erich Kästner and illustrator Walter Trier in their German children's novel *Emil and the Detectives* (*Emil und die Detektive*, 1929).[10] I begin this chapter by establishing the significance of trains in *Emil and the Detectives* and how this novel is situated in broader, cultural discourses on trains at the time. Drawing on scholarship of childhood reading, I then demonstrate the young author-illustrator's creative practice evident in *Pierre et Michelle* and "The Journey" as intergenerationally solidaristic: firstly, it builds on the text by an author and an illustrator of an older generation and, secondly, it creates a bond between herself and her parents in a period of separation as a consequence of forced migration. The final part of this chapter turns to an example of train travel in *When Hitler Stole Pink Rabbit* and finds that Kerr's intergenerational solidaristic practice continued in adulthood. In this example, the children's novel also forges a link between daughter and parents; the train in *Emil and the Detectives* can again be read as a departure point.

## TRAINS TO LIFE, TRAINS TO DEATH: THE CULTURAL SIGNIFICANCE OF TRAINS IN THE FIRST HALF OF THE TWENTIETH CENTURY

The Kerrs' experience of trains was not unique; indeed, trains played a variety of roles in everyday life and the conflicts that were taking place across Europe. Like many children and their families who escaped from Germany, the Kerrs stayed in several countries before settling in Britain. Each border crossing was more than a geographical movement: it also involved political, cultural, linguistic, and emotional upheaval. The experiences of the Kerr children are part of a much larger history of children's border crossings by train in the Nazi era. As commemorated by the bronze statue of Jewish child refugees and deportees at the Berlin Friedrichsstrasse railway station, *Züge ins Leben—Züge in den Tod* (*Trains to Life—Trains to Death*),[11] trains for many children in Nazi territories led to life, whether with their families, as in Judith Kerr's case, or by means of rescue programs such as the Kindertransport.[12] For many, however, train journeys ended in one of the death camps. Journeys by train, then, were fraught with ambivalence. This dark side to train travel had a long history. As a child, Judith Kerr would not have been conscious of this history in its entirety, but it would have informed the world in which she was growing up, her parents' perception of trains, and eventually, her account of the family's flight to safety on a succession of trains.

In a vignette entitled "The First Locomotive" ("*Die erste Lokomotive*"), the Marxist philosopher Ernst Bloch endows trains with a "demonic nature" ("*die Dämonie*," 208) arising from their historical associations. For Bloch, their use as modern war machines was a new manifestation of "the hellish face of the first locomotive," bringing noise, smells, and catastrophic accidents to the modern world (209). His characterization in part reflects the fact that since the Crimean campaign (1853–56), troop trains had acted as "extensions of battlefield logistics" in Europe (Beaumont and Freeman, 33), but most significantly for Bloch, the introduction of conscription in the First World War had seen a particularly dark use of locomotives. As Matthew Beaumont and Michael J. Freeman explain, at this time "the railway became the means by which men left home for their training camps and postings, their railway warrants forming a kind of universal currency to the conduct of war" (34). Given the carnage on the front lines of the First World War, railway warrants were for many effectively death warrants.

Bloch was writing very closely to the time of the publication of *Emil and the Detectives*, where the train's "black raging circles" ("*in dem schwarzen rasenden Kreise*," 63) gives it a demonic nature in the nightmare Emil has aboard the train on which he must travel alone to Berlin from his provincial hometown,

Neustadt. Scholars have argued that Kästner employs the train as a metaphor for the negative implications of modernity.[13] At the same time, the train acts as a brutal force that separates the young protagonist from his mother before he feels ready to leave her. In Emil's nightmare, the comparison of the train to a frenzied dog (*"Der Zug drehte sich um sich selber wie ein Hund, der sich in den Schwanz beißen will,"* Emil and the Detectives, 63) mirrors Kästner's earlier description of the howling and hissing it makes when it pulls into Neustadt station (*"Dann kam der Personenzug nach Berlin, mit Heulen und Zischen,"* 51). This beast-like train does not wreak death or destruction as the train does in Bloch's vignette, but it does cause Emil distress.

Trier's illustration of Emil running from the train in his nightmare with his arms outstretched also recalls the farewell between mother and son. As they had waited for the train, Emil took his mother by the arm (*"Er faßte die Mutter an Arm,"* 50) and then hugged her closely (*"Er drückte die Mutter fest an sich,"* 50–51), tightening his arms around her neck a little more when the train arrived (*"Emil fiel der Mutter noch ein bißchen um den Hals,"* 51). The lateral movement in the nightmare illustration is to the left; Emil reaches back in the story to his mother, just as he had clung to her at the train station. This movement is disconcerting; it also guides the reader's eye to the preceding rather than following pages. It emphasizes Emil's resistance to go to Berlin. Frau Tischbein might have thought that her son was "old enough" (*"er ist ja groß genug,"* 38) to travel alone by train from his home and mother, but Emil, in these two instances, is reluctant to do so.

Separation by train became a theme of children's artworks in the various conflicts that broke out in Europe in the 1930s.[14] As Zérane S. Giradeau et al. show in their study of child wartime drawings, "[a]t the individual level," it is family separations that "mark the real entry into the war for children, that is to say the moment when a vague concept—war—becomes intelligible and tangible, which can be experienced in the everyday life" (143). If war for children is understood to begin with family separation, then in the child war art the train can be read as an instrument and a symbol of this separation.

## REBUILDING THE TRAIN: JUDITH KERR'S WRITING AND DRAWING AS INTERGENERATIONAL SOLIDARISTIC PRACTICE

Discourses on childhood reading have established that children identify literary patterns and devices in books, which they carry in their memories and with which they can later write "something new, yet something old" (Greenway, xxii). The theme of separation by train in *Emil and the Detectives* provided the young

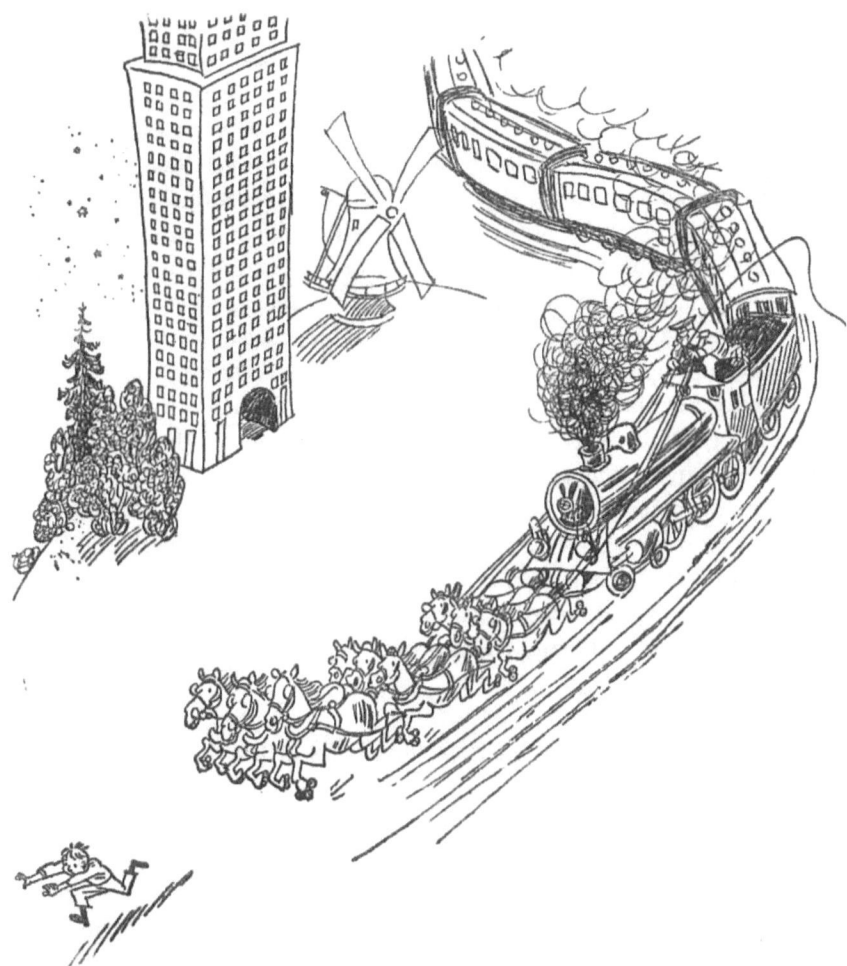

Illustration by Walter Trier for *Emil and the Detectives* showing Emil running from the train in his nightmare. © Atrium Verlag AG, Zürich.

Judith Kerr with material with which to shape her own fictional accounts of her experience of separation by train. I also argue that this children's novel had particular appeal to Kerr as a tyro author-illustrator because it encouraged its readers to collaborate with author and illustrator. In the preface, Kästner invites child readers to have a go at constructing the novel themselves before reading it. He places ten of Trier's vignettes between the preface and first chapter of the novel and implores child readers to treat them as "building blocks" and "build" the novel as they would a church or train station (*"Es ist eine Arbeit, als solltet ihr aus Bauklötzen, die man euch gibt, einen Bahnhof oder eine Kirche aufbauen,"* Emil and the Detectives, 16).¹⁵ The simile that Kästner chooses in his invitation is striking. A child can play with building blocks over and over again, each time using the same material to construct something new, or, at least in a slightly different way, placing for example, a red block where a green one had been. When child readers use these blocks in texts they craft themselves, then these texts contain an intertextuality that is intergenerational because they are built from a text by an author and an illustrator of an older generation.

In Kerr's case, the child writer and artist becomes adult author-illustrator who once again picks up and arranges Kästner's building blocks. This notion of the reading act evolving as the reader grows older is explored in discourses on childhood reading. Katherine Jones has proposed children's literature as generational literature because it "come[s] along" with readers over the course of the lives (305). For this very reason, it is also *inter*generational because it first passes from an adult author-illustrator to a child reader. Furthermore, as Kimberley Reynolds has observed, stories encountered by children "continue to unfold and inform how we interpret the world" (9) throughout childhood and into adulthood. Young Kerr's reading of *Emil and the Detectives* unfolds as she faces her own nightmarish train travel and then seeks to reconstruct it, firstly in childhood and then in adulthood.

## "UNE GRANDE BÊTE FURIEUSE": NIGHTMARISH TRAINS IN JUDITH KERR'S JUVENILIA

Kerr builds the trains in *Pierre et Michelle* with similar characteristics to the train in *Emil and the Detectives*. The train that carries Pierre and Michelle away from their parents is also described as a frenzied creature: as the train nears the French village where the children are to stay with their aunt and uncle, it "emerges from the nearby copse like a great, furious beast, dragging behind her all of the carriages like a long tail. The train arrives, hissing like mad. The white steam trails behind spreading an unpleasant smell" (*"la locomotive sort du bosquet voisin comme une grande bête furieuse, traînant derrière elle tous les wagons qui ont l'air d'une longe [sic] queue. Le train arrive sifflant comme fou. La vapeur blanche part en arrière répandant une odeur desagréable,"* JK/01/01/01/07). This beast delivers the children safely to their awaiting relatives because their uncle, Monsieur Bidon, as signalman, can control it. However, in an episode in the story's final chapter, where he cannot do so, the train's potential to wreak death and destruction is fully realized. Here, just as in Emil's nightmare, there is threat of a train accident; Pierre has lost the key to the signal room, so Monsieur Bidon cannot operate the signals to keep the train on track rather than derailing. Pierre sees in his mind's eye vivid images of "a great train, turned over by

Illustration by Judith Kerr for *Pierre and Michelle* showing Pierre averting the derailment. © Judith Kerr. Image courtesy of Seven Stories: The National Centre for Children's Books.

the signals, in flames," "children who search for their parents," "women who cry into their hands" and "newspapers with long articles entitled 'A terrible railway accident...'" ("*Dans son imagination il voit un grand train en flames renversé à côté d'une aiguille. Il voit des enfants qui cherchent leurs parents, des femmes qui pleurent leurs maris. Il voit des journaux avec de longs articles intitules «un terrible accident de chemin de fer...».*," JK/01/01/01/67). These images inspire him to act. Just in the nick of time, he saves the train by climbing up to the signal box, squeezing through its window, and operating the controls so that the train stays on track.

As Emil's train nightmare is intratextually linked with his departure by train at the beginning of the novel, so too is the nightmarish train in *Pierre and Michelle* coupled to the train earlier in the story. While the nightmare in Kästner's novel links intratextually to Emil's separation by train from his mother, this near nightmarish scenario in young Kerr's text highlights aspects of the children's anxiety about their separations by train from their parents. The focus on windows in the illustrations of Pierre averting the derailment achieves an intrapictorality with the illustrations at the beginning of *Pierre and Michelle* and "The Journey," which show the train carriage windows out of which the children lean and wave to their relatives as they approach their destinations. All three images emphasize the children's movement on and around trains. While Pierre stretches through the window and up to the signal board, the children stretch out of the train windows. Kerr's early talent as a visual storyteller is evident here. As William Moebius explains in his "Introduction to Picturebook Codes,"

> the frequent depiction in picturebooks of grates, doors, windows and stairs, of roads and waterways, and the changing representations of light, artificial and natural, to accord with different degrees of character understanding, are not accidental or fortuitous phenomena, but downright basic to the symbolic force of the story. A character who looks out of the window or stands in the door, as Max does in *Where the Wild Things Are*, is implicated in the unspoken meanings of thresholds. Whether stairs, steps or extended ramp, the incline may provide a measure of the character's stature or of progress towards a depth or height of understanding or confusion. (146–47)

The train windows, then, allow reading the train as a threshold. For the children leaning from the train windows, the train might be regarded as a threshold into exile. Both of the girls' faces and arms are positioned downwards. With Moebius's window code in mind, these young girls are arguably descending into exile with all its negative connotations. While these images are neatly framed, the children are not confined by the borders. As they lean out of the window in *Pierre and Michelle*, Michelle's handkerchief crosses over the line Kerr draws to mark the train carriage. Similarly, in "The Journey," the girl Puppi's arms extend past the window frame. The characters' movements in these images are depicted in ways that suggest that the children want to break away from exile just as Emil wanted to return to his mother. Moreover, the breaking the frame illustrates the child's desire to maintain a degree of intergenerational solidarity: Michelle reaches back to where she had been with her parents and Puppi towards her grandfather, eager to re-bond with the adult awaiting the children's arrival in Nice.

## CONNECTING TRAINS: CONTINUUM BETWEEN JUDITH KERR'S LITERATURE FROM AND ABOUT CHILDHOOD EXILE

The trains in Kerr's juvenilia separate the children from their parents, but, paradoxically, the two texts created a link between the child author-illustrator and her parents during a period of separation in the exile years. The train travel in

Illustration by Judith Kerr for *Pierre and Michelle* showing the children as they lean out of the train and wave to their aunt and uncle as they approach their destination. © Judith Kerr. Image courtesy of Seven Stories: The National Centre for Children's Books.

Illustration by Judith Kerr for "The Journey" showing the children as they lean out of the train and wave to their grandfather as they approach the train station in Nice. © Judith Kerr. Image courtesy of Seven Stories: The National Centre for Children's Books.

the juvenilia is omitted from *When Hitler Stole Pink Rabbit*,[16] but the children's novel also features some of the exilic train travel and forges a link with Kerr's parents, as she wrote the novel in memory of them. This intergenerational solidarity goes further as she wrote the book for her own children, in the process carrying the family story forward.[17] Each instance of train travel in the novel is with one or both parents so that the parents' as well as the children's stories can be foregrounded and the link between them can be portrayed. I take as an example in this section of the chapter the flight by train from Berlin, which stands as the first instance of train travel in the novel. Knowledge of Kerr's childhood reading of Kästner's novel sheds light on the construction of the railway carriage in which the protagonist, Anna, her brother, Max, and Mama travel the last, perhaps most important leg of their journey from Stuttgart to Zurich, where Papa awaits them.[18]

Kästner introduces the railway compartment in which Emil travels to Berlin as the third "building block" between the novel's preface and first chapter, titling it "A fairly important railway compartment" (*"Ein ziemlich wichtiges Eisenbahnabteil," Emil and the Detectives* 21). The significance of train carriages in Kerr's juvenilia—notably, the train carriage windows—has been discussed above; Kerr picked up Kästner's building block again many years later to

"A fairly important railway carriage". Illustration by Walter Trier for *Emil and the Detectives*. © Atrium Verlag AG, Zürich.

rebuild the train that crosses the German-Swiss frontier. There is an evident intrapictorality between Trier's and Kerr's illustrations of the railway compartment. The combination of economy and expressiveness in Kerr's line is similar to that of Trier's. Focusing on Kerr's vignette for the railway compartment in *When Hitler Stole Pink Rabbit* (33), we see that the luggage rack is drawn in the same cross detail as Trier's, and hatching is used in both illustrations to mark the spaces within the carriages. Kästner's caption draws attention to the varied characters that can be encountered in railway compartments; in turn, Kerr places a passenger who plays an integral role in the family's border crossing in her story. This passenger, "the lady with the basket" (36), acts as a foil to Herr Grundeis who gives ignorant Emil a highly exaggerated account of Berlin (*Emil and the Detectives*, 55–56). Although the lady sharing the compartment with Mama and the children is similar to Herr Grundeis in her possession of power stemming from her local knowledge of the destination, she does not abuse it. She answers Mama accurately each time the latter asks if they have reached the frontier when the train stops (*When Hitler Stole Pink Rabbit* 35–36). Moreover, the inclusion of this passenger in an otherwise empty compartment (35) positions Mama on a similar level to her daughter, whose

Copy of Judith Kerr's original artwork for the vignette of the railway compartment in *When Hitler Stole Pink Rabbit*. © Judith Kerr. Image courtesy of Seven Stories: The National Centre for Children's Books.

questioning, like Mama's, shows a lack of control of the situation. In the sudden flight from their Berlin home there is a kinship (Gubar, "Hermeneutics . . .," 300) between child and adult where their helplessness and unknowing is related rather than differentiated.

As with *Emil and the Detectives* and Kerr's juvenilia, attention is also drawn to the characters' arm movements. When the train pulls safely into Zurich railway station, "Papa, who was always so dignified, who never did anything in a hurry, suddenly ran towards them. He put his arms around Mama and hugged her. Then he hugged Anna and Max. He hugged and hugged them all and would not let them go" (*When Hitler Stole Pink Rabbit*, 38). Here, Kerr emphasizes the bond of the nuclear family unit by showing their reunion after their time apart rather than focusing on their separation, as she does in the juvenilia.

*When Hitler Stole Pink Rabbit* as a children's novel that fictionalizes a real child's experience of exile from Nazi Germany is widely read and acclaimed; Judith Kerr was awarded Officer of the Most Excellent Order of the British Empire (OBE) in 2012 for her contribution to children's literature and Holocaust education.[19] However, one unacknowledged factor that makes this novel unique is that it can be read alongside the child's verbal and pictorial texts crafted in the years in which the novel is set. When read in tandem, it becomes evident that Kerr began constructing the story of her family's exile in childhood. As this chapter has shown, Kerr drew on her reading of *Emil and the Detectives* so that, *with* paper, pencil, and pen she could, in one way, remain connected with her parents when they could not be together. Many years later, Kerr again picked up pencil, pen, and *Emil*'s train as a model, this time to put her parents *on* paper and in this way forge a connection with them. The adult-authored and -illustrated text is altered and revised, but it shares intergenerational solidaristic practice and concerns with the juvenilia. Marah Gubar draws attention to the fact that when children's literature is defined as literature *by* adults *for* children, where adults are characterized as "active, creative producers and children as passive, inert receivers, we set into motion [. . .] types of aetonormative amnesia. Children's participation in the production of youth culture is forgotten—and so, too, are the insights of adults who helped to enable that participation" ("Seen and Heard," 47). This chapter is one attempt to stall this amnesia by demonstrating how *When Hitler Stole Pink Rabbit* was the product of an active child reader, writer, and artist who became an adult author-illustrator who passed on the train building blocks from her childhood to new generations of child readers.

## NOTES

1. For biographical information on Alfred Kerr, see Vietor-Engländer (2016).
2. Judith Kerr also wrote about her family's flight from Nazi Germany in *Judith Kerr's Creatures: A Celebration of Her Life and Work* (8–10). The other volumes of Judith Kerr's autobiography are *Bombs on Aunt Dainty*, originally titled *The Other Way Round* (1975) and *A Small Person Far Away* (1978).
3. See chapter twelve of *When Hitler Stole Pink Rabbit*.
4. Judith Kerr explains how, as a child, to draw "seemed a normal way to pass one's time, just as it was normal for [her brother] Michael to kick a ball about" (*Creatures*, 8).
5. See the introduction to this volume for discussion of Weems's thesis on how texts can forge spatial connections between generations.
6. This correspondence is held in the Alfred Kerr Archive at the Akademie der Künste in Berlin. See, for example, AK, 453.
7. See Lathey (1998, 1999) and McGillicuddy (2014, 2016) on the depiction of childhood exile in *When Hitler Stole Pink Rabbit*.
8. Examples of the juvenilia have been published in *Creatures* (6, 9, 15–20), *A Pickled Childhood* (30–1), *Drawn from the Archive: Hidden Histories of Illustration* (Lawrance 2015), *Das rosa Kaninchen, Mog und die anderen—Die Bilderwelt der Judith Kerr (The Pink Rabbit, Mog and the Others—Judith Kerr's World of Pictures*, Liesen and Linsmann 2013), and *Judith Kerr* (Carey 2019). While Nicola Otten's doctoral thesis on the Kerrs' autobiographical writings does not include the material deposited to Seven Stories, it does offer close-readings of some of the poetry Judith Kerr composed and illustrated as a child that is held in the Berlin archive (130; AK, 2626).
9. In *Pierre and Michelle*, Pierre and his sister travel alone by train from Paris to rural France to stay with their aunt and uncle. While in "The Journey" ("Die Reise," JK/01/01/02), Puppi and Michel travel alone by train from Paris to Nice to stay with their maternal grandparents. It is difficult to date these two stories. In the compilation of material for Kerr's memoir, *Pierre and Michelle* was dated 1935 (*Creatures* 12). This date corresponds with archival evidence. Letters to her parents from Nice allude to a story that she was working on at the time (AK, 453). However, anecdotes in these letters are much closer to events narrated in the collection of illustrated stories entitled *Puppi and Michel in Nice* (*Puppi und Michel in Nizza*, JK/01/01/02), the first of which is "The Journey." Moreover, dating the letter from Pierre and Michelle's mother September 19, 1936 (*Pierre and Michelle*, JK/01/01/01/76) would suggest the story was written (or at least completed) in the autumn of that year. While there are strong parallels between Judith's 1935 letters and *Puppi and Michel in Nizza*, there are clues in the story that indicate that it too was, if not drafted, at least completed at a later date. In "A Day in Nice" ("Ein Tag in Nizza"), the second part of the story, the narrator explains that Puppi did not yet have the pink pyjamas she wears, but could not resist including them because they are so fine (*"Die rosa Pyjamas hatte ich damals noch nicht, aber ich konnte sie nicht widerstehen sie zu erwähnen—sie sind doch SO FEIN!,"* JK/01/01/02/F9a). Judith made the final section of the story, "Birthday Speech: the best grandma of all time" ("Geburtstagsrede: die beste Omama aller Zeiten") to celebrate the sixtieth birthday of her maternal grandmother, Gertrud Weismann, in 1937. The illustrations are also drawn in what appears to be a more mature hand than those in *Pierre and Michelle*.
10. See Judith Kerr's account of her childhood reading in Antonia Fraser (51–58) and Gillian Lathey's discussion of the novel's popularity among German Jewish children at the time surroundings its publication (104–105).

11. All translations in this chapter are my own. This memorial is part of a series of Kindertransport memorials made by sculptor Frank Meisler (1925–2018), himself a Kindertransportee. The other memorials can be found at London Liverpool Street Station (*Kinderstransport—The Arrival*), Gdańsk Główny Station (*The Departure*), and the Hook of Holland (*Crossing to Life*). The Kindertransport was a rescue program that saw 10,000 unaccompanied Jewish children from Nazi territories travel to safety in Britain between the November Pogroms in 1938 and the outbreak of the Second World War.

12. See my previous footnote.

13. See, for example, Haywood, 111.

14. See, for example, Anna Lehinger (57–62) on a collection of drawings children made in Switzerland in response to the Swiss mobilization of September 2, 1939; S. Girardeau (242) for the painting made by C. Frédéric, a primary school student in 1940 Paris; and the Spanish Civil War Collection, University of California and Children's Drawings of the Spanish Civil War, Columbia University Libraries Online Exhibition.

15. Kästner's preface is not translated into the English editions of the novel. The vignettes, with their lengthy captions, are dispersed throughout the text of the English editions, close to the events they illustrate.

16. There is a threat of separation in the novel (see chapter twenty-two), but here, the family's financial difficulties are remedied before they have to go through with it.

17. See the introduction to this volume for discussion of this element of intergenerational solidarity.

18. As a fictionalized autobiography, the characters do not bear the same names as the Kerrs. However, "Anna" was Judith Kerr's first name; she was born Anna Judith Helene Gertrud Kerr.

19. Judith Kerr did not receive the OBE for this novel alone; she is the author-illustrator of thirty-seven books, including the much-loved *The Tiger Who Came to Tea* (1968) and the series of *Mog* picture books (1970–2015).

## WORKS CITED

Beaumont, Matthew, and Michael J. Freeman, eds. *The Railway and Modernity: Time, Space and the Machine Ensemble*. Peter Lang, 2007.

Bloch, Ernst. *Spuren*. Suhrkamp, 1930.

Carey, Joanna. *Judith Kerr*. Thames & Hudson, 2019.

"Children's Drawings of the Spanish Civil War." *Columbia University Libraries Online Exhibition*, https://exhibitions.library.columbia.edu/exhibits/show/children. Accessed June 14, 2018.

Fraser, Antonia, ed. *The Pleasure of Reading: 43 Writers on the Discovery of Reading and the Books that Inspired Them*. Bloomsbury, 2015.

Giradeau, Zérane S., editor. *Déflagrations: Dessins d'enfants, guerres d'adultes*. Anamosa, 2017.

Greenway, Betty, ed. *Twice-Told Children's Tales: The Influence of Childhood Reading on Writers for Adults*. Routledge, 2005.

Gubar, Marah. "The Hermeneutics of Recuperation: What a Kinship-Model Approach to Children's Agency could do for Children's Literature and Childhood Studies." *Jeunesse: Young People, Texts, Cultures* 8, no. 1 (2016): 291–310.

Gubar, Marah. "Seen and Heard: Remembering Children's Art and Activism." *Los Angeles Review of Books* 20 (2018): 42–51.

Haywood, Susanne. *Kinderliteratur als Zeitdokument: Alltagsnomalität der Weimarer Republik in Erich Kästners Kinderromanen*. Peter Lang, 1998.
Jones, Katherine. "Getting Rid of Children's Literature." *The Lion and the Unicorn*, 30, no. 3 (2006): 287–315.
"Judith und Michael Kerr." *Alfred-Kerr-Archiv*, Akademie der Künste, Berlin, AK 453.
Kästner, Erich. *Emil und die Detektive*. 1929. Williams & Co., 1934.
Kerr, Judith. *Bombs on Aunt Dainty*. 1975. HarperCollins, 2017.
Kerr, Judith. *Eine eingeweckte Kindheit*. Argon, 1990.
Kerr, Judith. *Judith Kerr's Creatures: A Celebration of her Life and Work*. HarperCollins, 2013.
Kerr, Judith. "Pierre et Michelle." *Judith Kerr Collection*, Seven Stories: The National Centre for Children's Books, Newcastle upon Tyne, JK/01/01/01.
Kerr, Judith. "Puppi und Michel in Nizza." *Judith Kerr Collection*, Seven Stories: The National Centre for Children's Books, Newcastle upon Tyne, JK/01/01/02.
Kerr, Judith. *A Small Person Far Away*. 1978. HarperCollins, 2017.
Kerr, Judith. "Weihnachtsgabe Puppis für die Eltern." *Alfred-Kerr-Archiv*, Akademie der Künste, Berlin, AK 2626.
Kerr, Judith. *When Hitler Stole Pink Rabbit*. 1971. HarperCollins, 2013
Lathey, Gillian. "A Child's View of Exile. Language and Identity in The Autobiographical Writings of Judith Kerr and Charles Hannam." In *Keine Klage über England? Deutsche und Österreichische Erfahrungen in Großbritannien, 1933–1945*, ed. Charmian Brinson, 190–99. Ludicium, 1998.
Lathey, Gillian. "From Emil to Alice: The Hiatus in the Childhood Reading of Exiles from Germany and Austria, 1933–45." In *German-speaking Exiles in Great Britain*, ed. Anthony Grenville, 99–122. Rodopi, 2000.
Lathey, Gillian. *The Impossible Legacy: Identity and Purpose in Autobiographical Children's Literature Set in the Third Reich*. Peter Lang, 1999.
Lawrance, Sarah. *Drawn from the Archive: Hidden Histories of Illustration*. Seven Stories Publications, 2015.
Lehninger, Anna. *Vor-Bilder. Nach-Bilder. Zeit-Bilder. Kommerzielle Zeichenwettbewerbe für Kinder in der Schweiz, 1935–1985*. Chronos, 2015.
Liesen, Pauline, and Maria Linsmann, eds. *Das rosa Kaninchen, Mog und die anderen: Die Bilderwelt der Judith Kerr*. Burg Wissem Bilderbuch Museum der Stadt Troisdorf, 2013.
McGillicuddy, Áine. "From Germany to England: Girls in Exile in the Works of Judith Kerr and Irene N. Watts." In *Exile and Gender I: Literature and the Press*, eds. Charmian Brinson and Andrea Hammel, 188–206. Brill Rodopi, 2016.
McGillicuddy, Áine. "Out of the Hitler Time: A Life in Exile." In *Politics and Ideology in Children's Literature*, eds. Marian Thérèse Keyes and Áine McGillicuddy, 127–40. Four Courts, 2014.
Moebius, William. "Introduction to Picturebook Codes." *Word and Image* 2 (1986): 141–58.
Otten, Nicola. "*Mit Geschaffnem grüßt man sachte, was nur das Erleben brachte": Verfolgung, Flucht und Exil im Spiegel der autobiographischen Schriften der Familie Alfred Kerrs*. PhD thesis, Hamburg University, 2009.
Reynolds, Kimberley. *Radical Children's Literature: Future Visions and Aesthetic Transformations in Juvenile Fiction*. Palgrave Macmillan, 2007.
"Spanish Civil War Children's Drawings." *Spanish Civil War Collection*, University of California, https://library.ucsd.edu/dc/collection/bb4540678g. Accessed June 14, 2018.
Vietor-Engländer, Deborah. *Alfred Kerr: Die Biographie*. Rowohlt, 2016.

# 9

# NADJA HALILBEGOVICH'S *MY CHILDHOOD UNDER FIRE: A SARAJEVO DIARY*
## THE INTERGENERATIONAL SELF AND THE KINSHIP MODEL
Anastasia Ulanowicz

Since the emergence of children's literature studies and childhood studies in the late twentieth century, scholars have remained attentive to the role played by literary texts and other cultural artifacts in the rich and complex dynamics between children and their elders. Indeed, as the essays anthologized in this collection demonstrate, scholars have questioned how literary depictions of child-adult relationships address the possibility of, or otherwise test the limits of, expressions of intergenerational solidarity. Significantly, however, few, if any, studies in this field have explored the potential of adults' creative interaction with their former childhood selves. What would it mean to posit the individual self as inherently intergenerational? On what notions of childhood and subjectivity might such a proposition depend? And how might this concept of an intergenerational self, and the new possibilities of collaboration and solidarity it implies, become legible in books produced by and for young people?

If there is one text that invites these questions, it is Nadja Halilbegovich's *My Childhood Under Fire: A Sarajevo Diary* (2006). Like well-known works such as Anne Frank's *Diary of a Young Girl* (1947) and Zlata Filipović's *Zlata's Diary* (1995), *My Childhood Under Fire* is a reprinted and translated version of a childhood diary that Halilbegovich kept in order to bear witness to wartime conditions—namely, the siege of Sarajevo in the early 1990s. Much like the authors of these former texts, the teenaged Halilbegovich intentionally crafted her journal entries for eventual public consumption as a means of testifying to the daily experiences of children living under exceptional historical circumstances. Unlike these texts and other children's wartime diaries, however, this one features annotations produced by the adult Halilbegovich, who is now a writer and artist currently residing in Canada. In these annotations, Halilbegovich fills in significant gaps left open within the original narratives, and reflects on her initial impressions from the perspectives she has gained since her emergency evacuation, her emigration to North America, and her subsequent personal and artistic maturation. Read side-by-side, then, Halilbegovich's original entries and later annotations not only offer twin portraits of the same person at distinct stages of her individual development, but also suggest an intimate relationship between her past and present selves. On the one hand, Halilbegovich is careful to make a spatial and visual distinction between her original entries and her annotations, so as to distinguish between her childhood and adult selves and, what is more, to respect the integrity of her childhood voice. On the other hand, however, her added reflections position her adult voice and perspectives in relation to her earlier ones in such a way that suggests an additionally nuanced and textured depiction of a traumatic historical event. In this way, then, *My Childhood Under Fire* productively expands Marah Gubar's concept of a "kinship model" of children's literature and childhood, insofar as it intimates that collaborative projects undertaken by discrete but nonetheless interlinked child and adult agents may well extend to the adult writer's strategic and creative engagement with her own juvenilia and the articulations of selfhood within it.

## CONTENT: CHILDREN'S CREATIVE AGENCY AND INTRA-/INTERGENERATIONAL COLLABORATION

"I have lived three lives" (7). In this first, arresting, sentence of her introduction to *My Childhood Under Fire*, the adult Halilbegovich calls attention to how she perceives herself not as a seamlessly unified subject but rather as an individual who has been compelled to stitch together multiple experiences into a narrative that offers her at least a consoling sense of cohesion. As the author clarifies, her "three lives" correspond to the events immediately before, during, and after the siege of Sarajevo: the first marks her "comfortable" and "cheerful" existence in a "conventional middle-class family" in the former Yugoslavia (7); the second involves her experiences "under fire" in this erstwhile republic's capital city (7–8); and the third pertains to her adult life in North America, where she continues to be haunted by the memories of internecine warfare (9). If Halilbegovich regards her childhood diary as her "most valuable possession," then, this is not only because it documents her traumatic experiences but also because it effectively mediates her "three lives."

To this end, the diarist intuits Marah Gubar's contention that our "younger selves and our older selves are multiple and interlinked, akin to one another rather than wholly distinct" ("Risky Business," 454). Gubar's observation of the ultimately "interlinked" character of younger and older selves informs her critique of two dominant scholarly approaches to children and their texts, which she names the "deficit model" and the "difference model," respectively. The former approach involves the perception of young people as "lacking the abilities, skills, and powers that adults have (451). The latter approach stresses the "radical alterity or otherness of children, representing them as a separate species, categorically different from adults" (451). In order to counter these approaches, Gubar proposes a "kinship model" that is "premised on the idea that children and adults are akin to one another, which means that they are neither exactly the same nor radically dissimilar" (453). This alternate approach, she claims, draws on the basic premise that children, like adults, are "human beings," and as such, in possession of voice and agency (453): although their expressions of such voice and agency might vary "in degree" from those of adults, young people's creative and critical efforts nevertheless should be acknowledged in relation to, rather than radically separate from, that of adult producers (454). Thus, the kinship model challenges dominant readings of childhood that deny or otherwise overlook children's potential contributions to culture.

Halilbegovich's original entries and later annotations make dramatically clear the ways in which individual children can function as artistic agents and collaborate with both other young people and members of older generations on aesthetic projects. In order to demonstrate how they do so, however, it is first necessary to give a preliminary introduction to the book's basic structure—that is, the way in which it arranges its initial entries and subsequent notes. Such an exposition will not only place into relief how the text's form and content insist upon the child's potential to participate in the production of culture, but will also set the stage for a subsequent analysis of how its credence in the young person's capacities for creative collaboration informs the textual relationship that Halilbegovich establishes between her war-era and present-day self.

*My Childhood Under Fire* is characterized, first, by a strategic use of visual formatting and printed space. With the exception of a few illustrations and marginal doodles, the author's original entries are translated into English and rendered in comic sans font. The use of bold lettering makes these entries immediately visible; moreover, since comics sans is conventionally associated with childhood or a certain degree of playfulness, the font gives at least the impression of the original script produced by a child's yet unsteady hand.[1] By contrast, the author's later commentaries, which follow key original entries and are placed under the recurring subtitle, "Looking Back," are rendered in Joanna font.[2] In this way, the text beckons the reader to take in a set of original entries and then to pause and reflect on them at the promptings of the "Looking Back" annotations, which furnish greater historical and cultural context or focus on a specific detail in one of the preceding narratives in order to call attention to their social or affective significance.

For example, the first few entries of the diary, which Halilbegovich made between May and June of 1992, document the initial adjustments she had to make as she was suddenly propelled from her "first life" of peaceful middle-class comfort to her "second life" in besieged Sarajevo. They address how her perception of the war changed once it was no longer a television spectacle but rather an event that transpired literally in her backyard (11); how her increasingly "piled up feelings" about "deafening explosions" prompted her to keep a diary in which she might articulate her experiences and anxieties (11); and how her regular routine of school and play gave way to equally regular evacuations to a basement shelter (12). Immediately thereafter, the adult Halilbegovich's first annotation not only confirms the terror she experienced but also notes that her fears were compounded by witnessing, for the first time, her parents' own vulnerability: although she had long looked to her parents for "advice, comfort, and security," she became suddenly aware of how, in the dismal basement setting, they "couldn't hide" their fear, no matter how much they tried to reassure her (12). On the one hand, this annotation gives expression to, and thus respects the integrity of, a childhood intuition that Halilbegovich explicitly recalls registering but was unable to articulate in writing at the time—not least, perhaps, because she was already so (literally) shaken by immediate physical threats to her survival that any admission of her deeper psychological insecurities may have practically undone her. On the other hand, however, this "Looking Back" entry demonstrates how the author's spatial and temporal distance from this initial event, as well as her heretofore accumulated experiences, have allowed her to admit and actively engage with the fragility of human life from a perspective, and within a discourse, that was not immediately available to her as a child.

Throughout the diary, both the original entries and later annotations underscore the collaborative and often improvised efforts of young people to sustain creative production in the face of wartime deprivation. In an entry dated on September 16, 1992, Halilbegovich explains how she and the young friends she has made during regular evacuations to her building's basement establish a group they name the "Tenants of the Basement" (18). This group organizes an "exhibition of drawings of handicrafts" for which they produce "special handmade invitations for the eldest tenants of our building" (18). The second meeting of the "Tenants," recorded in a September 26, 1992, entry, involves the "exchanging of war-food recipes created by our mothers with a bare number of ingredients" (20). Although subsequent entries do not explicitly mention further "Tenants'" meetings, this club apparently continues to meet, since the diarist reports on June 6, 1993, that she, along with her young neighbors, have founded a child-written-and-produced newspaper entitled *Kids of Sarajevo*. This newspaper, which apparently is entirely conceived by the building's youngest tenants and has no adult moderator, demonstrates sturdy organization and a clear and equal division of labor: "Everybody has an assignment—some will draw pictures, some will write stories or poems. We will also include jokes, word puzzles, and war recipes from our mothers" (42). Moreover, it is motivated by an overarching activist impulse. According to the young Halilbegovich, the newspaper's production, which involves not only candid accounts of the war's effects but also playful experiments with different forms and media, demonstrates "the way children fight for freedom" (42). Halilbegovich's account of the "Tenants'" newspaper and their other creative endeavors makes evident the inventive capacities of children as well as their aptitude for self-organization.

Of course, it would be naïve to assume that Halilbegovich's "Tenants of the Basement" collective is purely *sui generis* or otherwise unmediated. Indeed, to do so would risk romanticizing this group of children, and childhood more generally, in such a way that ultimately leads to the discourses of the fundamental difference between children and adults against which Gubar warns. As Gubar argues, it is impossible to conceive of individual child agents, or even creative collectives of children, without first admitting that they—and, surely, the adults they eventually become—are radically influenced by the contingent cultural and material conditions into which they are born. All human beings, she maintains, "begin life in a compromised situation, a state of dependence in which key decisions about who we are and how we live our lives are being made for us, affecting how we conceive of ourselves and the world around us" ("Hermeneutics," 300). Each of the diarist's reports of the "Tenants'" activities acknowledges how they occur within, and in response to, a larger, profoundly adult-mediated social context in which they are initially implicated. For instance, the group's early recipe-exchange meeting, as well as their later publication of "war recipes from our mothers," implies at least the tacit involvement and approbation of the group members' caregivers. Likewise, another entry, in which Halilbegovich states that the "small party" of friends who assemble to celebrate her birthday do not "play, sing, or talk loudly" in an effort to respect the downstairs neighbors who had "just lost their son defending the Zuc Hill" suggests that the group's activities are not as spontaneous or entirely self-ruled as they might initially appear; instead, they seem to be mediated by the needs of adults and the social codes they observe (45). Even the children's entirely self-created newspaper suggests the influence of adults and, more broadly, the *a priori* existence of a socio-historical context in which its young creators are already sutured. Not only does its division of labor and textual organization mimic those of the adult-created periodicals, but also its activist purpose places into relief the "Tenants'" acknowledgment of their position within, and their critical response to, socio-historical circumstances beyond their own making.

It would be a mistake, however, to conclude that adult mediation invalidates children's creative potential. Rather, cultural institutions make possible various spontaneous, often surprising alliances between children and adults that effectively destabilize their culturally preordained separate roles. For example, the adult Halilbegovich relates her memories of a weekly radio quiz program that, although it was initially designed as a virtual schoolroom for children whose official coursework had been disrupted by the war, ultimately became an opportunity for young people to compete both with and alongside their elders. When the ambitious young Halilbegovich called in a response to a quiz question, her father and elder brother would occasionally join her, "shout[ing] different answers into phones in different rooms"—much to the consternation of the radio "teacher" confronted by "three stubborn players on the same line" (41–42). "These moments," the annotation states, "were both comic and exhilarating" since they allowed the family to "escape our stark reality, if only for a short time" (42).

As comical and escapist as this brief interlude may seem, it also demonstrates how wartime conditions radically disrupt such conventional oppositions as parent versus child, teacher versus student, and the public environment of school versus the private context of the family. Of course, this insight is not entirely new. After all, if children's wartime diaries continue to fascinate contemporary readers, this is at least in part because they demonstrate how young people who are expected to conform to Romantic expectations of carefree innocence are unceremoniously initiated into the realm of world-weary adulthood, even as their elders are subjected to childlike vulnerability. What is remarkable about Halilbegovich's annotated account of the radio contest, however, is that it refuses a narrative of wartime conditions wherein either the child is definitively forced into the position of the adult or the adult categorically assumes the position of the child. Rather, it depicts an intermediary context—literally, one managed by the medium of radio—in which children like Halilbegovich might take on the authoritative voices usually ascribed to adults even as their elders may dare to engage, if only momentarily, in the kind of playful performance usually associated with children. This is the intermediary space where adults and children might meet and compete as equals to sustain the creative production of knowledge in the face of its potential obliteration.

## FORM: DYNAMIC RELATIONSHIPS BETWEEN THE CHILD AND ADULT SELF

The content of *My Childhood Under Fire* offers a convincing case study of Gubar's kinship model of childhood studies, not least because it provides detailed examples of children's aesthetic agency, intra- and intergenerational forms of aesthetic collaboration, and the material and ideological circumstances that mediate such endeavors. This text does not simply represent the creative kinship between children and adults but rather incorporates and performs it within its very form: that is, as a book effectively co-written by Halilbegovich's childhood and adult selves. Indeed, upon a closer analysis of the precise relationships between the original entries and the later annotations, one can perceive the influence of the various expressions of kinship and collaboration depicted in its content on the ways in which the entries and annotations speak to one another in order to offer a richer depiction of the siege of Sarajevo. In other words, if in the first place Halilbegovich was inspired to publish a version of her diary that offers a veritable call-and-response between her childhood and adult voices, this may very well be because she was already well-acquainted with how children and adults may work together in order to offer a collective and textured response to and representation of their immediate circumstances.

Moreover, the central focus of the collective content of *My Childhood Under Fire* on the aesthetic kinship between, and shared vulnerability of, children and adults in besieged Sarajevo—rather than, say, on their differences in age, experience, and psychological maturity—suggests a strategy of reading its child-authored entries and adult-authored annotations that resists the privileging of one over the other. It would be tempting, for example, for a reader to consider Halilbegovich's childhood impressions of the siege as more raw, direct, or otherwise authentic than those that she offers from her more spatio-temporally distant, and certainly more materially secure, perspective as a North American adult. Likewise, a reader could just as well insist that Halilbegovich's later annotations, informed as they are by historical hindsight and accrued wisdom, provide a more objective, or at least comprehensive, perspective on her initial experiences. Ultimately, both readings are wanting: whereas the first overvalues the category of direct experience in trauma representation and privileges the child's voice to such an extent that it suggests its radical otherness from its adult counterpart, the second suggests that the child's entries fundamentally lack the authority and legitimacy of the adult's annotations. Indeed, since the content of both the original entries and the later annotations so strenuously insists upon the ways that, *pace* Gubar, children and adults may collaborate on aesthetic projects, *My Childhood Under Fire* effectively annuls the rhetoric of difference that informs the former reading of the text and the rhetoric of deficit that informs the latter. Rather, it suggests that an individual's child and adult selves may be perceived in various relationships that shift according to the contexts in which they appear together.

Certainly, there are moments in *My Childhood Under Fire* that require the clarification, contextualization, and perspective that can only be afforded through the adult Halilbegovich's retrospective efforts. Perhaps the most dramatic example might be the author's account of her ultimate escape from besieged Sarajevo. The final two diary entries, made on August 5 and 6, make clear the psychological toll that the war has taken on the young author: she reports long nights punctuated by nightmares of "bloody bodies" that prompt her to call to her mother "like a child" (102), as well as equally long days when she "can't even control [her] eyes that aimlessly stare at nothing" (102–103). What these entries do not divulge, however, is that, even at this moment, she was waiting to be selected for a caravan of children to be transported first to Croatia and then to the United States. Instead, her diary ends with a melancholic statement: "I wonder if I will always exist in some middle space between the painful memories of my past and the reality of my present—searching for the future" (103). Read in light of her ultimate evacuation, this statement—which presages, or rather establishes, her later claim to having lived "three lives"—gives some indication that she is aware of her potential flight, but nevertheless does not give her diary a satisfying conclusion. The final annotation, however, offers the context and resolution otherwise lacking in the last entry. Here, Halilbegovich documents her long-awaited selection by two humanitarian organizations; her ordeal of navigating security checkpoints and underground tunnels; and her final wrenching separation with her mother, who, although permitted to accompany Halilbegovich as far as Croatia, was obligated to return to Sarajevo.

However, if *My Childhood Under Fire* gives the adult Halilbegovich the last word, this is not necessarily because it imagines her as the final authority on her wartime experiences. Rather, it calls to attention the conditions that radically circumscribed the diarist's ability to represent her direct experiences and thus places into relief the veritable debt that the present-day author owes to her younger self. It would have been practically impossible for the author to record her flight from Sarajevo, not least because the urgency of the passage left no time to do so. Moreover, the new and constantly shifting circumstances that the author faced upon the completion of her journey—her separation from her mother, her brief and disorienting stay in Croatia, her flight to the US, and her adjustment to a new, surrogate family—all the more delayed her representation of, and reflection on, her abrupt exit. Consequently, she had little choice but to *defer to* an older version of herself, who might in good faith reassemble the fragments of memory scattered in the wake of a transatlantic journey. Read from this perspective, Halilbegovich's later annotations are not so much statements that legitimize her childhood ramblings with the imprimatur of detached or otherwise objective adult wisdom as they are the long-anticipated payment of a promise. After all, any act of deferral demands an eventual response, just as any act of deference implies a certain responsibility and reciprocity on the part of the relatively more powerful subject who receives it. In this way, then, Halilbegovich's annotations take the form of a long-due obligation: here, at last, the adult might deliver the narrative that her childhood self initially intended but was nevertheless thwarted from being immediately delivered.

If the conclusion to *My Childhood Under Fire* supplements the final passages of the original diary and thus calls attention to the adult author's fulfillment of a promise to her younger self, then other annotations amplify details that are already present within the initial entries but whose significance might potentially be lost on the reader. For example, over a course of matter-of-fact yet surprisingly cheerfully intoned entries produced between June 4 and June, 28, 1993, Halilbegovich introduces her reader to the various efforts that she and her friends and family members make to preserve a sense of normalcy in their relatively constricted community: for example, club meetings, music lessons, and birthday parties. However, just when the reader may be tempted to be caught up in the relative ebullience expressed in this series of passages, a "Looking Back" annotation effectively interrupts them with a more somber and affectively charged memory of this precise period:

> For months I didn't see a single piece of fruit. Then Sanel [Halilbegovich's elder brother] got a job as an interpreter for the United Nations, translating between Bosnian and English. When the soldiers asked him if he wanted to be paid in food or money, Sanel chose food. One afternoon, he brought me an orange. For hours I held it in my hand, laughing and crying. I felt as though I were holding the entire world in my hand. (45)

Whereas the original entries energetically, if not obstinately, call attention to efforts made by Halilbegovich and her fellow citizens to maintain an existence similar to that of their Western counterparts, this annotation reminds the reader that such attempts were made in the face of extreme want. Moreover, by offering a rather lyrical depiction of Halilbegovich's reception of the mere gift of an orange, this annotation arrests the flow of the matter-of-fact and action-based narrative in order to place into relief the more tender and reflective moments of vulnerability it explicitly occludes.

Crucially, however, this intervention does not seek to replace or otherwise override the original entries that precede it. In fact, it calls attention to details and nuances of preceding passages that readers might otherwise overlook: Halilbegovich's apparently surprising claim that, in the months documented by these passages, she "didn't see a single piece of fruit" might well impel readers to return to the earlier entries with a more discerning eye. For instance, in the June, 28, 1993, entry that immediately precedes the adult Halilbegovich's poignant narrative of the orange, the child diarist not only boasts that she has learned at last to ride a bicycle, but also notes that she spent part of her day lugging "seven ten-litre containers of water up the 252 steps" to her fourteenth-floor flat (44). Read on its own, this entry's assessment of this day as a "lucky" one might appear to pertain merely to the successful bicycle lesson (44). However, once readers consider this entry in relation to the following annotation—which offers a retrospective account of a wartime child's delight in otherwise taken-for-granted material goods—they might recognize how even the painstaking effort to transport a basic resource, and not simply a conventionally recognized childhood rite of passage, may be considered part of a particularly fortuitous day. In this way, Halilbegovich's annotations not only supplement the initial entries but also amplify their content: in an act that might well be considered one of tacit solidarity, the adult author's reflections make more visible and urgent the nuances implicit within the statements made by her childhood self.

There are moments in *My Childhood Under Fire*, however, that demonstrate not so much collaboration or amplification than the difference, and even competition, between the child-authored and adult-produced passages. This is especially evident in what may be the most harrowing and memorable portion of the text: its account of Halilbegovich's brush with mortality during the shelling of her neighborhood. In the original entry—made on October, 30, 1992, a mere twelve days after the immediate event and ostensibly written from her rest-bed—Halilbegovich offers a cogent and comprehensive narrative of her wounding and gradual recovery. Here, she describes perceiving an explosion and then registering, in quick succession, a "sharp stabbing pain" in her legs, a crowd of neighbors standing above her, and the sight of her "own blood on the walls and on the floor" (23–24). Additionally, she recounts her long wait in an overcrowded emergency room and her relief upon hearing her legs won't be amputated. However, as scrupulous as this narrative might be, it nevertheless omits details that a thirteen-year-old girl might understandably repress. It is only in the following "Looking Back" annotation that the reader learns that Halilbegovich's convalescence involved "having [her] nineteen-year-old-brother carry [her] to the toilet"—a daily exercise that left her "ashamed and frustrated" (27). Likewise, it is in this same annotation that the adult Halilbegovich divulges the painstaking process of reaching the bathroom without her brother's assistance. Here, she describes how she "rolled off the bed like a sack of potatoes" and dragged herself across the floor "like a wounded snake" (27).

Here, perhaps more than at any other moment in the text, one perceives a dramatic difference between the content of the child- and adult-authored entries—and presumably their intentions as well. Although Halilbegovich's original narrative certainly does not shy away from offering readers a graphic account of her radical vulnerability during the bombing and her subsequent hospitalization, it conspicuously excludes details of her rehabilitation: the diarist merely reports friendly visits from neighbors and fellow choir members. One can only speculate about the reasons why the young Halilbegovich chose not to elaborate on the conditions of her convalescence: she may well have repressed them in her recovery from an initial trauma; she may have wished to sustain the characteristically upbeat tone of her previous entries; or, perhaps most likely, she may have withheld certain details out of a sense of (preteenaged) shame or modesty. The adult Halilbegovich, however, appears to remember the conditions of her recovery in vivid detail—and what is more, she clearly has no reservations about describing her veritably abject position during this period. To this end, then, these two startling different accounts of the bombing's aftermath place into relief the substantially different subject positions from which they were written, as well as the extent to which their respective uses of tone and content cannot entirely be reconciled within a work that otherwise demonstrates the development and amplification of mutually shared perspectives.

## THE PALIMPSEST AND THE PERSPECTIVAL SHIFT

The extent to which *My Childhood Under Fire* involves such simultaneous blending and clashing of voices demonstrates how it is ultimately palimpsestic in form. Not unlike ancient documents in which two or more moments of inscription coincide on the material page, Halilbegovich's annotated diary makes evident the juxtaposition of two temporally distinct texts produced by equally distinct narrative personae that, once read in relation to one another, produce new and unanticipated interpretations of their respective content. In fact, the author's precise organization of her original entries and later annotations suggest her ever-shifting encounters with her childhood voice that include, alternately, corroboration, supplementation, amplification, and contestation. To this end, the palimpsestic nature of Halilbegovich's annotated diary offers something of a textual portrait of the postmodern subject, whose articulation of selfhood is mediated not only by the specific cultural and historical contexts that shape her consciousness but also by her constant re-evaluation and re-narrativization of her former memories—or, as it were, "lives." No less significantly, such a palimpsestic form offers a metaphor for the subject's fluctuating roles within intergenerational relationships. That is, just as a textual or photographic palimpsest involves the simultaneous blending and clashing of discrete voices, perspectives, and (literal) positions, the dynamics between older and younger generations extend beyond simple binaries or hierarchies of power. Instead, they are comprised of contextually contingent instances of collaboration and contestation.

Ultimately, a recognition of the palimpsestic character of *My Childhood Under Fire* assists in bringing about a "perspectival flip" that Gubar argues is so necessary to a kinship model of childhood and children's literature studies. Readers and scholars, Gubar argues, are so conventionally predisposed to perceiving children and adults as veritably separate species locked within predetermined structures of power that they often encounter great difficulty in imagining how young people and grown-ups actually share certain experiences in common—and, in turn, how the simultaneous similarities and differences between them might afford both complex (or "messy") interactions and potential acts of creative collaboration. "Because," Gubar insists, "we inhabit an aetonormative culture, stressing the similarities that link children and adults often involves a perspectival flip: instead of presuming that adults represent the norm and then investigating how children deviate from that norm, kinship-model adherents test out what happens when we regard the position that children generally inhabit as standard or shared" ("Hermeneutics," 300). Such a "perspectival flip," she maintains, begins with the overturning of the basic presumption that "adults are full-fledged autonomous agents" and that "children fail to live up to that standard" through the fundamental recognition that "all human beings begin life in a compromised position, a state of dependency" (300). It is through an acknowledgment of a radically shared vulnerability that scholars might predicate their studies of intergenerational relationships on the commonalities, rather than the differences, between young people and their elders.

If Gubar's perspectival flip begins with the detection of a primary vulnerability, then certainly a text such as *My Childhood Under Fire* offers additional opportunities that challenge conventional modes of thinking about the relationship between young people and adults. Firstly, it complicates easy binaries that distinguish adults in ostensibly full possession of agency and children whose capacities are relatively lacking. In turn, it suggests that ironically democratizing extreme political and material conditions places into relief the potential of young people and grown-ups to engage in collaborative creative efforts, rather than to remain determined by separate and essentialized roles. Secondly, the very form of *My Childhood Under Fire* invites exercises in "perspectival flipping" not least because it beckons readers to alternate—or as it were to flip—between the author's childhood and adulthood perspectives at such frequency that it forbids the privileging of one over the other. In doing so, it invites readers to perceive how the respective voices of children and adults ultimately enrich one another—and, what's more, how an individual adult's recognition of her earlier (textual) impressions and the multiple "lives" they represent produce a multidimensional and veritably intergenerational self.

## NOTES

1. As its name suggests, the comic sans font was initially used in the lettering in comic books. Consequently, it has accrued both positive and negative associations according to the contexts in which it has been used. Although its use is generally accepted in texts that suggest or perform values of "creativity" or "play," its deployment in ostensibly more formal or "serious" forms, such as advertising copy and legal documents, has been disparaged as irresponsible or even infantilizing. As I have noted above, the placement of Halilbegovich's original entries in comic sans appears to underscore the child author's initial creative efforts as well as to offer a print approximation of her juvenile penmanship. However, precisely because comic sans has been so often associated with a lack of sophistication, its use in the original entries of *My Childhood Under Fire* may be consciously read or unconsciously perceived as infantilizing, or otherwise detracting from, its urgent depiction of life under siege. To this end, then, the ambiguous connotations of this use of font places into relief the equally ambiguous categories of "child" and "adult" addressed and complicated by text's content and form.

2. I am grateful to Rebecca Vitkus for definitively identifying this font in Halilbegovich's text. Joanna font is a serif typeface developed by Eric Gill in the 1930s as an improvisation on earlier Renaissance-era designs. Certainly, the use of this typeface in Halilbegovich's later "Looking Back" annotations is as significant as its use of comic sans in her original entries, not least because its Renaissance influences suggest a certain sophistication or "worldliness" in her adult-authored statements that is ostensibly lacking in her original entries. As I argue above and below, however, other aspects of the content and form of *My Childhood Under Fire* significantly destabilize the binary between childhood ingenuity and adult sophistication implicitly suggested through its juxtaposition of comic sans and Joanna font, respectively.

## WORKS CITED

Filipović, Zlata. *Zlata's Diary: A Child's Life in Sarajevo*. Trans. Christina Pribichevich-Zori. Intro. Janine Di Giovanni. Penguin, 1994.

Frank, Anne. *The Diary of a Young Girl: The Definitive Edition*. 1947. Trans. Susan Massotty. Random House, 1991.

Gubar, Marah. "The Hermeneutics of Recuperation: What a Kinship-Model Approach to Children's Agency Could Do for Children's Literature and Childhood Studies." *Jeunesse: Young People, Texts, Cultures* 8, no. 1 (2016): 291–310.

Gubar, Marah. "Risky Business: Talking About Children in Children's Literature Criticism." *Children's Literature Association Quarterly* 38, no. 4 (2013): 450–57.

Halilbegovich, Nadja. *My Childhood Under Fire: A Sarajevo Diary*. Kids Can Press, 2008.

# 10

# IMAGINED GENOCIDES, MULTIDIRECTIONAL MEMORY, AND INTERGENERATIONAL SOLIDARITY

## IN RANSOM RIGGS'S *MISS PEREGRINE* TRILOGY

Marek Oziewicz

The notion of intergenerational solidarity describes a social compact made in the name of survival (see the introduction to this volume). In the world after the Holocaust and Stalin's genocides—the memory of which is considered a "basis for an emergent universal human-rights regime" (Craps and Rothberg, 518)—one cultural form intergenerational solidarity has taken is the survivors' testimony. Mobilizing the memory of past atrocities in the service of the future, such transmission of knowledge is taken to provide future generations with vital insights for the development of historical understanding and transcultural empathy. In literature, narrative accounts of the Holocaust and other genocides have traditionally been the domain of nonfiction and realist fiction. In the genres of memoir, autobiography, eyewitness account, and historical fiction, depictions of genocide command moral sway by virtue of representing historical atrocities perpetrated on real-world victim minorities. Predicated on truth-claims, such literature is appreciated as a form of testimony and warning.

How is intergenerational solidarity structured on the transmission of knowledge about historic genocides supported by genres in which the stamp of correspondence to the real has never been a value criterion? While this may sound counterintuitive, the mode of testimony and warning has been pronounced in speculative fiction and many award-winning works projected about-to-happen genocides as key conflicts in the plot. As John Rieder notes, even the most elaborate imagined genocides in science fiction rarely go beyond "the bare historical record of what happened to non-European people and lands after being 'discovered' by Europeans and integrated into the capitalist world economy" (373–74). Fantasy, in turn, has been *the* mode of testimony for the impossible. Extending the notion of the impossible to events so mind-boggling that they almost need to be invented to be believed, Gary Wolfe suggests that fantasy offers "means of sustaining our confrontation with the most shocking event of the twentieth century" that helps keep the Holocaust "from receding into the pale shadows of history" (11).

To posit that unbelievable events such as genocides must be "re-imagined for succeeding generations on their own terms" (10) entails a performative view of memory as a site of intergenerational articulation of affective kinship. This type of relational solidarity across generations, which Anastasia Ulanowicz has called "second-generation memory," plays a key role in Ransom Riggs's *Miss Peregrine* trilogy. Like any view of memory as a creative process, however, it raises questions about the blurring of reality and fiction. How can memories of organized violence be protected from imaginative distortions? Is imagination antithetical to historical memory in general, or to the memory of historical genocides in particular? What happens when an imagined genocide is couched within the account of the historical one? Finally, who has the right to claim the status of a witness? Such questions of memory, truth, and representation lie at the heart of any reflection on literary fiction about genocide. They are likewise relevant to a consideration of how different genres of memory support intergenerational solidarity based on transmission of remembrance. Framed by these questions, this chapter explores the proposition that our ability to experience imagined genocides is a necessary flip side of our capacity to imagine an experience of a genocide. Ransom Riggs's *Miss Peregrine* trilogy (2011–15) is read as a performance of second-generation memory in which Jake's slipping back in time—effectively stepping into his grandfather's shoes to complete Abe's life's mission—operates as a fantastic projection of intergenerational solidarity. Throughout, it is also suggested that within the framework of multidirectional memory representations of genocide in fantasy offer a valid set of tools to contemplate genocide as a historic and situated process.

Ransom Riggs's *Miss Peregrine* trilogy is a time-slip mythopoeic fantasy consisting of *Miss Peregrine's Home for Peculiar Children* (2011), *Hollow City* (2014), and *Library of Souls* (2015). Unique among recent works of fantasy in its incorporation of vintage photographs as narrative truth markers, the trilogy is thematically and structurally a two-part story. Part one, *Miss Peregrine's Home*, develops as a time-slip fantasy, in which fifteen-year-old Jake witnesses a mysterious death of his grandpa Abe, travels to the Welsh island Cairnholm where Abe stayed during World War II, and then slips back in time to interact with his grandfather's friends. These friends, like Abe, turn out to be peculiars—humans with special abilities—who hide in a time loop because they are haunted by a faction of peculiars bent on ruling the world. When the Cairnholm peculiars are raided, Jake discovers that he is also a peculiar, possessing a unique gift of being able to see—and thus kill—the otherwise invisible monsters called the hollowgast. After their guardian, Miss Peregrine, is abducted, Jake refuses to return to his own time. Instead, he rallies the other peculiars to free her and help Miss Peregrine regain human shape. That epic quest through time loops across the globe becomes the second part of the story, which spans books two and three. Time-slips and leapfrogging through time are normalized and the primary generic convention driving the narrative becomes mythopoeic fantasy, with its signature marker of the grand-scale conflict between good and evil. The quest to free Miss Peregrine and other *ymbrynes*—female peculiars who can manipulate time and act as guardians of time loops—turns out to be the quest to save the entire peculiardom and the human world too. The new experiment planned by the renegade faction would not only require the extermination of all non-complying peculiars but might also destroy the entire planet.

In so building the conflict, Riggs primes the audience to read the series as a story of imagined genocide against an imagined minority. That peculiars are an imagined minority is clear from the alternative taxonomy of human beings Riggs introduces. In the words of Miss Peregrine, the human species consists of two main lines: *coerlfolc*, ordinary humans, and *syndrigast*, or peculiars (*Home*, 149). Peculiars, or people with magical abilities, have existed all over the world since time immemorial. In many cultures, they were venerated as shamans, mystics, healers, shape-shifters, and the like. Eventually, the larger world turned against their otherness—as described in *Tales of the Peculiar* (2016)—driving peculiars out, burning them as witches, or banishing them as faeries. In search of places to hide, female peculiars called *ymbrynes* invented "temporal loops in which peculiar folk can live indefinitely" (*Home*, 151). This solution worked for several centuries. However, at the end of the nineteenth century, a splinter faction of peculiars challenged the logic of hiding. They began to advocate a view that peculiars should rule the world rather than hide from it. This would mean transforming what they take as "the common genetic trash of the human race" into slaves (322). In an attempt to re-harness the function of time loops from a place to a person, which would make that person effectively immortal, these dissatisfied peculiars set up an experiment in a disused loop in the Siberian tundra. The experiment went awry. It resulted in the Tunguska explosion of 1908 that transformed the participants into tentacle-mawed cannibalistic monsters. These hollowgast are somewhat immortal but exist as empty shells, forever driven by "insatiable hunger for the flesh of their former kin" (256). Peculiar flesh is their only hope of deliverance for when "a hollow gorges itself on enough peculiars, it becomes a wight" (256). Wights have no peculiar abilities and can pass for ordinary humans; they serve hollows as procurers of peculiar flesh and use them to terrorize peculiars and commoners alike. As Miss Peregrine puts it, "[i]t's a hierarchy of the damned that aims someday to turn all hollows into wights and all peculiars into corpses" (256).

In the universe of the *Miss Peregrine* trilogy, peculiars are thus a doubly persecuted minority. Long shunned by the common people, they are now poached by wights and hollows. Theirs is a story of an escalating genocide that will soon wipe them out. Confirming that it is indeed genocide, the novels establish unmissable links with the paradigmatic genocide story of the Holocaust. This occurs at least on three levels. First, Abe is a Holocaust survivor, and Jake's discovery of his grandpa's past frames how Jake will contextualize the hunt for peculiars that unfolds before his eyes. "Ours can be a life of trials and deprivations," Miss Peregrine explains, but "Abe's life was doubly so because he was born a Jew in the worst of times. He faced a *double genocide*, of Jews by the Nazis and of peculiars by the hollowgast. He was tormented by the idea that he was hiding here while his people, both Jews and peculiars, were being slaughtered" (*Home*, 248, italics mine).

When Abe leaves the island to join the war, he does so to fight both kinds of monsters: the Nazis and the hollowgast. He returns a changed man who no longer wants to hide. And while the war eliminates the Nazi threat, "the hollowgast emerge [. . .] stronger than ever" (248). His fellow peculiars remain hidden in the Cairnholm loop. Abe crosses the Atlantic as part of "a minor exodus of peculiars to America" (248), which, at that time, was a place where peculiars could blend in and try to live normal lives. At the same time, Abe's skills as a hollows hunter make him unique. American peculiars will ask him "to help eradicate troublesome pockets of hollows" (249), and Abe will remain the hunter of monsters until his death.

The other link between the two genocides is chronological. The main plot is set in blitz-time Wales, at the height of Nazi power in Europe, and unfolds from September 3, 1940, the date on which the Cairnholm loop is set. Miss Peregrine's home will eventually be destroyed by a Nazi bomb, though not before she is taken by the wight Golan, who leaves the island on a Nazi U-boat which has other wights on crew. The connection between the Nazis and wights is also operative on the level of ideology and language. Like the Nazis, wights are white supremacists bent on ruling the world. It may not be a coincidence that Riggs chose to dub them "wights"—an Old English word meaning both a supernatural creature and a human person—whose homonym, "whites," evokes associations with the ideology of white supremacy. Nor is it hard to miss that the other key term, the "hollowgast," can be read as an inflection of the Holocaust, establishing a link with planned, ideologically informed genocide and with the monsters who carried it out. Reinforcing the connection, the defeat of wights in *The Library of Souls* is followed by freeing crowds of peculiars from the wights' prisons and laboratories and brings to mind images of the liberation of Nazi death camps. The prisoners are depicted as "subjects of [. . .] horrible experiments," looking "thin and ragged," wandering in a daze (*Library*, 406), many "so shocked by what they'd experienced that they would not speak [. . .] as if they could not quite square the scene [of liberation] before them with the hell they had accepted as reality" (407). Whether or not Riggs intended it, the reconstruction of the peculiardom that follows resembles denazification that ensued after the fall of the Third Reich. Enslaved peculiar children are freed; the slavers, collaborators, and perpetrators are exposed or flee the country; tribunals, resembling the Nurenberg court, are established to deal with the traitors and wight criminals. Such individuals are hunted down and brought before justice (412).

How would the story be different if the Holocaust framing were removed? One answer to this question can be found in Tim Burton's adaptation. The film unfolds as Jake's romance with Emma is embedded within a quest to reverse Abe's death by defeating the monsters that will have caused it decades later. Jake's time-slip adventure is projected as a fantastic means of dealing with his personal guilt of not believing Abe's tales and thus contributing to his death. The focus remains on intergenerational solidarity; indeed, Jake's actions preclude Abe's murder. Still, their relationship is severed from the larger context of the Holocaust. The evil is a handful of monsters versus a small group of potential victims rather than an organized project to wipe out an entire racially coded minority. The film not only abandons the story of genocide in favor of intergenerational romance, but makes a number of deliberate moves to erase any links between genocide of the peculiars and the Holocaust. The term "hollowgast" is replaced with neutrally coded "hollows," and the term "wight" disappears in favor of "bad peculiars" (1:07:00). The wight Golan—who, in the novel, emerges as the leader of white peculiar supremacist movement—is played by a black star, Samuel L. Jackson, who is cast merely as a mad scientist. This move eliminates any parallels between white supremacy, Nazism, and the hunt for peculiars that the novel carefully constructs. Thus, while the original Golan leaves the island in a Nazi submarine, the filmic Mr. Barron takes a ferry. The context of World War II remains relevant only for the bombing scene, and the action of the film is pushed two years forward, to September 3, 1943, possibly in an effort to make it easier for the international audience to recognize it as wartime. With all these changes, Burton's film transforms Riggs's novel into a spectacle full of gory, eye-eating scenes, curiously weird humor, and slapstick skeleton battles that would not be out of place in *Pirates of the Caribbean*.

Unlike the film, the novels rely for their effect on casting Jake's experience as parallel to that of the Holocaust. Besides representing peculiars as a minority targeted for racialized genocide, they highlight another aspect of Jake's story: its utter unbelievability. As Holocaust scholars have noted, genocide, for survivors and commentators alike, challenges imagination. Its senselessness and incomprehensibility make any description of genocide inadequate and necessarily couched in "a curious air of unreality"—a phrase Hannah Arendt coined to refer to the tone of reports by survivors of Nazi and Soviet camps (233). In a similar way, one of the key challenges in Riggs's series is how to make the unbelievable conceivable.

This theme is introduced in the prologue to *Miss Peregrine's Home*, when Jake recounts his childhood fascination with Abe's accounts of his exciting travels. The tales, he recalls, were always told "like secrets that could be entrusted only to me" (*Home*, 8), and each telling brought in "some lurid new detail" (9). The telling of the tales and Jake's own conceptualizations of their content illustrate the practice of second-generation memory. As Ulanowicz has theorized it, second-generation memory involves an individual's conscious recognition of participation in past events that one did not directly experience, a consideration of memories of those close to one as part of one's own inheritance, and the creative incorporation—sometimes editing—of these memories "in order to construct a meaningful interpretation of [one's] own relationship to both the past and the present" (4). Second-generation memory is not limited to interactions between parents and children. It encompasses any intergenerational production of memory "that exists in a contingent, 'second' relationship to earlier articulations of the past" (5). All these elements describe Jake's relationship to Abe's tales through which the protagonist constructs his identity. As he grows up, however, Jake becomes threatened by a sense that his grandpa's amazing stories could not possibly be true. He first confronts Abe on this issue when he is seven. Abe is offended by this breach of trust, but then brings out the pictures. As they gaze at the yellowed prints of peculiar children, the awed boy asks, "Is it real?" (*Home*, 11). Abe assures him that it is, but seeing lingering doubt looks Jake in the eye:

"You don't believe me?"

I thought about it, looking at the pictures and then at my grandfather, his face so earnest and open. What reason would he have to lie?

"I believe you," I said.

And I really did believe him—for a few years, at least—though mostly because I wanted to, like other kids my age wanted to believe in Santa Claus. (16)

Soon a moment comes when Jake, after being taunted at school, declares that he no longer believes in Abe's stories. This denial of memory and its reframing as fiction breaks their affective kinship. Following Jake's outburst, Abe drops the subject so thoroughly that it makes Jake feel like he was lied to all along. The resentment becomes a wall between them. "I couldn't understand why he'd made up all that stuff," Jake broods, "tricked me into believing that extraordinary things were possible when they weren't" (17). Finally, a few years later, Jake's father explains that the stories were not exactly lies as "exaggerated versions of the truth" or "a truth in disguise" (17). The monsters, he says, were not tentacled creatures but humans wearing Nazi uniforms; the island was a refuge for peculiar children but their peculiarity was their Jewishness rather than any special powers; and the magic about their lives was survival—that they managed, in sometimes miraculous ways, to escape the ghettos and gas chambers. The truth of these facts is "banal" enough to be understood yet horrible enough to be unmentionable (17). Jake will never ask for another story; Abe will never tell one. That is, until one day, when "an extraordinary and terrible thing happen[s]" (18)—a day Jake realizes he should have asked for these stories and the dying Abe realizes he should have told Jake before. The tragic event re-establishes intergenerational solidarity between Abe and Jake, transforming the latter into what Ulanowicz calls "the bearer of second-generation memory" (15): Jake recognizes that his life is not entirely his own and he goes on to consciously incorporate the memory of Abe's experiences. For bearers of second-generation memory, this active remembrance is a survival strategy, embraced as if one's life depended upon it "because, in some sense, it does" (15).

The paradox of wanting to share an impossible story yet knowing it to be so unreal that it will not be believed is central to the series. It aligns the *Miss Peregrine* trilogy with the tradition of Holocaust literature and other genres of trauma fiction built around the need to reveal and conceal. This particular tension is never resolved. At the end of the last book, Jake considers explaining his disappearance to his parents but realizes that "the truth wouldn't work" (*Library*, 420). His experience blurs the line between fiction and reality. It becomes an unprovable fact that can only be communicated as a story; that is, accepted—or rejected—as a story in the same way as Abe's memories passed on to Jake. For the reader, the story is coded as "true" since the narrative confirms the validity of Jake's—and Abe's—otherwise uncommunicable experience. Slipping back in time, Jake performs second-generation memory by literally stepping into his grandpa's shoes. He interacts with Abe's peers, falls in love with Abe's sweetheart, and completes what would have been Abe's mission— had Abe stayed in Cairnholm until Miss Peregrine's home was raided. Like in Jane Yolen's *The Devil's Arithmetic* (1988), the device of time-slip enables the protagonist directly to experience the life of a past-generation family member who was the victim of the unspeakable. Becoming one's ancestor to live out their but also one's own story is the ultimate, albeit fantastic, projection of intergenerational solidarity, itself "a dimension of the self-reflective experience of second-generation memory" (Ulanowicz, 16). From the first time he crosses back in time and is mistaken for Abe, Jake is no longer a listener of Abe's stories but their protagonist and active creator. He becomes aware of how profoundly dependent upon Abe's experiences and memories his selfhood is. Within the framework of second-generation memory, his story becomes a memorate for Abe's experience.

"Memorate" is a term proposed by Carl von Sydow for an eyewitness account of an encounter with numinous or supernatural forces: a realistic, believable narrative about magical, unbelievable narratives—as Abe's tales appear to Jake. According to Brian Attebery, works of fantasy employ the structure of memorates to connect "the teller to a traditional belief or legend" (35). More generally, memorates in fantasy bridge the gap between the narrative and ordinary life. They confirm, through a story of personal experience, what has so far appeared impossible even to the tellers themselves. Such too is the case with Jake, the unbeliever, becoming an actor in Abe's tale. One marker of memorates in fantasy is that the characters are disbelieved. What they accomplished or sacrificed is not understood, "[y]et the stories have to be told" (Attebery, 115). This dynamic plays out in Jake's reception of Abe's tales and then in Jake's own story. Abe's tales are disbelieved even by his most devoted listener. Yet they need to be told, for without them Jake would never figure out how to complete Abe's mission. Just as Abe's stories are memorates for Jake, the novels—with Jake's first-person narration—perform the function of a memorate for the reader. They become a testimony Jake will not be able to share with his family or friends. As Attebery notes, disbelieved memorates are recounted in fantasy "not necessarily for the benefit of the listeners"—the book's audience—but to suggest "something important about the uses of fantasy, about the cultural work it can do" (115). That cultural work, in Riggs's series, seems to be the building of intergenerational solidarity centered on resistance to *any* form of racist ideology. Jake's story offers the reader a memorate which links the imagined genocide of peculiars with the history of the Holocaust. Reinforcing the theme of intergenerational solidarity in the series—one facet of which is the *ymbrynes*' mission to seek out and shelter young peculiars—Jake and Abe's solidarity takes the form of becoming witnesses to genocide, as well as its survivors.

To see them as such requires the reader's acknowledgment of the strong resonance between the genocide of the peculiars and the Holocaust. But, in evoking so many elements of the Holocaust story, is Riggs not guilty of instrumentalizing the Shoah? This is a valid concern, and scholars writing about Riggs's work have each felt compelled to address it. Maria Nikolajeva, for example, acknowledges the danger of fictionalizing the Holocaust but points out that "Abraham's metaphorical description of his persecutors as 'monsters' makes the story more universal" (70). Agata Zarzycka, in turn, argues that Riggs employs Gothic and supernatural themes "to centralize the cultural processing of war and Holocaust themes" (235). None of these valid points are enough, however, to alleviate the concern about misappropriation. It will haunt any interpretation of the *Miss Peregrine* trilogy as long as it is considered within the framework of competitive rather than multidirectional memory.

Competitive versus multidirectional memory are terms introduced by Michael Rothberg to facilitate discussion around the project of decolonizing comparative trauma studies. The key modern challenge in the fields of trauma and memory studies—both of which arose around the Holocaust as their archetypal topic—has been whether it is possible, and if so, how productive, to compare histories of different genocides without denying their uniqueness. After all, the emergence of a separate interdisciplinary field of the Holocaust studies was largely due to the claims of uniqueness that set it apart from postcolonial, African American, and other histories of systemic violence. In contemporary multicultural societies, however, "memories of colonialism, occupation, slavery, and the Holocaust bump up against one another" (Rothberg, "Gaza," 523). The challenge is how to remember any one genocide without erasing the memory of others—in other words, how to think about them together but resist "an ugly contest of comparative victimization" (Rothberg, *Multidirectional*, 7). Rothberg's answer is that memory wars are unavoidable only in the framework of competitive memory: when memory is understood as a zero-sum game in which "too much emphasis on the Holocaust is said to marginalize other traumas, or, inversely, adoption of Holocaust rhetoric to speak of those other traumas is said to relativize or even deny the Holocaust's uniqueness" ("Gaza," 523). However, in an alternative model of remembrance, which Rothberg calls multidirectional memory, collective memories of disparate genocides coexist in the public sphere in a dialogical engagement rather than in competition. In that framework, sustained attention to one phenomenon—often, but not necessarily the Holocaust—serves as a vehicle to sharpen our perception of other genocidal histories. The result, says Rothberg, "is not less memory, but more—even of subordinated memory traditions" (523). Multidirectional memory allows us better to conceptualize the otherwise unique histories of slavery or colonialism or the Holocaust or the Armenian genocide, freeing each from their memory siloes and providing "resources for other [marginalized or oppositional] groups to articulate their own claims for recognition and justice" (524).

My suggestion is that Riggs's use of the Holocaust as a couching for his story can be read as a form of appropriation only when considered in the framework of competitive memory. When read through the lens of multidirectional memory, however, Riggs's books make the memory of the Holocaust dialogically central to the series' impassioned case against oppression and political schemes based on assumptions of racial superiority. The implications of the distinction between competitive and multidirectional memory extend beyond the question of Holocaust appropriation, however. They shed light on the uses of fantasy as a vehicle for transmission of remembrance that supports intergenerational solidarity in the face of genocide even if—or, perhaps, especially when—this remembrance is explicitly fictionalized. While Rothberg projects the operations of multidirectional memory as a way to conceptualize the plurality of historical genocides, why would this plurality need to exclude imagined genocides? If, as he insists, "public memory is *structurally multidirectional*—that is, always marked by transcultural borrowing, exchange, and adaptation," and if memory's analogies and references "function as unavoidable building blocks or *morphemes* of public memory" ("Gaza," 524, italics in original), why should these references and analogies be limited only to historical genocides? My suggestion is that they need not be.

The first reason for this argument is that the capacity to distinguish between factual and fictional knowledge is a basic cognitive skill that equips one to create meaning out of literary representation. What is at stake in drawing attention, as Rothberg does, to the constructedness of transcultural and transgenerational memory is not the truth or falsehood of memory but the fact that human minds employ the same cognitive-affective apparatus to process factual and fictional accounts. While in moral terms the protagonist's trauma ought to feel less real to us when they are characters in a book rather than actual people, in cognitive terms the extradiegetic reality of characters appears to be a minor factor. According to Nikolajeva, "our brains are capable of responding to fictional worlds as if they were actual" (23). Nor is the epic journey of the survivor protagonist less emotionally meaningful than accounts of similar experiences in real-life. Constructedness also lies at the heart of second-generation memory, with its "improvisational" and "associative" modes of articulating relationships "that prevailing social norms do not regard as sanctioned or legitimate" (Ulanowicz, 18). Jake's second-generation memory performs the function of multidirectional memory for the reader; it extends beyond the factual and draws on the symbolic and imagined. If so, the concern that the novels' memory of the Holocaust must be protected against imaginative distortions appears less interesting than the concern about how effectively the employment of imaginative strategies brings home the reality of genocide, including the Holocaust, for the contemporary young reader.

The second reason that makes it possible to argue that our ability to experience imagined genocides is a necessary flip side of our capacity to imagine an experience of a genocide is an understanding of how fiction mediates information. Narrative fiction is a form of verbal representation, in which the author may take liberties with facts and truth. Since "the referentiality of fiction is in second degree" (Nikolajeva, 23), verbal signs in fictional narratives are only arbitrarily connected to referents in the real world. Their plausibility does not render them true. For instance, having a grandfather who is the Holocaust survivor—although possible in the real world—is not ontologically truer in Riggs's novel than slipping through time, which we take as impossible in the real world. This fundamental premise that "all fictional facts are equally possible; [that] there are no facts that are true or false, and 'false' facts have as much epistemic value as 'true' ones" (24) applies doubly to fantasy, which is even more unverifiable against reality than any other type of fiction. In fact, the cultural importance of fantasy is predicated on its *denial* of factuality: "The fundamental premise of fantasy," Attebery insists, "is that the things it tells not only did not happen but *could* not have happened. In that literal untruth is freedom to tell many symbolic truths" (4). When applied to Riggs's series, the effect of these principles is that both the Holocaust and the genocide of the peculiars are equally impossible-yet-real within the narrative since "different levels of embedding allow the same novel to be both fantastic and realistic" (38). This paradox allows the series to engage with the "symbolic truth" about genocide, making it knowable through a multidirectional memory relationship with the Holocaust. Expanding Nikolajeva's claim that "the structured [. . .] nature of a fictional world can *potentially* make it a better source of knowledge than the chaotic and ambiguous reality" (27), Riggs's fictional world may be said to engage readers in exploring affective rather than factual knowledge about genocide. Affective knowing matters: accessing the pain of others is always an imaginative experience since empathy is a facet of imagination too. This affective knowing is achieved by aligning readers with Jake's incredulity and incomplete knowledge throughout the story, in which they have to fill cognitive gaps as to what is fact and what is fiction. For example, when Jake sees the first hollow in the Florida woods, he and the reader are left to decide whether it was a stress-induced hallucination—as Jake's family and psychiatrist want him to believe—or a real phenomenon in the world of the story, as is confirmed later.

This process of making inferences based on textual evidence, projecting possible outcomes, and then verifying these guesses as the story develops is not just how stories work but how our minds work, too. One of the core discoveries that emerged from cognitive studies—foundational to my argument in *Justice in Young Adult Speculative Fiction* (2015)—is that human minds are hardwired for script-based narrative understanding. Our meaning-making proceeds through decoding sequences of action in a particular context and recognizing how content such as characters, plot, setting, and conflict fills the slots in particular scripts. Literature offers actualizations of scripts, including those of being a persecuted minority, and this has also been the case for stories about the Holocaust. As early as 1977, Eric Kimmel identified four types of Holocaust narratives, each defined by its story arc, setting, and a unique sequence of characteristic tropes: stories of Resistance, Flight, Occupation, and Death Camps. Barbara Krasner, in her presentation at the conference of the Children's Literature Association in 2016, proposed to add two other categories that emerged more recently: Rescue and Return. From the cognitive perspective, each of these types is a bundle of actualized scripts that have accrued to narrative descriptions of Holocaust stories in a similar way that Propp's functions have come to describe the structure of traditional Russian fairy tales. Seen through this lens, Riggs's series develops a number of scripts known from Holocaust literature. Jake's time-slip into 1940 is not structurally different from Hannah's time-slip into 1941 in Yolen's *The Devil's Arithmetic*; his interaction with Emma as his guide is not structurally different from Hannah's interaction with Rivkah; and his learning about the ongoing persecution of the peculiars is not structurally different from what Hannah learns about the Nazi persecution of Jews. Beyond these, the *Miss Peregrine* books actualize a number of other scripts, most of them having to do with hiding due to one's difference, being pursued by monsters, and fighting against the threat of horrible death. And while it is also concerned with individual survival, the series presents a tale of collective survival of a people. In all these ways, the key events that structure the narrative of Riggs's series articulate the genocide script that is most heavily and consistently overdetermined by its reference to the archetypal genocide script of the Holocaust.

Like fictionalized accounts of the Holocaust, the *Miss Peregrine* trilogy is a story of the unbelievable. It tests our capacity to imagine an experience of a genocide by immersing us in an experience of an imagined genocide. When the protagonist slips back in time to relive the past which is also the present, the novels invite the reader to experience the script of being a persecuted minority. They communicate the performative character of memory as a force that lies at the heart of intergenerational solidarity and makes the present possible. This insistence on the responsibility of the present generation to attend to specific historically and materially bound experiences of past generations forms the series' moral ground. The novels do not erase the distinction between real-world genocide and imagined genocide; instead, they put them in a productive relation within multidirectional memory. This act of dialogical imaginative extension is potentially transformative. In *Regarding the Pain of Others* (2004), Susan Sontag mentions how the inhabitants of besieged Sarajevo were offended by an exhibit in which the pictures of their destroyed city were displayed alongside the pictures from Somalia. "To set their sufferings alongside the sufferings of another people," Sontag writes, "was to compare them [...], demoting Sarajevo's martyrdom to a mere instance" (113). The citizens of Sarajevo felt that it was "intolerable to have one's own suffering twinned with anybody else's" (113). Like with the memory of the Holocaust, such comparison is intolerable, but only in the framework of competitive memory. If one wants to move beyond outrage and hurting to achieve transcultural empathy, however, the same emotion may become a productive, action-oriented force in the framework of multidirectional memory. The *Miss Peregrine* trilogy demonstrates the value of fantasy as a means to reframe historic genocides in contexts that move beyond the discourse of competition and hierarchy. While it offers a fantastic projection of intergenerational solidarity—Jake's slipping back in time to relive part his grandfather's life—the trilogy communicates that real-world solidarity among generations requires empathetic memory and that active performance of that remembrance empowers us to stand up against racist ideologies that make genocide possible.

## WORKS CITED

Arendt, Hannah. *Essays in Understanding*. Schocken, 1994.
Attebery, Brian. *Stories about Stories: Fantasy and the Remaking of Myth*. Oxford University Press, 2014.
Craps, Stef, and Michael Rothberg. "Introduction: Transcultural Negotiations of Holocaust Memory." *Criticism* 53, no. 4 (2011): 517–21.
*Miss Peregrine's Home for Peculiar Children*. Dir. Tim Burton. 20th Century Fox, 2016.
Nikolajeva, Maria. *Reading for Learning: Cognitive Approaches to Children's Literature*. John Benjamin's Publishing Company, 2014.
Oziewicz, Marek. *Justice in Young Adult Speculative Fiction: A Cognitive Reading*. Routledge, 2015.

Rieder, John. "Science Fiction, Colonialism, and the Plot of Invasion." *Extrapolation* 46, no. 3 (2005): 373–94.
Riggs, Ransom. *Hollow City*. Quirk Books, 2014.
Riggs, Ransom. *Library of Souls*. Quirk Books, 2015.
Riggs, Ransom. *Miss Peregrine's Home for Peculiar Children*. Quirk Books, 2011.
Riggs, Random. *Tales of the Peculiar*. Dutton Books, 2016.
Rothberg, Michael. "From Gaza to Warsaw: Mapping Multidirectional Memory." *Criticism* 53, no. 4 (2011): 523–48.
Rothberg, Michael. *Multidirectional Memory: Remembering the Holocaust in an Age of Decolonization*. Stanford Universiy Press, 2009.
Sontag, Susan. *Regarding the Pain of Others*. Picador, 2003.
Ulanowicz, Anastasia. *Second-Generation Memory and Contemporary Children's Literature: Ghost Images*. Routledge, 2013.
Wolfe, Gary. "Introduction: Fantasy as Testimony." In *The Fantastic in Holocaust Literature and Film: Critical Perspectives*, eds. Judith B. Kerman and John Edgar Browning, 7–12. McFarland, 2015.
Zarzycka, Agata. "The Gothicization of World War II as a Source of Cultural Self-Reflection in *Miss Peregrine's Home for Peculiar Children* and *Hollow City*." In *War Gothic in Literature and Culture*, eds. Agnieszka Soltysik Monnet and Steffen Hantke, 229–44. Routledge, 2016.

# PART FOUR

## CHILDREN'S LITERATURE AND INTERGENERATIONAL PROJECTS

# 11

# "SOMETHING THERE IS THAT DOESN'T LOVE A WALL"
## THE MEDIATING CHILD AND THE ETHICS OF COHABITATION
Blanka Grzegorczyk

Recent political discourse invokes vulnerability to others to justify recourse to coercive precautionary measures and explain the exercise of state power at the expense of collective dissent. At a time when various forms of terror and counter-terror permeate the world order, new divisions accompany the social and political transformations of the century, while walls and other border structures are being promised, erected, or rebuilt purportedly to allow contemporary society to inhabit this rapidly changing world more securely. That youth culture has become increasingly engaged with these difficult issues is clear, for instance, from the rise in popularity of political vocabulary among the young entrants to the BBC's creative writing competition 500 Words. As a result of research analyzing the entries, the Children's Dictionaries team at Oxford University Press declared "trump" to be the Children's Word of the Year in 2017 (with "wall," "Brexit," and "alternative facts" also featuring prominently across over 131,000 submissions [Pickles, n.p.]), a year after the title was awarded to the word "refugee," which had appeared in the vast number of just under 123,500 short stories written by children between five and thirteen years old (Erizanu, n.p.). The vulnerability of certain groups of people under the transformed conditions of the new century has influenced children's thinking and creativity. At the same time, the anxieties of a mainstream Western culture that shores up its borders against what it perceives as alien—and that relies on anti-Muslim and anti-immigrant paranoia narratives to reconstitute some imagined wholeness—have contributed to the proliferation of children's novels designed to foster ethical responsibility for the other.

A large group of diverse British children's authors, including Elizabeth Laird, Alex Wheatle, Alan Gibbons, Anna Perera, Bali Rai, Sarah Crossan, Brian Conaghan, Miriam Halahmy, Sita Brahmachari, and Rachel Anderson, have placed ethical emphasis on the exposure to and obligations towards one's others repeatedly in their writings. With an eye to the contemporary children's novel as an expression of a common humanity that involves young readers in a recognition of its fundamental condition of precariousness, I bring into critical conversation the discourses of postcolonialism, multiculturalism, cosmopolitanism, and human rights, as well as the ethics of cohabitation. This ethics, as understood by Judith Butler, follows from a particular kind of solicitation that compels us to recognize and enact the "bonds of solidarity that emerge across space and time," or to be responsive to those who are outside our immediate sphere of belonging but whom we cannot will away without undermining our humanity ("Precarious . . .," 135). Post-9/11 children's novelists have played a part in establishing children as agents of social change, mainly through constructing young protagonists as inherently empathetic and intensely responsive to those other lives. The child characters in the contemporary novel for the young are often described as making sense of the harms of othering and working to achieve new, cross-cultural, and cross-generational alliances that undermine the present differential way of regarding populations.

Critics like Sunaina Marr Maira and David Kieran have engaged with the complicated position of young people growing up in the post-9/11 era who find themselves caught between the ideologies of nationalism and the practices of social exclusion, but with no more than occasional investigations of the connections between children's fiction and the themes of racist paranoia, anti-immigrant hostility, and politicized identities. Speaking about an increasingly virulent racism against refugees and migrants, Butler argues that "a passionate commitment to the everyone and the anyone" is integral to "entering into a common world [. . .] with those who are at risk of not counting" (in Berbec, n.p.). The challenge, then, is to maintain an ethical obligation to those whose difference from us seems to be quite marked, including those who have been described by the state and the mainstream media as threats to the core of our culture, nationhood, and identity. The conflation of recent anti-terror laws and practices and the state regulation of migrant populations provides an operative framework within which certain lives are regarded as less worthy of protection. When situated within the postcolonial field, conventionally seen as concerned with the politics of division and separation, both the framing of recent British military interventions abroad as justified violence and the framing of immigration issues as a war fought on the home front can throw up colonial continuities and parallels (see, for example, Lazarus 2002; Gilroy 2005; Sivanandan 2006; Ware 2010). This chapter examines Rachel Anderson's *Asylum* (2011) and Sita Brahmachari's *Tender Earth* (2017) in the context of human rights and postcolonial ethics. The texts are concerned with the possibility of communication across the tribal divide between "us," young Britons, and "them," migrants and asylum seekers, which would speak a counter-narrative to the state's and the mainstream media's anti-immigrant rhetoric. Different kinds of intercultural cooperation are undertaken self-consciously by the central characters in these novels within and across generations. The chapter reads these alliances as embodying a form of multiculturalism that is based on an idea of mutuality, a shared understanding of communal values, and an active form of cosmopolitan solidarity against the treatment of immigrants in Britain. Anderson's and Brahmachari's young protagonists can be seen to come into their own as agents for change, often as a result of intergenerational conflict, or of finding agency within a critical relation to the present constructions of otherness; they then bring about among all generations a new form of responsiveness to migrants and manage to build more welcoming communities.

In Anderson's *Asylum*, the rather formulaic cast of minor characters who reside in Hawk Rise, a derelict tower block that migrants and asylum seekers share with an unnamed English city's poor and vulnerable, ensures that the reader is made aware of the links between Britain's immigration policies, social exclusion, and residential segregation. The chapters alternate between the perspectives of two young refugees, fifteen-year-old Sunday, who has been brought into the country illegally and given the (unpaid) job of being Hawk Rise's caretaker, and nine-year-old Rosa, who tries to navigate the highly complex immigration system while caring for her ill mother. Writing about Salman Rushdie's *The Satanic Verses*, Robert Spencer reminds us that the "migrant's perspective [. . .] is perforce a disenchanted one" (256), and Rushdie himself describes a "migrant's-eye view of the world" as disillusioned with the one-time certainties about the nature of reality and haunted by a suspicion of all truths and all narratives (394). In line with this vision of the migrant condition, Anderson's novel exposes us to a whole range of disjunctures, pressures, and constraints that lie at the heart of her young protagonists' predicament. The Britain that the two children reach after their respective journeys is far from the rosy picture of a "Wonderland [. . .] where [. . .] there would be no violence and the healthcare was the best in the whole world" (152), a picture painted by Sunday's and Rosa's relatives back at home as well as by other refugees heading in the same direction. Indeed, the country's weather and population seem equally unwelcoming. On seeing Hawk Rise for the first time, Rosa thinks that "[i]t must be where the vagrants, the hopeless and other worthless people were sent," and she feels "so angry that she clenched her fists inside her pockets. They'd been tricked into coming here. She was not worthless. She had the sachet of coloured felt-tip pens she'd won [at school for industry] to prove it" (38). Sunday, on the other hand, muses on the opening page that "Great Britain was never his country of first choice, nor second. He'd have preferred Canada or Germany or America. Best of all, Iceland which, so he'd heard, was cold and treeless but democratic and respectful of human life. Britain was where he ended up" (1). Early in the novel, the boy is told that the only people who wanted him in Britain are migrant smugglers and their cronies; throughout the book, he wishes he had argued with the smugglers to "send him to a more caring nation" that—unlike the British people, bombarded with popular media representations of young male refugees as threatening rather than vulnerable (see, for instance, Duffy 2016; and Chouliaraki and Stolic 2017)—would value a "strong, healthy, willing incomer" (173). Through these characters' complex relationships with their hosts and neighbors, Anderson demonstrates that, in their vulnerability, immigrants have no choice but to rely on the hospitality that others are prepared to offer them.

The systematic mistreatment to which immigrants are subjected in Anderson's story, ranging from verbal abuse to dehumanizing policies, does not accommodate what Edward Said in his essay "Reflections on Exile" (1984/2001) judges to be the twentieth-century state's reinvention of the term "refugees" to denote large groups of "innocent and bewildered people requiring urgent international assistance" (181). Rather, similarly to the recent Eastern European or Latin American incomers into British society, and much like the Commonwealth migrants after the Second World War, these new arrivals may be understood to carry with them not just an unwelcome reminder of the loss of imperial prestige but also the prospect of a reverse colonization, thus threatening, in the eyes of those who see the best source of solidarity in cultural homogeneity, the cohesion of the British nation (see Gilroy 2005, 2006). The socially and ethnically divided landscape of *Asylum* provides a warning that chimes with Malachi McIntosh's description of the dominant representations of immigration as sustaining the current schisms running through the nation: the political discourse in Britain has routinely presented new entrants as having the "potential to undermine the state through an essential disconnection from the nation," which is all the more affecting given the post-9/11 and -7/7 climate of heightened security concerns (73). While pressures on the government to restrict immigration to Britain dominate the news headlines found in the novel in ways which many readers might recognize from real life, Rosa soon learns that the immigration authorities "have to check each case thoroughly to ensure there's no threat to national security" and that her welfare support worker's role consists in teaching refugees who are granted temporary residence "what to do to tidy up their lives into the British way" (11, 34). Ironically, Rosa's (and Sunday's) experience in Britain is that of being repeatedly denied fundamental human rights—and of mobilizing cross-cultural solidarity, returning to the "dulled," "dejected" residents of Hawk Rise a sense of collective responsibility for the lives of one another (39)—rather than threatening the denial of them to others.

Sunday's mediator status is linked to his ability to take on the kind of responsibility that Emmanuel Levinas characterizes as "answering for everything and for everyone" (*Otherwise Than Being*, 114); that he prevails in his determination to anticipate the needs of the building's occupants and to respond to their many requests in the most positive and caring manner is significant both in terms of the Levinasian concept of subjectivity as realized through giving oneself up to others and of imposing an ethical obligation upon others to find forms of cohabitation distinguished by a commitment to equality and cooperation. For Levinas, one's subjectivity is formed through relations with others (we exist, he argues, "through the other and for the other" [*Otherwise Than Being*, 114]), and yet those who act upon us clearly remain other to us, with responsibility being derived not from sameness but from an exposure to otherness: "It is the 'here I am' said to a neighbour to whom I am given over, by which I announce peace" ("God and Philosophy," 184). Of course, there are contradictions in Levinas's position on being addressed by and bound up with others, and his affirmation of certain forms of nationalism raises key questions about the conditions for moral responsiveness; accordingly, after Butler, I read Levinas against himself here, or against the exclusionary assumptions by which his philosophy is sometimes supported (see Butler 2012). If Anderson's protagonists make various kinds of sacrifices in acting for others, their Levinasian subjectivity emerging "for the other," there is also a Butlerian undercurrent in the novel of an apparent "intertwinement" between all those other lives and the characters' own that "extend[s] beyond the religious and cultural communities" which Levinas sees as a "necessary condition and limit" to ethical relations ("Precarious," 140). Having lived through terror and violence, and been forced to leave their elderly relatives behind, the two young refugees find themselves caring for, and then being cared for by, a group of people of various ages who have themselves experienced uncertainty, displacement, and violence. When Rosa spends the night in the flat of Mrs. Ndebele (who says that "it [i]sn't right for Rosa to be alone" after her mother is taken to hospital, even while Rosa decides that "it [i]sn't safe for [an . . .] old woman with shaky hands to be left on her own, specially when the stairwell outside was so dark" [238]), the girl discovers that the childhood home back in Asia that Mrs. Ndebele lost in her youth before marrying a British soldier was in a rural village very much like Rosa's own. The legal status of many of the residents of Hawk Rise is as precarious as that of the newcomers, too, and Sunday is often asked to help his neighbors with documents like visa applications, being more attentive to the vulnerable than the welfare workers at People's Advice Bureau, as attested to by all those he helps (90).

In *Asylum*, the council-owned tower block provides not just a backdrop but also a means of focusing relations of care: Sunday is prepared to devote his life to others yet is also dependent on those others, and the residents, young and old, quickly agree to keep an eye on the boy who lives "in the comfortless, cookerless, windowless storeroom next to the boiler room" (95), taking turns to leave food and domestic items for him to find; in a similar way, Rosa's persistent efforts to create a vegetable garden among the "piles of refuse and small patches of sour dust" in the building's forecourt win her the help of the initially sceptical tenants (207). Even though the communal sampling of the radishes grown in the garden that occurs in the final sections of the novel is overshadowed by the approaching demolition of Hawk Rise, the memories of such get-togethers later cause the again-homeless Sunday to reflect that "it was not the quality of the construction but the quality of the people which rendered a place habitable" (274). The clear call to community is also a call to cross cultural boundaries—to ignore "some of the very terms through which contemporary global conflicts are conceptualized" and extend our ethical obligations to those who appear to test our sense of belonging (Butler, *Frames*, 156)—while moving towards the recognition of our common humanity. This is the kind of recognition that Rosa's mother, Lila, edges towards in her dazed, dreamlike state when she thinks that "[p]erhaps the many countries of the world were not so far apart as she had feared." But maybe, Lila adds, "they were further and nobody ever got back to where they started" (67), and so there is a suggestion in all of this that what is shared is a generalized condition of precariousness, a frailty that relies on a conception of the subject as fundamentally dependent on a world of others who constantly challenge the horizons of the life that they hold in common.

In the case of Anderson's novel, the life that the young immigrants share with their new neighbors is alienatingly non-rural: "There were rules about urban life he was going to have to learn quickly," Sunday realizes, "He prayed that, in God's good time, he would fit into this ugly landscape as if he belonged" (13). On the other hand, being denied growing space is felt most acutely by

Rosa, who wants fresh vegetables similar to those her grandfather grew before their village was destroyed yet struggles to clear enough space to put in any seeds, since "[i]t seemed that the wasteland around Hawk Rise was well recognized [. . .] as the most convenient dumping ground" in the city (134). In addition, through episodes such as the one in which Sunday suffers racist abuse from a smartly dressed couple who stop their car in the building's courtyard to dispose of an old, broken-down fridge, as well as bags of rubbish, and who comment loudly that the "whole block was a blooming garbage tip," the novel demonstrates that what makes anti-immigrant attitudes possible is the failure to see all lives as valuable, recognizable, or indeed worth preserving—a "waste of space," the couple call all "foreigners" as they mock the boy (116). At the same time, the literal and figurative wasteland surrounding Hawk Rise is transformed through the two children's persistence into a thriving oppositional space marked by what Butler would describe as a "sustainable interdependency" established on the grounds of equality ("Precarious," 149).

Unable to partake in the totality of the city in which they live—a city sheltering ongoing antagonisms that can be linked to the imprint of colonial history on its carefully regimented social spaces—Anderson's protagonists may be said to transform this particular space into a "dwelling place" in accordance with the Heideggerian notion that "mortals ever search anew for the essence of dwelling" and that "they *must ever learn to dwell*" (363, italics in original). Thus, to properly dwell in this complex cultural reality, where precariousness cuts across categories of identity, we need not just *build* but also *think* about the wider question of dwelling, for "[b]uilding and thinking are [. . .] insufficient for dwelling so long as each busies itself with its own affairs in separation, instead of listening to the other" (362). In *Asylum*, whose lives count as valuable, and whose stories are eligible for cultural and institutional recognition, matters for how the community is (re)built. Particularly important, then, is the voicing of Sunday's and Rosa's perspectives in ways that counter dominant Western narratives. These narratives are presented in various forms, including immigration workers' framing of asylum seekers as "illegals who arrived with invented tales of political suffering in order to scrounge off the UK's medical system" (166–67), which is challenged throughout the novel by the resurfacing of the children's traumatic memories of the very real violence from which they escaped, and by colonial-period fictions like *The Secret Garden*, used by the girl's friend from school, Jules, to describe Rosa's attempts to create her garden ("You know, the lonely waif who comes from far-off Eastern lands where everybody's died and then she turns out to have green fingers"), to which Rosa replies matter-of-factly: "No green fingers. [. . .] All very clean. And no secret. This is share for all the peoples of my home" (218).

Despite the narrative impetus towards cross-cultural, intergenerational collaboration, the laying bare of the problems that have to be addressed in order for British society to embrace a new, redemptive inclusiveness is accompanied by an equally powerful recognition of the limitations of individual acts of solidarity. The burden of acting upon, or ethically soliciting, others to live together across differences falls entirely on the young protagonists, who have already been let down by ineffective adult figures such as Rosa's mother. The girl reflects on how "[i]t was hard being strong for two of them. Some days, [she] wanted to howl like Granpap's dog pulling on its chain" at their support worker (33–34), who herself "knew she hadn't shown enough commitment to these two. One of the difficulties was she hardly knew them. She hadn't had time to study their file. They'd been passed on to her, like a pair of nearly new shoes" (166–67). The scripted response of the immigration officers who interview Sunday appears similarly inadequate, and they too are aware of their own passivity. "Doesn't make sense, does it?" one of them mutters. "Picking up kids like this, then chucking them out on the streets. We ought to be doing more for them than that" (188). The children seem more suited to the task of actively contesting the status quo, since what is needed, as Rosa puts it, is "[l]ess talk talk"—something which, in Rosa's experience, does not necessarily lead adults to action, which she believes is desperately needed—and "more work work" (199–200). Moreover, the communitarian ties forged by these characters at Hawk Rise are only temporary. After its former residents are rehoused, and the building itself is demolished, the alliances inevitably fall apart; no longer proximate to the children in a physical sense, the dispersed Hawk Rise community cannot protect Rosa from further racist attacks and remains ignorant of Sunday's deportation. By highlighting the discrepancy between local assertions of community bonds and global forms of ethical connections, the novel makes clear the need for a global connectedness with, and obligation to, those whose lives are not always conceived as counting.

Brahmachari's *Tender Earth* is a good example of the representation of ethical obligations emerging not just within but also outside the cultural contexts of a shared life grounded in physical proximity. The third novel in a series that tells the story of the Levensons, a London-based family with Indian and Jewish roots, *Tender Earth* shows how Laila, the family's youngest member, comes into her own as a moral agent while asserting a degree of independence from a large cast of characters already committed to safeguarding the lives of those who are far away—to name but a few, her sister Mira, who has traveled to Kolkata to help out at their aunt Anjali's refuge for street children; Laila's friend Kez's family, who have sponsored a little disabled girl from the refuge; or Mira's friends, Jidé and Millie, who are leaving for Rwanda to do volunteer work with the poor. Thus, at the same time as Laila makes her own commitment to the other—and, in Hegelian terms, finds her moral consciousness while retaining a sense of self within the family, where she has the "self-consciousness of [her] individuality in this [familial] unity" of self and other (148)—child readers' attention is directed to issues that they are likely to have encountered only from a geographical or cultural distance. Such encounters occur in the novel through campaigns run by charities to raise awareness of the greater precariousness of certain kinds of lives (incorporated into the novel in the form of an "I am a Refugee" poster that Laila sees on the underground) or through news accounts of the sufferings of the displaced from conflict-torn regions and reporting of public demonstrations organized in the West to highlight these vulnerable people's plight (here shown to elicit affective responses from Leyla, Laila's Iraqi refugee friend's mother, and Dara, Kez's Kindertransport refugee grandmother). "When I watch the news it never feels like the world is all connected up like this," Laila says upon discovering that her late grandmother, the activist Nana Josie, marched against a war that later affected Pari's family (254), and together with Laila, readers learn to see these forms of connectedness in ways that confront the problem of how "community" is to be understood and compel them to register in the public sphere their resistance to perceived injustices. Missing family members tie *Tender Earth* and *Asylum* together, allowing British-born characters like Laila to empathize with migrants' experiences of displacement, loss, and separation ("Our whole town was shelled [. . .] flattened," Pari tells Laila in a scene that ends with the girls holding hands and crying, "Grey rubble and dust, houses turned into coffins. My grandmothers and grandfathers were buried there, and my cousins" [322]); these losses also reveal precariousness—linked by Butler with a more specifically political notion of "precarity," or a "condition in which certain populations suffer from failing [. . .] networks of support and become differentially exposed to injury, violence, and death" (*Frames*, 25)—to be a shared condition of human life.

Part of *Tender Earth*'s consideration of a generalized precarity as a promising site for alliances that are not grounded in physical proximity or even identification unfolds through its synthesis of past and present that bears on the narrated relation between self and others. Laila wonders if the "Connected Lands" category—which her schoolteacher encourages all children to use when introducing themselves to others in their new tutor group—"isn't just about countries in the world; maybe it means the lands of the past too" (96), and her exposure to the perspectives of her grandmother (after she acquires, unbeknownst to the rest of the family, Nana Josie's "Protest Book," which chronicles her activist struggles) and Dara (whose stories of Jewish refugees displaced in the Second World War Laila hears firsthand) has a crucial impact on the girl's ethical growth. Kristen Renwick Monroe has reminded us that the "psychological forces at work during the Holocaust partake of the same political psychology underlying other political acts driven by identity [. . .] from prejudice and discrimination to sectarian hatred and violence" (4), but when Laila cites learning lessons from past traumas like the Holocaust as one of the reasons for studying history, she realizes that "[her] list is homework and [war refugee Pari]'s is actually her life," and that "if you're involved in things it feels different" (251–52).

By acknowledging the contaminating effects of genocidal practices and unequal political conditions, together with the damage inflicted by past violence on the living tissue of the present, the novel achieves more than a lesson in how history repeats itself; the reader is drawn into the interrogative processes of a narrative whose protagonist learns to constantly question the taken-for-granted character of the norm that determines whose lives will count as valuable and to challenge what Butler has termed "First World complacency" to try to build different modes of sociality and politics "on the basis of vulnerability and loss" (*Precarious*, 8, 20). Whereas characters like Dara and Pari are haunted by past losses, Laila dwells on present failings and silences. Horrified at the defacement of graves (including Dara's husband's) in the Jewish cemetery, the anti-immigrant sentiment Pari has been facing both in and outside school, and the racist aggression and abuse she sees Janu suffering on a London tube train, Laila is moved to act: "I have to think of something I can DO about this. [. . .] This is not a time to stay quiet. Nothing's healed. I'm not going to let [Dara] think that it's all happening again and we're just going to sit by and watch" (376). Indeed, with the suffering of others in mind, Laila organizes an antiracist vigil dedicated to Dara and her husband during which she and her schoolfriends go barefoot in the snow-covered cemetery to gather struggles against racism within a cross-cultural and cross-temporal framework; their bodily enactment of vulnerability is shown to be "for others," as Levinas would say, extending ethical connections beyond what we might rightly call global ones, to the bodily sensations that bind together different temporal modes, or what has been and what could be done to produce a radically new future. Such creation of affective bonds between first-generation trauma survivors and a new generation of Britons is a strategy often used by contemporary British novelists to convey the "possibility of regeneration and renewal" (Pellicer-Ortín, 56). In highlighting that Laila witnesses the pain of past and present traumas by adoption through acts of empathetic solidarity, with other characters becoming inspired to make ethical moves towards their others, Brahmachari articulates young people's potential for forging connections across cultures and generations.

But if Brahmachari's novel, in reaching for the bonds of a shared humanity that could broker difference, sets home against world—and sees the particular as inevitably bound up in the global (and historical)—it is also the case that it testifies to both the urgency and the difficulty of a global ethics in a time when, in the words of Elleke Boehmer, "[i]ntricate and deathly forms of terror and counter-terror [. . .] interpenetrate the global order" (146). For the older generation depicted, it is a shock to watch whole populations plunged into insecurity and fear. "[A]ll these apartheids now," Nana Josie's friend Simon observes with reference to the post-9/11 climate, "all harder to fight against in their own way" (156). Living in the city, for instance, is framed within the current anti-terror discourses as already a "security risk" (4); at the same time, the practices of fingerprinting and video monitoring schoolchildren sustain an atmosphere of constant emergency and non-specific alarm (82–83). In mainstream media, immigrants tend to be discursively constructed as less than human. "Listen to the language they use!" Dara exclaims. "Quotas, swarms [. . .] as if people are insects—or vermin!" (189). Yet echoes of populist rhetoric are evident even among the views voiced by Laila's classmates, and when a girl from Laila's group is told that attending secondary school can open the door to other languages, cultures, and religions, she mumbles under her breath, "Like we need any more doors open? I know where I'm from!" (72). Asked to remain in a state of perpetual alert, and in response to the conditions of heightened susceptibility to injury, many of Laila's fellow Londoners turn to reactionary populism and prejudicial perception of Britain's immigrants, but there are many other people in Brahmachari's novel who take to the streets to oppose the newly intensified racialized ways of seeing and judging others in the name of national security, with Laila herself taking part in her first large protest march only weeks before she organizes the vigil. As in *Asylum*, it is the moral transformation of *Tender Earth*'s young protagonist that is pivotal in how it provides vehicles for both the reader and most of the other characters to enter sympathetically into the lives and the suffering of others.

Laila's feeling of dissatisfaction with her level of social involvement and her longing to be "part of something bigger than [herself]" are used to signal her readiness to enter into a new stage of moral understanding (235). This type of development, or the child's induction into the "philosophy of right," is linked in Hegel's ethical theory to the individual's self-actualization as a subject and citizen (Hegel 1820/1893; see also Sainsbury 2013), as is the young characters' questioning of "where [they] belong in the world," their "waking up to what's ahead of [them]," which is part of this developmental framework (188). This is also clearly present in Laila's father's childhood interviews with his own father about his anti-fascist struggles. The girl's father describes these exchanges as his younger self, saying, "I want to understand what's going on in the world, I'm not a kid any more" (266). Reading is offered here as another transformational activity, a form of being called up in ways that compel one's concern, in keeping with Boehmer's recent characterization of the practice as an "engagement with other consciousnesses and other imaginations" to an extent that makes transnational identifications possible (12). Interestingly, Laila's overnight reading of books like *I Am Malala*, kept secret from her family, both indicates her rebelliousness and marks her as a privileged character, who, unlike Pari, for instance, can not only afford books but also has a comfortable, warm space in which to read them. In fact, embodied in Laila's interactions with others throughout the novel is her growing recognition of her own cultural privilege and rights-bearing status. It is through committing to affirm the lives of those commonly regarded as culturally alien and morally suspect, while assuming responsibility for mobilizing new social formations bound not by the presumption of familiarity but by an enduring obligation to others, that the girl finds a sense of purpose in a capacity for relational intimacy and gains a fresh perspective on the value of togetherness.

If *Tender Earth*'s main protagonist becomes less and less solipsistic as the novel progresses, towards the end of the book she is capable of seeing herself objectively, with the kind of detachment that is usually shown by an omniscient narrator, as both an individual subject and a "link" between the different groups of people coming together around her (350). The expressions of solidarity that Laila witnesses and inspires during the protest march and the vigil allow her to remain hopeful about the possibility of a better future to come, which leads Laila to a more qualified understanding of what Nana Josie tries to convey in her "Protest Book"—namely, "how standing together makes you feel stronger, even if you can't see how it changes things straight away" (391). Again, however, the burden of responsibility to the other is located with (if eagerly taken up by) the young generation: even while Laila's and Kez's parents try to shield their children from the images of conflict, violence, and death whenever they appear on the TV screens in their homes, other adults (including Dara) firmly believe that "it's up to [young people] now to get the heart of this world beating again" (344). At the protest, Laila sees London's communities as she has never seen them before; there are whole families there, carrying newborns and pushing prams, and "total strangers are actually talking to each other, laughing and joking," thus making efforts of solidarity habitual to the young (229). Adding to Laila's attempts to forge new alliances that assemble across distances so as to achieve their ethical goals are her cousin Priya's creation of a "Holi Spring" music video in which child dancers in Kolkata merge with a group of dancers in New York in a fusion of colors, as well as Janu's barefoot journey around the world, both operating as forms of ethical solicitation that go beyond the collection of funds for a new orphanage in India. Significantly, by the end of the novel Laila's family learns the truth about her activist achievements and celebrates them with their own gestures of inclusive solidarity with their extended community. The young characters of *Tender Earth* emerge as sources of hope precisely because they are "trailblazers in their different ways" (37); ultimately, it is the younger generation's ingenuity and commitment to equality that promote various forms of solidarity and facilitate ethical life in the novel, thereby encouraging young readers to work thoughtfully through its moral reckonings.

In what could be considered an expression of solidarity between their adult authors and child readers, books like *Asylum* and *Tender Earth* invest in young characters as willing subjects who are ready to engage in and mobilize alliances aimed at sustaining life on egalitarian terms. These young protagonists help the books appeal to the audiences which are more inclined to respond in a like-minded fashion, and which often trump difference with sameness; therefore, any opening up to the impositions coming across linguistic, cultural, or national borders must at this stage be regarded as provisional. While such texts do not offer an assurance that the struggles to extend equality regardless of background or circumstance are likely to cease soon, they clearly recognize young people's growing sociopolitical agency and put their trust in children's ability to think their way into future solidarities that would break the barriers of the post-9/11 experience and cast of thought. The opening of these communities to new political and social possibilities demands some critical reflection from readers themselves to consider how a shared condition of precariousness bears on our ethical obligations to one another. There is a new mode of connectedness that is coming to consciousness in the contemporary children's novel, one that tears down cultural walls and collapses spatial and temporal distances.

## NOTE

A reworked version of Blanka Grzegorczyk's chapter appeared as chapter 5 in her monograph *Terror and Counter-Terror in Contemporary British Children's Literature* (Routledge, 2020).

## WORKS CITED

Anderson, Rachel. *Asylum*. Hodder Children's Books, 2011.
Boehmer, Elleke. "Differential Publics—Reading (in) the Postcolonial Novel." *Cambridge Journal of Postcolonial Literary Inquiry* 4, no. 1 (2017): 11–25.

Boehmer, Elleke. "Postcolonial Writing and Terror." In *Terror and the Postcolonial: A Concise Companion*, eds. Boehmer and Stephen Morton, 141–50. Wiley-Blackwell, 2010.

Brahmachari, Sita. *Tender Earth*. Macmillan Children's Books, 2017.

Butler, Judith. *Frames of War: When Is Life Grievable?* Verso, 2009.

Butler, Judith. *Precarious Life: The Powers of Mourning and Violence*. Verso, 2004.

Butler, Judith. "Precarious Life, Vulnerability, and the Ethics of Cohabitation." *Journal of Speculative Philosophy* 26, no. 2 (2012): 134–51.

Butler, Judith. "We Are Worldless Without One Another." Interview by Stephanie Berbec. *Other Journal*, June 26, 2017, https://theotherjournal.com/2017/06/26/worldless-without-one-another-interview-judith-butler/. Accessed February 12, 2018.

Chouliaraki, Lilje, and Tijana Stolic. "Rethinking Media Responsibility in the Refugee 'Crisis': A Visual Typology of European News." *Media, Culture & Society* 39, no. 8 (2017): 1162–77.

Duffy, Kate Scarlett. "There's a Reason the Teenage Boys I Work with from the Calais Jungle Look So Old." *The Independent*, October 21, 2016, https://www.independent.co.uk/voices/calais-jungle-children-teenage-boys-refugees-young-men-look-older-age-assessment-reason-why-a7373146.html. Accessed October 2, 2018.

Erizanu, Paula. "'Refugee' is Children's Word of the Year." *The Guardian*, May 26, 2016, https://www.theguardian.com/childrens-books-site/2016/may/26/refugee-is-childrens-word-of-the-year. Accessed March 2, 2018.

Gilroy, Paul. "Multiculture in Times of War." *Critical Quarterly* 48, no. 4 (2006): 27–45.

Gilroy, Paul. *Postcolonial Melancholia*. Columbia University Press, 2005.

Hegel, Georg Wilhelm Friedrich. *The Ethics of Hegel: Translated Selections from His 'Rechtsphilosophie'* [1820], ed. James Macbride Sterrett. Ginn, 1893.

Heidegger, Martin. "Building, Dwelling, Thinking." In *Basic Writings*, 343–64. Harper & Row, 1977.

Lazarus Neil. "Spectres Haunting: Postcommunism and Postcolonialism." *Journal of Postcolonial Writing* 48, no. 2 (2002): 117–30.

Levinas, Emmanuel. "God and Philosophy." 1975. *The Levinas Reader*, Trans. Richard A. Cohen and Alphonso Lingis. Blackwell, 1989.

Levinas, Emmanuel. *Otherwise Than Being, or, Beyond Essence*. 1974. Trans. Alphonso Lingis. Kluwer Academic, 1991.

McIntosh, Malachi. "The Exigencies of Exile and Dialectics of Flight: Migrant Fictions, V. S. Naipaul, Kiran Desai." In *Reworking Postcolonialism: Globalization, Labour and Rights*, eds. Pavan Kumar Malreddy et al., 72–86. Palgrave Macmillan, 2015.

Monroe, Kristen Renwick. *Ethics in an Age of Terror and Genocide: Identity and Moral Choice*. Princeton University Press, 2012.

Pellicer-Ortín, Silvia. "The Ethical Clock of Trauma in Eva Figes' In *Winter Journey*." In *Ethics and Trauma in Contemporary British Fiction*, eds. Susana Onega and Jean-Michel Ganteau, 37–60. Rodopi, 2011.

Pickles, Matt. "'Trump' Revealed as Children's Word of the Year." *Oxford Arts Blog*, June 15, 2017, http://www.ox.ac.uk/news/arts-blog/trump-revealed-childrens-word-year. Accessed March 2, 2018.

Rushdie, Salman. *Imaginary Homelands: Essays and Criticism, 1981–1991*. Granta, 1991.

Said, Edward. "Reflections on Exile." 1984. In *Reflections on Exile and Other Literary and Cultural Essays*, 173–86. Granta, 2001.

Sainsbury, Lisa. *Ethics in British Children's Literature: Unexamined Life*. Bloomsbury, 2013.

Sivanandan, Ambalavaner. "Race, Terror and Civil Society." *Race & Class* 47, no. 3 (2006): 1–8.

Spencer, Robert. "Salman Rushdie and the 'War on Terror.'" *Journal of Postcolonial Writing* 46, no. 3 (2010): 251–65.

Ware, Vron. "The White Fear Factor." In *Terror and the Postcolonial: A Concise Companion*, eds. Elleke Boehmer and Stephen Morton, 99–112. Wiley-Blackwell, 2010.

# 12

# A GRAND CAUSE

## REPRESENTATIONS OF CHILDREN'S CONTRIBUTIONS TO REGENERATIVE AGRICULTURE IN PICTUREBOOKS

Michelle Superle

Fact: The United Nations Convention on the Rights of the Child (UNCRC) is anchored by a group of articles focused on children's rights to provision, including Article 24, which promises the right to nutritious food.

Fact: One out of every six children in the United States experiences food insecurity; those of low socioeconomic status living in cities are more likely to suffer from the lack of access to nutritious food (Flores and Amiri, 38). The "food deserts" in American cities adversely affect people's access to healthy foods (Evans et al., par. 2).

Fact: The UNCRC has been critiqued for allegedly promoting overprotection (Arts–72).

Fact: Approximately one hundred million children worldwide today are engaged in harmful child labor in the agricultural sector ("Child Labor in Agriculture").

Fact: In the United States today, "large farms with over one million dollars in sales account for only 4 percent of all farms, but 66 percent of all sales" (Koba).

Fact: Industrial mass agriculture utilizes unsustainable methods that harm the environment; small-scale farming is a more sustainable, equitable method of agriculture (Woodhouse, 437).

Fact: In 1861, 84 percent of Canadians lived in rural areas, and "Canada's economy was based mainly on the primary sector—chiefly agriculture"; but by

2011 only 18.9 percent lived in rural areas ("Canada Goes Urban"). Further, "in 1921, agriculture was the single most common occupation, employing 1 million Canadians and accounting for one-third of all jobs. By 2008, about 327,000 people were primarily employed in agriculture, accounting for 1.8% of the labor force" ("Agriculture"). This shift parallels similar changes throughout developed nations.

Assertion: Children are capable of participating in regenerative agriculture, particularly on small, local and/or urban farms.

Assertion: An astonishing body of picturebooks for young children portrays farms, farming, and/or life on a farm.

In the light of the above, I contend that increased regenerative agriculture that both involves and benefits children is urgently needed. Picturebooks can help to inspire and normalize this empowering activity that provides ways for children to fulfill their rights by collaborating with adult advocates.

## FOOD AND BOOKS — FAST TRACK TO A BETTER WORLD

Historically, virtually all children participated in agriculture, a norm that changed in the West less than one hundred years ago (Effland, 281). In fact, children were once integral to agriculture. For example, they completed important daily chores on small family farms, participated in community harvests on larger farms (often as paid laborers), and worked as slaves on plantations. Without children's varied contributions to farming, food security could not have been achieved throughout most of human history. Today, however, most children in developed nations will experience agriculture solely through their reading material; this vicarious experience begins immediately, with books for the youngest children. The causes of this reality are multifaceted and complex, but they include the UNCRC, a human rights treaty that ensures children's rights to protection and provision, emphatically prioritizing their education, and large corporations that control broad swathes of agricultural production worldwide. There can be no doubt that today's food production lacks any official place for children.

However, the growing North American "Good Food Movement" has sparked a renaissance of urban agriculture and the small hold family farm in their "new" incarnations as the seat of sustainable, organic, "regenerative" agriculture. This movement is touted as "a grand cause" with the capacity to "solv[e] our biggest problems" because "food is everything" (Preston, 318). In scholarly terms, this worldwide food sovereignty movement can be understood in the context of "agroecological initiatives" that aim at transforming industrial agriculture partly by transitioning the existing food systems away from fossil fuel-based production largely for agroexport crops and biofuels towards an alternative agricultural paradigm that encourages local/national food production by small and family farmers based on local innovation, resources and solar energy. (Altieri and Toledo, 587)

Is there a place for children's contributions in this "new" model of farming, with its potential to improve human health, help level socioeconomic disparity, and reverse environmental degradation? Many educators believe so, although broader discussions on the topic produced for adult audiences generally omit children's roles—even while positioning them as beneficiaries of this enterprise. Nevertheless, some picturebooks for children tell a very different story.

As I will show, a small yet significant body of contemporary English-language picturebooks position children's contributions as central to this new regenerative agriculture: works such as *On Grandpa's Farm* (Sathre 1997), *Sleep Tight Farm* (Doyle 2016), and *Anywhere Farm* (Root 2017) portray children as valuable partners in agricultural activities.

This is important because regenerative agriculture is labor intensive. It is a practice that

has at its core the intention to improve the health of soil or to restore highly degraded soil, which symbiotically enhances the quality of water, vegetation and land-productivity. It typically employs techniques that are used more generally in organic agriculture, with the aim to preserve/build soil organic matter, including minimum tillage, growing cover crops and green manures, composting, mulching and crop rotation. Its best practices mandate an avoidance of artificial inputs—pesticides, fertilisers, herbicides—that damage the living organisms in the soil. (Rhodes, 105)

When children collaborate with adults to ensure sustainable food security on a small but impactful scale, particularly when this collaboration also involves regenerative practices, it is a powerful practice indeed. Textual representations of such activities have immense inspirational potential to both swell the ranks of the Good Food Movement with enthusiastic new participants of all ages—which is necessary because this labor-intensive method of agriculture relies extensively on "hand work"—and plant seeds of hope in children's minds. Some recent picturebooks about farming extend the empowering promise that children can participate in both feeding themselves and saving the world *right now* through ethical food production—while simultaneously creating a healthier future for everyone. Such an endeavor would go a long way towards fulfilling many children's rights as they are enshrined in the UNCRC, including their health, education, provision, and participation rights.

## IGNORANT DREAMERS

Farms, livestock, and food production are prevalent settings, characters, and themes in children's literature. Impressive quantities of board books, picturebooks, easy readers, and middle-grade fiction—both classic and contemporary—position some aspect of farm life as central to the narrative. Martha Kruse has speculated that this phenomenon stems from adults' nostalgic yearning for a romanticized pastoral past (24). This seems likely to be true, but in this chapter I discuss only a handful of recent American picturebooks that are as forward-looking as they are nostalgic; their core shared quality is their potential to empower children to exercise their rights by collaborating with adults in regenerative agriculture projects. However, it is also important to acknowledge that, despite the impressive prevalence of children's books about farm life, many picturebooks about agriculture are prescriptive information-based works that position child readers as ignorant and needful of correction. For instance, a robust body of recent publications such as *Working on a Farm* (Marsico 2008), *A Year at a Farm* (Harris 2009), *Before We Eat: From Farm to Table* (Brisson 2014), *A Year on the Farm* (Unstead 2015), and *On the Farm, at the Market* (Karas 2016) lack central child characters and seem dedicated to filling a perceived knowledge void in child readers. Equally disempowering are texts that perpetuate soft-focus, outdated images of both childhood and agriculture. For example, *When I Visit the Farm* (Beshara 2009), *On Uncle John's Farm* (Fitz-Gibbon, 2009), *On the Farm* (Elliott 2012), and *A Day at the Farm* (Cordier 2013) all feature child characters blissfully reaping the rewards of old-fashioned farm life on traditional small holds without contributing to it—playing with animals, frolicking in the landscape, and feasting on produce. These dreamy, romanticized children are passive recipients of agriculture.

Such limited and highly constructed images of childhood are also present in the scant scholarship about picturebooks that portray farming. Some discussions have taken issue with technological accuracy, clearly positioning the texts as teaching tools for children presumed ignorant about food production (Eppley 2010); others have focused on ideological issues such as gender (Hamilton et al. 2006), class (Beck 2009), and various stereotypes (Koller 2013). This research (with the exception of Beck's) generally centers around the portrayal of adult characters, emphasizing the importance of their role in agriculture and sole responsibility for food security. For example, Nancy Chu concludes her *Rural Educator* article (1993) by admonishing that "parents and teachers" should "selec[t] and shar[e] a range of informational books, picturebooks and even poetry" about farming to "help children recognize the fact that farming is accomplished by people whose skillful use of technology, knowledge of the environment and science, and sense of commitment are crucial to our society" (14). Of course, the "people" she refers to are adults. A later *Rural Educator* article expresses the same concerns (Czarney and Terry 1998). Similarly, in "Aprons, Overalls, and So Much More: Images of Farm Workers in Children's Picturebooks" (2001), Martha Kruse worries that because this body of children's literature "might serve as an urban child's only window onto rural ways of life, these texts should not perpetuate negative stereotypes or factual inaccuracies that may permanently distort the reader's image of agrarian workers" (22). Kruse identifies several particularly harmful images—"farmer as solitary, farmer as comic buffoon, and farmer as old-fashioned"—which are deemed problematic because they contradict the reality that "agrarian work is a cooperative, intellectually demanding, and sophisticated enterprise" (22).

Such emphasis on adult characters largely excludes children: in fact, given that these discussions focus on books for children, their exclusion comprises a sort of prejudice against children. This exclusion is also uncomfortably ironic, given that agriculture was historically and remains today an area of serious rights violations against children. I will discuss this paradox further later; here, I am concerned with the paucity of children portrayed as capable participants in the crucial enterprise of ensuring food security through agriculture—both in picturebook representations and scholarly discussions. As Nina Christensen so aptly reminds us, because picturebooks portray children they project suggestions about what child readers might be capable of: "Portraits, narratives, and implied readers are expressions of certain perceptions of childhood" (360). What are we to make, then, of picturebooks about agriculture that omit or fail to position child characters in any meaningful role—and the scholarship that similarly discusses child readers as problematically ignorant about agriculture? I would go so far as to contend that they are childist. In her groundbreaking work, *Childism: Prejudice Against Children* (2012), psychoanalyst Elizabeth Young-Bruehl argues that it is adults' "*attitudes* towards [children] that matter most" (15, emphasis in original) and explains that corrosively prejudiced attitudes resting upon assumptions that children are illogical and incompetent date back thousands of years (25). Here, my focus on and attitude towards children (both readers and characters) differs from previous research on this topic: consequently, this discussion is the first to take a "child-centered" approach to picturebooks about agriculture.

In my initial definition of this approach, I insisted that the UNCRC must anchor such literary discussions ("The United Nations Convention . . .," 152): thus, I use it accordingly here. And, as I have argued previously, a child-centered picturebook "proceeds from a child-centered foundation that acknowledges children's uniqueness, competence, and curiosity" ("How to Choose . . .," par. 15). Using a child-centered approach, scholars can "consider the literary constructions at play by looking at how child characters are portrayed" and "ask whether the book provides representations of children that" (par. 17), among other things, "[a]cknowledge children's competence, [v]alue children's contributions to their families and communities, " and "[p]osition children and adults as allies in collaborative, mutually beneficial relationships" (par. 18). I have cautioned that "few picturebooks tick all these boxes"; many "contain both childist and child-centered qualities" (par. 19), but those I discuss in this chapter do, indeed, include all these child-centered representations. As child-centered picturebooks, the sample texts about agriculture I examine here show that children are valuable members of society right now, portray child characters respectfully, and have the potential both to inspire and to empower child readers.

## TOWARDS EVERYWHERE FARMERS

Since these texts are picturebooks, their visual representations of childhood and agriculture are paramount: all three sample texts include many illustrations of children and adults collaborating on agriculture projects that seem to incorporate regenerative practices. However, in terms of social variables beyond age, *Anywhere Farm* is by far the most visually empowering, while *On Grandpa's Farm* is the least progressive because it portrays only one Caucasian child working alongside "their" grandfather to complete regular daily chores in the late summer harvest season (depicted using bright sunshine, blooming sunflowers, ripe berries, and haying) on a "traditional" North American small hold farm. This child is pictured androgynously, with a "bowl" haircut, wearing black gumboots, blue jeans, and varied shirts throughout the day—a white T-shirt, a pinkish-red sweater, and a green button-down shirt. The narrative progresses chronologically, beginning with breakfast, finishing with dinner, and detailing all the chores in between. Many of these chores focus on procuring food that the characters soon consume (harvesting corn, tomatoes, berries, and fish). Both the joy with which the child is depicted working and frolicking around the farm and the late-summer season create a holiday air. In terms of the individual child's work on the farm, the visual depiction in *On Grandpa's*

*Farm* affirms the character's competence. Aside from dropping one egg, the child is shown working happily and capably alongside Grandpa: together, they muck livestock paddocks, tend to chickens, weed the vegetable plot, mend a fence, bale hay, catch fish, and prepare dinner. These activities, largely completed by hand (aside from the mechanized haying), align with regenerative agriculture practices and promise impressive food security for the characters.

While the child's task-based competence is indubitably empowering, the book's socioeconomic underpinnings are not. The entire agricultural system shown in this text is predicated on private ownership of an impressive parcel of land—as specified in the title, this is *Grandpa*'s farm: the illustrations portray large, well-maintained buildings, a small lake, and sprawling pastures. It is unlikely to be coincidental that Grandpa is white. Hence, although the visual representations of gender and age promise that children can participate meaningfully in regenerative agriculture, the representation of class and race is exclusive, positioning this sort of agriculture in a decidedly white, middle-class, capitalist milieu.

Similarly, *Sleep Tight Farm* uses an old-fashioned artistic style to portray a traditional small hold (red barn, white farmhouse, silo, and fencing) that appears to be privately owned by a white family utilizing it for both homesteading and as a market garden to stock their farm stand. Most of the twelve double-spread illustrations show members of the unnamed family collaborating to complete the necessary harvest and winterizing chores that will ensure continuity of their personal food security and agricultural business. These illustrations employ a sort of "time-lapse" style that shows both harvest and winterization activities.

The children take an active role in both. They are visually gendered as a boy and girl by clothing and hairstyles recognizably coded as male and female in early twenty-first century North America. However, their activities are equally demanding and functionally interchangeable. The girl is shown harvesting strawberries, hauling firewood, helping her mother spread groundsheets over crops, feeding chickens, winterizing beehives, and staffing the farm stand. The boy is shown clearing dishes away from the table, winterizing the strawberry field with his mother, pruning raspberry canes with his father, hauling firewood, harvesting tomatoes, collecting eggs, and staffing the farm stand. By working with their parents to complete the labor-intensive tasks associated with regenerative agriculture by hand, these child characters are shown as integral members of the family farm team, participating in provisioning their own well-being through food security, contributing to the family business, and, crucially, having a good time while doing so; their facial expressions are consistently depicted as focused and calm with slight smiles. Here, as in *On*

*Grandpa's Farm*, the portrayal of childhood is empowering through gender and age. Here again, though, the portrayal of class and race is exclusive. (In fairness, both of these texts do include an author's note clarifying that the story is inspired by the author's own life.)

*Anywhere Farm* is an extreme departure from the traditional, idyllic, capitalist system of small hold farming. And although the two texts discussed previously *imply* regenerative agriculture practices, *Anywhere Farm* actually *shows* them in action. This picturebook promises that everyone can farm everywhere, showing people of varied ages, genders, races, and abilities collaborating to transform a barren inner-city landscape into lush, abundant urban farmland. With colorful, cartoon-like illustrations, children are depicted completing the agricultural tasks, while adults initially look on as supportive bystanders and eventually become customers. Indeed, this text is such a departure from its capitalist predecessors that it even shows children engaged in economically subversive activities like pilfering supplies from dumpsters and merchants, not to mention reclaiming civic space for their endeavor; they cover a "No Dumping" sign with a handmade "Neighborhood Garden" banner.

These enterprising children are depicted working individually and together on a range of agricultural activities that begin with seed germination and culminate in the harvest and sale of crops such as tomatoes and flowers. They start seeds, devise an irrigation system, source planters, transfer seedlings, designate protective walkways, and engage in marketing activities. However, not all child characters are actively involved: some become consumers when their parents purchase produce from the farmers' market, while others look on longingly, with wistful expressions on their faces. These onlookers, one depicted outside the fenced area of the farm, and the other shown gazing down from a nearby balcony, seem to create space for child readers to become inspired and begin wishing to be "anywhere" farmers. As Junko Yokota proposes, children can "enter [picturebooks] and have agency" by "enter[ing] and [creat]ing unstated aspects of the story" and/or by "enter[ing] and rul[ing]" (210). In *Anywhere Farm* the children's initiative and leadership does garner them a sort of "ruling" power—after all, they are the ones not only producing the life-sustaining food, but are also being rewarded financially for it. However, the child characters portrayed as onlookers also seem to promise that, sooner or later, any child could get involved.

Such scrutiny of the illustrations in the three sample picturebooks demonstrates that, through their visual portrayals of children collaborating competently, effectively, and happily with adults in regenerative agricultural activities, these texts have the potential to inspire child readers to take similar action. Beyond the illustrations, elements of fiction are also empowering, particularly the point of view. Unlike prescriptive, information-based picturebooks about agriculture that employ a didactic, omniscient third-person narrator which distances readers, the three sample texts use point of view to include readers. *On Grandpa's Farm* employs first-person singular, while *Sleep Tight Farm* uses first-person plural. Most empowering of all, *Anywhere Farm* relies on second-person narration.

The use of a first-person singular narrator in *On Grandpa's Farm* creates an "authentic" tone, providing a sort of proof that the child protagonist is capably engaged in the agricultural activities shown, since they are the one reporting on their experience. While the narrator refers to themself directly only twice throughout the spare text, these phrases draw attention to their accomplishments: "I find," and "I hammer." By establishing this point of view, the protagonist takes responsibility for the rest of the narrative even when they are merely reporting on their surroundings with observations such as, "Queenie scampers. Shadows stretch." Thus, the concluding phrase in the book, "Supper sizzles," takes on more resonance, especially in conjunction with the illustration showing the child working alongside Grandpa to cook the fish they have caught and the vegetables they have harvested. This phrase demonstrates the child's responsibility for, awareness of, and satisfaction with their role in contributing to provision rights through food security.

Similarly, the first-person plural narration in *Sleep Tight Farm* signals to readers that all four members of the family participate in the crucial, valuable, and challenging work of farming. This collaboration is established in the first page spread: "*We* are busy putting the farm to bed" (emphasis mine). While the illustrations show precisely which members of the family are engaged in each task, the narration conglomerates this work as a collective: "We shake straw over berry plants. [. . .] We dig for the last carrots, beets, and potatoes. [. . .] We stack wood. [. . .] We board up the chinks in the chicken coop. [. . .] We build a windbreak for the beehives." Similarly, the plural narration clearly indicates that everyone involved in the farm work benefits from it: "We lick our lips, remembering [the strawberries]. [. . .] [The wood] will heat our home all winter. [. . .] We feast on homegrown treats—vegetable soup and berry pie." The narrator assures readers that this collaboration has resulted in prosperity: "There's plenty for us and plenty to sell!" The point of view in *Sleep Tight Farm* emphasizes the value of children's contributions to a family farm, which support food security, financial gain, and enjoyment for all concerned.

Going a step further, the second-person narration in *Anywhere Farm* makes this text the most inclusive and inviting of the sample. The direct address to readers begins immediately, with the first words of the text: "For an anywhere farm, here's all that you need: soil, and sunshine, some water, a seed." This address provides an invitation for readers to become involved in a regenerative agriculture project. Every single page includes a direct address to readers, often in the form of questions and answers that emphasize child readers' potential for capably making crucial and enjoyable decisions. For example, the question "where can you plant your anywhere farm?" is ultimately answered as follows: "Plant an anywhere farm anywhere that you like." Similarly, the answer to "what can you plant on your anywhere farm?" is "on your anywhere farm, plant whatever you please." While the speaker seems to be an adult authority figure that initially positions child readers as ignorant, the narrator also provides space for children to express their opinions on matters that affect them—just as Article 12 of the UNCRC decrees.

Similarly, children's collaborative work on such valuable projects is emphasized at the end of the story, when the narrator promises, "one day all our anywhere farms anywhere might turn into . . . an everywhere farm—everywhere." The concluding words of the story promise readers that "it all start[s]" with "[j]ust one farmer—you—and one little seed." While indubitably prescriptive due to its authoritative adult-like voice, the use of second-person narration in *Anywhere Farm* also has the potential to empower child readers by offering them the inspirational awareness that they can exercise their human rights, make choices, and take action that will improve the landscape, help achieve food security, and bring communities together. In other words, they can be farmers.

## GROWING TOGETHER—CO-CREATING THE FUTURE TODAY

Collaborating to ensure food security is visceral, valuable work. It is also physically demanding work. For environmental reasons, regenerative agriculture eschews mechanization whenever possible, relying heavily on manual labor. Therefore, this highly necessary endeavor should—and, perhaps ultimately *must*—involve everyone in a society, including its youngest members. By no means is this a call to return to the "bad old days"; I am not disputing the current construction of childhood as it is enshrined in the UNCRC. It is vital to prioritize children's rights to safety, education, and leisure. However, when children work with adult advocates on regenerative agriculture projects, they can simultaneously fulfill their health, education, provision, and participation rights (the latter if children are invited to express their views about crops and other key agricultural decisions, for example). Indeed, this updated vision of children's involvement in crucial agricultural initiatives is fully in line with a contemporary construction of childhood that is gaining traction: the "empowered child."

Books such as *Anywhere Farm*, with its radically inclusive vision of regenerative agriculture, have immense inspirational potential to launch and anchor projects such as school-based community gardens that involve children starting in kindergarten in collaboration with adults to both transform the landscape and support food security and regenerative agriculture across socioeconomic borders. Nor is this vision a top-down initiative; children themselves report a desire to grow food. For example, results from a participatory research project described in the article "Ask Them" demonstrate that children ages four through seven prioritize food security and yearn for food-producing gardens at school: "Many children described their ideal school as farm-like, with animals and vegetable gardens" (Finelli et al., 230). Both adults and children agree that regenerative agriculture is beneficial and should involve children.

However, all too often adults overlook children's potential involvement in such projects (a notable exception to this trend is Barbara Kingsolver's *Animal, Vegetable, Miracle* [2007]). Brent Preston's memoir, *The New Farm: Our Ten Years on the Front Lines of the Good Food Revolution* (2017), offers a case in point. Concluding the chronicle of his family's trial-and-error attempts to run a small organic farm, Preston claims his children now "have the confidence and independence of farm kids" (310). While this suggests they were involved in the enterprise, the memoir itself rarely mentions his son and daughter, and when it does, it is usually to position them as obstacles threatening the completion of urgently time-sensitive agricultural work. For example, Preston describes scrambling to fulfill their first large wholesale order, which was accomplished by "almost killing [them]selves" to meet the deadline, and admits that he "honestly [doesn't] remember what [they] did with the kids that day. On many weekends they were left to their own devices" (151). His children were five and seven years old at that time.

Later, Preston confesses that the demands of the farm caused significant family strife in the early days. Not only did it compromise his marriage, but he was also impatient with and resentful of parental duties that detracted from his farm work (298). Far from being involved in or contributing to this "new" sort of farming—typical regenerative agriculture, which is really just a modern (organic, sustainable) return to the small hold family farm—Foster and Ella Preston at times seemed to threaten its precarious viability. Preston's memoir is far from unusual; in serious discussions of the future of agriculture, children's roles are decidedly not the focus.

Yet Preston dedicates the book to his children. In ultimately touting the rewards of this "new" farming model, Preston claims that it "provides us with everything we need: great food, clean water and enough money to do pretty much whatever we want. We have time to spend with our children and a safe, stimulating environment for them to grow up in" (321). Thus, even when children are not directly involved in regenerative agriculture, they provide the impetus for it, benefitting from it in the short term by experiencing ideal physical and social conditions, and ultimately reaping its long-term rewards in the future. In this sense, such endeavors help adults ensure children's rights in the short and long term. But, according to this narrative, farming is serious business: it is not child's play.

Preston's position is not unique. Indeed, it is eerily similar to children's literature scholars who examine how agriculture is portrayed in picturebooks. Ironically, even scholarship specifically *about* children's involvement in food security, such as "Farm to School in British Columbia: Mobilizing Food Literacy for Food Sovereignty" (Powell and Whitman 2018), barely mentions children beyond a few statistics about them. While this view is not surprising in itself (given still influential past constructions of childhood), it is somewhat perplexing in the context of the integral ways that actual children have contributed to agricultural enterprises throughout history. Yet, in light of agriculture's fraught past and current status as a site of minor misdemeanors and major atrocities against children—especially through slavery—it is understandable. Thus, the paradoxical contemporary adult focus seems inevitable: farming is not for today's children, yet children will ultimately reap its greatest rewards.

Similarly, many picturebooks about agriculture either omit the presence of children or portray them as dreamy recipients of the bounteous pastoral beauty that (some) farms provide. Nina Christensen suggests that the main possibilities for picturebooks come from adopting a "'prescriptive' approach, which depicts childhood as it ought to be," a "'retrospective' approach," which "indicates an archaic or deliberately timeless setting," and/or texts that "promote 'progressive' ideals concerning children and society," which means they "have participated in the transformations over time of ideals concerning childhood" (365). Although each approach is present in all the sample texts I have discussed, it is largely the third that has informed my examination of agricultural picturebooks from a child-centered perspective.

Despite the small sample discussed here, I am confident that an emerging body of children's picturebooks about farming tells a different story than either their predominantly childist corollaries or the adult narratives that more often comprise discussions about food security. A significant few recently published picturebooks about farm life position children as capable team members making valuable contributions to the farm's viability. The sample books discussed here suggest an alternative view of the relationship between food production and children—and thus, ultimately, survival. In this view, children are involved and competent. Working with adult advocates, they contribute to a viable future by helping to co-create it right now. These books provide the youngest readers with compelling portrayals of agriculture as a collaborative activity, suggesting that there is a realistic, manageable way for children to contribute to the "grand cause" of ensuring their own and others' survival while simultaneously helping to save the planet.

## WORKS CITED

"Agriculture." Statistics Canada. 2018, 150.statcan.gc.ca/n1/pub/11–402-x/2011000/chap/ag/ag-eng.htm. Accessed December 31, 2018.

Altieri, Miguel, and Victor Manuel Toledo. "The Agroecological Revolution in Latin America: Rescuing Nature, Ensuring Food Sovereignty and Empowering Peasants." *Journal of Peasant Studies* 38, no. 3 (2011): 587–612, DOI: 1080/03066150.2011.582947.

Arts, Karin. "Twenty-Five Years of the United Nations Convention on the Rights of the Child: Achievements and Challenges." *Netherlands International Law Review* 61, no. 3 (2014): 267–303, proxy.ufv.ca:2048/login?url=http://search.ebscohost.com. proxy.ufv.ca:2048/login.aspx?direct=true&db=a9h&AN=100382613. Accessed December 30, 2015.

Beck, Scott. "Children of Migrant Farmworkers in Picture Storybooks: Reality, Romanticism,and Representation." *Children's Literature Association Quarterly* 34, no. 2 (2009): 99–137.

Beshara, Crystal. *When I Visit the Farm*. Lobster, 2009.

Brisson, Pat. *Before We Eat: Farm to Table*. Illus. Mary Azarian. Tillbury House, 2014.

"Canada Goes Urban." Statistics Canada, 2018, 150.statcan.gc.ca/n1/pub/11-630-x/11-630-x2015004-eng.htm. Accessed December 31, 2018.

"Child Labor in Agriculture." *Food and Agriculture Organization of the United Nations*, 2019, ao.org/childlabouragriculture/en/. Accessed December 31, 2018.

Christensen, Nina. "Picturebooks and Representations of Childhood." In *The Routledge Companion to Picturebooks*, ed., Bettina Kummerling-Meibauer, 360–70. Routledge, 2018.

Chu, Nancy. "A Review of Children's Literature about Farming and Rural Life." *Rural Educator* 15, no. 2 (1993): 11–15.

Cordier, Severine, and Cynthia Lacroix. *A Day at the Farm*. Owlkids, 2013.

Czarney, Sarah, and Lucinda Terry. "What do Real Farmers Look Like? Rural Life in Children's Literature." *Rural Educator* 19, no. 3 (1998): 43–48.

Doyle, Eugenie. *Sleep Tight Farm: A Farm Prepares for Winter*. Illus. Becca Stadtlander. Chronicle, 2016.

Effland, Anne. "Agrarianism and Child Labor Policy for Agriculture." *Agricultural History* 79, no. 3 (2005): 281–97, jstor-org.proxy.ufv.ca:2443/stable/3745070. Accessed September 17, 2018.

Elliot, David. *On the Farm*. Illus. Holly Meade. Candlewick, 2012.

Eppley, K. "Picturing Rural America: An Analysis of the Representation of Contemporary Rural American Picturebooks for Children." *Rural Educator* 32, no. 1 (2010): 1–10.

Evans, Alexandra, et al. "Increasing Access to Healthful Foods: A Qualitative Study with Residents of Low-income Communities." *International Journal of Behavioral Nutrition and Physical Activity* 12, no. 1 (2015), doi: 10.1186/1479–5868–12-S1-S5.

Finelli, Manuel, et al. "Ask Them: Child Participation in the Development of Educational Services." *Canadian Journal of Children's Rights* 1, no. 1 (2014): 219–34, ojs.library.carleton.ca/index.php/cjcr/article/view/19. Accessed February 14, 2018.

Fitz-Gibbon, Sally. *On Uncle John's Farm*. Illus. Brian Deines. Fitzhenry and Whiteside, 2006.
Flores, Heather, and Azita Amiri. "Addressing Food Insecurity in Vulnerable Populations." *American Journal of Nursing* 119, no. 1 (2019): 38–45, doi: 10.1097/01.NAJ.0000552585.15471.a7.
Hamilton, M. C., D. Broaddus, and K. Young. "Gender Stereotyping and Under-representation of Female Characters in 200 Popular Children's Picturebooks: A Twenty-First Century Update." *Sex Roles* 55, no. 11–12 (2006): 757–65.
Harris, Nicholas. *A Year at a Farm*. First Avenue, 2009.
Karas, Brian. *On the Farm, at the Market*. Henry Holt, 2016.
Kingsolver, Barbara. *Animal, Vegetable, Miracle: A Year of Food Life*. Harper Perennial, 2007.
Koba, Mark. "Meet the '4%': Small Number of Farms Dominates US." *CNBC*, May 6, 2014, cnbc.com/2014/05/06/state-of-american-farming-big-producers-dominate-food-production.html. Accessed December 31, 2018.
Koller, Kathryn S. "Portrayal of Agriculture in Children's Literature: Contemporary Stories in Picturebooks, Traditional Tales, and Nonfiction." Department of Curriculum and Instruction, Division of School Library Studies University of Northern Iowa, 2013, digital.library.uni.edu/cdm/ref/collection/mast/id/237. Accessed March 12, 2018.
Kruse, Martha. "Aprons, Overalls, and So Much More: Images of Farm Workers in Children's Picturebooks." *Journal of Children's Literature* 27, no. 2 (2001): 22–28.
Marsico, Katie. *Working on a Farm*. Cherry Lake, 2008.
Powell, Lisa Jordan, and Hannah Wittman. "Farm to School in British Columbia: Mobilizing Food Literacy for Food Sovereignty." *Agriculture and Human Values* 35 (2018): 193–206, doi-org.proxy.ufv.ca:2443/10.1007/s10460-017-9815-7. Accessed December 31, 2018.
Preston, Brent. *The New Farm: Our Ten Years on the Front Lines of the Good Food Revolution*. Random House, 2017.
Rhodes, Christopher J. "The Imperative for Regenerative Agriculture." *Science Progress* 100, no. 1 (2017): 80–129, doi: 10.3184/003685017X14876775256165.
Root, Phyllis. *Anywhere Farm*. Illus. G. Brian Karas. Candlewick, 2017.
Sathre, Vivian. *On Grandpa's Farm*. Illus. Anne Hunter. Houghton Mifflin, 1997.
Superle, Michelle. "How to Choose Picturebooks that Will Enlighten, Not Damage, A Child." *The Conversation*, August 20, 2017, theconversation.com/how-to-choose-picture-books-that-will-empower-not-damage-a-child-82112. Accessed October 20, 2018.
Superle, Michelle. "The United Nations Convention on the Rights of the Child: At the Core of a Child-Centered Critical Approach to Children's Literature." *The Lion and the Unicorn* 40, no. 2 (2016): 144–62, doi:10.1353/uni.2016.0017.
United Nations. "Convention on the Rights of the Child," 1989. UNICEF, November 2, 2013, ohchr.org/EN/ProfessionalInterest/Pages/CRC.aspx. Accessed March 27, 2016.
Unstead, Sue. *A Year on the Farm*. DK Children, 2015.
Woodhouse, Philip. "Beyond Industrial Agriculture? Some Questions about Farm Size, Productivity and Sustainability." *Journal of Agrarian Change* 10, no. 3 (2010): 437–53.
Yokota, Junko. "Finding the Spaces Within: Picturebooks and Child Agency." In *Child Autonomy and Child Governance in Children's Literature*, eds. Christopher Kelen and Björn Sundmark, 207–17. Routledge, 2017.
Young-Bruehl, Elisabeth. *Childism: Confronting Prejudice Against Children*. Yale University Press, 2012.

# 13

# GARDENING AND INTERGENERATIONAL SOLIDARITY IN CONTEMPORARY AMERICAN CHILDREN'S LITERATURE

Aneta Dybska

Since the 1990s, Americans have witnessed the publication of an abundant crop of picturebooks for children and stories for young adults that contribute to the growing popularity of urban gardening across the country. A distinctive strand of American literature for children, DyAnne DiSalvo-Ryan's *City Green* (1994), Sarah Stewart's *The Gardener* (1997), Paul Fleischman's *Seedfolks* (1997), Jacqueline Briggs Martin's biographical *Farmer Will Allen and the Growing Table* (2013), and Rebecca Elliott's *The Last Tiger* (2012) all resonate with the urban revolution in American cities[1]—the gardening and farming initiatives that are part and parcel of grassroots regeneration and beautification projects, be it at the scale of the neighborhood block, the city, the region, or the country. A shared feature of the books is their aetonormativity with respect to the conduct and practices of citizenship.[2] In their didactic function, the stories effectively combine civic education with child agency and it is the interplay of social norms and individual aims that holds potential for place-based transformation. In what follows, I will argue that the fictionalized gardening projects foreground intergenerational solidarity as a foundation for civic renewal, weaving together the community and the nation. Yet, rather than look for the ritualized forms that bring the nation into existence, such as "parades, remembrance ceremonies, anniversary celebrations, monuments to the fallen, oaths, coinage, flags, eulogies of heroes and memorials of historic events" (Smith, 162), I will explore the fleeting and unspectacular reiterations of what Michael Billig calls "banal nationalism" in children's literature—the daily "flagging" of the nation, "so familiar, so continual, that it is not consciously registered" (6): the planting of flowers or vegetables in unlikely urban locales. These are micro-scale projects that couple the American pastoral ideal with the idiom of citizenship.

Solidarity usually refers to social unity or cohesion as achieved through collective responsibility, shared interest, and a sense of moral obligation towards a group (Scholz, 18–20). Solidarity can also be defined as a function of enhanced social capital, understood as

> connections among individuals—social networks and the norms of reciprocity and trustworthiness that arise from them. In that sense social capital is closely related to what some have called "civic virtue." The difference is that "social capital" calls attention to the fact that civic virtue is most powerful when embedded in a dense network of reciprocal social relations. A society of many virtuous but isolated individuals is not necessarily rich in social capital. (Putnam, 19)

A building block of social solidarity, contemporary sociologist Robert Putnam's notion of social capital is reminiscent of Émile Durkheim's classical concept of mechanical solidarity, characteristic of premodern societies where individuals share a collective consciousness (norms, ideas, beliefs, attitudes, and so on).[3] Such solidarity is an intergenerational force, leaving an imprint on the individual's identity and on their sense of moral obligation towards a social group (63, 79).

While mechanical solidarity entails a high degree of social and moral similarity, modern capitalist societies, Durkheim notes, are bound by so called organic solidarity, linked to the high division of labor and specialization, whereby individuals depend on one another to perform diverse, yet complementary, tasks. Relations among dissimilar individuals are regulated by law and contract. It is economic interdependence and social difference and a new secular morality, encoded in law, that reinforce organic solidarity (Kieran and O'Boyle, 40). Significantly, Durkheim's model holds that, rather than appear in succession at distinct stages of social evolution, the two kinds of solidarity coexist in most societies (Lukes, xxix; Szacki, 385). I find those insights a useful theoretical backdrop for the analysis of children's books' engagement in place-based regeneration that promotes active citizenship and intergenerational connectivity.

The discussion that follows zooms in on grassroots gardening and farming projects, especially their investment in contemporary civil society in line with de Tocquevillian "principle of self-interest rightly understood." The principle promotes public-spirited attitudes among fellow citizens who engage in "daily *small acts of self-denial*" and "*willingly sacrifice* a portion of their time and property to the welfare of the state" (de Tocqueville, vol. II, ch. 8, emphasis mine). Civic involvement is closely related to enhanced social capital and constitutes a key tenet of republican citizenship. An inherent element of a functioning democracy, this mode of citizenship prioritizes communal goals over the pursuit of narrow self-interest and self-government, protects individuals against the controlling power of the state, and significantly, makes the vibrant civil society the center of politics (Dagger, 148–50).

It is precisely the micro-politics of change that drives the plot of the children's books analyzed here. Yet to unfold the varied fictional manifestations of intergenerational solidarity, it is necessary to foreground civic nationalism as a major force of cross-generational bonding, unity, and cohesiveness. American civic nationalism unites diverse individuals into a polity of citizens bound by the national creed which is "the cement in the structure of this great and disparate nation" (Myrdal, 3). It stands for a set of political ideals and principles to live by—namely, the belief in individual liberty, democracy, constitution, and the rule of law, as well as cultural and political equality (Myrdal, 8; Lieven, 19). This chapter investigates the ways in which the discourses of citizenship as well as the American pastoral myth partake in the production of place-based intergenerational solidarity.

## THE URBAN PASTORAL AS A SOURCE OF SOCIAL SOLIDARITY

Children's books thematically focused on urban gardening rely on the archetypal pastoral design.[4] This pertains to the structure of the literary work in which there is a conflict between the pastoral landscape and the anti-pastoral forces of industry and technology. The two antithetical forces are ideologically moored in different value systems and social philosophies (Marx 27). If, in the mid-nineteenth century, the industrial was symbolized by the machine encroaching on the pastoral ideal, today the reverse is true: the pastoral ideal is re-embedded in an urban setting and functions as a vehicle of fostering social and, in some instances, interspecies solidarity.[5] Rather than the machine interrupting the idyll, the agrarian re-enters the contemporary post-industrial landscape.

Sarah Stewart's *The Gardener* is a Depression-era story of a young resolute white country girl named Lydia Grace Finch who is sent to New York to temporarily live with her Uncle Jim because her family is in financial straits. Uncle Jim runs a bakery in a typical mixed-use neighborhood of narrow car-filled streets lined with tenement houses. Though he is surrounded by people, he comes across as unhappy and dour. The story is told through letters written by Lydia to her uncle in the city and, once there, to her parents and grandparents who remained on the farm. At the outset, readers learn that she is an avid gardener, for as soon as she embarks on the city-bound train, she starts dreaming of gardens. Once in the city, she initiates a small-scale gardening project, ordering flowering plant seeds from a catalogue, planting them, and watering them until they bloom in window boxes and in front of the bakery.

Lydia Grace exhibits a missionary zeal for gardening, which becomes a magnet of social life around Uncle Jim's bakery. Her growing of marigolds, zinnias, radishes, onions, lettuce, and other plants in window boxes draws the neighbors to share their plants, to pass by, to window shop, and finally to buy bread, rolls, cookies, and muffins at the shop. As the bleak, empty, or simply boring, street corner acquires radiance, Uncle Jim's bakery becomes a lively third place,[6] attracting crowds of would-be customers. The colorful flowers ornamenting the tenement's facade add a new aesthetic quality to the place, which, as vividly depicted in David Small's drawings, encourages contact and increases interage connectivity: neighbors sharing plants with Lydia Grace make an investment in the place. An agent of change, the child protagonist successfully cross-pollinates the urban with the pastoral; her beautification project acts as a magnet for neighbors on errands, passers-by, and strangers, casting them into many fleeting encounters that foster "an emotional tone in conduct" characteristic of small-town life (Simmel, 12). The cumulative effect of such chance meetings on the sidewalk, urban journalist Jane Jacobs argued in a different context, breaks down anonymity and creates "a feeling for the public identity of people, a web of respect and trust, and resource in time of personal and neighborhood need. The absence of this trust is a disaster to a city street. Its cultivation cannot be institutionalized. And above all, *it implies no private commitments*" (56, emphasis in original).

Never short of energy or enthusiasm, the resolute niece goes so far as to plant a secret roof garden for Uncle Jim's private use, all in the hope of making him happy. She does so with the help of an African American couple, Emma and Ed, who work at the bakery. Emma shares Lydia's secret, supports her in the endeavor, and, upon Lydia's departure, becomes the plants' caretaker. Whereas the relationship that develops between the two female characters engenders cross-racial and cross-generational solidarity, Uncle Jim remains distant and morose, expressing the opposite of Lydia's high-spirited nature. Unwavering in her resolution to eventually see him smile, she displays innocence and purity of motive, as well a filial gratitude for taking her in. Yet neither Lydia nor the readers are privy to the cause of Uncle Jim's condition.

I propose that Georg Simmel's classic essay "The Metropolis and Mental Life" (1903), which resonates with Durkheim's notion of social solidarity, offers an interpretive key to Uncle Jim's emotional withdrawal. Presumably a migrant from the countryside, he reveals the symptoms of a blasé type who has learned to deal with the overstimulation of metropolitan life with an attitude of "reserve" and mask of "indifference" that conceals his genuine feelings and reactions (Simmel, 15). Or it may well be that, when faced with the individualistic, rational, and "calculating exactness of practical life" (13), he withdrew into nostalgia for the smells, looks, and the natural rhythms of rural life back home.

When looked at in this light, Lydia's gardening project, which evolves over a period of ten months, transplants the civic spirit of small-town America into the modern urban landscape. Her movement in space and time is a progression away from the pastoral ideal, but one that relies on the train—the "machine in the garden"—to carry the Arcadian dream into the realm of progress, two countering components of the pastoral design, as defined by Leo Marx (27). The city is the antithesis of the open fields, meadows strewn with flowers, and bountiful gardens; it stands for American societal development, measured with the grand architecture of Penn Station, which is Lydia's gateway to the city, or, more generally, as a distance from Thomas Jefferson's ideal of agrarian democracy. Jefferson believed that America's political uniqueness could be maintained if it remained a country of yeoman farmers who tilled their own land: "Those who labor in the earth are the chosen people of God, if ever he had a chosen people, whose breast he has made his peculiar deposit for substantial and genuine virtue." Self-subsisting and industrious, they were free from the pressures of the market economy and dependence on "the casualties and caprice of customers," which "begets subservience and venality, suffocates the germ of virtue, and prepares fit tools for the designs of ambition" ("Query XIX"). Jefferson's yeoman farmers embodied republican virtue, integrity, and happiness. Coded in this description is his anti-urbanism, his distrust towards industrial economy and the factory system, competitiveness, and pursuit of monetary gain—counterforces that could threaten America's democratic ideals of equality and individual freedom (Marx, 122–23).

If *The Gardener* operates ideologically at the scale of an urban neighborhood, Rebecca Elliot's *The Last Tiger* does so at multiple levels, bringing together the abstract space of urban planners and the concrete space of lived experience (Lefebvre, 361–62). *The Last Tiger* is set in a post-apocalyptic urban landscape that attests to the modernist project's cannibalistic tendency to eat away at the fruits of its own making. The belching factory chimneys, impersonal office towers, and panoptic command centers hover over the industrial ruins of a once thriving metropolis. Technological rubble has replaced nature. Faceless masses live in this dark and gloomy landscape in a state of amnesia, having lost memories of the world as it used to be as well as a sense of collective purpose.

*The Last Tiger* tells the story of a little white boy named Luka who befriends the eponymous last tiger living amidst the industrial ruins. Told using third-person narration and addressed to younger audiences than Stewart's *The Gardener*, the lavishly illustrated story begins with Luka's unusual encounter with the animal. The relationship develops when Luka sets the tiger's paw free from an old can. The tiger reciprocates the favor by presenting Luka with a potted flower—a precious and unusual gift, given that the natural ecosystem has been destroyed, the flora and fauna depleted. Thus begins a secret friendship that involves exchanges of smiles, jubilant and trusting play, and attachment. When the tiger as the only surviving specimen of animal life is captured, caged, and put on public display, the resourceful boy negotiates the animal's freedom on condition that it shows humans its secret garden.

Lush, verdant, filled with the smell of colorful flowers, and alive with the noise of bees and the flutter of butterflies, this is a truly mythical garden that restores the humans' memories of the past and a nostalgia for the premodern American idyll. Immersion in nature and the experience of its rich biodiversity, along with the peaceful symbiosis of plants and animals, triggers within the visitors strong emotional responses. When brought to this fairy-tale place, the urbanites of different ages and ethnicities, many of them Luka's peers, instinctively turn to nature: their mouths start smiling at the sight of squirrels, snails, mice, and butterflies. They start playing with animal friends, jumping, and moving their bodies freely to the rhythms of nature. This emotional/affective process fosters interspecies solidarity, which, in turn, initiates the re-embedding of the pastoral ideal in the post-urban landscape. The book ends with Luka and the tiger sitting next to each other, contentedly admiring the transformation: a stream meandering through parklike surroundings, game roaming freely against the bright cityscape of soaring glass towers. In a manner of engineers supervising construction work, the two gardeners have relied on wild animal labor in the recovery of the ecosystem (Coulter, 64) and have shown concern for the well-being of all stockholders. A reader familiar with urban utopian projects cannot fail to see that Elliott's visualization of the future city harks back to Frank Lloyd Wright's concept of Broadacre city (1932), which aimed to reconcile technological progress with Jefferson's agrarianism in a grand vision of suburban America.

## SOCIAL CAPITAL AS SOLIDARITY

The ideal of the American garden as the organizing theme and structural element of the stories entails investments in social capital within the realm of the civil society. Putnam distinguishes two kinds of social capital, both of which result in social cohesion based on relationships of trust, care, and reciprocity: the bonding type, which describes social ties that exist between members of culturally homogenous groups, and the bridging type, which develops across social divisions of ethnicity, economic status, education, or religion (22–23).[7] It is in the latter kind of social capital where diversity finds expression and multiple identities coexist. If we were to analyze the selected children's books through the prism of social capital, the *City Green* neighborhood abounds in social capital prior to the gardening project, while gardening initiatives in *The Growing Table*, *The Last Tiger*, and *The Gardener* parallel investments in scarce social capital. Indeed, wherever a sense of connectivity and shared interests and feelings develop, bonds of solidarity emerge. Regardless of the geographical and political scale, the civil society brings citizenship and place solidarities in a productive interplay.[8]

Two of the children's books discussed in this chapter, Jacqueline Briggs Martin's *Farmer Will Allen and the Growing Table* and DyAnne DiSalvo-Ryan's *City Green*, end with instructions on how to implement the ideals permeating the narratives in the child readers' own lives. Of course, children's books necessarily target a crossover audience that includes adults: parents, teachers, and caregivers, who make the books accessible, whether in a public library or at home, and guide children's reading choices. The instructions on how to start one's own garden presuppose intergenerational solidarity as built into a child's reading experience, but they encourage mutual engagement in more than reading. I am mostly interested in the political philosophy undergirding those extra materials and its consequences for intergenerational solidarity.

The protagonist of DiSalvo's book, Will Allen, is a living black basketball-player-turned-urban-farmer whose biography served as a model for Martin's fictional character. Raised on a farm, Will escapes the drudgery by excelling at basketball and moving to Belgium. But while there, he realizes that he loves growing things and feeding people, so he learns to make compost by using wriggler worms. When his sports career ends, he returns to the United States, where he converts an abandoned city lot into a vegetable garden. With the help of neighbors, young and old, he expands his business, enacting a grand vision of an ever-growing table laden with organic food.

At the end of *The Growing Table* is a letter written by the real-life Allen to readers, stressing the value of food literacy and farming skills as tools with which to live better and healthier lives. This letter is more than a list of recommendations for young readers enticed by the idea of eating sustainable food grown with the helping hand of their families. Allen sees the individual effort of each individual child as the force with which to make the world a better place to live. His far-fetched vision of a worldwide good food revolution resonates with Tocqueville's principle of self-interest properly understood. Individuals' actions are not guided by a "disinterest" in others, but by a feeling of solidarity that reaches beyond the legal and geographical borders of the nation-state. While transcendence of the nation may be seen as a recognition of what Ulf Hannerz calls the global ecumene—"the interconnectedness of the world, by way of interactions, exchanges and related development" (7)—the concern instantiates Americans' belief in their nation's providential destiny, the uniqueness of their political institutions, and civilizational achievements.

This message becomes even more apparent in the pictures accompanying the text in *The Growing Table*. On a two-page spread, Will Allen is depicted as a national hero, a messenger of the gospel of sustainable farming, who "sees what others cannot see"—the potential of buying private property in declining urban areas and investing his labor to bring about social change. A self-driven, determined, enterprising, and creative farmer, the saint-like leader discovers a way to turn abandoned lots, factories, and warehouses into economic opportunities inseparable from the promise of a more just world, where people grow their own healthy food. With arms stretched out in a self-confident, embracing gesture, his figure is the source of godly energy radiating outwards onto his followers. They applaud by raising their hands high in the air, hands holding farming tools, carrots, and tomatoes, and *The Good Food Revolution* written by Allen himself.

The story closes with the following lines: "Will you be on Will Allen's crew? Will you grow vegetables for your family, your neighbors, on your porch, or roof, or yard? How big will YOUR table be?" Those words are printed over a brightly colored landscape of urban rooftops turned into gardens, with a huge Statue of Liberty in the foreground, symbolically legitimizing Allen's faming project. Instead of the torch in her raised arm, the statue holds a handful of beetroots; instead of the tablet bearing the date "4th July 1776," she holds a basket of colorful vegetables (squash, carrots, broccoli, tomatoes, cucumbers, and lettuce). In the bottom right-hand corner stands the tiny figure of Farmer Will Allen, who waves at the reader from one of the verdant rooftops, among raised beds of vegetables.

Interestingly, he does not rely on public institutions, whether local or national. What he does is not challenged from without, either by the controlling state or legal limitations. His vision catches on and gains a following in the free marketplace of ideas. If people join in the farming project spontaneously and voluntarily, it is because they identify with the public-spirited attitude, and if equality of opportunities (equal access to healthy food) is their concern, they will make extensive use of their individual freedom and the free market to pursue their own ends, without the state interfering. This vision of social change begins at the grassroots level, and it is within the robust civil society that the hope for a better future is deposited. "Growing Power," the name of Allen's Milwaukee city farm, alludes to Will Allen's life philosophy. It is representative of liberal citizenship that places responsibility in the hands of individuals and seeks solutions to problems outside the purview of an interfering state (Schuck, 131–34). Yet some credit for Will's farming success goes to the red wriggler worms that turn garbage into compost. When the worms start dying, Will and his child-helpers work hard to ensure their survival by finding the best garbage diet. The mutual dependence of the farmer on the worms and of the worms on a steady supply of organic waste expands the traditional notion of liberal citizenship to include interspecies solidarity, a relationship which is subsumed under sustainable gardening and farming.

Whereas in *The Growing Table* it is one exceptional adult's initiative, know-how, and inventiveness that attracts neighbors of all ages, in DyAnne DiSalvo-Ryan's *City Green* social change comes out of a young black girl's and an old white woman's shared love of growing plants in coffee cans. When a building in their Philadelphia neighborhood is demolished, the girl Marcy and her friend, Miss Rosa, seize the opportunity to turn it into "one big coffee can." On the advice of a neighbor, they form a civic committee that goes to the city hall and follows the legal procedure of applying for a lot to cultivate a collective garden.

The text and images emphasize group agency rather than good leadership. Unlike in *The Growing Table*, where only one character, Will Allen, was named by the third-person narrator, in *City Green* the child-narrator, Marcy, names many of the characters and acknowledges their contribution to the gardening project. The setting of *City Green*, a single urban block, is already a neighborly place where community-minded neighbors know and visit each other or have contact in the street. One source of narrative tension is, of course, the problem of the derelict house, after whose demolition "this block now looks like a big smile with one tooth missing." The other is Old Man Hammer, a cantankerous widower who contests the garden project. As in the case with Uncle Jim in *The Gardener*, the question is whether Old Man Hammer can be brought into the neighborly fold and made happy again.

After successfully applying for the lot and paying a symbolic dollar for the lease, Marcy and her neighbors—retirees, mothers and fathers with children, a girl in a wheelchair, a nun—clear the land. They plant their seeds, picnicking in the reclaimed public space. Someone donates fence slats, someone else, bright paint. Eventually, even Old Man Hammer sneaks into the garden at night to plant his row of seeds by the back fence, a fact Marcy observes through her bedroom window.

As with *The Growing Table*, *City Green* ends with an appeal to the reader. In the latter book, the appeal takes the form of an instruction manual titled "Starting a Community Garden" written by the American Community Gardening Association.[9] A natural follow-up to Marcy's fictional success, it calls on young readers to "make something happen" in their real-life neighborhoods, to turn "ugly lots into beautiful gardens." This is followed by a six-step process that involves identifying the owner of a vacant lot, finding a city-run gardening program to navigate the initiative, getting permission for the use the lot and, if necessary, paying a small fee, and finally, appropriating the land for a community garden. What is striking when we compare this manual with Will Allen's letter is the emphasis on following legal procedures and respecting private property as prerequisites for any civic action. Whereas Will Allen, a model of liberal citizenship, builds up his enterprise without any reference to the noninterfering government, Marcy and her neighbors rely on the local government, which acts as a facilitator of change and protector of individual rights. In fact, throughout the picturebook the community garden project is framed in such a manner as to deliver on the promise inherent in the American creed: individual freedom, democratic participation, equal opportunities, and equal protection by law. Marcy may be the catalyst of the beautification project, but her neighbors equally commit and devote energy to the common endeavor. They are drawn together not only by attachment to place or the existing social capital, but also by the bonds of national identity. Committed to the common cause, they volunteer work and time. Even the individualistic Will Allen relies on an army of volunteers to bring to life his vision of the growing table. Republican citizenship is the force that binds the fictional gardening communities across the divides of race, gender, class, religion, and, most notably, age.

All the picturebooks discussed here highlight the interdependence of humans and the natural environment, for instance by showing how contact with nature can bring emotionally withdrawn characters back into the communal fold. Perhaps more interestingly, two of the books explore the theme of interspecies solidarity. Elliott's eponymous last tiger puts the inhabitants of the urban jungle back in touch with nature and with their natural, playful selves. Meanwhile, the red wriggler worms in *The Growing Table*, when properly nurtured, collaborate with Will Allen to fertilize the soil that allows him to grow food. But no less significantly, children's books on the theme of urban gardening serve as a vehicle for building intergenerational solidarity. While they highlight the child-protagonists' individual agency, they also show that urban gardening relies on the collective power deposited within the civil society. Liberal and republican citizenship coexist as sources of intergenerational solidarity needed to start and sustain gardens. Both rely on the vibrant civil society and on investments in social capital. Pursuing the agrarian ideal in the urban setting brings children and adults together, not necessarily in close relationships, but in a solidarity rooted in proximity, attachment to place, sidewalk encounters, and neighborly familiarity.

## NOTES

1. Elliott's picturebook, although published in the United Kingdom, is targeted at English-language audiences in general. Sold by American online bookstores, it has elicited a warm reader response in the United States.

2. Maria Nikolajeva's concept of aetonormativity relates to "adult normativity that governs the way children's literature has been patterned. [...] Nowhere else are power structures as visible as in children's literature, the refined instrument used for centuries to educate, socialize and oppress a particular social group. [...] Yet, paradoxically enough, children are allowed, in fiction written *by adults* and for the enlightenment and enjoyment of children, to become strong, brave, rich, powerful, and independent—on certain conditions and for a limited time" (*Power*, 8, 10).

3. Mechanical solidarity depends on a consensus of values, orientations, and norms, and as such dovetails with the consensual dimension of solidarity. See Maria Amparo Cruz-Saco, "Intergenerational Solidarity."

4. For a recent ecocritical discussion of the functions of the pastoral nature in children's literature, see Zoe Jaques's "'Tiny Dots of Cold Green': Pastoral Nostalgia and the State of Nature in Tove Jansson's *The Moomins and the Great Flood*."

5. "Interspecies solidarity" is a relatively new term related to a project of fostering human-animal relations, built on expanded empathy and understanding, recognition of animals' needs, desires, and their contribution to labor and economic processes, as well as an ethical concern in providing for their well-being. For more, see Kendra Coulter, *Animals, Work and the Promise of Interspecies Solidarity*.

6. Sociologist Roy Oldenburg defines third places as informal gathering places where individuals regularly meet on a neutral ground, where they "may come and go as they please, in which no one is required to play host, and in which we all feel at home and comfortable" (22). They are characterized by inclusiveness, social leveling, and conversation (28). Significantly, "a radically different kind of setting from the home, the third place is remarkably similar to a good home in the psychological comfort and support that it extends" (42).

7. Putnam's definition of social capital dovetails with Maria Amparo Cruz Saco's notion of intergenerational solidarity discussed in the editors' introduction to this volume. For more, see *Intergenerational Solidarity: Strengthening Economic and Social Ties* (2010).

8. I discuss community gardening as enhancing social capital and place-based solidarity in an article titled "Paul Fleischman's Seedfolks: Community Gardening and Urban Regeneration" and in *Regeneration, Citizenship, and Justice* (pp. 109–25). I argue that Fleischman's children's novella serves as an example of social interdependence embedded in Durkheim's notion of organic solidarity. The neighborhood garden is a proxy for the multicultural state, where the volunteer gardeners—strangers of different ages, ethnicities, and social backgrounds, newcomers and old-timers, immigrants and transient workers—use their diverse skills and cultural experiences to grow culturally appropriate food as long as their practices do not impinge on the liberty of other gardeners. The community garden is a microcosm of the nation-state, while

the local community, bound by a shared sense of place and emotional attachments, serves as the building block of solidarity on the level of the larger society.

9. On the copyright page, DiSalvo-Ryan acknowledges the help of American Community Gardening Association, among others, informing readers that "a portion of the author's royalties will be donated" to the organization. Thus, she is making a statement about her book's political agenda. Philadelphia was one of the first American cities to foster community gardening initiatives, and, as such was featured in the documentary series Edens Lost & Found titled "Philadelphia: A Holy Experiment" (dir. Hary Wiland, 2006).

## WORKS CITED

Billig, Michael. *Banal Nationalism*. Sage Publications, 1995.
Coulter, Kendra. *Animals, Work and the Promise of Interspecies Solidarity*. Palgrave Macmillan, 2016.
Cruz-Saco, María Amparo. "Intergenerational Solidarity." In *Intergenerational Solidarity: Strengthening Economic and Social Ties*, eds. María Amparo Cruz-Saco and Sergei Zelenev, 9–34. Palgrave Macmillan, 2010.
Dagger, Richard. "Republican Citizenship." In *Handbook of Citizenship Studies*, eds. Engin F. Isin and Bryan S. Turner, 145–57. Sage Publications, 2002.
de Tocqueville, Alexis. *Democracy in America* and *Two Essays on America*. 1835/1840. Trans. Gerald E. Bevan, introduction and notes by Isaac Kramnic. Penguin Books, 2003.
DiSalvo-Ryan, DyAnne. *City Green*. Morrow Junior Books, 1994.
Durkheim, Émile. *The Division of Labor*. 1893. Trans. W. D. Halls. Palgrave Macmillan, 2013.
Dybska, Aneta. "Paul Fleischman's *Seedfolks*: Community Gardening and Urban Regeneration." *Polish Journal for American Studies* 8 (2014): 167–80.
Dybska, Aneta. *Regeneration, Citizenship, and Justice in the American City since the 1970s*. Peter Lang, 2016.
Elliott, Rebecca, *The Last Tiger*. Lion Children's Books, 2012.
Fleischman, Paul. *Seedfolks*. Harper Trophy, 1997.
Hannerz, Ulf. *Transnational Connections: Culture, People, Places*. Routledge, 2016.
Jacobs, Jane. *The Death and Life of Great American Cities*. 1961. Vintage Books, 1992.
Jaques, Zoe. "'Tiny Dots of Cold Green': Pastoral Nostalgia and the State of Nature in Tove Jansson's *The Moomins and the Great Flood*." *The Lion and the Unicorn* 38, no. 2 (2014): 200–216. Project MUSE, doi:10.1353/uni.2014.0015.
Jefferson, Thomas. "Query XIX." Notes on the State of Virginia," 1787. xroads.virginia.edu/~HYPER/JEFFERSON/ch19.html. Accessed March 3, 2018.
Kieran, Allen, and Brian O'Boyle. *Durkheim: A Critical Introduction*. Pluto Press, 2017.
Lefebvre, Henri. *The Production of Space*. 1974. Trans. Donald Nicholson-Smith. Blackwell, 1991.
Lieven, Anatol. *American Right or Wrong: An Anatomy of American Nationalism*. Oxford University Press, 2004.
Lukes Steven. Introduction. *The Division of Labor*, by Emile Durkheim. 1893. Trans. W. D. Halls. Palgrave Macmillan, 2013, xxv–xlvi.
Martin, Jacqueline Briggs. *Farmer Will Allen and the Growing Table*. Illus. Eric-Shabazz Larkin. Readers to Eaters, 2013.
Marx, Leo. *The Machine in the Garden: Technology and the Pastoral Ideal in America*. 1964. Oxford University Press, 2000.

Myrdal, Gunnar. *An American Dilemma. The Negro Problem and Modern Democracy*. 1944. Harper & Row, 1962.
Nikolajeva, Maria, *Power, Voice and Subjectivity in Literature for Young Readers*. Routledge, 2010.
Oldenburg, Roy. *The Great Good Place: Cafes, Coffee Shops, Bookstores, Bars, Hair Salons, and Other Hangouts at the Heart of a Community*. 1989. Marlowe & Company, 1999.
Putnam, Robert D. *Bowling Alone: The Collapse and Revival of American Community*. Simon & Schuster, 2000.
Scholz, Sally J. *Political Solidarity*. Pennsylvania State University, 2008.
Schuck, Peter H. "Liberal Citizenship." In *Handbook of Citizenship Studies*, eds. Engin F. Isin and Bryan S. Turner, 131–44. Sage Publications, 2002.
Simmel, Georg. "The Metropolis and Mental Life." 1903. In *The Blackwell City Reader*, eds. Gary Bridge and Sophie Watson, 11–19. Wiley-Blackwell, 2002.
Smith, Anthony D. *National Identity*. Penguin Books, 1991.
Stewart, Sarah. *The Gardener*. Illus. David Small. Farrar Straus Giroux, 1997.

# PART FIVE
## REWRITING AETONORMATIVITY WITH YOUNG READERS

# 14

# THE "LYNX-EYED SAGACITY" OF THE "SCHOOLBOY"

## WILLIAM GODWIN AND THE JUVENILE LIBRARY (1805-1825)

Malini Roy

> I am accustomed to consult my children, in this humble species of writing in which I have engaged: I placed the two or three first sections of this work in their hands, as a specimen; their remark was, *How easy this is! Why! we learn it by heart, almost as fast as we read it!* Their suffrage gave me courage, and I carried on my work to the end.
> (William Godwin, preface, *History of England*, v–vi)

William Godwin, author of the foundational treatise of philosophical anarchism, *Enquiry Concerning Political Justice* (1793), as well as a number of novels, plays, and pedagogical and journalistic writings, also wrote books for children of schoolgoing age.[1] These books were brought out through the "City French and English Juvenile and School Library" (1805–1825), a small publishing-cum-bookselling enterprise in London that Godwin ran with his second wife, Mary Jane Godwin (St. Clair, *Godwins and Shelleys*, 284–87; Clemit, "William Godwin's Juvenile Library").[2] Godwin's *History of England* (1806), presented under the pseudonym Edward Baldwin, affirms the collaborative creation of the book with the participation of his five children—one of these being the future writer Mary Shelley. In Godwin's arch self-deprecation of "this humble species of writing," his admission that he was "accustomed to consult" his children, while he intended to persuade potential (adult) customers of the utility of the book, may come across as a shared wink of condescension towards mere children. But his positioning of the noun "suffrage" is also arresting, given its resonance of political enfranchisement, a topic whose implications he had discussed at some length in *Political Justice*. The term "suffrage" also invokes the older sense of intercessory prayers in liturgical practice, bearing the secular import of the children's endorsement of the book before its release into the market (*PPWG* 3, 226–27; *Oxford Dictionaries*).[3] In both these senses, Godwin's declaration exemplifies a relationship of "generous reciprocity" between adults and children, which he had envisaged as an ideal pedagogical state in the essay "Of Choice in Reading" in the collection, *The Enquirer* (1797) (*PPWG* 5, 136). This relationship appears to be confirmed by another of Godwin's first child readers, his stepdaughter Claire Clairmont. According to Claire, "[a]ll the family worked hard, learning and studying: we all took the liveliest interest in the great questions of the day" (Claire Clairmont, *Clairmont Correspondence* 2, 617–18). In Clairmont's reminiscence of her childhood home, the Godwin family life seems to have been lived in perpetual performance of a platonic dialogue shared cordially between children and adults. Moreover, the Godwin family used to live on the floor just above the bookshop. The family atmosphere may well have exemplified, in Clairmont's account, that of the bookshop, which used to double up, in Godwin scholar Pamela Clemit's accurate phrasing, as an "intellectual salon": a run-off of the eighteenth-century English traditions of cultivated sociability ("William Godwin's Juvenile Library" 90). This chapter demonstrates that in envisioning his children as muses and editors of his Juvenile Library books, Godwin's texts propose a similar process of intergenerational dialogue with the children who comprised his initial audience, and whose feedback shaped what he offered to the public at large.[4] This chapter investigates the characteristics and complexities of this dialogue, arguing that Godwin's endeavor to cultivate a relationship of "reciprocity" with his child readers is pioneering as an attempt at cross-generational solidarity, if it is less than entirely "generous" in nature.

## "INSIDIOUS AND DANGEROUS"

Godwin's adoption of the pseudonym "Edward Baldwin"—along with his other pseudonyms "Theophilus Marcliffe" and "William Scolfield"—was not exactly a matter of choice (St. Clair, *Godwins and Shelleys*, 279, 285–87).[5] The Juvenile Library was poised upon political quicksand: Godwin was known to many as the author who had animadverted against the very existence of the State and its authority in *Political Justice*, a book that he himself would later characterize as the "child of the French Revolution" (*PPWG* 2, 163–65).[6] Unsurprisingly, Godwin was subject to the backlash against British Jacobins who had supported the revolution by the government headed by Prime Minister William Pitt the Younger, in the wake of fears of a similar revolutionary upsurge in England and the opening of war against France in 1793; the so-called Pitt's Terror had broiled into the era of the Napoleonic Wars (1803–1815) (St. Clair, *Godwins and Shelleys*, 192; Hilton, 66–74, 87–213). Pamela Clemit has unearthed a crucial piece of evidence that points to the frisson generated by the Juvenile Library books, in the form of the report of a spy for the Home Office in 1813, entitled "A few particulars concerning Godwin's Juvenile Library which ought to be made generally known." The spy was worried that Godwin was fomenting "every" egalitarian "principle professed by the infidels and republicans of these days" by selling books, moderately priced within the range of a few shillings to a few pence, that were produced to "allure schools of a moderate and lower class."[7] The report appears to image Godwin as a spider at the center of a printing web: "it is very little known that the proprietor is *Godwin*, the author of *Political Justice*" (italics in original); he was spinning "a regular system through all his publications to supersede all other" books in schools, offering an alternative to the previous books favored by schoolteachers and possibly parents (quoted in "William Godwin's Juvenile Library," 90–91).

Despite the spy's purple imagery, the Juvenile Library books do not appear to have struck all customers as products on the radical fringe. In fact, as Robert Anderson has astutely noted, a number of the books "were even purchased by members of the royal family" (130). The jackets of the books were often embellished with appreciative reviews from leading periodicals, including those located at the opposite end of the political spectrum. In the list of "New Books for Children" in the *Life of Lady Jane Grey*, for instance, one finds an advertisement inserted for *Fables, Ancient and Modern* by Edward Baldwin, with a review comment from *The Anti-Jacobin Review and Magazine*: "They are unquestionably written" for "making an impression on, and conveying instruction to, those for whose use they are designed." That the Juvenile Library books were meant to appeal—for the sake of business—to a common denominator of tastes can be gleaned textually from *Life of Lady Jane Grey*, written by Godwin's nom de plume "Theophilus Marcliffe," which I will discuss later in this chapter. This book centers on the tragic history of the Tudor noblewoman who was persuaded, through a political conspiracy hatched by her uncle John Dudley, the Duke of Northumberland, to become the "Nine Days Queen of England" in 1554, in contravention of the stronger claims of the princesses Mary and Elizabeth (later Mary I and Elizabeth I, respectively). Godwin begins by pointing to Lady Jane as a role model for girls: she "is the most perfect model of a meritorious young creature of the female sex, to be found in history" (v–vi). His panegyric to Lady Jane as a learned woman possibly recalls his first wife Mary Wollstonecraft's clarion call for women to be educated in the same way as men, to "have power," as she had said, "over themselves" (138). However, Godwin also forestalls a misogynistic parody of his protagonist as an eighteenth-century bluestocking by emphasizing that Lady Jane did not "fall into any neglect of those more useful and ornamental arts, which are peculiarly to be desired in the female sex" (8–9). These "arts," Godwin elaborates, comprise "needle-works," "various instruments of music," and singing in a "voice peculiarly sweet." Godwin offers here a list of skills close to the clichéd ladylike "accomplishments" (*Jane Grey*, 9) gently mocked by Jane Austen in *Pride and Prejudice*, where Bingley is astonished at the young ladies who "all paint tables, cover skreens [sic] and net purses" (Austen, 28).

The growing body of critical studies on Godwin's Juvenile Library books has tended to appreciate the Juvenile Library books as a development of Godwin's radical political thought and liberal pedagogies in the 1790s. According to William St. Clair, Godwin worked "quietly away at influencing the next generation"—child readers who would eventually grow into adults (*Godwins and Shelleys*, 283; "William Godwin," 165–81).[8] Pamela Clemit's approach shows that Godwin's subversive politics often lies in the books' "formal strategies, designed to foster the moral autonomy of the child reader," who is not dictated an interpretation of the text by the author, but given the freedom to choose ("William Godwin's Juvenile Library," 92).[9] However, given the mixed messages of these books, if we can take the example above from *Jane Grey* as representative, my approach comes closest to that of Robert Anderson, which is alive to "the moral complexity and ambiguity" in these books (126). According to Anderson, the content reveals "authoritarian tendencies" as well as liberal messages; critical approaches that interpret these books as a continuation of Godwin's radical agenda also "tend to gloss over the contradictions" (126, 142).

In view of this broad critical consensus on the politically radical elements within the Juvenile Library books, I would suggest that perhaps the most important reason for the perception of these books as inflammatory by some of Godwin's contemporaries lies in their attempt at cultivating at the dialogic relationship of "reciprocity" with child readers that I have indicated at the beginning of this chapter.[10] This aspect appears to have been overlooked in the otherwise excellent studies of the Juvenile Library books, seemingly focused on authorial intent and predicated upon a rather hazy notion of a (universalized and essentialized) child reader. While the notion of a generic child reader becomes difficult to abandon altogether as a cognitive category in serving as a useful locus of distinction from adult readers—and will not, therefore, be jettisoned altogether in this chapter—I would assert that Godwin's dialogue with his child readers, as compared to his adult readers, can reveal some surprising turns of "reciprocity."

Here, let me first recapitulate Godwin's reflections on the activity of reading in the essay-collection *The Enquirer*, which appear to be extraordinarily prescient of twentieth-century reader-response theory. In the essay "Of Learning," he asserts that the ideal reader "will have a greater number of ideas that are passing through his mind, than of ideas presented to him by his author" (*PPWG*, 5, 237). Most significantly for the present discussion, Godwin's ascription of agency to the reader applies equally to the child reader. In the essay "Of Choice in Reading," the educator ought to allow the child reader, at least "in some instances," "to select his own course of reading." "Suffer him," enjoins Godwin, "to wander in the wilds of literature" (*PPWG*, 5 142). As Susan Manly's investigation of the Juvenile Library books has revealed, a number of contemporary reviewers of *The Enquirer* took exception to Godwin's ideal of the child's uncensored, active, and creative reading: "the *Critical Review*, *Monthly Review* and the *British Critic* all expressed reservations" (138).

Manly has made a singularly productive identification of the controversial and iconoclastic portent of Godwin's advocacy of free reading for the child. Like the reviewers, the spy seems to have found Edward Baldwin's *The Pantheon* to be "an insidious and dangerous publication," on the grounds of a careful reading of the text. Following a preface that "professes to exalt the purity and show the superiority of Christianity over the heathen morality taught in the Grecian and Roman mythology," the book's content, according to him, "improperly excites the curiosity of young persons to read the grossest stories on the subject, and artfully hints the wisdom of the morality of the heathen world" (Clemit, "William Godwin's Juvenile Library," 91). The fact that Godwin attempted to address "young persons" who "read" his books "artfully" rattled the spy, who, I would posit, had hit the bull's eye without knowing it. In *The Enquirer*, Godwin generally seconds the child as "an individual being, with powers of reasoning, with sensations of pleasure and pain, and with principles of morality" (*PPWG*, 5, 119). He argues therefore that the child "has a claim upon his little sphere of empire and discretion; and he is entitled to his appropriate portion of independence." However, that "sphere," he notes, is also "little," while he regulates the quantity of "independence" to that merely "appropriate" (*PPWG*, 5, 119). Godwin's counter-impulse to control the child, even while claiming human subjectivity for the latter, springs, probably, from his adult imperative to socialize the child. In the Juvenile Library books, Godwin's urge to contain the child from his position as a caregiver becomes especially evident if one compares them with the nearly contemporaneous novel *Fleetwood* (1805), which features several representations of the child for adult readers' consumption. Reading can be shown to be an activity that controls the child reader benevolently in *Jane Grey*. Contrapuntally, given Godwin's recognition—and, indeed, sanction—of the child as an "individual being," Godwin's preface to Edward Baldwin's *Fables* (1805) also states: "If we would benefit a child, we must become in part a child ourselves. We must prattle to him; we must expatiate upon some points; we must introduce quick, unexpected turns, which, if they are not wit, have the effect of wit to children" (iii–iv). Here, Godwin seems to accept that the expectations of child readers may be different from those of adults. The child's short attention span requires continual coaxing through "quick, unexpected turns" in Godwin's attempt to connect with his readers in the venture of telling stories, despite his rather patronizing adult's stance in the contention that children understand but the "effect of wit" (*Fables*, iii–iv). The adult author's always already doomed attempt to "become a child" appears to be only ever "in part" successful; the child may well recognize the imitated product. I would suggest that Godwin's cognizance of the "child" as an other, coupled with the need of "consulting" his children that he mentions in the preface to *History of England*, forms the locus for a liberatory agenda for child readers. This agenda can be read as a valiant proto-intergenerational act that might hoodwink the regulatory imperatives of his adult book buyers. As I will demonstrate in *Jane Grey*, Godwin achieves this goal by building in rhetorical procedures that undermine the text's own impulse to control the child reader, allowing multiple ways of reading by children. These children may be individually different, a fact Godwin knew well, if we are to trust the voice of the protagonist in *St. Leon* (1799): "One exquisite source of gratification, when it is not a source of uneasiness, to speak from my own experience, which a parent finds in the society of his children, is their individuality" (*CNMWG*, 4, 114–15).[11] In fact, as I will show, Godwin presents certain passages that foreground, provocatively, multiple ways of reading these texts. Godwin's passages radically demonstrate the varied possible meanings embedded within rather than, as Clemit has argued, straightforwardly and unambiguously "foster[ing] the moral autonomy" of the child reader ("William Godwin's Juvenile Library," 92).

## THE CHILD READER AND THE CHILD READ

In *Jane Grey*, when the rightful heir Mary I ascends the throne of England, Lady Jane is convicted of high treason—a circumstance hinting at Pitt's Terror—and is finally "beheaded in the Tower" of London, "in the Seventeenth

Year of her Age," as announced in Godwin's epigraph on the title page. If the mention of Lady Jane's youth deploys affect in order to intrigue the interest of school-aged readers by rousing empathetic identification, Godwin pursues his advantage by showing that scholastic skills form the very bedrock of his protagonist's selfhood. Lady Jane is not "fortunate in her parents," the Marquis and Marchioness of Dorset, who perform their parental roles as per the norms of stereotypically wealthy and disengaged aristocrats (3). They are "desirous" that their child "should be accomplished, but they did not know the best way of going about it," and the best they can do is to "procure" her a set of "instructors and masters" to do their bidding (3). Godwin narrates an account of a day in Lady Jane's life at the age of thirteen. This, he says, is related in "a book, entitled the Schoolmaster" by the scholar Roger Ascham, tutor to "the princess Elizabeth" (later Elizabeth I), which Ascham wrote to illustrate that "love" is more effective than "fear" as a pedagogical method (*Jane Grey*, 16; Ascham, 39).[12] Quoting nearly verbatim from Ascham's account, Godwin offers an endearing portrayal of inter-age friendship in narrating a visit by Ascham to his "lovely young friend" Lady Jane before departing for a trip to Germany (12). At this time, Lady Jane's parents are outdoors, living up to their assigned roles—from Godwin's middle-class perspective—as decadent aristocrats in the epicurean pursuit of fox hunting. Meanwhile, Lady Jane stays in her own apartment—a "divine virgin diligently studying the divine Phædon of the divine Plato in the original Greek"—as Ascham gushes later, in a letter written from his Continental travels to Lady Jane herself (18). At the time of Ascham's visit, however, Lady Jane, rather less impressed by herself, explains that her addiction to books forms a bulwark against her emotionally neglectful family; "in presence either of father or mother," every action of hers must be performed "perfectly," otherwise she is "so sharply taunted, so cruelly threatened, yea presently sometimes with pinches, nips, and bobs" (12–16). In contrast to her hypercritical parents, her tutor, John Aylmer, compensates through an affectionate pedagogy structured "so gently, so pleasantly, with such fair allurements to learning" that she reports: "[W]hatsoever I do but learning, is full of grief, trouble, fear, and wholly misliking unto me. And thus my book hath been so much my pleasure, and bringeth daily to me more pleasure and more" (14).

Perhaps there is an element of self-staging in Lady Jane's retreat to her "book" as an alternative pastoral to the sylvan space of the fox hunt. As biographer Eric Ives has noted, this retreat "looks like teenage rebellion" (52). This episode, however, also shows an adolescent insisting doggedly that "learning" forms a substitute for emotional deprivation. Perhaps the lady doth protest too much? Godwin offers an exegesis: "This little story, thus simply told by this admirable child, affords a striking example, how wrong that system of education is, which treats a free and apt disposition with severity, and, as it were, applies the whip and spur to that horse which, from the prompting of his own nature, would go as fast as any master ought to desire him" (15–16). In pointing to the child's "free and apt disposition," the obtrusive narrator appears to transpose Godwin's advocacy in *The Enquirer* of the child's free choice in reading. Oddly, however, he compares the child to a horse, whose "own nature" is apparently already keen to perform the master's "desire." Lady Jane's sublimated rebellion is not seriously likely to displease her parents, who have in any case wished to make her "accomplished" (3). The horse's willingness to perform the master's bidding without "severity," at this instant, begins to feel a tad more troubling than the fictive representations of reading children, which as Matthew Grenby has observed, were common to portraits, novels, and children's books of the era. These representations, according to Grenby, served a "highly didactic purpose": while "children were being encouraged" to value their books, "adults were slyly being educated in their book-buying and usage duties too" (18–19).

Reading thus works as a safety valve for the child's rebellious feelings in *Jane Grey*. This becomes clear if we compare Godwin's portrait of a child in the novel *Fleetwood*, who is faced with a situation of (admittedly much greater) oppression. The character Ruffigny, a friend of the protagonist Fleetwood's father, is orphaned. He is tricked by his supposed guardian, an evil uncle, into joining the silk mills of Lyons in France. This narrative circumstance enables Godwin to direct the adult reader's attention towards the dehumanizing phenomenon of child labor, prevalent in the textile industries of England as well in the early years of the Industrial Revolution (Hilton, 5). Prefiguring the concept of what we would now understand to be children's rights, Ruffigny's retrospective narration satirically relates the claim of the character Vaublanc, a figure in cahoots with his uncle, that Vaublanc's "town is a perfect paradise." The child laborers, barely "four years of age" or even younger, comprise horrifyingly efficient worker ants; they "are quiet, and orderly, and attentive, and industrious." In contrast to Vaublanc's optimistic portrait, Ruffigny draws his reader into commiseration with the children's deformed bodies and the "stupid and hopeless vacancy in every face" (*CNMWG*, 5, 89). Ruffigny's description, in a degree of searing detail almost Dickensian in intensity, underlines that the mechanized rituals of factory work affront the very being of children. In an echo of philosopher John Locke's notion of the infant's mind as a blank slate or tabula rasa, Ruffigny declaims that "[t]he mind of a child is essentially independent; he does not, till he has been formed to it by hard experience, frame to himself the ideas of authority and subjection" (*CNMWG*, 5, 89–90). The child's mind, therefore, seems to have no innate notion of authority, except as a product of the social conditioning of "hard experience." Ruffigny observes further: "The mind of a child is no less vagrant than his steps; it pursues the gossamer, and flies from object to object, lawless and unconfined: and it is equally necessary to the development of his frame, that his thoughts and his body should be free from fetters" (*CNMWG*, 5, 89–90). The child's mental freedom finds a corporeal correlate, as Ruffigny eventually escapes the drudgery at the silk mills to become a "vagrant." His "steps" grow "lawless and unconfined" as he takes to the road. Despite being a child, he becomes something of the picaresque hero in eighteenth-century novels—a role usually reserved for adult protagonists—as he encounters various episodic adventures (even getting robbed once), perhaps reflecting Godwin's reading of Henry Fielding's *The History of Tom Jones, A Foundling* (1749) a few years before the composition of *Fleetwood* ("William Godwin's Diary").[13] Ruffigny also becomes "a friendless outcast and an exile," and concludes: "I belonged to no one" (*CNMWG*, 5, 93, 107). Ruffigny's escape from an oppressive environment may be said to embody Godwin's uninhibited expression of the child's autonomy for adult readers, but this autonomy appears to get compromised when he addresses child readers in *Jane Grey*. Indeed, when Godwin's own daughter, Mary Shelley, ran away from home with his intellectual protégé, Percy Bysshe Shelley, with Claire Clairmont in tow in the summer of 1814, Godwin felt utterly scandalized (St. Clair, *Godwins and Shelleys*, 362–63).

However, Godwin also appears to build in rhetorical procedures within *Jane Grey* that enable the relinquishing of adult control. This can be seen, in *Jane Grey*, in Godwin's strikingly elaborate description of the physical circumstances of Lady Jane's imprisonment, which almost feels supernumerary for the sake of plot development. The conditions of a prison, Godwin begins, "are what no one," generally, and "not a prisoner" specifically "would desire." "Persons committed to a fortress for imputed crimes against the state" have at least three watch guards in close proximity, and besides, "[a] guard sleeps in their chamber." Moreover, if the prisoners are let into the open air for short walks, "a gentleman-jailor (as he is called) walks close behind them, to observe their motions, and overhear their words." Further on, he continues:

> A prison is a dreary abode, and, if the prisoners desire any amusement, they must apply for leave to have a book, a pen, or paper, which is sometimes granted, and oftener refused. Every thing depends upon the caprice of their superintendents, who are seldom indisposed to make those who are under government feel their power. The prisoner is rarely permitted to see his friends, rarely even (perhaps once a week, if he is particularly favoured) his nearest relations. The husband is not left alone with his wife, nor the father with his child. (71–74)

On one level, this passage may simply draw the child reader to sympathize with Lady Jane as a young prisoner tipped onto the wrong political bandwagon by older family members. However, in showing how the prisoners are brutalized through incessant surveillance mentally, if not through physical torture, Godwin's description echoes his own arguments for free speech during Pitt's Terror. In a letter written to the *Morning Chronicle*, "Liberty," Godwin had asserted, "consists in delivering us from the empire of spies and informers in not subjecting to us to perpetual watchfulness and reserve" (*PPWG*, 2, 24–26). In hindsight, Godwin's passage from *Jane Grey* almost certainly recalls his visits to radical friends and associates in Newgate Prison in 1793, especially if we consider Godwin scholar Jon Mee's persuasive claim, based upon documents of the period, that "Government repression" was often pictured by the radical camps as "an invasion of privacy" (Mee, 148–49, 155–56). Certainly, Godwin's ruminations on the operation of power through mechanisms of omniscient visibility anticipates Michel Foucault's much later reflections in *Discipline and Punish* (1975) on the "the major effect of the Panopticon" designed by Jeremy Bentham, which "induc[es] in the inmate a state of conscious and permanent visibility that assumes the automatic functioning of power" (201). Godwin's rhetorical sleight of hand, however, leaves it to his child reader to decipher any possible connection between the hoary past and current political realities without saying so.

In contrast to such nebulous messages in *Jane Grey*, *Fleetwood* appears to work on a more forthright moral division between the fallen adult world and the prelapsarian world of the child, where the represented child's voice serves an oracular function. Ruffigny's uncle, addressing his charge as "a very perverse and wicked boy," insults his intelligence in claiming that "you do not know what is good for you, and must trust to the better discernment of your elders" (*CNMWG*, 5, 82). Ruffigny knows very well that the supposed "elders" are abusing his "trust"; their "better discernment" is nothing but mere "cant" that he has "incessantly heard" (*CNMWG*, 5, 49). The child's desire for moral clarity is doubled in a more satirical vein elsewhere. In remembering his schoolboy years, the protagonist Fleetwood remarks that when "boys grow up to be men, the dullard will frequently play his part to the great satisfaction of the spectators; and not only outstrip his more ingenious competitor in the road of fortune, but even be more highly esteemed, and more respectfully spoken of, by the majority of those who know him" (*CNMWG*, 5, 49). Here, Godwin's *theatrum mundi* of the adult world of the "dullard" and his rapt spectators appears to be little removed from the world of realpolitik, whereas Fleetwood elaborates that the dullard's reign is one that "lynx-eyed sagacity and frolic malice of schoolboy against schoolboy are sure to discover and expose" (*CNMWG*, 5, 49).

In counterpoint, the ethical landscape of *Jane Grey* appears to be relatively polychromatic. Godwin describes the boy king, Edward VI, being visited occasionally by his half-sibling Princess Elizabeth (the future Queen Elizabeth I) and their cousin Lady Jane, depicting relative concord between the three children. Explaining the social dynamics in this group, Godwin characterizes Elizabeth as being "distinguished for her talents and literary turn," drawing perhaps upon Ascham's description of her "excellency of learning and knowledge of divers tongues" (*Jane Grey*, 6–8; Ascham, 66). However, the "young king," Edward VI, Godwin continues,

> gave her the good-humoured nick-name of his *Lady Temper*. It is a little difficult to know what Edward VI meant by this name. Was it given in allusion to the sagacity she possessed beyond her years, and the prudence and propriety which, as they marked all her actions in the sad period of her adversity, may be supposed to have discovered themselves even now? Or, is it possible, as Elizabeth when queen of England, though she was the most extraordinary and deep-judging of her sex, showed herself occasionally a woman of very violent passions, that she teased her poor brother thus early with the quickness of her resentments, and the tartness of her replies? (6–8)

Here, Godwin offers two possible interpretations of the teasing nickname "Lady Temper." The first possible "allusion," however, is an absurd match for Elizabeth's "sagacity" or "prudence and propriety." With the rhetorical question beginning with "is it possible," Godwin directs the child reader towards the more likely answer: the "quickness of her resentments, and the tartness of her replies." Godwin thus mottles the aura of the Virgin Queen. However, more than Godwin's anti-monarchical jibe at Elizabeth's "violent passions," the text's self-reflexive demonstration of the different ways in which a text can be read is what, I would argue, makes Godwin's address to child readers truly radical. As Manly has noted, the conservative philanthropist Sarah Trimmer criticized Godwin's *Bible Stories* for not "*bringing every thought into captivity to the obedience of* CHRIST" (*Guardian of Education* I, 247–48; quoted in Manly, 138). Godwin, on the other hand, disrupts any pretense to a feudal ethos of "obedience" towards God, Church, or King, positioned in vertical relationships of higher authority. Instead, he insinuates coyly to the child reader that the text—or, indeed, the world outside the text—might be "a little difficult to know" (*Jane Grey*, 6–8).

In Lewis Carroll's *Through the Looking-Glass* (1872), Alice asks the character Humpty Dumpty "whether you can make words mean different things" (186), anticipating the theoretical concerns of twentieth-century post-Saussurean linguists. Godwin's hint in *Jane Grey* seems to pave the way for Alice's question.

The allusive quality of Godwin's dialogic addresses to child readers, in contrast to the monovalent bent of the child he represents for adult readers in *Fleetwood*, advocates the radical potential of reading, permitting an intergenerational bond between adult author and the child editor or reader that can be said to escape the usual confines of parenting, formal education, and even Romantic-era ideologies of childhood.

## NOTES

1. Unfortunately, most of the books authored by Godwin are not available in quality print editions today. Some are found in special collections of early printed books, some have been digitized, and others have been reissued in the form of facsimile reprints. For details of titles published, please see the Works Cited. The pagination of the Juvenile Library books I have cited here reflects my consultation of print copies at Bodleian Library in Oxford, UK, and the Baldwin Library of Historical Children's Literature, Gainesville, Florida. I would like to thank the Children's Literature Association for a research grant in 2012 that enabled me to examine the Juvenile Library books at length in the Bodleian Library.

2. See Clemit, 93. The shop was first registered in the name of the manager Thomas Hodgkins, who was later dismissed for stealing money. See also Clemit, "Philosophical Anarchism," 44.

3. I am using the abbreviation *PPWG* for the standard critical edition *Political and Philosophical Writings of William Godwin* in seven volumes, with Mark Philp as general editor. The respective volume number is inserted in the parenthetical citation.

4. This is, however, not an archival study of traces of the reception of Godwin's book by his own children or by child readers at large, of the kind that Matthew Grenby has memorably performed in *The Child Reader* (2011): this would be a fruitful line of inquiry but is beyond the scope of the present essay, which emphasizes nuances within Godwin's own texts.

5. William St. Clair discovered that Godwin had used the pseudonym "William Scolfield" for *Bible Stories* (1802), which he wrote for the publisher Richard Phillips.

6. Godwin's reference to the French Revolution can be found in "Thoughts occasioned by the perusal of Dr. Parr's Spital Sermon, preached at Christ Church, April, 15, 1800: being a reply to the attacks of Dr. Parr, Mr. Mackintosh, The Author of an Essay on Population, and others."

7. These prices can be found on the jackets of each Juvenile Library book: *Jane Grey*, for instance, features a long list of "New Books for Children" at the back with respective prices.

8. For earlier studies of the books in terms of publishing history, see Margaret Kinnell, "Childhood and Children's Literature," and Brian Alderson, "'Mister Gobwin' and His "Interesting Little Books.'"

9. Janet Bottoms, in "'Awakening the Mind,'" reveals continuity between Godwin's liberal pedagogical philosophy in *The Enquirer* and his Juvenile Library books by "Edward Baldwin." Susan Manly's treatment sharpens the political edge in perceiving these books as a development of Godwin's "earlier work on the subject of treason, sedition, and the censorship of free thought and discussion" (135). Suzanne L. Barnett and Katherine Bennett Gustafson's introductory essay to their scholarly digitized edition of Godwin's *Fables*, in *New Romantic Circles*, emphasizes the personal touch to Godwin's experience as a "parent and social reformer," who "was keenly aware of the pedagogical needs of young readers and of the insufficiency of the books available to them." I am very grateful to John-Erik Hansson for having allowed me a

preview of his essay on the Juvenile Library books in a forthcoming collection, *Romanticism and the Cultures of Infancy*, edited by Cian Duffy and Martina Domines Veliki. Hansson's essay illuminates Godwin's politically progressive stance in his histories compared to other children's histories in his era.

10. For an approach that does not perceive the Juvenile Library books as distinctively political, see Matthew Grenby, "Politicizing the Nursery."

11. I am using the abbreviation *CNMWG* for the standard critical edition *Collected Novels and Memoirs of William Godwin* in eight volumes, with Mark Philp as general editor. The respective volume number is inserted in the parenthetical citation.

12. Ascham's *The Schoolmaster* is available on the website Internet Archive, albeit with spelling modernized to a certain extent.

13. This is noted in the diary on December 20, 1796 (Godwin's entries are usually very short).

## WORKS CITED

Alderson, Brian. "'Mister Gobwin' and His 'Interesting Little Books, Adorned with Beautiful Copper Plates.'" *Princeton University Library Chronicle* 59 (1998): 159–89.

Anderson, Robert. "Godwin Disguised: Politics in the Juvenile Library." In *Godwinian Moments: From the Enlightenment to Romanticism*, eds. Robert M. Maniquis and Victoria Myers, 125–46. University of Toronto Press, 2011.

Ascham, Roger. *The Schoolmaster* (*The Scholemaster*). 1570. Cassell, 1909. Internet Archive, https://archive.org/details/schoolmasterooaschuoft. Accessed December 22, 2017.

Austen, Jane. *Pride and Prejudice*, ed. James Kinsley. Oxford University Press, 2004.

Bottoms, Janet. "'Awakening the Mind': The Educational Philosophy of William Godwin." *History of Education* 3, no. 33 (2004): 267–82.

Carroll, Lewis [Charles Lutwidge Dodgson]. *The Complete Illustrated Lewis Carroll*. Wordsworth Editions, 2008.

Clairmont, Claire, Charles Clairmont, and Fanny Imlay Godwin. *The Clairmont Correspondence: Letters of Claire Clairmont, Charles Clairmont, and Fanny Imlay Godwin*, vol. 2, ed. Marion King Stocking. Johns Hopkins University Press, 1995.

Clemit, Pamela. "Philosophical Anarchism in the Schoolroom: William Godwin' s Juvenile Library, 1805–25." *Biblion: The Bulletin of the New York Public Library* 9 (2000–2001): 44–70.

Clemit, Pamela. "William Godwin's Juvenile Library." *Charles Lamb Bulletin*, no. 147 (2009): 90–99.

Foucault, Michel. *Discipline and Punish: The Birth of the Prison*. Revised ed., 1977. Trans. Alan Sheridan. Vintage, 1995.

Godwin, William. *Collected Novels and Memoirs of William Godwin*, 8 vols., ed. Mark Philp. William Pickering, 1992.

Godwin, William. [Edward Baldwin]. *Fables, Ancient and Modern, Adapted for the Use of Children*, ed. David L. Greene. Juvenile Library, 1805. Garland, 1976.

Godwin, William. [Edward Baldwin]. *The History of England, for the Use of Schools and Young Persons*. Juvenile Library, 1806. Revised ed., London, 1854.

Godwin, William. [Edward Baldwin]. *History of Greece: From the Earliest Records of That Country, to the Time in Which it was Reduced into a Roman Province. Illustrated with Maps and Portraits*. Juvenile Library, 1822. *History of Greece by William*

*Godwin*, http://curi.us/files/History-of-Greece-William-Godwin.pdf. Accessed March 28, 2018.

Godwin, William. [Edward Baldwin]. *History of Rome: From the Building of the City to the Ruin of the Republic. Illustrated with Maps and Other Plates. For the Use of Schools and Young Persons.* 2nd ed., 1809. Juvenile Library, 1811.

Godwin, William. [Theophilus Marcliffe]. *Life of Lady Jane Grey, and of Lord Guildford Dudley, Her Husband.* Juvenile Library, 1806.

Godwin, William. [Theophilus Marcliffe]. *The Looking-Glass. A True History of the Early Years of an Artist; Calculated to awaken the Emulation of Young Persons of both Sexes, in the Pursuit of every laudable Attainment: particularly in the Cultivation of the Fine Arts.* Juvenile Library, 1805. Revised ed., 1885.

Godwin, William. [Edward Baldwin]. *The Pantheon: or Ancient History of the Gods of Greece and Rome for the Use of Schools, and Young Persons of Both Sexes.* Juvenile Library, 1806.

Godwin, William. [Edward Baldwin]. *The Pantheon, Or, Ancient History of the Gods of Greece and Rome: Intended to Facilitate the Understanding of the Classical Authors, And of the Poets in General; for the Use of Schools, and Young Persons of Both Sexes.* Juvenile Library, 1806. Hathi Trust Digital Library. Accessed February 2, 2018.

Godwin, William. *Political and Philosophical Writings of William Godwin*, 7 vols., general ed. Mark Philp. William Pickering, 1993.

Grenby, Matthew. *The Child Reader, 1700–1840*. Cambridge University Press, 2011.

Grenby, Matthew. "Politicizing the Nursery: British Children's Literature and the French Revolution." *The Lion and the Unicorn* 27 (2003): 1–26.

Hilton, Boyd. *A Mad, Bad, and Dangerous People? England, 1783–1846*. Clarendon, 2006.

Ives, Eric. *Lady Jane Grey: A Tudor Mystery*. Blackwell, 2009.

Kinnell, Margaret. "Childhood and Children's Literature: The Case of M. J. Godwin and Co., 1805–1825." *Publishing History* 24 (1988): 77–99.

Manly, Susan. "William Godwin's 'School of Morality.'" *Wordsworth Circle* XLIII, no. 3 (2012): 135–42.

Mee, Jon. *Conversable Worlds: Literature, Contention, and Community, 1762–1830*. Oxford University Press, 2011.

*New Romantic Circles Edition: William Godwin's Fables Ancient and Modern*, eds. Suzanne L. Barnett and Katherine Bennett Gustafson, July 23, 2014, https://www.rc.umd.edu/blog_rc/new-romantic-circles-edition-william-godwins-fables-ancient-and-modern. Accessed November 2, 2018.

*Oxford Dictionaries*. https://en.oxforddictionaries.com/definition/suffrage. Accessed March 29, 2018.

St. Clair, William. *The Godwins and the Shelleys*. W. W. Norton, 1989.

St. Clair, William. "William Godwin as Children's Bookseller." In *Children and their Books: A Celebration of the Work of Iona and Peter Opie*, eds. Gillian Avery and Julia Briggs, 165–81. Clarendon, 1989.

Wollstonecraft, Mary. "A Vindication of the Rights of Woman." In *A Vindication of the Rights of Men and A Vindication of the Rights of Woman*, ed. Sylvana Tomaselli, 65–294. Cambridge University Press, 1995.

# 15

# BUILDING BRIDGES
## INTERGENERATIONAL SOLIDARITY IN THE WORKS OF AIDAN CHAMBERS
Vanessa Joosen

Since children's literature is a discourse produced by adults for children (as well as other adults), these books are a form of intergenerational dialogue by definition, even if it does not necessarily take the form of solidarity or collaboration. Although many children's literature critics reflect on the fact that children's authors are usually adults, they rarely consider in more specific terms the phase in life that these authors are in, and even in age studies, extensive reflections on the author's life stage are fairly rare (Henneberg 2006). Adulthood, after all, ranges from young and emergent adulthood to deep old age, spanning over eighty years, and some authors' careers stretch over several decades (Joosen 2018). How does an author's phase in life impact on the themes they write about and the literary perspectives and techniques they use? How many of their own generational concerns do they address in their children's books, and how do they do so in a way that can appeal to young readers? The British author Aidan Chambers (born 1934) is particularly interesting to study in this context. When Chambers won the Hans Christian Andersen Medal in 2012, the jury motivated their choice by praising his "clear understanding of the adolescent mind" (IBBY). Chambers is best known for the so-called *Dance* sequence, which is named after *Dance on My Grave* (1982) but begins with *Breaktime* (1978). It spans six young adult novels, concluding with *This Is All* (2005). Chambers started working on the *Dance* sequence in the late 1970s, when he was in his mid-forties, and continued work on it until his late seventies. Despite his advanced age, he managed to write about adolescence in a way that appealed not only to adult critics, but also to various adolescents, several of whom started corresponding with him. How did he bridge his temporal distance from this stage in life? And how did real adolescents contribute to this process?

I explore these questions with a multidisciplinary approach that draws on genetic criticism, age studies, and reception studies. Genetic criticism is related to textual philology and text-critical analysis but focuses on the so-called *avant-texte*, the documents preceding the publication of a literary work, as interesting material in their own right—regardless of whether they made it to the final version or not. These include notebooks, schemes, sources, and manuscripts. The goal of genetic criticism is to reconstruct "the movement of writing" (Deppman et al., 2) and raise "awareness that the published text is less of a finished product than it may seem" (Van Hulle, 4). Recent genetic criticism has been inspired by, among others, narratology, cognitive studies, and digital humanities. Theoretically informed genetic criticism is only occasionally applied to children's literature studies (see Connolly, Dalrymple, Mason), rarely combined with age studies, and hardly ever mentioned as a field in and of itself. A genetic study can give insight into Chambers's construction of age, especially if the study of those documents can be supplemented with interviews, as I have done. Age studies is a multidisciplinary field that investigates the social construction of age (Green 2010). It has aided in gaining a better understanding of the different stages in life as governed not just by biology, but also by cultural factors and expectations.

This chapter also contributes to deconstructing the restrictive view of young readers as only passive consumers of children's books. Various other researchers have recently shown that young people have played a more active role in the production of cultural artifacts addressed at them than they have been credited with, pointing out the intergenerational collaboration that lay at the basis of theatre productions and television programs (Gubar), as well as children's books (Gubar, Smith). Some of the most famous children's books originated in letters or read-aloud sessions for real children or to entertain specific children. Authors as diverse as Hans Christian Andersen, Lewis Carroll, Beatrix Potter, and J. K. Rowling come to mind here. We know from Victoria Ford Smith's *Between Generations* (2017) that child audiences of the past were often "active listeners" who shared their opinions and contributed ideas to the stories. A combination of genetic studies and age studies can further lay bare how members of different generations have connected in the creative processes of more contemporary books.

The genetic analysis in this chapter is focused on the notebook that Aidan Chambers used for composing *The Toll Bridge* (1992). The first entry in the notebook dates back to July 1985, and the final entries are dated September 1991, when Chambers started work on *Postcards from No Man's Land* (*Notebook*, 232). In *The Toll Bridge*, the protagonist, Jan, has fled his parents and girlfriend to live and keep toll at the eponymous bridge. The novel is concerned with themes of identity construction, knowing others, child-parent relations, and coming of age. While it describes intergenerational conflicts, especially between Jan and his parents, it also shows that some stages in life are more akin than what might appear at first sight. Chambers's construction of adolescence is particularly well documented and informed by, among others, texts from psychology and sociology, as well as newspaper clippings about adolescents, and a rich body of other literary works, aimed at both adults and adolescents. In the construction of adolescence in his writing process, elements from all these sources were often blended. His archive, held at his home and in Seven Stories Newcastle, also contains correspondence with readers of various ages. These letters endorse his approach to adolescent literature, and can shed light on how adolescents and young adults have informed the character construction in his later works. I have supplemented the genetic study of the notebook for the *Toll Bridge* with interviews with Chambers himself and three of the former adolescents who were in touch with him for several years: Karin Kustermans, Bart Moeyaert, and Marieke Dilles.

## MEMORIES AND DIARIES

In writing for adolescence, Aidan Chambers drew inspiration from various sources. His notes make tangible how his memories and diaries from youth continued to inspire him in middle adulthood and old age. As Haru Takiuchi (2016) has detailed, for example, Chambers used his experience as a so-called "scholarship boy" to construct the class conflict between Ditto and his father in *Breaktime*, which Greenway calls his "most autobiographical novel" (16, also cited in Takiuchi, 37). Whereas for some authors, childhood memories prevail over adolescence as an inspiration for their work, it is the latter period that Chambers keeps returning to:

> it is in adolescence that we come to full consciousness of all the major aspects of life: who and what we are, what we believe and don't believe, work, love, sex, politics, gender, nationality, money, independence, authority, career, death, war, etc etc. Adolescence is about beginnings rather than ends. And this fascinates me. I suppose some critics would suggest, perhaps correctly, that I write youth fiction in order to make sense of my own adolescence and growth to adulthood. (Chambers, personal interview)

As this quote makes clear, he connects his exploration of adolescence with a search for understanding adulthood.

Throughout his writing process, Chambers connects his personal memories, diaries, and experiences with secondary sources. The notebook for *The Toll Bridge* suggests two strong preoccupations in the early stages of the writing process: one with bridges—visiting an actual toll bridge was an important source of inspiration in developing the book—and one with amnesia as an idea that he toyed with as a trigger for the protagonist's identity crisis (and which he ended up using for another character, Adam). Chambers found further inspiration in Oliver Sacks's *The Man Who Mistook His Wife For a Hat*, and writes down the following citation:

> The world [for a Korsakov sufferer] keeps disappearing, losing meaning, vanishing—and he must seek meaning, <u>make</u> meaning, in a desperate way, continually inventing, <u>throwing bridges of meaning over abysses of meaninglessness, the chaos that yawns continually beneath him</u>. (*Notebook* January 2, 1987, 10; emphasis and square brackets in original)

A few months into the creative process for *The Toll Bridge*, Chambers had found in Sacks an author who linked his two preoccupations of the bridge and amnesia. Interestingly, immediately following this quote is an entry that describes how he is "[i]dly glancing at a diary [he] kept in '56" (when he was twenty-one):

> 8 July: I am inevitably alone: each man is. That is the hardest thing to accept. It is a painful realization. I strive here [at college] to make a contact—a real bridge across which all things may pass. But no one will, <u>no man can</u>, accept.
>
> I am striving to synthesise. (*Notebook* January 2, 1987, 11; emphasis and square brackets in original)

The feeling of being alone is central to Jan's escape in *The Toll Bridge*. He has fled his parents and girlfriend after he has been plagued by bouts of depression, which he feels are caused by the social pressure to perform certain roles that do not match with who he truly is. He struggles to discover what lies underneath those performances of social roles. In the course of the novel, however, Jan's identity construction keeps being informed by human contact—both with new people and with those he left behind. Building bridges seems inevitable and runs as a red thread through *The Toll Bridge* and all the other *Dance* novels, which are marked by formative experiences of human exchange. In *The Toll Bridge*, the most influential people on the development of Jan's character are his peers, but in other works, in particular *Postcards from No Man's Land* and *Dying to Know You*, intergenerational exchanges also foster the adolescent's coming of age. That process of collaboration between people at different stages in life takes place on various levels besides the content, including the genesis of the book.

## KINSHIP BETWEEN STAGES IN LIFE

In addition to his memories and sources, the kinship between the stages in life helped Chambers to connect with the experiences of teenagers while he was in midlife and old age. In *Dying to Know You* (2012), the connection between an older author and an adolescent who is in love is the central plot feature. In other books, the kinship between the two stages in life is developed more marginally, but studying his archive helps to understand how Chambers became interested in developing certain aspects of adolescence because he could relate them to his own life stage. "Kinship" is the term that Marah Gubar (2014) uses as an alternative to the so-called "difference model" that stresses the otherness of childhood and adulthood. The kinship model that she proposes instead highlights the shared humanity and experiences in these phases in life. Other critics have also stressed that some of the experiences that are typically ascribed to adolescence are by no means unique for that phase. Lydia Kokkola points out that the emphasis on the Sturm und Drang of adolescence obscures the fact that other periods in life can also be marked by stress and turmoil (6). The midlife is one such period (see also Green), as becomes apparent from both *The Toll Bridge* and the notebook.

For genetic studies, discarded paths in the writing process can be equally revealing as the trajectory towards the published book. This is also true for Chambers's construction of age and kinship between the generations. Early on in the notebook for *The Toll Bridge*, Chambers considers a section of a poem by his friend Alan Tucker as an epigraph to his novel. The poem, entitled "The Toll Bridge," illustrates how previous stages in life can catch one by surprise: "Memory is a sealed room I did not know I possessed. / It is as though my childhood of days broke into it, / burst in, shouting and laughing." Chambers eventually decided against using the poem in the published version of his novel. Although *The Toll Bridge* was also inspired by memories of his youth, it was not so much informed by reminiscences of childhood happiness as by the experience of re-living of teenage angst. Central to Chambers's take on the kinship between various stages in life is the idea of "recognition," which played an important part in *The Toll Bridge* in particular. As the published novel itself reveals, and its genetic dossier further elucidates, Chambers parallels the turmoil of adolescence with that of midlife. He conceived of *The Toll Bridge* as a modern "recognition story," or *anagnorisis*, as described in Aristotle's *Poesis* and exemplified in, among others, *Oedipus Rex*. As Chambers explains in a fax to his Dutch publisher Jacques Dohmen, "the key feature of adolescent fiction, what marks it out, is that it is (a name I gave it years and years ago) the Literature of Recognition. [. . .] What interested me especially is that 'recognition' means 're-cognize.' That is, a change from ignorance to knowledge [NOW I KNOW] but a change such that there is a recovery of something once known rather than a shift from ignorance to knowledge" (Chambers, fax to Jacques Dohmen, August 5, 1993, 1; see also *Notebook*, 138). This act of recovery, of re-knowing something once known, proved not to be unique to adolescence, but also appears in the midlife, as Chambers describes feeling reconnected in midlife to experiences from adolescence.

During the writing of *The Toll Bridge*, Chambers was inspired by Terence Cave's *Recognitions* (1988), a book that taught him why, as a middle-aged man (Chambers was fifty-eight in 1993), he would feel so akin to adolescence. Cave's book, Chambers explains to Dohmen,

> helped me see how (the fictional, adolescent) Jan's story meshed with my own (this-world, middle-aged) story: "The crisis of the adolescent is re-enacted in the crisis of the middle-aged man: recognition narratives characteristically juxtapose two moments of fictional biography in this way, sketching the structure of life and in many cases suggesting the precariousness of the structure, its proneness to collapse." (Chambers August 5, 1993, 2; see also Paul, 65 and *Notebook*, 139)

Dohmen pointed out a flaw in the analogy between the adolescent and the middle-aged man: "Jan is at the *beginning* of adolescence and you more or less at the *end* of your 'middle years'" (August 9, 1993). While Dohmen highlights the differences, Chambers stresses—both in his letters and the book itself—that both are moments of change and potential crisis. As Chambers's notebook makes clear, both words in the "toll bridge" matter. A bridge connects two phases in life and takes you "[f]rom known to unknown" –that is the idea of recognition. This crossing comes with a toll: "You pay for passage: a transaction for movement" (*Notebook* July 21, 1985). Jan's stay at *The Toll Bridge* comes with intense moments of self-doubt and feelings of betrayal and rejection.

Jan is not the only character in the novel to experience a crisis at a moment of transition. *The Toll Bridge* includes a letter by his father in which he describes his wife's mental breakdown after Jan has left home. It highlights various moments in an adult's life course where change can be painful: the father talks about losing a child, the mother's separation anxiety, his jealousy of Jan, and so on. In his effort to build intergenerational understanding, the father highlights the similarities between adolescence and midlife, stating that "the menopause is the middle-aged counterpart of adolescence, and its effects are comparable, and as natural." These effects are detailed as a series of physical changes and sudden impulses of the body that are beyond a person's control, as well as emotional turmoil and depression. In the writing process, the idea of this letter came rather late; it is missing from the first overviews and only begins to emerge on July 24, 1988. There Chambers notes: "Can't recall a teenage book that reveals the mother's curious actions are the result of menop., which is a frequent cause, presumably, of difficulties between teens and their mothers? (Or, at least, that mothers have to live through this state at a time when their children are at their most strong willed or 'difficult,' as they break away from their dependence)" (128).

Recalling this passage in his letter to Dohmen a few years later, Chambers elaborates: "I believe it to be common to both men and women: that is, a period in the middle-age when they go through again the questions that first posed themselves during adolescence—re-cognize them, in fact" (August 9, 1993, 2). *The Toll Bridge* then reflects not just the teenager's anxiety when confronted with the major existential questions of life, but also "the crisis of the author as he re-enacts his adolescent crisis and in which he confronts his own middle-aged crisis" (2). Later in the letter, he phrases it as follows: "[T]he author re-cognizes his current self through the recognitions of the adolescent self in the protagonist, and this is much more difficult to probe and understand than simply to equate the author's middle-aged biography with events in the book" (3–4). In short, it would be a step too far to project the feelings that Jan experiences onto the author himself, but they do share some of the basic existential questions that have produced Jan's crisis and that are explored through the story.

The kinship that Chambers sees between the life stages of adolescence and old age can help to understand why he proved to be so successful as an author of young adult literature. Dohmen at least explains that the concept of "recognition" helps him understand why he finds reading good young adult literature more fulfilling than literature for adults (August 9, 1993). Chambers retorts that recognition also explains his own attraction to "teenage" literature. His connection with adolescence is devoid of nostalgia, which would require distance, but is rooted in an intense awareness of kindship and re-experience during the writing process as "imminent present": "That is, as ab-reactions: the adolescent state, the adolescent crisis lived again as if it were in the present, as *now*. Yet with this difference [. . .]: the author imports into the consciousness of his protagonist understandings that only the middle-aged author can actually achieve" (fax to Jacques Dohmen, August 9, 1993, 2). The combination of kinship with experience is what characterizes Chambers's middle-aged construction of adolescence in his novels. That sense of kinship was further reinforced by his conversations with actual teenage readers.

## TEENAGE INSPIRATIONS

In addition to Chamber's memories and sources, the writing process for several of his books involved personal contacts with adolescents and young adults, which he established first as a teacher and school theatre director, and later as an author: "All my working life," he says, "I have been in constant contact with young people aged eleven to twenty-five. I observe them, listen to them, and sometimes ask them about aspects of their lives I need to know about and 'make my own'" (Chambers, personal interview). His archive includes intimate letters of some of these teenagers and young adults. In order to respect their privacy, I chose not to disclose these letters but opted for interviews in which I asked three of Chambers's former teenage contacts to share their views on the relationship with Chambers and his works. All three responded quickly and enthusiastically, stating that their contacts with the author had been valuable experiences during their teens and/or early twenties.

Karin Kustermans is one of the teenagers with whom Chambers corresponded and met regularly. Karin was fifteen when she read *Dance on My Grave*, admiring both its content and form, as she explained during the interview: "Hal's story touched me deeply—in a way that you can only be emotionally affected in your adolescent years—but I was impressed at least as much by the way the author told the story. The play with chronology, narrative points of view and textual genres, the intertextual references (even though I didn't know that word at the time), the suggestive understatements, those kinds of things" (Kustermans).[1] Contacts with adolescents who appreciated the literary techniques that he used and the philosophical questions he was raising confirmed Chambers's belief that people in this phase in life have a wide range of interests, including the kinds of "intellectual pursuits" that mark many of the young characters in his novels (Chambers, personal interview).

Karin first met Chambers in 1988, when she was seventeen and he delivered a talk in the Flemish town of Baarle. When Karin approached him afterwards, they had a long conversation about reading, literature, school, and also about "how I thought about friendship, and how I experienced life in general as a seventeen-year-old" (Kustermans). The conversation continued over the following years, in letters, occasional phone calls, and meetings, when Chambers also shared his ideas and thoughts about his work in progress, sometimes with very specific questions:

> Some of his questions had to do with a new book, sometimes I would only notice that later, after it was published. I remember a meeting in Amsterdam, a lunch, after which he took me to the Rijksmuseum, to show me a portrait that Rembrandt had made of his son Titus. I remember that he really wanted to know what I saw in that painting, how I experienced it, and told me afterwards what he thought about it—as if he wanted to test his "views" against mine, a young person.

In *Postcards from No Man's Land*, the teenage protagonist Jacob indeed visits the portrait and reflects on it. Chambers also consulted Karin to check the credibility of his characters' speech and to connect with youth culture in the Netherlands, where *Postcards* is set. She introduced him to lyrics by Bram Vermeulen that he used in *Postcards*. Karin observes that Chambers also needed her help to bridge a gender gap and construct female adolescence in particular. This is also apparent from the input from young people that he sought when he was writing *This Is All: The Pillow Book of Cordelia Kenn*, the only novel in the *Dance* series with a female protagonist. For this book, two pregnant women in their twenties kept diaries for him, describing their experiences (Chambers, personal interview).

At times, the intergenerational collaboration was more indirect. The Flemish author Bart Moeyaert was a student in his early twenties when he first met Aidan Chambers in 1986, and the latter invited him to his house. Moeyaert was coming to terms with his homosexuality and his aspirations as a young writer; he had made his debut three years earlier, at age nineteen. Hungry for knowledge and input, and more eager to listen than to talk, Moeyaert himself doubts that Chambers learned anything from him. Chambers played a mentoring role, and although their age difference of thirty-one years did not raise any barriers to conversation topics, it did situate Moeyaert in the role of disciple, and Chambers in the role of teacher (Moeyaert, personal interview). Yet I would argue that even this role was a form of intergenerational dialogue that indirectly fed into Chambers's poetics. Moeyaert, after all, was mostly interested in *Dance on My Grave* for its form. Reading it provided a double shock for him, raising his awareness not just about the kinds of loves that people can experience, but also the forms in which these narratives can be expressed. His literary awareness, curiosity, and acknowledgment of Chambers' expertise must have functioned as an endorsement for the mentor that his approach and knowledge were valid. Chambers, moreover, told Moeyaert he admired his open-mindedness, which encouraged the older author to play the mentoring role. Moeyaert feels that their contact faded as he grew older, and the balance in the mentor/mentee relationship shifted (April 18, 2018).

Strikingly, the three people interviewed all mentioned a distinct interest in poetic forms in their former teenage selves. Moreover, several of Chambers's works are inspired by the writing of authors in their late teens and early twenties, who contributed to his image of the intellectually, verbally, and emotionally competent adolescent.[2] Chambers's books have been criticized for being too artistic and intellectual for a teenage readership (see, among others, Moss 46), with characters who are larger than life. Various passages in the notebook also testify to regular feelings of failure. On December 12, 1989, he writes: "I have to see—make myself accept—that my books do matter" (166), while one of the final entries reads: "Deep anxiety about quality & narrative success fo of the book. Sense of disappointment" (*Notebook* August 31, 1991, 232). The adolescent readers and aspiring writers who were in contact with Chambers supported him in his conviction that his young characters were not too intellectual to be credible and that there was an audience who loved his books. At the same time, he is equally convinced that his narratives should not necessarily mimic, but can also surpass reality. Chambers's works offer to his readership both points of recognition and potential for growth, and the adolescents that he met and corresponded with endorsed him in the idea that he had struck the right balance. They proved to him that his books *did* matter. Whereas Chambers ended the notebook for *The Toll Bridge* on a pessimistic note, the reception of the book, in particular its adaptation to a play directed by Dirk Terryn (1998), who directly sought Chambers's creative input for the script, was a source of deep satisfaction for him. Among other reasons, this is because of the intense collaboration with the actors, who were in their mid-twenties in the summer of 1997, when Chambers joined them. Given that Chambers was sixty-two at the time, their co-creation is a further form of intergenerational collaboration, which Chambers calls "one of the happiest experiences of my career."[3] To date, he is still in touch with Robby Cleiren, who performed the part of Jan (Chambers, personal interview 2018).

Is there a limit to this type of intergenerational collaboration? Does it change as the author grows older? In the course of his writing career, Chambers has passed on from middle adulthood to old age, and the temporal distance with his teenage self and young readership has also risen. Asked whether he found it harder to write about adolescence as his own age increased, Chambers replies:

I didn't used to. Adolescence was always alive in me and "inhabited" me. I knew it viscerally, so to speak. But after *This Is All* I began to lose that sense of being inhabited by youth. At the same time, the culture began to change considerably. Just to take one example. It would be impossible now to write a youth novel set in the present day without social media, and the digital forms of communication, entertainment, opinion, and fact-finding being part of the story. I do not use the social media (in fact, I thoroughly detest it). And because I always write about current life, I wouldn't be able to write a youth novel that includes modern youth daily experience. [. . .] In short, I no longer feel I belong to "the age between." And this has caused a crisis in my writing life. (Chambers, interview)

As Victoria Ford Smith argues in *Between Generations*, intergenerational collaborations are always marked by their "particular cultural moment" (242). To this, I would add that the age of the participants involved also matters and inevitably shifts in time, as they enter different stages in life. As youth culture changed, and Chambers grew increasingly distant from it, the intergenerational connection with teenagers ultimately faded, even though his personal contacts with young people in their late teens and twenties have so far persisted.

Chambers's oeuvre and archive are rich both in examples of intergenerational solidarity and in their potential for future research that makes use of genetic criticism and age studies. This kind of research may be driven both by adult scholars and by younger people who are interested in his books; the depth of the conversations that Chambers had with his readers shows that young people too have important insights to offer on his works. The genetic approach that I have presented in this chapter may be argued to clash with one of the fundamental tenets of Chambers's view on literature, however: the freedom of the reader to construct meaning. In various publications and lectures, he has testified to being influenced by Roland Barthes's distinction between authors and writers, and between "readerly" and "writerly" texts (see, among others, *Reading Talk*, 14). Whereas his earlier writing was informed by efforts to guide his audience to meaning, his *Dance* series was developed along different lines, less driven by the needs of young readers than by the artistic form that the story needed to be told. As a consequence of his poetics, Joanna Klinker stresses, Chambers's novels demand an active reader, corresponding to the "writerly" text in Barthes's terminology: "Chambers encourages his readers to become engaged with texts, breaking them apart, filling holes, and creating meanings that are pertinent to them" (260). His novels allow for multiple meanings, which are co-created by the reader. Genetic criticism puts the emphasis back on authorial intention, reviving the author that Barthes had declared dead to open up space for the reader. However, the intergenerational collaboration that genetic research on Chambers's works helps lay bare shows that this authorial intention was dialogic from the start. The notebooks and manuscripts make apparent how many different voices resonate through Chambers's novels. Rather than closing down avenues for interpretation, this kind of research can open up new ones, drawing attention to passages that might otherwise be easily overlooked, or that never made it to the final novel but were crucial steps in its development and that are interesting to study in their own right. Adolescent and young adult voices were crucial to many of those steps—sometimes directly, more often indirectly. Chambers's works and writing process testify to the kinship between these phases in life, and the reception of his works by at least some adolescent readers endorsed the success of this intergenerational collaboration, which, in turn, fed into his writing process.

## NOTES

1. The interview with Karin Kustermans was conducted in Dutch; all translations of these quotes are my own.
2. Anne Frank's diary has proven to be highly influential on Chambers' own views on adolescence, as are Raymond Radiguet, Françoise Sagan, S. E. Hinton, Mary Shelley, Alec Waugh, Clarice Lispector, and Francoise Mallet-Joris (interview 2018).
3. http://www.aidanchambers.co.uk/toll.htm. Accessed February 11, 2019.

## WORKS CITED

Cave, Terence. *Recognitions: A Study in Poetics*. Clarendon, 1988.
Chambers, Aidan. 1982. *Dance on My Grave*. Red Fox, 2000.
Chambers, Aidan. *Dying to Know You*. Amulet, 2012.
Chambers, Aidan. Fax to Jacques Dohmen, August 5, 1993. 3pp. Photocopied at Aidan Chambers's home in 2015.
Chambers, Aidan. Fax to Jacques Dohmen, August 9, 1993. Photocopied at Aidan Chambers's home in 2015.
Chambers, Aidan. Fax to Jacques Dohmen, August 12, 1993. Photocopied at Aidan Chambers's home in 2015.
Chambers Aidan. Notebook for *The Toll Bridge*. Photocopied at Aidan Chambers home in 2015.
Chambers, Aidan. 1995. *Now I Know*. Red Fox, 2000.
Chambers, Aidan. Personal interview, January 17, 2018.
Chambers, Aidan. 1999. *Postcards from No Man's Land*. Red Fox, 2000.
Chambers, Aidan. 1992. *The Toll Bridge*. Red Fox, 2012. Kindle.
Chambers, Aidan. *This Is All: The Pillow Book of Cordelia Kenn*. Random House, 2012.
Chambers, Aidan. *Reading Talk*. Thimble Press, 2001.

Connolly, Ruth. "Using Manuscripts to Research Children's Literature." In *Children's Literature Studies: A Research Handbook*, eds. M. O. Grenby and Kimberley Reynolds, 56–60. Palgrave Macmillan, 2011.

Dalrymple, Nolan. "Case Study—Working with the Seven Stories Archive." In *Children's Literature Studies: A Research Handbook*, eds. M. O. Grenby and Kimberley Reynolds, 60–62. Palgrave Macmillan, 2011.

Deppman, Jed, Daniel Ferrer, and Michael Groden. "Introduction: A Genesis of French Genetic Criticism." In *Genetic Criticism: Texts and Avant-textes*, eds. Jed Deppman, Daniel Ferrer, and Michael Groden, 1–16. University of Pennsylvania Press, 2004.

Dilles, Marieke. Personal interview, April 10, 2018.

Dohmen, Jacques. Fax to Aidan Chambers, August 9, 1993. Photocopied at Aidan Chambers's home in 2015.

IBBY. "Hans Christian Andersen Awards 2002," http://www.ibby.org/subnavigation/archives/hans-christian-andersen-awards/2002/?L=0.

Green, Lorraine. *Understanding the Life Course: Sociological and Psychological Perspectives*. Polity Press, 2010.

Greenway, Betty. *Aidan Chambers: Master Literary Choreographer*. Scarecrow, 2006.

Gubar, Marah. "The Hermeneutics of Recuperation: What a Kinship-Model Approach to Children's Agency Could Do for Children's Literature and Childhood Studies." *Jeunesse* 8, no. 1 (2016): 291–310.

Henneberg, Sylvia B. "Of Creative Crones and Poetry: Developing Age Studies Through Literature." *NWSA Journal* 18, no. 1 (2006): 106–125.

Joosen, Vanessa. *Adulthood in Children's Literature*. Bloomsbury, 2018.

Klinker, Joanna J. "The Pedagogy of the Post-Modern Text: Aidan Chambers's The Toll Bridge." *The Lion & the Unicorn* 23, no. 2 (1990): 257–70.

Kokkola, Lydia. *Fictions of Adolescent Carnality: Sexy Sinners and Delinquent Deviants*. John Benjamins, 2013.

Kustermans, Karin. Personal interview, March 11, 2018.

Mason, Karen M. "The Case of the Missing Manuscripts: Doing Archival Research on Children's Series Authors." In *Rediscovering Nancy Drew*, eds. Carolyn Stewart Dyer and Nancy Tillman Romalov, 170–78. University of Iowa Press, 1995.

Moeyaert, Bart. Personal interview, April 18, 2018.

Moss, Geoff. "Metafiction, Illustration, and the Poetics of Children's Literature." In *Literature for Children: Contemporary Criticism*, ed. Peter Hunt, 42–66. Routledge, 1992.

Paul, Lissa. "Dancing in the Hall of Mirrors." In *Reading the Novels of Aidan Chambers: Seven Essays*, ed. Nancy Chambers, 62–72. Thimble, 2009.

Smith, Victoria Ford. *Between Generations: Collaborative Authorship in the Golden Age of Children's Literature*. University Press of Mississippi, 2017.

Takiuchi, Haru. "Aidan Chambers' *Breaktime*: Class Conflict and Anxiety in the Work of a Scholarship-Boy Writer." *Children's Literature in Education* 47, no. 1 (2016): 36–49.

Tucker, Alan. "The Toll Bridge." In Chambers, *Notebook*.

# 16

# THE MINGLING OF TEENAGE AND ADULT BREATHS

## THE DUTCH *SLASH* SERIES AS INTERGENERATIONAL COMMUNICATION

Helma van Lierop-Debrauwer and Sabine Steels

In 2006, Dutch children's author Edward van de Vendel launched the so-called *Slash* series, a run of young-adult novels depicting the lives of "special youngsters" (described on the back cover of each book). The first novel in the series was published in 2008, the most recent one in 2017. The novelty brought by the *Slash* books into Dutch children's literature in 2008 is its being a form of "collaborative life writing" (Smith and Watson, 264): a cooperative effort between young adults and well-known children's authors, with the former telling their life stories to the latter, who subsequently wrote these down. By mingling "the breath of young heroes with the breath of stubborn authors," Van de Vendel hoped the series would blur the traditional age divide between children and adults: "Children's literature can make clear how close we are to each other. How our breath, once blown, always, always mingles" (128; our translations throughout). The series thus constitutes an interesting example of YA-books that connect adults and young people and that emphasize the importance of intergenerational alliance.

In this chapter, we discuss how the idea of intergenerational communication underlying the *Slash* series is put into practice. Firstly, through interviews with four authors and four young adults participating in the *Slash* series, we explore to what extent the cooperation between adult author and young informant manages to live up to the ethical principles of egalitarian partnership in collaborative life writing projects as outlined by Thomas Couser (2004). Here we focus on *the process* of telling and writing, which John Paul Eakin calls "the story of the story" ("Relational Selves," 63). Secondly, through close-reading of *Voor jou 10 anderen* (*Ten a Penny*), written by Mirjam Oldenhave (2008) and based on the life story of Cynthia van Eck, a girl who was raised together with many other children by a completely incapable foster mother, we analyze if and how in this book the protagonist's and the author's breaths are mingled. In this second part, the emphasis is on the representation of the young informant in the published book as *the product* of the partnership between the author and the young adult. The overall aim of the chapter is to provide insight into the way this YA-series supports Marah Gubar's view of childhood and adulthood as related instead of separated (453).

## THE ETHICS OF EGALITARIAN PARTNERSHIP IN COLLABORATIVE LIFE WRITING

In *The Company We Keep: An Ethics of Fiction* (1988), Wayne Booth poses the question whether or not authors of fiction have unlimited freedom "to expose, in the service of art or self, the most delicate secrets of those whose lives provide the material" (130). He relates this question to fiction, but the issue of the author's freedom in exposing other people's lives becomes even more urgent in collaborative life writing projects such as the *Slash* series. According to Couser, the ultimate ethical principle in such projects is that both parties should benefit from the process and have a maximally egalitarian relationship. However, in reality this is very difficult to achieve. Although collaborative life writing projects are based on relationships that are voluntary and satisfying for the participants, "there are thin and not always clear lines between making, taking, and faking the life of another person in print" (36). Firstly, this is so because the term collaborative life writing in itself is misleading: both partners having an equal share in the writing process is an exception rather than the rule. Most of the time, they have clearly distinguished roles, with one partner telling the story and the other one writing it down. Secondly, as Couser argues, this difference between the partners' contributions often goes together with a power hierarchy between them, caused by social differences with respect to race, class, gender, or age (37). In the case of the *Slash* series, both threats to an egalitarian partnership are present. The marketing surrounding the series consistently presents the authors, known for their literary skills, as the ones who have written the stories based on the life narratives told by the young adults. Because the informants are younger than the authors, there is also the risk of an imbalance of power. Power based on age difference is a defining feature of children's and young adult literature. To address this fact, Maria Nikolajeva introduced the concept of aetonormativity (8). In children's and young adult literature, adulthood is the norm; that is, children's books represent a form of communication that is, by definition, created and controlled by adults. In this chapter, we explore how the authors and the young informants of the *Slash* series have dealt with both the disparity in roles and the power hierarchy resulting from age difference. We reflect on the question as to what extent and how the series as a collaborative life writing project challenges the predominantly aetonormative character of children's and young adult literature.

To minimize the risks of an unequal relationship during the process of life writing and to avoid a misrepresentation of the person whose life story is told, Couser makes use of the ethical principles of biomedicine. The most important ethical principle is respect for the informant's autonomy—that is, the right to determine what will happen to his or her life story (18). This means that informants must know that someone is writing about them and they must give their informed consent to the writing and the publication. Authors must actively inform them about the consequences, the advantages and the risks of the project. Finally, yet significantly, informants must be given control over their life stories. In other words, respect for the informant's autonomy implies what Couser calls "transactional visibility," which means that the partnership's conditions "are made available for inspection" by the informant (25). Related to the principle of autonomy is the principle of "nonmaleficence and beneficence" (Couser, 26). Whereas in biomedicine this is a moral duty, in life writing the principle of doing no harm is a moral aspiration; the biographer will not be punished for maleficence, but avoiding harm and warding off exploitation of the informant is highly appreciated (Couser, 27).

We focus on how the *Slash* series exemplifies principles of an egalitarian relationship in collaborative life writing and how it fleshes out the idea of intergenerational solidarity, which Van de Vendel expressed, using the metaphor of "the mingling breaths."

### "YOUNG PEOPLE FROM WHOM WE CAN LEARN"

The *Slash* series consists of fourteen life stories about boys and girls who grew up under difficult, frequently traumatic circumstances. The name of the series is a deliberate choice: the slash on the cover, with the author's name to the left of it, and the young informant's name to the right, emphasizes that collaboration between them is the main characteristic of the books. For Van de

Vendel, the aim of this project of collaborative life writing was twofold: he hoped, on the one hand, that it would push authors of young adult novels closer to today's reality and, on the other, that it could have "the possible effect of pulling young adults closer to literature as well" (127). The latter aspiration was fed by the belief that "reality, verisimilitude, honesty still have a growing magnetic power" (127) for young readers. Some of the books in the series deal with public trauma, experienced by many people at the same time, such as war or migration. An example of this is the first book in the series, *De gelukvinder* (*The Fortune Finder*), written by Edward van de Vendel and Anoush Elman (2008). It is a life narrative about a young Afghan fugitive told against the political backdrop of the Taliban oppression in Afghanistan, on the one hand, and Dutch society at the beginning of the twenty-first century, on the other. Other books are about individual trauma, such as gender dysphoria or child abuse. The latter is the case in *Voor jou 10 anderen* (*Ten a Penny*), which will be discussed below.

We interviewed four authors and four informants who worked together on books in the *Slash* series: Edward van de Vendel, the initiator of the series, and Anoush Elman; Mirjam Oldenhave and Cynthia van Eck, who coauthored *Voor jou 10 anderen* (2008); Anke Kranendonk, who collaborated with Lieke Kranendonk on *Alles is weg* (2009; *Everything is Gone*), a book dealing with the loss of a best friend; and finally, Anna Woltz and Vicky Janssen, who were partners on *Meisje van Mars* (2011; *Girl from Mars*), a book about gender dysphoria. Cynthia van Eck and Anoush Elman are pseudonyms: Anoush chose another name because he did not want to jeopardize the asylum procedure his family was involved in at the time, while Cynthia did not want to use her own name out of solidarity with people who were part of her past. The photos of young adults on the covers of the four books were a joint decision of the publisher, the authors, and the adolescents. They are pictures of anonymous young people and not of the informants.

Our interview questions concerned the ethics of egalitarian partnership. Through the interviews, we explored how the adult author and the young adult worked together, to see whether their collaboration was an example of the kinship model of childhood proposed by Marah Gubar (2013). This model rests on the premise that adults and children "are akin to one another, which means they are neither exactly the same nor radically dissimilar." Keywords in this model of childhood are "relatedness" and "connection," as opposed to "otherness" and "deficiency." Both adults and children are human beings, differing in degree, not in kind (453–54). The interview questions pertained to the start of the project, the young informant's knowledge about the content and the form of the book, the existence of a contract, the division of roles, the possibility of withdrawing from the project, the right to read and edit the manuscript before publication, and the feelings of the two partners about the result.

## "THE STORY OF THE STORY"

In each of the four projects, it was the adult author who took the initiative to write the book. However, in two instances the young adults played a crucial role in choosing the subject of the book. The fact that in both these cases the author and the young informant knew each other beforehand contributed to the development of the idea. Cynthia van Eck is the foster daughter of Mirjam Oldenhave,[1] and Lieke Kranendonk is a cousin of Anke Kranendonk. Cynthia van Eck suggested that her foster mother use her life experiences for the book in the *Slash* series. However, Mirjam Oldenhave hesitated for quite some time, because she felt it was somewhat opportunistic to "use" her foster daughter. Moreover, the fact that they were not only participants in a temporary project but were also living together was another issue that bothered Oldenhave. Eventually, she accepted the offer, because Cynthia had an intriguing story to tell. Her doubts show that the author was well aware of the possible harm the project could do to her foster daughter. In the case of *Alles is weg*, Lieke Kranendonk asked her aunt for help, because she knew Anke Kranendonk was a professional author. She wanted to make a memory book for one of her best friends who died in an accident. After they had made this little book for private use, Kranendonk asked her cousin if she could also use her story for the *Slash* series. The young adult gave her consent, based on her aunt's explanation of the book's format. Right from the start, her aunt told her that she could always quit if telling the story turned out to be too painful.

Edward van de Vendel and Anna Woltz did not know their informant beforehand. Their point of departure was determined by the oversimplified news reports about migrants and a personal interest in gender issues respectively. Van de Vendel googled the keywords "fugitive" and "life story," finding an item on Anoush Elman, who had written a play about his experiences during secondary school. He subsequently contacted Elman through the latter's teacher and they met a few months later. Van de Vendel explained what the book would be about and that it was up to Anoush to decide if he wanted to participate. It took Anoush six months to answer Van de Vendel's question. In the interview, Anoush Elman emphasized that in all these months Van de Vendel had never pushed him, which helped him to make an informed decision. He never regretted his agreeing to participate despite the fact that it caused many painful memories to come back. He had been assured that in the course of the process he would always be free to withdraw if he had second thoughts about his decision.

Anna Woltz announced her plan in an email which she posted on the site of a foundation for people with gender dysphoria. Nineteen young adults responded, six of whom she invited for an interview. Eventually, she decided to continue the project with Vicky Janssen, who was not only able to tell her story in a lively way but also seemed to be ready for the process of telling and publishing her life narrative. Working together with Anna, Vicky never once considered withdrawing from the project.

It is clear that all young adults participated voluntarily after they had been informed about the format of the series. All four adolescents had private as well as more public motives behind their decision to participate. The private motives had to do with the expectation that telling their story would likely be therapeutic, helping them come to terms with what they had been through in their lives. The more public motives included that their story might be of help to people with comparable experiences or might give people fresh insights into complex issues. Anoush Elman, for example, agreed to participate because he hoped that telling his story would help bridge the gap between Dutch people and migrants such as himself.

All respondents mention signing a contract, which, as they remember it, mainly concerned deadlines and royalties. The authors and the young informants would get an equal share in the royalties. As stated, right from the start, the authors explained what kind of book it would be, and together author and informant divided the roles between them. The writers particularly emphasized that they wanted to do justice to the life stories of the young informants. However, they also told them that they would not tell the events exactly as they had happened. The authors all stressed that the book was to be a novel, meaning that one character could be based on more than one person in real life, that names and the order of the events could be changed, or that some of the informants' experiences might be left out altogether. All the young adults agreed to go along with the genre, and none of them felt that injustice would be done to their story if it was adapted in this way. On the contrary, they all said they were very satisfied with the result. In fact, for Lieke Kranendonk, it was the choice of the novel form that made her feel that it was her story. After her friend had died, she was interrogated by the police. The report of that interrogation only consisted of facts, which did not reflect how she had experienced it: "Anke brought my story to life, because she knew how to capture my emotions." Reflecting on the result, all authors show respect for the contribution of the young adults and stress that the project was a joint venture. Anna Woltz, for example, said:

I recognize my own voice, because I had to add a lot of details and dialogs. I see exactly what choices I made to build tension and to foreground certain themes, how the chronology is sometimes changed and how I structured the story. [. . .] At the same time, I stay very close to the truth, and Vicky has a fabulous memory. Therefore, many details are hers not mine. Moreover, she has a very powerful voice, which I have adopted as much as possible—so yes, I definitely have the feeling that *Meisje van Mars* does justice to Vicky's story. I think she feels the same.

In her interview, Vicky confirms Anna's perception. She said that when she read the book for the first time, she cried for quite some time, because she was so happy: "Anna did such a good job, with my voice in the story being 95% and hers only 5%." Anna Woltz's quotation shows that the authors could not do without the young adult's voice. Just like Edward van de Vendel, who emphasizes how much he benefited from Anoush's visual way of telling, Anna Woltz underscores that the two roles in the process were different, but equally important.

On looking closer at the process, we notice different patterns with respect to the number of sessions that took place and in terms of the control the young adults had or wanted to have over their story. Edward van de Vendel and Anoush Elman had over fifty sessions, in addition to which the author also spoke with Elman's family. Besides the sessions, they also had more informal contact, walking on the beach, for instance, or going to the theatre. They both feel that they became friends in the process and that the age difference did not matter. The other authors and adolescents all had fewer sessions. All the young informants said that they had control over their life story. In three of the four cases, they read chapters of the book after the author had finished them. Vicky Janssen first read the book after Anna Woltz had completed it, but before it was published. They all felt that they could fully participate in the process and that there was trust. None of the young adults felt the need to edit the manuscript before publication. All the youngsters were also informed about the publicity that might ensue after publication. Both the authors and the young informants more than once stressed the openness of the process and the feeling of connectedness.

The interviews show that *the process* of this collaborative life writing project is intergenerational solidarity put into practice, acknowledging as it does the abilities and strengths of both partners. At first sight, the creative agency of the young informants might seem less than that of the authors, because the latter write the stories down, adding and deleting information, and using their literary skills. However, both the authors and the young respondents agree that the way the adolescents told their stories was decisive for the result. They perceived each other as partners, in the sense outlined by, among others, Ford Smith, who proposes an alternative approach to authorship. Instead of focusing on "common definitions of professional authorship" that "often exclude children or elide their participation," she fosters a perspective that is "attentive to young people as social actors" (21). By acknowledging the agency and creativity of the adolescents, the adult authors of the *Slash* series take the same stance.

## AUTHENTIC REPRESENTATION AS AN INDICATION OF INTERGENERATIONAL SOLIDARITY

To gain further insight into how intergenerational communication is fleshed out in the *Slash* series, we now shift our focus from *process* to *product*. Through a close-reading of *Voor jou 10 anderen* by Mirjam Oldenhave and Cynthia van Eck, we discuss the way the young informant in the novel is *represented* tells us about intergenerational solidarity. To answer this question, we use the concept of authenticity, a key notion in life writing studies. Authenticity has to do with being trustworthy and with telling the truth, which scholars generally perceive as being essential to life writing (Eakin, 3). At the same time, many of them, among others Lejeune, admit that totally and unambiguously telling the truth in life narratives is impossible. However, Lejeune argues, this does not relieve life writers of the obligation to tell the life story as authentically as possible. This implies that both the factual historical reality in which the autobiographical subject or, in this case, the subject of collaborative life writing lived, and his or her subjective, personal experience should be represented in a way that is true to life (36). Relating this "ethics of authorial performance" (Parker, 53) to the *Slash* series, we argue that an authentic portrayal of the young informant in the novel is an indication of intergenerational solidarity, acknowledging the creative contribution of this young adult.

### An Authentic Representation of Historical Reality

Every life takes place in a social context. Therefore, any textual element that refers to an identifiable, contemporary, or historical context in a life narrative—be it symbolic motives, verifiable events, subtle details, or a specific vocabulary—contributes to the authenticity of a life story (among others, Kokkola, 68–79). *Voor jou 10 anderen* tells a three-part story. In the first part, Cynthia, along with a bunch of other kids, is living in an illegal foster home. Mommy Riet is their foster mother. She is poor, mentally impaired, and unable to take on this responsibility. The children do not go to school and are fed dry bread for dinner. When they quarrel, she threatens to send a child molester after them. The most painful thing about the children's predicament is that for quite some time they perceive their situation as completely normal. After the children have lived together this way for more than half a decade, social workers come to take them away from their foster mother and to separate them from each other. Cynthia is in shock, feeling betrayed by Mommy Riet, who does not care about "her" children being taken away from her. The young girl is now put in a children's home. She is completely traumatized and unable to remember or feel anything (part two). When she gets older, she moves to a young adult shelter where she finally gets a better grip on her life (part three).

Cynthia is living in an unnamed Dutch city during the 1990s. However, to set the scene in a historical context, the text displays a combination of verifiable events, subtle non-iconic details and slang that contribute to the historical authenticity. For example, there is an explicit reference to Marc Dutroux, the Belgian child rapist and murderer caught in 1996. Moreover, there are a lot of telling details in the text that evoke a recognizable contemporary setting: Mommy Riet watches American sitcoms on television (19), they buy their groceries at Aldi's (26), a well-known supermarket chain in the Netherlands, and there is a reference to Lara Croft, a fictional character in an internationally known video game and action movie (109). The language used in the novel also contributes to its historical authenticity. Many slang expressions, like "even moeven" (46) en "mmereet" (122), reveal a particular social environment, while other sentences are typical of young people today. However, this spoken informal language is not used all the time.[2] The text shows a balance between the author's concern for an authentic portrayal of the protagonist and the setting and her ambition to write a story in her own style, making her own voice heard. This issue of "voice" is one of the aspects of the "ethics of form" (Steels, 19); that is, the preconditions for an authentic and ethical representation of lived experiences in traumatic life writing.

## An Authentic Representation of the Subjective Personal Experience through the Ethics of Form

The ethics of form consists of three prerequisites for a reliable and trustworthy portrayal of a life: the use of "the shriek of silence" (Patterson 1992) instead of graphic details, the recognition of the limits of memory, and the fragmentation and polyphony of "the self" (see, among others, Douglas, 88). The first precondition has to do with the way the lived experience is represented, the second refers to what is portrayed, and the last relates to whose life story is being told. We now focus on these three prerequisites.

In his study *The Shriek of Silence: A Phenomenology of the Holocaust Novel* (1992), Dave Patterson was the first to conceptualize "the shriek of silence" as a way authors deal with the difficulty of finding an adequate language for traumatic experiences. He argues that by creating silence, authors of narratives about trauma do more justice to a person's emotions than by providing graphic details. The first part of *Voor jou 10 anderen* recounts the life in the foster home with Mommy Riet as seen through the eyes of young Cynthia. When the child protection authorities show up and take Cynthia away, the girl feels betrayed by Mommy Riet. This traumatic betrayal is evoked by using one simple but significant sentence: "Usually one realizes things very slowly, but sometimes you understand something *at once*" (69, italics HvL and SS). The phrase "at once" is repeated at the end of the second and the third parts of the book, when Cynthia once again is going through traumatic experiences. The repetition of exactly the same words at crucial moments and the omission of details underline the importance of these emotional moments and the impact they have on the protagonist. Instead of using graphic details, the created silence tells us more about the child's inability to express her deepest emotions than detailed information could have done.

*Voor jou 10 anderen* is based on the memories of Cynthia van Eck. In life writing studies, the loss of memory is perceived as inherent to (auto)biography in general and to traumatic life narratives in particular. Douglas notices that autobiographies of traumatic childhood experiences are often fragmented in their representation of the past due to the inaccuracy of memory in general and to the mechanism of forgetting which is characteristic of trauma. Such fragmented representations of the past emphasize the limitations of memory and are thus considered to be important devices for an authentic representation of the subject of the life narrative (119). In *Voor jou 10 anderen*, the loss of memory is emphasized several times. When it comes to details in her life, Cynthia admits more than once that she forgot about them, either by saying explicitly that she no longer knows, or by using words that suggest that her memory fails, or both: "I was *probably* shouting the loudest of all, but *I don't remember*" (65, italics HvL and SS). Cynthia's explicit acknowledgment of memory loss contributes to the truthfulness of her life story.

However, there are other details that the young adult did not forget. She vividly remembers asking her foster mother questions about her real mother, as well as longing for sincere confirmation. She also remembers Mommy Riet's answer: "'I am your mother. I take care of you, don't I? You are my children.'

That sounded so sweet that I sat down. I still remember that we looked at a beer advertisement. Something funny happened that we both had to laugh at" (20-21). Because these are details related to key moments in her life, they are still part of her memory. The loss of memory because of traumatic experiences is particularly visible in part two, which consists of many fragmented and inconsistent memories and indications of Cynthia's inability to remember more. Instead of ironing out the inaccuracy of memory, Oldenhave validates Cynthia's story by presenting it as much as possible as it was told to her.

Finally, the "presentation of the self" is a decisive element in an authentic representation of personal experience. Douglas, among others,[3] points out that autobiographical narratives never speak with one clear voice. Because these narratives are always a rewriting of the past, "they are conventionally polyvocal" (88), being a dialogue between the voice of the subject's present self and of their past self. Therefore, both voices are heterogeneous and fragmented, which contributes to an authentic representation. *Voor jou 10 anderen* is written from the perspective of Cynthia, who is nineteen and looks back on her childhood and adolescence. The narrative voice is the voice of this nineteen-year-old. However, the voice of the child Cynthia is also heard and this does not go unnoticed, because the older Cynthia comments on her. An interesting example of such dialogism is the passage in which nineteen-year-old Cynthia tells about what young Cynthia said when she left Mommy Riet years ago: "'Thanks for everything and may be see you later.' *I did not recognize my own voice*, but I did say it to Mommy Riet" (71, italics Hvl and SS). Here, the overt intervention of the voice of the present self puts the voice of the past self into perspective. According to Kokkola, such interventions have the same effect as the exposure of a failing memory. Both contribute to the credibility of the protagonist as a real flesh-and- blood person (124).

Collaborative life writing projects such as the *Slash* series rely not only on a dialogue between the voices of the present and the past self, but also on a third voice, the mediating adult author. In *Voor jou 10 anderen*, this voice is mainly visible through the careful application of the ethics of form or the composition of the text. This creates a "paradox of authenticity": while the ethics of form is applied to guarantee a true-to-life representation of the adolescent protagonist, it simultaneously reveals the voice of the adult author, which theoretically reduces authenticity. However, as the interviews have made clear, this is not how it is perceived by the partners in this collaborative life writing project. All authors and adolescents emphasized that, for the stories to be told, they could not do without each other's voices.

Marah Gubar rightly criticizes the fact that the story most scholars tell about children's literature "rules out the possibility that young people can function as artistic agents, participants in the production of culture" (452). Victoria Ford Smith is one of the scholars who counters this traditional story by presenting cultural artifacts from the past that "all make space for the possibility of the agentic, creative child, inside and outside the book" (13). The *Slash* series presented here is a contemporary example of collaborative life writing that contests the idea of children's literature as one-way traffic; that is, created and controlled by adults only. The run-up to the process, as well as the process itself, provides evidence of relatedness, respect, and trust between two partners for whom age is irrelevant. There was transparency about the aim and the context of the series and about the role of each partner. Moreover, both the adult and young adult felt that in the result their contributions are closely intertwined. We have shown that a close-reading of *Voor jou 10 anderen* supports this perception. Carefully applying the ethics of form, the adult author portrayed the protagonist's emotions, her inconsistent memory, and her polyvocal self in an authentic way, while still preserving her own writing style in the process. The mingling of breaths in this creative project acknowledges the young adult's agency as equally important as the adult's agency. As much as the young adults learned from their cooperation with the experienced authors, the authors also learned from the personalities of the young informants. In the words of Edward van de Vendel: "I see the book as something invaluable that Anoush has given to me" (Van de Vendel, research interview, January 22, 2018).

## NOTES

1. Oldenhave is not the foster mother who figures in *Voor jou 10 anderen*.
2. In English: close to "back off."
3. See also Smith and Watson, 86, 216–18, and Kokkola, 97–100, 106–107.

## WORKS CITED

Booth, Wayne. *The Company We Keep: An Ethics of Fiction*. University of California Press, 1988.
Couser, G. Thomas. *Vulnerable Subjects: Ethics and Life Writing*. Cornell University Press, 2004.
Douglas, Kate. *Contesting Childhood. Autobiography, Trauma, and Memory*. Rutgers University Press, 2010.
Eakin, John Paul. "Introduction: Mapping the Ethics of Life Writing." In *The Ethics of Life Writing*, ed. John Eakin, 1–16. Cornell University Press, 2004.
Eakin, John Paul. "Relational Selves, Relational Lives: The Story of the Story." In *True Relations: Essays on Autobiography and the Postmodern*, eds. G. Thomas Couser and Joseph Fichtelberg, 63–81. Greenwood, 1998.

Eck, Cynthia van. Research interview, February 5, 2018.
Ford Smith, Victoria. *Between Generations. Collaborative Authorship in the Golden Age of Children's Literature*. University Press of Mississippi, 2017.
Gubar, Marah. "Risky Business: Talking about Children in Children's Literature." *Children's Literature Association Quarterly* 38, no. 4 (2013): 450–57.
Janssen, Vicky. Research interview, January 16, 2018.
Kawous, Ramin. Research interview, February 7, 2018.
Kokkola, Lydia. *Representing the Holocaust in Children's Literature*. Routledge, 2003.
Kranendonk, Anke. Research interview, January 9, 2018.
Kranendonk, Lieke. Research interview, January 24, 2018.
Kranendonk, Anke, and Lieke Kranendonk. *Alles is weg*. Querido, 2009.
Lejeune, Philippe. *Le Pacte autobiographique*. Editions du Seuil, 1975.
Nikolajeva, Maria. *Power, Voice and Subjectivity in Literature for Young Readers*. Routledge, 2010.
Oldenhave, Mirjam. Research interview, February 6, 2018.
Oldenhave, Mirjam, and Cynthia van Eck. *Voor jou tien anderen*. Querido, 2008.
Parker, David. "Life Writing as Narrative of the Good: *Father and Son* and the Ethics of Authenticity." In *The Ethics of Life Writing*, ed. John Eakin, 53–72. Cornell University Press, 2004.
Patterson, Dave. *The Shriek of Silence: A Phenomenology of the Holocaust Novel*. University Press of Kentucky, 1992.
Smith, Sidonie, and Julia Watson. *Reading Autobiography: A Guide for Interpreting Life Narratives*. 2nd ed. University of Minnesota Press, 2010.
Steels, Sabine. "Ethiek en life writing in jeugdliteratuur. Bouwstenen voor ethisch verantwoorde levensverhalen over trauma en de toepassing ervan op de Slashreeks voor jongeren." Master's thesis, Tilburg, 2015.
Vendel, Edward van. "Over adem." *Literatuur zonder leeftijd* 20, no. 71 (2006): 118–28.
Vendel, Edward van, and Anoush Elman. *De gelukvinder*. Querido, 2008.
Vendel, Edward van. Research interview, January 22, 2018.
Woltz, Anna. Research interview, January 14, 2018.

# AFTERWORD
## THE CASE OF THE EVIL (STEP)MOTHER, OR THE IMPOSSIBILITY OF INTERGENERATIONAL SOLIDARITY

Maria Nikolajeva

"I'll be damned," said Douglas. "I never thought of that. That's brilliant! It's true. Old people never *were* children!"

"And it's kind of sad," said Tom, sitting still. "There's nothing we can do to help them."

(Ray Bradbury, *Dandelion Wine*, 87)

The title of my chapter manifestly alludes to the title of Jacqueline Rose's book (1984), which, after more than thirty years, still serves as a starting point for any discussion of the nature and purpose of literature marketed for young audiences. Rose's argument, with its psychoanalytical flavor, focuses on the author, whether real or implied, whose adulthood distances them from the genuine experience of the child. Rose wrote this influential work long before contemporary memory studies confirmed that the so-called childhood memories are confabulations (see, for example, Foster 2009); however, her main premise opened the ongoing debate about representation of child/adult hierarchies in children's fiction that do not necessarily reflect the actual state of the matter, as described by childhood studies. Fiction after all is fiction and not fact precisely because it deliberately deviates from fact. Thus, the primary role of parents in children's literature is to be absent, preferably dead, which allows child protagonists agency generally unavailable to real children. The primary role of parents in young adult fiction, as Roberta Trites points out in *Disturbing the Universe* (2000), is to be the target of parental revolt. Between these two categories, there is not much room for intergenerational solidarity. There are, of course, exceptions, many of which are treated in the present volume. Yet, when it comes to fiction targeting a young audience, intergenerational solidarity is an oxymoron, a contradiction in terms. The premise of children's and young adult fiction as a specific form of storytelling is that the older generation is either comfortably removed, to allow the young protagonist a carnivalesque agency, or equally comfortably reintroduced, to present a rival in the struggle for survival of the fittest.

Here is where the storytelling conventions come to conflict with the educational and ideological intentions of children's literature. Again, as contributors to this and other volumes (for instance, Joosen 2018a; 2018b) persuasively demonstrate, representations of harmonious child/adult relationships in children's literature are not only possible but frequently successful in their assertion that generations should be mutually understanding and supportive. This harmony is an educational agenda that in children's literature shares space with issues such as gender equality and social justice. Therefore, paradoxically, such diverse genres as fairy tales and Bildungsroman—in other words, fiction featuring young people, but targeting a mature audience—offer a more accurate reflection of the real-life generational tensions that are far from harmonious. The purpose of this concluding chapter is not to question the prominence of positive child/adult portrayals in texts for young readers, but to suggest additional ways of looking at these texts than through the lenses of critical theory and constructivism. In my argument, I am deliberately provocative in order to draw attention to major inconsistences between the didactic—in the most positive sense—nature of children's literature and two interdependent facets that put this didacticism on trial: firstly, the narrative demands of storytelling; and secondly, the evolutionarily conditioned rift between generations that children's literature may attempt to gloss over. Let us consider the following story:

> Once there was a girl whose nickname was Red Riding Hood. One day her Mum said:
> 
> "It has been a while since we visited Granny. I have baked a cake and made some blackcurrant juice. Let's go and visit Granny."
> 
> Red Riding Hood was browsing the Web, but she was always happy to spend some time with her Mum and Gran. Off they went. As they were walking through the forest, Red Riding Hood said:
> 
> "You know, Mum, Granny toiled all her life cooking and cleaning and making Granddad happy, and I see you toiling morning till night cooking and cleaning and making Dad happy. I don't want this kind of life. I want to be a scientist."
> 
> "That's great," said Mum. "You will be the first in our family to go to university."
> 
> They came to the old people's home where Granny lived. It was a very good home that Mum and Dad had chosen with great care, and Granny was happy

there. Red Riding Hood, Mum and Granny sat on a veranda, eating cake and drinking juice, and Mum told Granny about Red's decision to become a scientist.

"That's great," said Granny. "I have savings after Granddad died. I have enough money to send you to Cambridge."

"Thank you, Granny," said Red Riding Hood. "It's very nice of you to support my dream."

Red Riding Hood and Mum went home, where Mum hurried to cook dinner before Dad returned from work. They had dinner, watched *Downton Abbey*, and went to bed.

This is a perfect story of intergenerational solidarity. Mother and daughter are good friends; mother is good toward *her* mother; and grandmother is grateful for her children for arranging the best care for her, in addition to supporting her granddaughter's ambitions. Possibly, the father could do some chores, but apart from that, this is a complete idyll.

However, it is not only an exceptionally boring story, but a story full of lies. Real life is not like that. Art is not like that either. Good storytelling needs some recognizable patterns, or as cognitive literary scholars call them, schemas and scripts (see, for example, Stockwell 2002; Hogan 2003). At the very least, a story needs a complication, a conflict. For the sake of argument, I will use implements from cognitive poetics, more precisely, mind-modeling (Zunshine 2006; Stockwell 2009; Stockwell and Mahlberg 2015), which implies readers' understanding of literary characters' thoughts and feelings, as well as of their thoughts about each other's thoughts. Below the idyllic surface, there are a number of potential conflicts of my conflictless story.

Applying mind-modeling to the mother might suggest that she is jealous of Red. The daughter is young and pretty, while the mother is aging. The daughter will soon compete with the mother for suitors. The script is recognizable from *Snow White*. But rather than sending the daughter into the woods, the mother is overprotective and does not allow her daughter any agency. She knows that there are suitors in the woods, but if she keeps the daughter company she will scare them off. The daughter, in turn, resents her mother's protection. She has a secret suitor, a certain Jack Wolf, whom she met at an online dating site that her mother has no control over. Red has arranged to meet Wolf in the woods next time she goes to visit her Grandmother. She is outraged when her mother suggests they go together, but must not reveal it.

The mother hates her mother-in-law who has always been a busybody and made her life hell on earth. She only pretends to be nice to her because the old hag will die soon and leave all her hoarded money to her only son. The marriage is a disaster, but the mother must endure it because she can never gain financial independence. She is a victim of patriarchy. She resents her daughter's dream of education. She is all the more outraged when the grandmother supports Red and offers to pay for her education. What a waste of money! What if the old witch has written a will in which she leaves all her money to her granddaughter?

The grandmother has always believed that her son married below his status. She thinks the slut deliberately got pregnant to snare him. She has ruined his career. Grandmother hates being dispatched to a care home, and she hates visits from her daughter-in-law whose cakes taste like toilet paper. She has written a will in which she leaves all her money to Wolf Protection Trust. She likes imagining the day when the will is opened. But she will pay her granddaughter's education just to spite the daughter-in-law.

I could go on, bringing in both the father and Mr. Wolf, but I have made my point. A story that is idyllic on the surface is rife with conflicts. Story after story, myth after myth, folktale after folktale, novel after novel, are all based on conflicts, most of which are intergenerational. Children try to liberate themselves from their parents' oppression; parents try to prevent their children, mostly unsuccessfully, from taking over. In Greek mythology, Cronus castrates his father and devours his children. Similar motifs occur in every culture. Depending on whether the story is told from the perspective of one generation or the other, one will be presented as victim and the other as perpetrator.

There are many good reasons for stories utilizing this script, and I will consider two of these: bio-psychological and aesthetic. The first approach employs the framework of evolutionary literary studies (e.g., Gottschall and Wilson 2005; Beer 2009; Boyd 2009; Boyd et al. 2010; Carroll 2011; 2012; Gottschall 2012; Davis 2012) to explore intergenerational relationships in a broad evolutionary perspective, that is, considering why child/adult hierarchies are portrayed the way they are, both in arts in general and in children's literature in particular. From the aesthetic point of view, the whole premise of children's literature is generational conflict, whether you view it from structuralist, psychoanalytical, feminist, postcolonial, posthuman, or cognitive perspectives. In my previous work, I have proposed the concept of aetonormativity to describe this phenomenon (Nikolajeva 2010), and I argue that as soon as aetonormativity is eliminated, the purpose of children's literature disappears. True, aetonormativity is frequently subverted, mostly through carnivalesque narrative devices, yet it can never be completely dismissed. There are numerous examples of children's texts in which an adult—typically a grandparent, a teacher, and occasionally a stranger—is portrayed as supportive; this figure, or a schema, as cognitive criticism would call it, goes back to the figure of the Wise Old Man or Woman in archaic thought whose role is to take young people through initiation. Once initiation is complete, the guide is usually discarded. There are other scripts in which child/adult relationships are depicted as harmonious or in which intergenerational memory is empowering, and it is easy to provide examples that contradict my argument. However, in this chapter I am not discussing specific texts, but general lines.

From the evolutionary perspective, children's literature, and literature and arts in general, are imagined orders: activities that have no immediate connection to evolution, as opposed to natural orders. The latter, in an oversimplified sense, originate from successful reproduction and natural selection. In contrast, imagined orders include arts, science, economics, religion, ethics, property, law, social hierarchies, interpersonal relationships, social justice, and education—that is, aspects of human life that do not directly contribute to evolution (see, for example, Harari 2011, 102–118). At the same time, one of the main disagreements among evolutionary scholars is exactly the question of what imagined orders are *for*, a question posed in an early work by evolutionary scholar Ellen Dissanayake, *What is Art For?* (1990). There is no consensus on whether art is a form of sexual display, whether it has an adaptive function, or whether it is a spandrel (a side effect of other adaptive processes [e.g., Boyd 2005; Davies, 121–88]). It is, however, frequently emphasized that imagined orders regulate human societies in various ways that contradict and counteract the purpose of evolution; some examples are regulations of property, opposition to violence, racial intolerance, ethics, and social justice (see, for example, Harari 2011, 2016; Pinker). In short, imagined orders help human beings to resist evolutionarily conditioned behavior, for their individual good and for the good of humanity as a whole. At the same time, evolution may favor imagined orders that in the long run contribute to evolutionary goals.

How, then, can we use insights from evolutionary studies to consider intergenerational relationships as depicted in children's literature? Unless we subscribe to the claim that art is a spandrel, which I find problematic, it is logical to assume that if evolution supports imagined orders beneficial for survival, it presumably follows that children's literature has survival advantages. Evolutionary theory suggests that the adults' motivation to instruct or amuse children through stories has a crucial adaptive purpose. Nonhuman animals educate their young through individual training, which may include finding food and shelter, distinguishing between good food and bad food, recognizing prey and predator, and thus avoiding danger. Much of this education is based on play, and for many evolutionary scholars play is already a form of art, a predetermined script—for instance, for hunt or fight (see, for example, Boyd 2009, 80–98). Yet this script is transmitted as individual experience, from parent to child, and each child has to learn it all over again. What possibly makes humans distinct from nonhuman animals is that we eventually acquired the capacity to share scripts about things beyond immediate sensory perception—stories built on memories and previous experience, both individual and communal. Evolutionary criticism claims that humans are storytelling animals, who have survived as a species thanks to their ability to tell stories (see, for example, Boyd 2009; Carroll 2012; Gottschall 2012), and that early stories are likely to have been told by adults to the young, for survival purposes. Storytelling, as well as play, is the most effective way of generational knowledge and experience transmission, far more effective than straightforward instruction. However, let us consider what kind of evolutionarily beneficial knowledge and experience children's literature endorses.

Evolutionary studies emphasize that one of the most essential factors in all animals' survival strategy, human and nonhuman animals alike, is the ability to distinguish between in-group and out-group, between "us" and "them." Moreover, the two central categories that are immediately recognizable are gender and age. Gender recognition supports the decision whether a stranger is eligible for mating; age recognition supports the decision whether a stranger presents a threat and also what power hierarchies are at play—is the stranger younger, a peer, or an elder; stronger or weaker; higher or lower in social hierarchy? The moment of recognition and subsequent decision is the starting point of most narratives. However, I would argue that gender recognition plays a more prominent role in fiction addressing adult audience, precisely because the goal is selecting a suitable mate. In contrast, the most important children's literature specific element in the us/them divide, largely absent from general literature, is the divide between children and adults, portrayed from a child's point of view.

Adult/child subordination is an imagined order that can be viewed from various perspectives, from repression, as suggested by Roberta Trites (2000), to subversion, as proposed by Clémentine Beauvais (2015). This subordination is supported by evolution because in the natural order human children need protection for a significantly longer period than most other species. The imagined order, however, prescribes a child's gradual liberation from adult protection, which children's literature portrays through various carnivalesque devices, when social hierarchies are temporarily inverted. In carnivalesque children's literature, child characters are empowered in ways that seemingly subvert evolution; yet evolution benefits from survival of the fittest, and fictional children are allowed to take over the world from less adaptive adults. This script also conveys the message that adults are not necessarily omniscient and omnipotent—to put it plainly, that children have the potential to make the world a better place.

The script that we can call transformative, following Clémentine Beauvais's (2015) model, is plausible because, as an imagined order, children's literature can potentially counterbalance the notorious selfish gene (Dawkins 2016) through ethics, solidarity, and social justice. In the natural order, children should unconditionally obey adults, for their own good. Yet, evolution and natural selection depend on spontaneous mutations, and each slight mutation in the imagined order of child/adult relationship may cause a radical change if it is beneficial for survival. It is, for instance, almost universally accepted today that respecting children's rights is a more efficient educational implement than punishment (cf. Pinker, 228–32), which we clearly see if we consider children's literature in a historical context. All shifts in the values and attitudes in children's literature are conveyed from the older to the younger generation through schemas and scripts.

There are species in which it is habitual for females to evict their young as soon as they become pregnant again. This makes sense so that the new babies get the mother's undivided attention, but the prerequisite is that the young animal can fend for themselves. If they haven't learned well enough, or if the mother has failed in supporting survival skills, the young animal will perish. Human babies are, for a number of good natural reasons, unable to take care of themselves considerably longer than other animals; therefore, a human child still needs parental support when a new baby is on the way. In addition, the imagined order of parental love makes it inconceivable that a human mother may want to get rid of her older child to take care of the new one. However, this script is frequently used in children's books in which protagonists feel anxious about the arrival of a new sibling. The script reflects a suppressed, archaic natural order in which a young human was indeed in danger of being abandoned or at least neglected when a new child arrived (a script, one may add, that society supports since it is beneficial). In a children's book, the script is typically resolved in a number of ways: the parents manage to persuade the protagonist that they love them just as much as before; the protagonist gets a puppy as compensation, or a new friend. Alternatively, the mother is narratively replaced by a stepmother, where rejection may seem less offensive. A stepmother either brings her own offspring, a stepsibling, or gets a new baby, a half-sibling, or both. In any case, an imagined order is employed to gloss over the natural order, but in the end, everybody becomes friends. This is just one example that demonstrates how an intergenerational conflict based on evolutionary premises is resolved in a satisfactory manner to assure young readers that their evolutionarily conditioned hostility toward a new sibling is meritless, and that societal practices, including child/parent relationships, will protect them from a bio-psychologically dictated threat.

Some other common scripts involve gender as well as age. All stories portraying intergenerational relationships operate with one or several of the four possible combinations: mother-daughter, mother-son, father-daughter, and father-son. Of these, the mother-daughter script is perhaps the most frequent, evoking Cinderella, Snow White, Rapunzel, and numerous children's novels and films (see, for example, Crew 2000). Once again, imagined orders in all cultures regulate relationships within close communities, such as families. Let us return, for instance, to the figure of the evil stepmother. From an evolutionary point of view, the stepmother's actions are not only acceptable and justifiable but also highly rational. Her goal is to pass on her genes, of which her daughters carry 50 percent, while her stepdaughter carries none. Moreover, she must ensure that her daughters find suitable mates, sufficiently wealthy and powerful, so that 25 percent of the genes are passed on to the next generation. The stepmother's oppression of the stepdaughter is a way to make her unattractive for potential suitors (for instance, by giving her worn-out clothes and smearing her face with ashes) to ensure that she dies without having reproduced.

According to many folktale scholars, both within psychoanalytical (Bettelheim 1976) and socio-historical (Zipes 1983) schools of thought, the evil stepmother is a late circumscription of the biological mother, since it ostensibly renders the mother/daughter conflict less disturbing, particularly in the Snow White-type stories. However, the biological mother script makes little sense from the evolutionary point of view. Why would a mother wish her daughter, who carries 50 percent of her genes, dead before she has procreated? (The only possible reason might be that the mother knows or believes that her daughter's genes are defective, but this is a far-fetched explanation). The stepmother script is therefore more convincing than the psychoanalytical account of the aging mother's envy and jealousy of the daughter's fertility. Portrayal of dysfunctional parent/child relationships is an imagined order that goes against the evolutionarily supported script and, indeed, proves unsustainable. Either a substitute parent or society must intervene, because a human child cannot as a rule care for themselves (stories of feral children are rare, while stories of child superheroes presuppose certain genre conventions).

The next question is why, if the stepmother's actions are justifiable, all stepmother scripts promptly punish the stepmother and her children, while rewarding the oppressed stepdaughter with a powerful and wealthy mate even though she has done nothing to deserve it. Let us remember that evolution is not interested in social justice, even though it can support altruism when it is beneficial for the survival of a genetic pool. The stepmother's actions, however, are not altruistic; she simply wants her stepdaughter eliminated. Here is where imagined orders enter. The idea of justice demands that those who oppress others be punished and the oppressed be rewarded. To justify the reward, the script makes the oppressors particularly nasty (ugly, spiteful, greedy—that is, positioned as an out-group) and the oppressed articulately virtuous and humble, eliciting recipients' empathy. Ethics, the imagined order that regulates our concepts of good and evil, virtue and vice, is introduced in stories, especially stories targeting children, to encourage the underdog to change their status either by disposing of the adversary or by seeking and conquering another territory. But even the nicest, most supportive biological mother will sooner or later encourage the daughter to leave, find a suitable mate and pass on the genes.

The father-son script also reflects intergenerational conflict, but is affected by the gender-specific behavioral differences. In many species, females are prompted by evolution to mate with as many males as possible. This behavior also guarantees that males will not kill offspring since they can never be sure that they do not kill their own and thus jeopardize gene reproduction. Males, in turn, are prompted not just to mate with as many females as possible, but to prevent all other males from mating, including their own sons. A son competes with the father, but not because he desires his mother, as the Oedipal script in psychoanalysis proposes. From an evolutionary perspective, there is no point in desiring the mother because the son already carries 50 percent of her genes. Instead, the son's evolutionary goals are, firstly, to replace his father in mating with non-related females and pass on his genes, and secondly, to protect both the mother and his existing and potential siblings who carry 50 percent of his genes. The script in which a son supports his mother and even protects her from the father is frequently reflected in children's books (see, for example, Coats and Fraustino 2015). At the same time, I would argue that this is not entirely based on solidarity, or rather altruism, but on evolutionarily conditioned egoism. A young male benefits from his mother's and siblings' survival, while the father presents a rival for the son's successful reproduction. Patricide is therefore fully justifiable from the evolutionary perspective, and we seldom have objections to male protagonists in children's literature killing their father figures, like Peter Pan or Harry Potter. However, the imagined order of filial affection counterbalances the patricidal script, as we see clearly in numerous children's novels depicting father-son reunion and reconciliation. By contrast, the imagined order of a son's selfish desire for his mother, emphasized in psychoanalytical discourse, unhelpfully blurs the natural order of the son's altruistic affection for and protection of the mother. In other words, regarding the mother/son relationship, the psychoanalytical imagined order is superimposed on the natural solidarity.

Finally, the father-daughter script, while possibly the least prominent in children's literature, is the most straightforward, as it is based on the unconditional taboo against incest. In children's literature, this taboo is frequently disguised as general abuse or neglect, which is sufficiently offensive. In evolutionary terms, a father benefits from keeping his sons away from eligible females, but he equally benefits from protecting his daughters. An abusive or neglecting father is a script in which the imaginary order of a functional family is used to highlight the father's fault. Again, the conflict is resolved either by the father's reform or by introducing a substitute, preferably one without reproductive potential. A recurrent script in young adult fiction is a girl having a crush on a male teacher who is clever and responsible enough to channel her desires toward a peer.

The common denominator of all these scripts is the fact that generations have distinctly different evolutionary goals. Three interdependent goals of adults dictated by evolution—wealth, status, and procreation—are the narrative engines of general fiction, while they are essentially irrelevant for children. Instead, children's literature focuses on the most salient aspects of childhood: safety and nutrition. Further, while adulthood aims at stability, childhood is by definition unstable and ever-changing, a fact duly reflected by children's literature. Yet children should preferably develop awareness of adult survival strategies and priorities, such as sexuality and upward social mobility. Therefore, children's and adolescent fiction explores, in a safe mode, young people's tentative ventures into adulthood: leaving the security of home and family, revolting against parental and social authorities, catering for themselves, initiating peer relationships, and behaving responsibly when it comes to both other individuals and society as a whole. All these activities imply a disruption of the established child/adult hierarchies through various carnivalesque devices. Some children's and particularly young adult novels take their protagonist closer to adulthood; some revert to childhood after the carnival is over. The border can easily become fluctuant, yet it can never be fully eliminated in a book that either purports to portray a child, or to address a young audience, or both. Here, I believe, Marah Gubar's (2011; 2016) kinship model fails since it attempts to blur the border, which, at the extreme, questions the very purpose of identifying childhood, and consequently children's literature, as a separate category.

As already mentioned, a common schema of an intergenerational relationship in children's literature is an older person, such as a grandparent who acts as a substitute parent when the real parent is absent or dysfunctional. Charlie's grandfather in *Charlie and the Chocolate Factory* is one good example; another is Mister Tom in Michelle Magorian's *Goodnight, Mr Tom* (see Joosen 2017). This figure is interesting from the evolutionary perspective. Seemingly, a person beyond an age of fertility becomes superfluous since they no longer have the capacity to pass their genes to the next generation. While this circumstance doubtless contributes to the increasing physical decay of older people due to weakened autoimmune system, evolutionary studies offer the so-called grandmother hypothesis (see, for example, Hawkes) which suggests that although women beyond an age of fertility are useless in terms of procreation, they still contribute to survival of the young by taking care of them while the parental generation is engaged either in providing food or in courtship and mating. Grandchildren carry 25 percent of grandparents' genes; therefore by protecting the grandchildren, grandparents contribute to group survival. We know of this behavior in many nonhuman animal species, and there are also numerous examples of childless aunts who assist in taking care of their nieces and nephews carrying 25 percent of the aunt's genes. In children's literature, a grandparent's role can be replaced by any elderly person, not necessarily related, yet this figure is a schema based on natural order. Moreover, evolution generally supports altruism when it is beneficial for the survival of a group, not just an individual. Being altruistic implies acting in ways that are advantageous to other individuals without any gain for oneself. An elderly stranger taking care of an orphan or an otherwise neglected child contributes to the well-being of an in-group—for instance, community, school, religion, nation, species, or a football team. Contemporary children's literature particularly promotes inclusion and tolerance, enhancing age-based divisions by other alterities, including race, disability, or sexual orientation. In this way, intergenerational solidarity also emphasizes social justice.

In his influential work *Signs of Childness in Children's Literature*, Peter Hollindale proposes that there is a certain set of qualities that characterize a child, which he calls "childness," claiming that it includes the child's awareness of being a child: "A child is someone who believes on good grounds that his or her condition of childhood is not yet over" (30). This self-awareness, as I see it, is a key element in Hollindale's concept of childness, as opposed to childhood that is predominantly defined by adults' awareness, or "belief on good grounds," of a human being's condition of childhood. This view has been questioned by some contemporary scholars, notably, Marah Gubar (2016), who oppose the binary of childhood/adulthood and prefer to see a continuum with strong bonds between generations. It is certainly impossible and counterproductive to point at a particular boundary between childhood and adulthood, not least because these concepts, whether biological or sociological, are historically and culturally determined. Yet there are both biological and cognitive differences between childness, in Hollindale's sense, and adultness, which, by analogy, is a state of awareness "on good grounds" of being adult. Good grounds may include financial independence, social status, and reproductive capacity, the latter not merely implying sexuality or sexual activity but the capacity to care for the offspring. In my recent response to Hollindale (Nikolajeva 2018), I argue that adults can no more understand the childness of a child than the batness of a bat—in other words, that the cognitive discrepancy between children and adults is insurmountable, that children's authors' claims of their childhood memories are based on false premises, and that children's literature as it is often understood is indeed impossible, although for different reasons than those proposed by Jacqueline Rose. Yet we see clearly that children's literature persists, and that children's authors' pursuit of childness is an aesthetic challenge, just as any attempt to capture and convey another subject's experience is an aesthetic challenge. It is there, I believe, children's authors endeavor to bridge the generational gap.

This brings me to the final part of my argument, the aesthetic reasons for the omnipresence of generational conflict. Obviously, behavioral and cognitive scripts are directly connected to narrative elements. As already mentioned, the absence of parental authority is one of the defining elements of a children's book plot. This element goes back to the fundamental structure of myths and folktales, described by structuralist scholars such as Vladimir Propp in *Morphology of the Folktale* and Joseph Campbell in *A Hero with the Thousand Faces*. This narrative element, in turn, is believed to originate in archaic initiation rites, when novices were removed from family protection and put on trial before they were returned to society as its approved members. Most children's books, if not all of them, start with the character either being abandoned by parental figures or displaced into an environment where such figures are beyond reach. This narrative element is also present in Aristotelian poetics as peripeteia, or complication (Aristotle). It is next to impossible to construct a plot without a complication, and what is the most natural complication for a child if not the threat of lost security, the fear of being abandoned and vulnerable. The plot is persistent in children's literature because it reflects a child's ineluctable dependence on adults for nutrition and protection.

While this necessary abandonment is dictated by the bio-psychological conditions I described earlier, from the narrative point of view it is simply indispensable for a successful plot construction. In real life, we may experience prolonged periods without radical conflicts or complications. However, the purpose of storytelling is to present readers or listeners with situations that they may not be exposed to in real life—that is, situations of conflict and crisis where their survival skills and ethical values can be tested. Such stories offer readers vicarious experiences that they probably would prefer to avoid in real life, including being abandoned, neglected, or abused by parental figures.

Again, in real life such conflicts are not always resolved. Children's literature, and to a certain extent also young adult literature, can offer satisfactory conflict resolutions, either through a reunion with parental figures or a successful introduction of substitutes. Such resolution confirms aetonormativity, restoring the initial power hierarchy and returning the child to dependence on adults. From an evolutionary point of view, this is not the optimal solution, since the young person will eventually need to leave adult protection behind and engage in peer relationships that lead to reproduction. However, from an aesthetic point of view, intergenerational conflict resolution, frequently referred to as a happy ending, is valuable, since it provides young readers with the sense of protection they need until they are ready to care for themselves. As has been already pointed out, human young require a much longer period of adult protection than most other animals; as such, the sense of security is necessary at least until mid-adolescence. Incidentally, adolescence in the Western world has recently been officially extended to the age of twenty-four (Sawyer et al. 2018), which implies that young people remain dependent on adults significantly longer than even fifty years ago. In his fascinating study *Entranced by Story: Brain, Tale and Teller, from Infancy to Old Age* (2014), Hugh Crago suggests that readers at different stages of life respond more readily to narratives most relevant to their age, such as safety in childhood, risk-taking in adolescence, reproduction in adulthood, and decay in senescence. While this classification may seem oversimplified, it does identify central scripts for each category.

Intergenerational conflict, then, is a recurrent narrative element of children's literature, its centerpiece and engine. While solidarity may be represented on certain conditions, it is fundamentally incompatible with children's literature aesthetics. Yet, just as "the impossibility of children's literature," proclaimed by Jacqueline Rose, has not stopped scores of brilliant writers to accept the challenge, the cognitive and aesthetic impossibility of intergenerational solidarity has not prevented authors from exploring this complex issue.

## WORKS CITED

Aristotle. *Poetics*. Oxford University Press, 2013.
Beauvais, Clémentine. *The Mighty Child: Time and Power in Children's Literature*. John Benjamin, 2015.
Beer, Gillian. *Darwin's Plots: Evolutionary Narrative in Darwin, George Eliot and Nineteenth-Century Fiction*. 3rd ed. Cambridge University Press, 2009.
Bettelheim, Bruno. *The Uses of Enchantment: The Meaning and Importance of Fairy Tales*. Knopf, 1976.
Boyd, Brian. "Evolutionary Theories of Art." In *The Literary Animal. Evolution and the Nature of Narrative*, eds. Jonathan Gotschall and David Sloan Wilson, 147–76. Northwestern University Press, 2005.
Boyd, Brian. *On the Origin of Stories: Evolution, Cognition and Fiction*. Harvard University Press, 2010.

Boyd, Brian, Joseph Carroll, and Jonathan Gottschall, eds. *Evolution, Literature and Film*. Columbia University Press, 2010.
Bradbury, Ray. *Dandelion Wine*. 1957. Avon, 1999.
Campbell, Joseph. *The Hero with a Thousand Faces*. Pantheon, 1949.
Carroll, Joseph. *Reading Human Nature: Literary Darwinism in Theory and Practice*. State University of New York Press, 2011.
Carroll, Joseph. *Literary Darwinism: Evolution, Human Nature, and Literature*. Routledge, 2012.
Coats, Karen, and Lisa Rowe Fraustino, eds. "Performing Motherhood: Introduction to a Special Issue on Mothering in Children's and Young Adult Literature." *Children's Literature in Education* 46 no. 2 (2015): 107–109.
Crago, Hugh. *Entranced by Story: Brain, Tale and Teller, from Infancy to Old Age*. Routledge, 2014.
Crew, Hilary S. *It is Really "Mommie Dearest"? Daughter-Mother Narratives in Young Adult Fiction*. Scarecrow, 2000.
Dawkins, Richard. 1976. *The Selfish Gene*. Oxford University Press, 2016.
Dissanayake, Ellen. *What is Art For?* University of Washington Press, 1990.
Davies, Stephen. *The Artful Species: Aesthetics, Art, and Evolution*. Oxford University Press, 2012.
Foster, Jonathan K. *Memory: A Very Short Introduction*. Oxford University Press, 2009.
Gottschall, Jonathan. *The Storytelling Animal: How Stories Make Us Human*. Houghton Mifflin Harcourt, 2012.
Gottschall, Jonathan, and David Sloan Wilson, eds. *The Literary Animal: Evolution and the Nature of Narrative*. Northwestern University Press, 2005.
Gubar, Marah. "On Not Defining Children's Literature." *PMLA* 126, no. 1 (2011): 209–216, doi.org/10.1632/pmla.2011.126.1.209
Gubar, Marah. "The Hermeneutics of Recuperation: What a Kinship-model Approach to Children's Agency Could Do for Children's Literature and Childhood Studies." *Jeunesse: Young People, Texts, Cultures* 8 no. 1 (2016): 291–310, doi:10.1353/jeu.2016.0015.
Harari, Noah Yuval. *Sapiens: A Brief History of Humankind*. Harvill Secker, 2011.
Harari, Noah Yuval. *Homo Deus: A Brief History of Tomorrow*. Harvill Secker, 2016.
Hawkes, Kristen. "Human Longevity: The Grandmother Effect." *Nature* 428 (2004): 128–29, doi:10.1038/428128a.
Hogan, Patrick Colm. *The Mind and Its Stories: Narrative Universals and Human Emotions*. Cambridge University Press, 2003.
Hollindale, Peter. *Signs of Childness in Children's Books*. Thimble Press, 1997.
Joosen, Vanessa. "Age Studies and Children's Literature." In *Edinburgh Companion to Children's Literature*, eds. Clémentine Beauvais and Maria Nikolajeva, 79–89. Edinburgh University Press, 2017.
Joosen, Vanessa. *Adulthood in Children's Literature*. Bloomsbury, 2018a.
Joosen, Vanessa, ed. *Connecting Childhood and Old Age in Popular Media*. University Press of Mississippi, 2018b.
Nikolajeva, Maria. *Power, Voice and Subjectivity in Literature for Young Readers*. Routledge, 2010.
Nikolajeva, Maria. "What is it Like to be a Child? Childness in the Age of Neuroscience." *Children's Literature in Education*, 2018, doi.org/10.1007/s10583-018-9373-7.
Pinker, Steven. *Enlightenment Now: The Case for Reason, Science, Humanism, and Progress*. Penguin, 2018.
Propp, Vladimir. *Morphology of the Folktale*. University of Texas Press, 1968.
Rose, Jacqueline. *The Case of Peter Pan, or The Impossibility of Children's Fiction*. Macmillan, 1984.

Sawyer, Susan M., Peter S. Azzopardi, Dakshitha Wickremarathne, and George C. Patton. "The Age of Adolescence. *The Lancet* 2 no. 3 (2018): 223–28, doi.org/10.1016/S2352-4642(18)30022-1.

Stockwell, Peter. *Cognitive Poetics: An Introduction*. Routledge, 2002.

Stockwell, Peter. *Texture: A Cognitive Aesthetics of Reading*. Edinburgh University Press, 2009.

Stockwell, Peter, and Michaela Mahlberg. "Mind-Modelling with Corpus Stylistics in David Copperfield." *Language and Literature* 24, no. 2 (2015): 129–47, doi.org/10.1177/0963947015576168.

Trites, Roberta Seelinger. *Disturbing the Universe: Power and Repression in Adolescent Literature*. University of Iowa Press, 2000.

Zunshine, Lisa. *Why We Read Fiction: Theory of Mind and the Novel*. Ohio State University Press, 2006.

Zipes, Jack. *Fairy Tales and the Art of Subversion*. Wildman, 1983.

# ABOUT THE CONTRIBUTORS

**Aneesh Barai** currently works in Education and Digital Literacies at the University of Sheffield. His research interests include representations of education in fantasy literature and film, intersections of modernism and children's literature, ecocriticism, and children's film. He has published on children's literature by T. S. Eliot, James Joyce, Sylvia Plath, Gertrude Stein, Langston Hughes, and Antoine de Saint-Exupéry. His current project is on modernism and school stories.

**Clémentine Beauvais** is a senior lecturer in English in Education at the University of York (UK). She has worked on children's literature theory, the history and cultural sociology of childhood, and is now working on literary translation in education. She is the author of *The Mighty Child: Time and Power in Children's Literature* (2015) and the coeditor, with Maria Nikolajeva, of *The Edinburgh Companion to Children's Literature* (2017).

**Justyna Deszcz-Tryhubczak** is associate professor of Literature and director of the Center for Young People's Literature and Culture at the Institute of English Studies, University of Wroclaw, Poland. She is the author of *Yes to Solidarity, No to Oppression: Radical Fantasy Fiction and Its Young Readers* (2016). She is a Kosciuszko, Fulbright, and Marie Skłodowska-Curie fellow. She has served as a member of the board of the International Research Society for Children's Literature.

**Terri Doughty** teaches in the English Department at Vancouver Island University. She has edited *Selections from the Girl's Own Paper, 1880–1907*, coedited *Knowing their Place? Identity and Space in Children's Literature*, and published on girls' adventure stories, YA fantasy fiction, and steampunk fairy tales. Her current interests include fairy-tale picturebooks as well as gender, fairies, and flora in illustrations.

**Aneta Dybska** is associate professor at the Institute of English Studies, University of Warsaw, Poland. Her book, *Regeneration, Citizenship and Justice in the American City since the 1970s* (2016), engages scholarly debates on revitalization and gentrification, theorizations of the "right to the city" idea, as well as grassroots struggles for the urban commons.

**Blanka Grzegorczyk** teaches at the University of Cambridge and Manchester Metropolitan University. She is the author of *Discourses of Postcolonialism in Contemporary British Children's Literature* (Routledge, 2015) and *Terror and Counter-Terror in Contemporary British Children's Literature* (Routledge, 2020).

**Zoe Jaques** is university lecturer in Children's Literature at the University of Cambridge. She is the author of *Children's Literature and the Posthuman: Animal, Environment, Cyborg* (2015) and coauthor of *Lewis Carroll's "Alice's Adventures in Wonderland" and "Through the Looking-Glass": A Publishing History* (2013). She is the general editor of the forthcoming three-volume *Cambridge History of Children's Literature in English*.

**Vanessa Joosen** is associate professor of English Literature and Children's Literature at the University of Antwerp, where she leads the European Research Council project "Constructing Age for Young Readers." She is the author of *Adulthood in Children's Literature* (2018) and has edited *Connecting Childhood and Old Age in Popular Media* (2018).

**Maria Nikolajeva** is professor emerita at the University of Cambridge. She is the author of numerous books on children's literature, most recently *Power, Voice and Subjectivity in Literature for Young People* (2009) and *Reading for Learning: Cognitive Approaches to Children's Literature* (2014). She coedited, with Clémentine Beauvais, *The Edinburgh Companion to Children's Literature* (2017). In 2005, she received the International Grimm Award for lifetime achievements in children's literature scholarship.

**Marek Oziewicz** is professor of Literacy Education at the University of Minnesota and holds the Sidney and Marguerite Henry Chair in Children's and Young Adult Literature at the College of Education and Human Development. He studies how literature helps young people become global citizens of a multicultural world, develop environmental awareness, and justice literacy. He is the author of *Justice in Young Adult Speculative Fiction: A Cognitive Reading* (2015).

**Ashley N. Reese** is a digital teaching fellow at the University of South Florida. She received her PhD.in Children's Literature from the University of Cambridge. Her current research focuses on gender and religion in turn-of-the-century, North American girls' books. She is the author of the forthcoming *The Rise of Girls' Literature*.

**Malini Roy** is penning down her experiences on having worked as a teacher trainer at the nonprofit organization Nanritam, which is located in a remote village in the state of West Bengal, India. She has written on childhood in British Romanticism, particularly in women's pediatric writing by Mary Wollstonecraft, and also on South Asian graphic novels. She blogs at https://theruminationsofsvanhildwall.blog/.

**Sabine Steels** is a cultural entrepreneur in Belgium. She inspires children and adults to engage with art. Sabine studied history and economy in the late 1990s and graduated in 2015 with a master's degree in Children's Literature from the Tilburg University. She received an honorary mention or her thesis "Ethics and Life Writing in Children's and Young Adult Literature," awarded by the Miep Diekmann Thesis Jury. She has a broad interest in children's literature and children's education.

**Lucy Stone** holds a Research Excellence Academy Studentship at Newcastle University, UK. Her doctoral project explores Judith Kerr's and Tomi Ungerer's literature from and about childhood exile in the Nazi era. Stone was a David Almond Fellow at Newcastle University and Seven Stories: The National Centre for Children's Books, UK, in 2016 and is a member of the IRSCL and UK section of IBBY.

**Björn Sundmark** is professor of English literature at Malmö University, Sweden, where he teaches "Children's Literature in a Global Perspective." He has published numerous articles and chapters on children's literature, and is the author of the study *Alice in the Oral-Literary Continuum* (1999) and the editor of *The Nation in Children's Literature* (2013) and *Child Autonomy and Child Governance in Children's Literature* (2016).

**Michelle Superle** is an associate professor in the English department at the University of the Fraser Valley. Her work has been published in *The Lion and the Unicorn* and *International Research in Children's Literature, Papers*. She is the author of *Contemporary, English-language Indian Children's Literature* (2011). She has served on the Children's Literature Association's International

Committee and currently sits on the editorial board of *Children's Literature in Education*.

**Nozomi Uematsu** is lecturer in Japanese Studies at the University of Sheffield in the School of East Asian Studies. She is a comparative literary scholar specializing in gender, sexuality, and neoliberalism in Japan and the UK. She has published on Doris Lessing, Jeanette Winterson, and Yoshimoto Banana, and on relations between women's happiness and labor (both giving birth and work). She is currently writing on women's masochism in Japan.

**Anastasia Ulanowicz** is associate professor of English at the University of Florida, where she teaches courses in children's literature, graphic narrative, trauma theory, and historical fiction. Her book, *Second-Generation Memory and Contemporary Children's Literature: Ghost Images* (2013), received the Children's Literature Association Book Award. Her current research involves representations of Eastern Europe in children's fiction and graphic narratives.

**Helma van Lierop-Debrauwer** is professor of Children's Literature at Tilburg University. She has published in national and international peer-reviewed journals and books on the history of children's literature, adolescent novels, picturebooks, and life writing. She coordinates a master's degree program on Children's Literature at Tilburg University and, together with other EU partners, she developed the Erasmus Mundus International Master's program "Children's Literature, Media, and Culture."

**Jean Webb** is professor of International Children's Literature at the University of Worcester. She has published widely on children's literature, including "Sickness and Literature for Children" in *The Edinburgh Companion to Children's Literature* (2017), edited by Maria Nikolajeva and Clémentine Beauvais.

# INDEX

Aarne-Thompson-Uther index, 10
Activism, xi, 120–21, 155, 159
Aetonormativity, xviii, xxiv, xxvin7, 31–33, 59, 67, 71, 112, 127, 176, 186n2, 220, 234, 243
Agency, 39, 96, 149, 165, 195, 232–33; of adults, xix, 79, 128, 229; of children, xix–xx, 18, 31–32, 59, 159, 169, 176, 185, 225, 229, 231; creative forms of, 117, 122, 224; of groups, 184; kinship-based, 33, 118
Akimoto, Daisuke, 81
Albert, Steven M., 89
Alderson, Priscilla, xvi
Altieri, Miguel, 164
Anderson, Rachel, xiv, xxiv, 148–53, 155, 157, 159
Anderson, Robert, 193–94
Animals: as distinctive to humans, 236–37; fantasies of, 56; interspecies solidarity, 86n5; representations of children and, 11–12, 164–74, 181–82
*Anne of Green Gables* (Montgomery), 19, 60, 75
*Anywhere Farm* (Root), 164, 167, 169–72
Aristotle, 210, 242
Arsenault, Isabelle, 8
Ascham, Roger, 197, 201
*Asylum* (Anderson), xiv, xxiv, 148–53, 155, 157, 159
Attebery, Brian, 137, 140
Austen, Jane, 194
Autobiography, 7, 101, 130, 207, 227–28

*Bambi* (Disney), 87
Banting, Keith, xvii

*Barack Obama, Son of Promise, Child of Hope* (Grimes and Collier), 8
Barthes, Roland, 90, 93, 95, 215
Beaumont, Matthew, 103
Bengtson, Vern, xii–xiii, 19, 25–26, 65
Bernstein, Robin, xviii
*Big* (Gracie Films), 71–72
Biggeri, Mario, xix
Biggs, Simon, xii, xvi
Bildungsroman, 5, 72, 75, 232
Billig, Michael, 177
*Billy Elliot* (Burgess and Hall), xxii, 47, 51–53
Biography, xxii, 3–4, 7–10, 15, 182–84, 210–11
Bloch, Ernst, 103–4
Boehmer, Elleke, 157–58
Bondoux, Anne-Laure, xxii, 14–15
Booth, Wayne, 219
Brahmachari, Sita, xiv, xxiv, 148–49, 154–59
*Breaktime* (Chambers), 205, 207
Buckingham, Will, xxii, 11–12
Burgess, Melvin, xxii, 47, 51–53
Burton, Tim, 134–35
Butler, Judith, 148, 151–53, 155–56
Butts, Donna, xii, 85

Carroll, Lewis, 201
Cattell, Maria G., 89
Cave, Terence, 210
Chambers, Aidan, xxiv, 205–16
Children's rights, xvi, 162–63, 165, 171, 198, 237
Christensen, Nina, 166, 173
Chu, Nancy, 166

Citizenship, 176–78, 182, 184–85
*City Green* (DiSalvo-Ryan), xxiv, 176, 182–85
Clemit, Pamela, 192–96, 202n2
*Cloth Lullaby* (Novesky and Arsenault), 8
*Coco* (Disney-Pixar), 86, 91–96
Cognitive studies, 139–41, 206, 233–34
Cohen, Dan, 20
Collier, Bryan, 8
Coulter, Kendra, 186n5
Couser, Thomas, 219–20
Covarrubias, Alexandra Mendoza, 94
Crago, Hugh, 243
Crandall, Nadia, 85
Craps, Stef, 130
Cross, Julie, xix
Cruz-Saco, María Amparo, xii–xiii, xiv–xv, 186n3, 186n7

Dagger, Richard, 178
*Dance on My Grave* (Chambers), 205, 212–13
*Dawn Will Be Magnificent* (*L'aube sera grandiose*, Bondoux), xxii, 14–15
*Dementia Diaries* (Snyman / Social Innovation Lab Kent), xxii, 47, 56
*Devil's Arithmetic, The*, 137, 141
Diary, 34, 38, 53, 56, 116–28, 119, 216n2
DiSalvo-Ryan, DyAnne, xxiv, 176, 182–85
Disney-Pixar, xxiii, 85–97
Dohmen, Jacques, 210–12
Douglas, Ann, 19
Douglas, Kate, 226–28
Downham, Jenny, xxii, 47, 51–53
Doyle, Eugenie, 164, 168–70
Durkheim, Émile, 177, 180, 186n8
*Dying to Know You* (Chambers), 209

Eakin, John Paul, 219, 225
Eastland, Katherine, 62
Effland, Anne, 163
Eisenstein, Sergei, 82
Elliott, Rebecca, xxiv, 176, 180–82, 185
*Emil and the Detectives* (Kästner), xxiii, 102–10, 112
Emil series (Lindgren), xxii, 31–42
*Emile* (Rousseau), 8
Environmentalism, xvii, 164, 171
Evolutionary literary studies, 234–43

Fairy tales, 10, 85, 141, 181, 232
Fantasy, 12, 56, 64, 70–83, 83n1, 131–42
*Farmer Will Allen and the Growing Table* (Martin), 176–85
Festivals: Christmas, 24–36, 40; Día de Muertos, 92–95; Tanabata, 74
Film, xxiii, 58, 60–62, 70–83, 85–96, 134–35, 238
Fine, Anne, xxii, 47–51, 53, 55
Finelli, Manuel, 172
*Fleetwood* (Godwin), 196, 198–200, 202
Flynn, Richard, xix–xx, 59
Folk tales, 10, 33, 85, 234, 238, 242
Foucault, Michel, 200
Fowkes, Katherine, 71–72
Freeman, Michael J., 103
Fuss, Diana, 74

*Gardener, The* (Stewart), 176, 178–82, 184
Genetic criticism, 206, 215–16
Gibbs, Frederick, 20
Giradeau, Zérane S., 104
*Girl of Limberlost, A* (Stratton-Porter), 19
Godwin, William, xiv, xxiv, 191–202
Gomila, Antònia, 90
*Grandpa's Great Escape* (Walliams), xxii, 47, 54–56
*Granny Project, The* (Fine), xxii, 47–51, 53, 55
Greenway, Betty, 104, 207
Grenby, Matthew, 198, 202n4
Grimes, Nick, 8
Griswold, Jerry, 19
Gubar, Marah, xviii–xx, 32–33, 37–38, 112, 117–18, 120, 122–23, 127–28, 206, 209, 219, 221, 228–29, 240–41
Gusmano, Michael K., 88

Halilbegovich, Nadja, xiii, xxiii, 116–28
Hall, Lee, xxii, 47, 51–53
Hannerz, Ulf, 183
Happala, Irja, xv
*Harry Potter* series (Rowling), 5–6, 31, 239
Hausknecht, Simone, 66
Hegel, Georg Wilhelm Friedrich, 155, 157
Heidegger, Martin, 153
Hockey, Jenny, 92
Hollindale, Peter, 241

Holocaust, 112, 130–31, 133–36, 138–42, 156, 227
Hopkins, Peter, 64
Horne, Jackie C., 18
*Howl's Moving Castle* (Studio Ghibli), xxiii, 70–72, 77–83
Hunter, Sarah, 66
Huxhold, Oliver, 65

Illustration, 29, 61, 101–13, 118, 167–70, 181
Immigration, xxiv, 148–57, 221
International Childhood and Youth Research Network, xvii
*Invention of Hugo Cabret* (Selznick), xxiii, 58–60
Ives, Eric, 197

Jackson, Rosemary, 71
James, Allison, 92
Jones, Diana Wynne, xxiii, 70, 79
Jones, Katherine, 106
Joosen, Vanessa, xxi, 4, 61, 64, 88, 92
*Journey, The* (*Die Reise*, Kerr), 102, 107–9, 113n9

Kästner, Erich, xxiii, 102–10, 112
Kerr, Judith, xxiii, 101–13
Kieran, Allen, 177
Kimmich, Matt, 78–79
Kinship: affective, 131, 136; between life stages, 206–16; and family structures, 90, 95; as "model" (Gubar), xx–xxiv, 32–42, 112, 116–29, 240
Klinker, Joanna, 215
Kokkola, Lydia, xviii, 5, 10, 209, 225, 228
Kruse, Martha, 165–66
Kustermans, Karin, 207, 212
Kymlicka, Will, xvii

*Lady Windermere's Fan* (Wilde), 62
Larkin, Elizabeth, 88, 90
*Last Tiger, The* (Elliott), xxiv, 176, 180–82, 185
Lee, Nick, xvi
Lejeune, Philippe, 225
L'Engle, Madeleine, 87
Levinas, Emmanuel, 151, 156
*Life of Lady Jane Grey* (Godwin), 193–202
Life writing, 218–21, 224–29

Lindgren, Astrid, xiii, 32–42
Lurie, Alison, 74

Mahlberg, Michaela, 20
Mahne, Katharina, 65
*Man Who Mistook His Wife For a Hat, The* (Sacks), 208
Manly, Susan, 195, 201, 202n9
Martin, Jacqueline Briggs, 176, 182–85
*Marvels, The* (Selznick), xxiii, 58–68
Marx, Leo, 178, 180
Mauro de Vasconcelos, José, 6
McIntosh, Malachi, 150
Mee, Jon, 200
Memoir, 7, 113n9, 130, 172
Memory studies, 138, 231
Mendlesohn, Farah, 78
Migrancy, 148–50, 180
Mills, Alice, 18
*Miss Peregrine* trilogy (Riggs), xiii, xxiii, 130–42
Moebius, William, 108
Moeyaert, Bart, 213–14
Monroe, Kristen Renwick, 156
Montgomery, L. M., 19, 60, 75
Multiculturalism, 148–49
Museums, 54–55, 60–64
*My Childhood Under Fire: A Sarajevo Diary* (Halilbegovich), xiii, xxiii, 116–28
*My Sweet Orange Tree* (Mauro de Vasconcelos), 6
Myrdal, Gunnar, 178
Myth, 11, 131–32, 178, 181, 195, 234, 242

Nationalism, 148, 151, 177–78
Natov, Roni, 58, 66
Nelson, Claudia, 24
Nikolajeva, Maria, xviii, xxvin7, 3, 6, 31, 59, 71, 78, 87, 138–40, 186n2, 220
Nodelman, Perry, xx, 6, 31, 61, 72
Novesky, Amy, 8

O'Boyle, Brian, 177
O'Keefe, Deborah, 23
Oldenberg, Roy, 186n6
*On Grandpa's Farm* (Sathre), 164, 167–70
Orphan, xxii, 19, 22–27, 58–60, 65, 159, 198, 241

Otherness, 32, 118, 122–23, 132, 149, 151, 209
*Out of the Hitler Time* (Kerr), 101

Pain, Rachel, 64
Palimpsest, xxiii, 126–28
Parker, David, 225
Parliament: Polish, xv; Neighborhood Children's (South India), xvii
Pastoral, 88, 165, 173, 177–80, 186n4, 197
Patterson, Dave, 226–27
Paz, Octavio, 92
Pearce, Philippa, 12–14, 64
Pellicer-Ortín, Silvia, 156
Photography, 67, 89–90, 93–95, 127, 131, 221
Picturebooks, xxiv, 8, 56, 108, 162–74, 176–86
*Pierre and Michelle* (*Pierre et Michelle*, Kerr), 102, 106–9, 113n9
*Pollyanna* series (Porter), xxii, 18–29
Population aging, xiv–xv, xxi, 47
Porter, Eleanor H., xxii, 18–29
*Postcards from No Man's Land* (Chambers), 207, 209, 213
Postcolonial studies, xxiv, 138, 148–49, 234
Pratt, Annis, 19, 26
Preston, Brent, 163, 172–73
*Pride and Prejudice* (Austen), 194
Propp, Vladimir, 141, 242
Protest march, xi, 157–58
Prunes, Mariano, 82
Putnam, Robert, 177, 182, 186n7

Racism, 148, 156
Refugee, 103, 136, 147–51, 154–56
Reynolds, Kimberley, 106
Rhodes, Christopher J., 164
Rieder, John, 131
Riggs, Ransom, xiii, xxiii, 130–42
Robinson, Joan G., xxiii, 70
Robinson, Laura, 23, 75
Romanticism: child as symbol of, xviii, 18–29, 60, 120–21, 202; and education, 8; and pastoral, 165
Root, Phyllis, 164, 167, 169–72
Rose, Jacqueline, xx, 71, 87, 231, 242–43
Rothberg, Michael, 130, 138–39
Rowling, J. K., 5–6, 31, 240

Sacks, Oliver, 208
Said, Edward, 150
Sánchez-Eppler, Karen, xviii
Sanders, Joe Sutliff, 19, 24
Sathre, Vivian, 164, 167–70
Scholz, Sally, 177
Schrader, Sandi S., xiii, 19, 25–26
Schuck, Peter H., 184
Seale, Clive, 93
Second World War, 81, 114, 150, 155
Seelye, John, 25
Selznick, Brian, xxiii, 58–68
Seven Stories, Newcastle, 102, 113n8, 207
Simmel, Georg, 179–80
*Slash* series (Vendel), xxiv, 218–29
*Sleep Tight Farm* (Doyle), 164, 168–70
Smith, Anthony D., 177
Smith, Sidonie, 218
Smith, Victoria Ford, xix–xx, 89, 206, 215, 225, 229
*Snow White and the Seven Dwarfs* (Disney), 85
Snyman, Matthew, xii, 47, 56
Social Innovation Lab Kent, xxii, 47, 56
Song, 34, 63, 95
Sontag, Susan, 142
Spencer, Robert, 149
Spitz, Ellen Handler, 87
Stereotypes, 87, 90, 133, 165–66
Stewart, Sarah, 176, 178–82, 184
Stonely, Peter, 24
Stratton-Porter, Gene, 19
Studio Ghibli, xxiii, 70–83
Sustainability, 162–64, 172, 182–84

Takiuchi, Haru, 207
*Tangled* (Disney), 85
*Tender Earth* (Brahmachari), xiv, xxiv, 148–49, 154–59
Terrorism, 147–48, 151, 157
*This Is All: The Pillow Book of Cordelia Kenn* (Chambers), 205, 213, 215
*Through the Looking-Glass* (Carroll), 201
Thunberg, Greta, xi
Tocqueville, Alexis de, 178, 183
Toledo, Victor Manuel, 164

*Toll Bridge, The* (Chambers), 206–11, 214
*Tom's Midnight Garden* (Pearce), 12–14, 64
Trains, 60, 101–13, 156, 179–80
Trier, Walter, 102–10, 112
Trimmer, Sarah, 201
Trites, Roberta Seelinger, 5–6, 231, 236
Tucker, Alan, 209
Tyler, Dennis, 96

*Unbecoming* (Downham), xxii, 47, 53–54
United Nations, xiv, xvi, 124, 162, 167, 171
*Up* (Disney-Pixar), 86–91, 95–96
Urbanization, 86–87, 152; and community programs, 88–91; and farming, 163, 166, 169; and gardening, 176–86

Vendel, Edward van de, xxiv, 218–29
Voyant Tools, 20–21

Wagner, Logan, 92
Wall, John, xvii
Walliams, David, xxii, 47, 54–56
Watson, Julia, 218
Weems, Lisa, xviii–xix, 102
*When Hitler Stole Pink Rabbit* (Kerr), xxiii, 101–2, 109–12
*When Marnie Was There* (Studio Ghibli), xxiii, 70, 72–77, 82
Whitley, David, 87
Wilde, Oscar, 62
Wilkens, Matthew, 20
Wilson, Carl, 81
Wilson, Garrath T., 81
Wolfe, Cary, 131
*Wonderstruck* (Selznick), xxiii, 58, 60–68
World War II, 81, 114, 150, 155

Yolen, Jane, 137, 141
Young adult literature, 5–6, 14, 205–16, 218–29, 231–32, 240, 242
Young-Bruehl, Elizabeth, 166

Zarzycka, Agata, 138
Zelenev, Sergei, xiii–xiv
Zimmerman, Virginia, 62–63

www.ingramcontent.com/pod-product-compliance
Lightning Source LLC
Chambersburg PA
CBHW030612230426
43661CB00053B/1954